1981

Corrections

It is recorded somewhere in the history of human experience that a father once gave his eight-year-old son, as a gift, a jigsaw puzzle of the world. Because of its complexity, as well as the tender youth of the child, it was not reasonable to expect the boy to complete the puzzle—if, indeed, he could complete it—in anything less than a protracted period of time. The father was astonished, therefore, when the lad brought him the completed puzzle within the hour. "My son," he inquired, "how on earth did you manage this incredible feat?" The boy responded, "It was easy, father. There was a picture of a man on the back of the world. I just put the man together, and the whole world fell into place."

Corrections: Treatment and Philosophy

LOUIS P. CARNEY

Chapman College
Orange, California

Prentice-Hall, Inc., Englewood Cliffs, New Jersey 07632

Library of Congress Cataloging in Publication Data

Carney, Louis P
  Corrections, treatment and philosophy.

  Includes bibliographical references and index.
  1. Corrections. 2. Corrections—United States.
I. Title.
HV9275.C36   364.6   79-22444
ISBN 0-13-178236-3

Editorial/production supervision and interior design: Marian Hartstein
Cover design: Wanda Lubelska Design
Manufacturing buyer: John Hall

Printed in the United States of America

10 9 8 7 6 5 4 3 2 1

Prentice-Hall International, Inc., *London*
Prentice-Hall of Australia Pty. Limited, *Sydney*
Prentice-Hall of Canada, Ltd., *Toronto*
Prentice-Hall of India Private Limited, *New Delhi*
Prentice-Hall of Japan, Inc., *Tokyo*
Prentice-Hall of Southeast Asia Pte. Ltd., *Singapore*
Whitehall Books Limited, *Wellington, New Zealand*

For
my wife, Bunny
my sister, Mary
my friend, Pat Boyd
and
Justine
each of whom sustained me

Contents

3

CRIMINAL DEVIANCE 43

4

THEORIES OF DEVIANT BEHAVIOR 66

5

CORRECTIONAL MODELS 84

6

PSYCHOTHERAPEUTIC STRATEGIES 105

7

THE PRACTITIONER'S BASIC TREATMENT TOOLS 131

8

CORRECTIONS AND PSYCHIATRY 157

9

INSTITUTIONAL TREATMENT   173

10

COMMUNITY-BASED STRATEGIES   210

11

THE JUVENILE JUSTICE SYSTEM   242

12

DIFFERENTIAL TREATMENT   270

13

SPECIAL TREATMENT PROBLEMS   285

14

THE PAST IS PROLOGUE 320

Preface

After the "Roaring Sixties," which featured sustained social unrest and protest, criminal justice theorists became introspective in the 1970s. One dramatic result of this introspection was the development of a cynical attitude toward correctional treatment, highlighted by the emergence of a punitive model, variously termed the *punishment, justice,* or *equity model.* The credentials of those espousing this approach are impressive, and the reverberations of the new battle cry have been commanding.

Because of the clamor, it has been assumed in some quarters that, as God was once proclaimed dead in a revolutionary brand of theology, treatment is dead in corrections.

This text is not so presumptuous as to profess to be the definitive *Fidei defensor* with respect to the treatment philosophy, but as a text on correctional treatment it cannot avoid an affirmative stance. The fundamental intent of this work, however, is to provide the student aspiring to a career in corrections with a coherent picture of the philosophy of treatment and its concomitant strategies in the field of corrections.

It is also designed to provide an updated sourcebook for the non-clinical professional correctionalist in probation, parole, prison, and community correctional endeavors. In a field that is constantly changing, it is imperative for both the student and the practicing professional to be conversant with contemporary philosophy and the operational tactics employed in the restorative mission of the correctional arts.

Despite the inimical attitude that has recently been expressed toward correctional rehabilitation (treatment), a great army of professionals and paraprofessionals, public citizens and private citizens, clinicians and non-clinicians is engaged daily across this country in an endeavor to redirect the delinquent and the felon out of the criminal justice system. What they do and how they do it is the heart of the treatment thrust.

In the recurring ideological battle between punishment and treatment, it is felt that the intrinsic merit of a *rational* treatment approach will be so self-evident that a profound philosophic *apologia* will be both unnecessary and implicit.

Among the many, I must especially thank Lorene Vance, for her sus.. ned support; Janet Campbell, for her prodigious sense of logistics; S. D. and J. Z. for their modest frivolity; Madonna M. R. Skinner, for her ineffable charm always, and help when I needed it; CONtact, Nebraska, for being a magnificent organization; Howard Loy and Dick Ennen, for intellectual stimulation; Henry Garcia, for timeless wisdom; Stephen Cline, for being not only a wise and patient editor, but also a very gracious one; and, above all, Louis Patrick, for without him and Bunny, nothing was possible.

Louis P. Carney

Corrections

1 Punishment in Perspective

The reward or punishment that comes to you is inherent in the governance of people.

Marcus Tullius Cicero

On January 7, 1946, the city of Chicago, and the nation, were shocked by the discovery of the decapitated and dismembered body of a six-year-old child, Suzanne Degnan. The shock had not subsided before two additional murders were uncovered. This time the victims were adult females, one stabbed and the other shot to death. There was no evidence that any of the victims had been sexually molested. The murderer, obviously driven by some irresistible compulsion, had scrawled on a wall in one victim's apartment, with her lipstick, the fearfully urgent message:

For heavens
sake catch me

Before I kill more
I cannot control myself

The murderer was eventually caught. He turned out to be a seventeen-year-old freshman at the University of Chicago, William Heirens.

It transpired that Heirens had been engaged in considerable criminal activity, including burglary and robbery in addition to the three murders which he had committed. At his arraignment, he pleaded guilty to thirty charges, including twenty-four burglaries, one robbery, and the three murders. He received concurrent sentences of one year to life on twenty-four burglary counts; one to twenty years on the robbery, running consecutively; a consecutive one to fourteen years on an assault to commit murder charge; and Natural Life on the three murders, to run consecutively.

It was subsequently determined that Heirens had been a transvestite from the age of nine and, despite the fact that three court-appointed psychiatrists had found him "not suffering from any psychosis,"[1] another examing psychiatrist later described him as "a disassociative psychotic schizophrenic."[2]

In 1972 Heirens became the first inmate in the history of the Illinois prison system to obtain a college degree while a prisoner. As this book is being written, he is still a prisoner, well into his fourth decade of incarceration. Although he has been a model prisoner, he has consistently been denied parole.

Entwined in this true story are all the elements that plague and challenge us as we endeavor to give meaning to *justice* in the criminal justice process. What is the nature of criminal man? What is appropriate punishment for a given offense? To what degree should insanity mitigate? To what degree can we precisely determine a psychotic condition? What is justice for the victim? For the deceased victim? Does punishment deter? Are treatment and rehabilitation legitimate aims of the criminal justice system? Can individuals freely choose nonconforming modes of behavior and are they, having thus freely chosen, automatically liable for prescribed sanctions? Can treatment take place in a prison? Should it? Can it take place anywhere? What is treatment? Should punishment replace treatment as the "correctional" disposition? Can punishment and treatment be joined in an effective partnership?

The distinguished English jurist, Sir William Blackstone, in his monumental *Commentaries on the Law of England,* declared that a madman is punished by his madness alone (*furiosus furore solum punitur*). Does

[1]Foster Kennedy, Harry R. Hoffman, and William H. Haines, "Psychiatric Study of William Heirens," *Journal of Criminal Law and Criminology,* 38, no. 4 (November-December 1947), 312.
[2]Lucy Freeman, *Before I Kill More* (New York: Pocket Books, Inc., 1956), p. 250.

forty—or fifty—years of such punishment atone for the deeds perpet-rated by a William Heirens? What would?

When are we entitled to initiate redemption?

The issues raised in the preceding section will be examined through-out this text. At this point we will examine those key issues and aspects of punishment which the student must ponder as he or she takes up the study of criminal behavior and its remediation.

PUNISHMENT: NATURE AND OBJECTIVES

In one of those quick, commercial blurbs which give a taste of the news to come, a prominent TV newscaster announced, "The publisher of *Hustler* magazine was given twenty-five years in Ohio. Film at eleven." In report-ing this in one of the major newspapers, an impish reporter commented, "Twenty-five years in Cincinnati ought to straighten anyone out."

This comment contains obvious humor, but it also contains the seed of the persistent belief that punishment deters. The general feeling is that if punishment is somehow fearful enough, or sufficiently punitive, it will dissuade the individual from continued criminality. We will deal with the question of deterrence shortly, but before doing so it is essential to acquire some insight about punishment and the philosophic foundations upon which it rests.

Defining Punishment

Scholars have been performing intellectual autopsies on punishment theory for centuries. So it is not surprising that we have inherited a variety of theories and definitions. Some writers have taken an uncompromising stand against punishment; others have insisted that punishment is the *sine qua non* of social control. The range of sentiment and theory is impressive. For example, Ives, in his classical and scholarly work on the subject, con-siders punishment "concessions allowed to unreasoning cruelty."[3] A con-temporary punishment theorist, van den Haag, on the other hand, has proclaimed that "Punishment—if not the only, or the first, or even the best means of making people obey laws—is ultimately indispensable."[4]

In the distinguished report on crime and punishment by the Ameri-can Friends Service Committee, it is compellingly alleged that the distinc-tive characteristic of punishment is "the application of force to another person against his or her will."[5] In the traditional utilitarian view, the es-

[3]George Ives, *A History of Penal Methods* (Montclair, N.J.: Patterson Smith Reprint Se-ries, 1970 [originally published 1914]), p. vi.

[4]Ernest van den Haag, *Punishing Criminals* (New York: Basic Books, Inc., Publishers, 1975), p. 262.

[5]American Friends Service Committee, *Struggle For Justice* (New York: Hill & Wang, 1971), p. 22.

sence of punishment is pain or unpleasantness. Obviously influenced by such writers as Grotius and Antony Flew,[6] Hart has aptly constructed the traditional model, defining "the standard or central case of 'punishment' in terms of five elements:

1. It must involve pain or other consequences normally considered unpleasant.
2. It must be for an offence against legal rules.
3. It must be of an actual or supposed offender for his offence.
4. It must be intentionally administered by human beings other than the offender.
5. It must be imposed and administered by an authority constituted by a legal system against which the offence is committed."[7]

Hart takes what is known as a utilitarian view. Utilitarianism is embedded in the Classical tradition, which we shall review shortly. In subjecting Hart's punishment criteria to the briefest of critical analysis, we might observe that it is a presumption that punishment necessarily obliges the imposition of pain. Deprivation, with the consequent unpleasantness of unfulfillment, might be a more rational criterion.

Hart emphasized the fact that punishment must ensue from an infraction of law that is administered by constituted authority. If the law is such, then punishment has legitimacy (if not rationality). In speaking of a "constituted authority," Hart echoes the thirteenth century dictum of St. Thomas Aquinas about the law itself, namely, that to bear the hallmark of legitimacy, it must be an ordinance of right reason, promulgated by the *duly constituted authority,* for the common good.[8]

With the natural bias of his legal training evident, Packer takes exception to Hart's definition, only because of its lack of inclusiveness. Packer contends that a sixth characteristic should be added to Hart's model: "It [punishment] must be imposed for the dominant purpose of preventing offenses against legal rules or of exacting retribution from offenders, or both."[9] The addition of doctrinal qualifications, it would seem, lends

---

[6]Grotius was a brilliant, seventeenth century Dutch jurist, noted for his *De jure belli ac pacis* ("Concerning the Law of War and Peace"), considered to be the first text on international law. For a precise account of Flew's definition, see Antony Flew, "Definition of Punishment," in Rudolph J. Gerber and Patrick D. McAnany, *Contemporary Punishment: Views, Explanations, and Justifications* (Notre Dame: University of Notre Dame Press, 1972), pp. 31–35.

[7]H.L.A. Hart, *Punishment and Responsibility* (Oxford: Oxford University Press, 1968), pp. 4–5.

[8]*Summa theol.* (Pegis ed.), Vol. 2, Question 90, Article 4: *Lex est quaedam rationis ordinatio ad bonum commune ab eo qui curam communitatis habet, promulgata).*

[9]Herbert L. Packer, *The Limits of the Criminal Sanction* (Stanford: Stanford University Press, 1968), p. 31.

support to Hart's contention that punishment theories are not really theories but moral claims.[10]

Before we examine the broad major conceptualizations in punishment theory, it is advisable to obtain a basic, working definition of punishment. Van den Haag succinctly captured the essence when he defined punishment as "a deprivation or suffering, imposed by law."[11] This is, as we have said, merely a working definition, and it does not imply the endorsement of van den Haag's particular philosophy. The element of suffering in punishment is classically a retributivist dogma. The student will recall that Hart said that punishment theories are in reality moral claims. The retributivist theory of punishment, in fact, has the morality of punishment as its fundamental foundation.

All theories of punishment largely fall into three broad conceptual categories: retribution, deterrence, or reformation. The rationale for punishment ranges from the view that offenders *deserve* to be punished to the view that punishment is a catalyst for regeneration. Comment on the last named will be reserved for Chapter 2. At this point we will review retribution and the deterrence-utilitarian school of thought. It will be obvious as we proceed that the lines of demarcation are sometimes quite fuzzy.

Retribution

The retributivist position can be very simply stated. The "morally derelict," to use Packer's term,[12] deserve to be punished. Punishment is not a question of dissuasion, nor of utility; and whether or not regeneration takes place subsequent to punishment cannot be the guiding principle of punishment. Man is considered a free, responsible, moral agent, who should be punished for his misdeeds just as he should be rewarded for his good deeds. According to retributivists, this is rooted in the very nature of man and, hence, it does not really require any justification.

Retribution subsumes vengeance and expiation, and it is as old as man. One of the oldest known codifications of law, the Code of Hammurabi (c. 1750 B.C.), was based on retributive theory, or *lex talionis* as it is called. The philosophy of retribution has endured and is, perhaps, the position to which most people subscribe, consciously or unconsciously. It is, in fact, the bedrock foundation of the contemporary Punishment Model, to which we shall refer in greater detail later in this chapter.

[10]Hart, *Punishment and Responsibility*, p. 72.

[11]Van den Haag, *Punishing Criminals*, p. 8.

[12]Herbert L. Packer, "The Justification for Punishment," in Gerber and McAnany, *Contemporary Punishment: Views, Explanations, and Justifications*, p. 183.

Retributivists accept the concept of free will, and consider its exercise a moral issue, and its misuse punishable. As a contemporary proponent of this view expressed it, "We pay the penalty because we owe it."[13]

Retributivism has been espoused by a great many philosophers of stature, most notably by Immanuel Kant (1724–1804) and Georg Hegel (1770–1831), with respect to criminal behavior. Because retribution invokes vengeance, and sounds harsh, it has been generally denounced by modern correctional theorists. Despite the severe sound of the word, retribution does not necessarily imply the need for severe sanction. A modern retributivist, Nigel Walker, for example, takes the position that retribution and severe sanction are not necessarily inclusive. In what he defines as "compromising retributivism," Walker maintains that

> . . . the penal system should be designed to exact atonement for offences in so far as this would not impose excessive unofficial retaliation, or inhuman suffering of the offender, and in so far as it would not increase the incidence of offences.[14]

Walker points out that retribution has to be considered in three senses: (1) *Retaliatory* retribution refers to the intentional infliction of an appropriate amount of suffering on a competant individual who has breached some code. (2) *Distributive* retribution means that retribution is restricted to individuals who have committed offenses. (3) *Quantitative* retribution involves the limitation of sanctions so that inordinate suffering is not imposed.

Whatever the favorable or unfavorable attributes associated with a retributivist philosophy, this posture has ancient roots. Aristotle defended it, as did St. Thomas Aquinas, although he doctored it with humanism. It colored the old Jewish law, and found its pure metaphysical form in Kant's *Philosophy of Law*. And the distinguished American jurist, Jerome Hall, insisted that there was an inescapable connection between law and morality, so that punishment is not only legal but moral. Of profound significance is the fact that the retributivist philosophy has so unabashedly begun to seep through the bulwarks of the heretofore antiretributivist ship of state in contemporary corrections.

Deterrence

It is an enduring assumption that punishment or the fear of infamy has a deterrent effect on proscribed behavior. It is common knowledge that where a crime persistently recurs, or a so-called "crime wave" occurs, the

---

[13]Sir Walter Moberly, "Expiation," in Gerber and McAnany, *Contemporary Punishment,* p. 73.

[14]Nigel Walker, "Varieties of Retributivism," in Gerber and McAnany, *Contemporary Punishment,* p. 83.

general clamor is for enhanced penalties, which evidences the sublime faith in deterrence.[15] This was apparent in the Federal Narcotic Act of 1956. Passed at the height of the drug scare, it incorporated a death penalty provision for a second conviction of sale of drugs to a minor. As could have been predicted—*because the penalty was inordinate*—no single individual was ever sentenced to death under this law. Nor did the sale of drugs abate.

As far back as the first century, the Greek essayist Plutarch (died c.120) spoke of the efficacy of infamy in reducing undesirable behavior. It seems that there had been an epidemic of suicides by young girls. To cope with this distressing occurrence, a law was passed which required that the bodies of individuals who had died at their own hands were to be hung naked on a public gallows. That law, it is recorded, had "a beneficial effect."[16]

In the endless battle between the retributivists and their "humanitarian" adversaries, the question of deterrence is a central issue. Ordinarily, the debate peaks on the question of capital punishment. The humanitarians denounce the possibility of a deterrent effect in capital punishment, particularly in view of the fact that most murders are crimes of passion. Their opponents sardonically observe that the executed are assuredly deterred.

For the past several decades, the humanitarian philosophy had been in the ascendancy in correctional thought. Consequently, an endless stream of books and tracts have come forth "affirming life" and placing the onus for the most heinous of human behavior at the door of "social conditions." This affronts the retributivists because, in effect, it denies man responsibility for his own destiny and it de-moralizes human interaction. What are the facts about deterrence?

The truth of the matter is that, aside from an occasional article of pertinence, there had not been a significant scientific effort to test the validity of the presumption about deterrence until Zimring and Hawkins published their exploratory work in 1973.[17] The best that can be said without controversion is that punishment is an effective deterrent for those who are not predisposed to commit a crime, and a questionable deterrent for those who are criminally disposed.

When Packer, whom we cited earlier, spoke of punishment "preventing offenses against legal rules," he was introducing deterrence. If the punishment "prevents," it follows that it must deter. In the traditional

[15] It is worth noting, parenthetically, that Karl Menninger describes deterrence as "a cloak for vengeance": *The Crime of Punishment* (New York: The Viking Press, 1968), p. 206.

[16] Frederick Howard Wines, *Punishment and Reformation*, rev. ed. (New York: Thomas Y. Crowell Company, 1910), pp. 84–85.

[17] Franklin E. Zimring and Gordon J. Hawkins, *Deterrence* (Chicago: The University of Chicago Press, 1973).

view, deterrence has been accepted as the *sine qua non* of punishment. But there has always been a degree of skepticism about the effectiveness of deterrence, and Hart maintains that "a cloud of doubt . . . has settled over the keystone of 'retributive' theory."[18]

The most obvious—and the most distressing—thing about the deterrent philosophy is that it necessarily deindividualizes. There is a sublime faith that penalty X will have the same influence whether applied to transgressor A, B, C, or D. As Zimring and Hawkins expressed it, "this style of thinking imagines a world in which armed robbery is in the same category as illegal parking, burglars think like district attorneys, and the threat of punishment will result in an orderly process of elimination in which the crime rate will diminish as the penalty scale increases. . . ."[19]

In deference to scientific scrupulosity, however, the deterrent theory should not be dismissed out of hand, any more than its efficacy should be uncritically assumed. In an earlier work, Professor Zimring suggested that studies which profess to show a negative correlation between *long* prison sentences and deterrence should not permit a similar assumption with respect to *short* prison sentences. The belief that there is a deterrent benefit to be derived from a brief exposure to incarceration is, in fact, the operating principle behind the practice known as "shock probation," which we will deal with in a later chapter. Continued experimentation with shorter sentences is indicated to further test the deterrent theory, according to Zimring.[20]

The Evidence for Deterrence

There exists, furthermore, some compelling evidence that certain types of sanctions, under cetain types of circumstances, may influentially deter. Chambliss conducted a study on a midwestern university campus to assess the impact of a drastic increase in the certainty and severity of punishment for parking infractions. The random sample was composed of 43 faculty members who had been resident faculty for at least 2 ½ years before the target year of the study. Each professor was interviewed and asked to "discuss the parking situation at the university." Little prompting was needed, as all were clearly quite aware of and concerned with the problem. The number of infractions, before and after the drastic increase in penalties (fines went up from $1 to $5 for the third infraction, and

---

[18]Hart, *Punishment and Responsibility*, p. 1.
[19]Zimring and Hawkins, *Deterrence*, pp. 19-20.
[20]Franklin E. Zimring, *Perspectives on Deterrence*, National Institute of Mental Health, Center for Studies of Crime and Delinquency (Washington, D.C.: U.S. Government Printing Office, January 1971), pp. 106-7.

faculty were held to the same accountability as students) were recorded. Subclasses were grouped on the basis of the frequency or infrequency of past violations. The findings gave "evidence that an increase in the certainty and the severity of punishment deters violation of parking regulations. . . ." and "the most outstanding changes took place among the most frequent violators."[21]

Andenaes, in another context, speaks of the efficacy of peremptory jail sentences for drunk driving offenses in his native Norway. In Norway, jail sentences are given for "unfit driving," in which the defendant has a blood alcohol content of 0.05, far below that which would constitute drunk driving in the United States. In California, for instance, an individual would have to have a blood alcohol content twice that amount (0.10) before intoxication could be legally assumed. Andenaes claims that, as a result of the severe sanctions imposed, an attitude is developed by which the average Norwegian culturally relates injudicious drinking with anticipated penalties. While he does not provide hard data to evidence a reduction in recidivism, and acknowledges that a considerable number are annually arrested for drunk driving, he claims "the fact that violations occur does not interfere with our conclusion that the severity of the legislation has to a high degree limited the incidence of driving after drinking."[22]

He offers what is, perhaps, a more dramatic evidence in support of his general thesis regarding deterrence when he refers to the Norwegian resistance to the German invasion. A large number of the Norwegian population, who were actively engaged in resistance to the German invaders during the occupation in World War II, refrained from active resistance after the Germans introduced capital punishment for this activity.[23] As LaPiere very wisely observed some time ago, "physical sanctions . . . depend on the individual's reaction to pain and injury. They can be effective only to the extent that he fears being physically hurt."[24] The principle to be elicited is that the response of the individual to the sanction, whether physical or nonphysical, is what determines the effectiveness or the ineffectiveness of deterrence.

There is another phenomenon implied, and that is the phenomenon of perception. How does the prospective offender perceive not only the

[21]William J. Chambliss, "The Deterrent Influence of Punishment," *Crime and Delinquency*, 12, No. 1 (January 1966), 70-75.

[22]Johannes Andenaes, "The General Preventive Effects of Punishment," in Leon Radzinowicz and Marvin E. Wolfgang (eds.), *Crime and Justice Volume II: The Criminal in the Arms of the Law* (New York: Basic Books, 1971), p. 91.

[23]*Ibid.*, p. 89.

[24]Richard T. LaPiere, *A Theory of Social Control* (New York: McGraw-Hill Book Company, 1954), p. 221.

threat of punishment, but also the prospect of certitude of punishment? In one recent study it was found, with respect to skyjacking, at least, that "the certainty of punishment acts as a better deterrent than increasing the severity of punishment."[25] The tactic employed in the study was to plot the points in time where an abrupt change took place in the publicizing of the severity, or the certitude of punishment for skyjacking. Certitude of punishment was more formidably perceived than was severity.

The concept of deterrence is more doctrine than theory. Indeed, Gibbs says that the doctrine is "a congery of vague ideas. . . ."[26] The primary reason for this state of affairs is that it is impossible to posit an exclusive cause and effect relationship between legal sanction and conformity. There are "extralegal" factors which have an influence in producing conformity. The fear of public ridicule, for example, can result in conformity where no physical sanction has been imposed. The role of the extralegal component, in fact, has been receiving increasing attention from social scientists, as deterrence continues to be so incompletely understood.[27]

Special and General Deterrence

(Before concluding our probe of deterrence, we should point out that it is customary to consider deterrence in two ways. *Special deterrence* refers to deterrence of individual offenders from further criminality. *General deterrence* refers to the broadly intended dissuasion of the general public from the commission of crime.) This distinction is significant. Professor Lehtinen employed this distinction in an interesting argument in favor of the death penalty. She based her argument on general deterrence rather than specific deterrence, that is, the effect on the general public rather than the effect on the murderer.[28] Cole, admitting that the evidence does not support the supposition that the criminal sanction has been effective, in terms of special deterrence, significantly adds, "But even if the evi-

---

[25]Robert Chauncey, "Deterrence: Certainty, Severity, and Skyjacking," in Stephen Schafer (ed.), *Readings in Contemporary Criminology* (Reston, Va.: Reston Publishing Company, Inc., 1976), p. 187. For another contemporary view, which holds that "perceptual considerations are truly central in the deterrence doctrine," see Maynard L. Erickson, Jack P. Gibbs, and Gary F. Jensen, "The Deterrence Doctrine and the Perceived Certainty of Legal Punishments," *American Sociological Review*, 42, No. 2 (April 1977), 305–17.

[26]Jack P. Gibbs, *Crime, Punishment, and Deterrence* (New York: Elsevier Scientific Publishing Company, Inc., 1975), p. 5.

[27]For an interesting and pertinent article on the dominance of the extralegal influence in the prosecution of marijuana offenses, see Robert F. Meier and Weldon T. Johnson, "Deterrence as Social Control: The Legal and Extralegal Production of Conformity," *American Sociological Review*, 42, No. 2 (April 1977), 292-304.

[28]Marlene W. Lehtinen, "The Value of Life—An Argument for the Death Penalty," *Crime and Delinquency*, 23, No. 3, (July 1977), 237-52.

dence would show that the criminal justice system had failed as a special deterrent, it might still perform the very important function of a general deterrent."[29]

It is clear that a great deal of research is needed to develop the parameters of deterrence. In 1978, the National Institute of Law Enforcement and Criminal Justice, a subdivision of the Law Enforcement Assistance Administration (LEAA), responding to that need, announced "the initiation of a program of research in the theory of general deterrence." No one can question the need to "increase the quantity and quality of empirical evidence and scientific understanding of the effectiveness of criminal justice penalties to deter criminal activity on the part of would-be offenders."[30]

The Objectives of Punishment

Sir James Fitzjames Stephen, one of the towering legal minds of Victorian England, is noted for his punishment-marriage analogy. According to Stephen, punishment maintains the same relationship to the appetite for revenge that marriage does to the sexual appetite. He saw vengeful punishment as the natural expression of the community's fear of criminality and hatred for it. Moberly placed this vengeful predisposition in "some instinctive basis in the animal impulse to resent aggression and to retaliate on the aggressor."[31] Ironically, the 1973 Nobel prize-winning ethologist, Lorenz, considered aggression a survival mechanism which assured the preservation of the species.[32] So much for the state of the art!

The objectives of punishment are implied throughout this chapter. From a practical point of view, what society intends to accomplish through punishment can be recapitulated as follows: Punishment expresses the collective societal disapproval for certain types of misbehavior. It provides an opportunity for atonement or expiation. It is designed to deter the offender and others from recidivism. It is a catalyst for reformation. It seeks to secure the common good. Punishment of the offender vicariously rewards those who obey the law.

These are the ostensible objectives. Whether or not they are achieved is a question the student should be able to answer after reading this book.

---

[29]George F. Cole, *The American System of Criminal Justice* (North Scituate, Mass.: Duxbury Press, 1975), p. 41.

[30]National Institute of Law Enforcement and Criminal Justice, LEAA, U.S. Department of Justice, *Criminal Justice Research Solicitation: Theory of General Deterrence* (Washington, D.C.: LEAA, 1978), p. 1.

[31]Sir Walter Moberly, *The Ethics of Punishment* (Hamden, Conn.: Archon Books, 1968), p. 379.

[32]Konrad Lorenz, *On Aggression* (New York: Harcourt, Brace & World, 1966).

HISTORIC DEVELOPMENTS IN
PUNISHMENT THEORY

In 1764, Cesare Bonesana, Marquis of Beccaria, published his "little tractate," which became "the sensation of the day."[33] His essay was entitled *Dei delitti e delle pene* ("Crimes and Punishments"), and it was a sensation because it fearlessly attacked the widespread, official use of torture against those accused of crime. Eighteenth-century European criminal law was barbaric and repressive. In fact, decades after Beccaria (as he is generally referred to) published his memorable work, psychotics were being placed in dark dungeons in England so that the darkness would enlighten their understanding.

Beccaria felt that the sovereign should exercise the right of punishment only when the common good was jeopardized. His teachings and principles were the foundation of the Classical School of criminology.

The Classical-Utilitarian Heritage

The principles underlying the American criminal justice system derive, in the main, from this eighteenth-century Classical School of criminology. If one principle permeated this school of thought it was that the punishment should fit the crime. The student will recognize this as a still popular belief, recalling, perhaps, that the executioner in the Mikado said, "The object of all sublime is to make the punishment fit the crime." The belief that the punishment should fit the crime has received a contemporary re-emphasis. In 1976, the eagerly awaited Report of the Committee for the Study of Incarceration was published. That report denigrated rehabilitation as the object of punishment, reiterating the dogma of the Classical School: "We conclude that the severity of the sentence should depend on the seriousness of the defendants' crime or crimes—on what he *did* rather than on what the sentencer expects he will do if treated in a certain fashion."[34]

Another basic premise of the Classical School was that man possessed free will. Criminal behavior was considered rational and deliberate behavior, and man was motivated by the pleasure-pain principle. It was the

[33]Frederick Howard Wines, *Punishment and Reformation*, rev. ed. (New York: Thomas Y. Crowell, 1910), p. 94.

[34]Andrew Von Hirsch, *Doing Justice, Report of the Committee for the Study of Incarceration* (New York: Hill and Wang, 1976), pp. xvi-xvii. For further perspective, see also "Stepped-Up Drive to Make Punishment Fit the Crime," *U.S. News & World Report* (Sept. 5, 1977), 47–48.

function of the criminal justice system to offset the pleasure of criminal activity by an adequate amount of counterbalancing pain (punishment). The *spiritus rector* of the Classical School of thought, Cesare Beccaria (1738-1794), however, did not believe in severe punishment. He maintained that punishment should be impartially imposed. Towards this end, judges would merely impose predetermined sanctions, for only the legislature had the right to determine the nature of those sanctions.[35] When Beccaria was putting those views in his famous treatise, the concept of the social contract, popularized by Rousseau, was in vogue. According to the social contract theory, man was born essentially free, but had to yield a measure of his freedom to the state in order to contract for the continued protection of his individual rights. It follows that Beccaria would oppose capital punishment, for an individual would "place in the public fund only the least possible portion [of his personal liberty], nor more than suffices to induce others to defend it."[36] The state had one major purpose, in Beccaria's view, and that was to facilitate the greatest amount of happiness for the greatest number of people, a principle which philosophers refer to as the *summum bonum*.

The man co-equally mentioned with Beccaria as the theoretician behind the Classical School of criminology was the erudite English scholar, Jeremy Bentham (1748-1832). He and Beccaria were contemporaries. It was Bentham who taught that the pleasure of crime must be outweighed by the pain of the penalty attached to it. This was based on Bentham's teaching that man was a rational animal who consciously chose pleasure and avoided pain, a doctrine which he called *felicific calculus*. This is a hedonistic principle, and Bentham is classified as a utilitarian hedonist.[37] The word "utilitarian" means that which has usefulness. Bentham's utilitarian principle was the *summum bonum* ("the greatest good for the greatest number"), a philosophy that permeates our democratic and criminal justice systems. Utilitarians also place great stock in the deterrent capacity of punishment. Although Beccaria believed that prevention of crime was "the ultimate end of every good legislation,"[38] he also believed in the dissuasive influence of punishment. The Classical-Utilitarian school of thought stands in opposition to the Retributivist position, because the former considers suffering to be an evil which the government should not be instituting. With behavioristic and positivistic condiments

---

[35]Cesare Beccaria, *On Crimes and Punishments,* trans. Henry Paoluccu (Indianapolis: The Bobbs-Merrill Co., 1963), p. 13.

[36]*Ibid.,* pp. 12-13.

[37]Sue Titus Reid, *Crime and Criminology* (Hinsdale, Ill.: The Dryden Press, 1976), p. 110.

[38]Beccaria, *On Crimes and Punishments,* p. 93.

added later, the student will recognize that free will, the pleasure–pain priniciple, a commitment to deterrence, and an effort to make the punishment fit the crime have strongly characterized our criminal justice disposition.

Positivism and Behaviorism

The nineteenth-century Positive School of criminology, prominently represented by Enrico Ferri (1856–1929), repudiated the traditional belief in free will, and began to lay heavy emphasis on the environment, much as the behaviorists in psychology did. Although he believed that an individual could be born with criminal predispositions (atavism), Ferri taught that favorable environmental surroundings could nullify those predispositions.[39] Because science is fundamentally deterministic, the positivist's rejection of free will was considered a facilitation of the scientific approach to the study of criminal behavior.

Ferri holds kinship with modern behavioristic psychologists. In expressing his inability to understand how anyone could accept the doctrine of free will, he said that behavior is not the result of volition but "the result of an interaction between the personality and the environment of man."[40] This is a bedrock principle of behavioristic psychology.

Orland uses the term "behavioral" to denote the contemporary "variant" of the utilitarian position, and one that is contraposited with retributivism in the great punishment debate.[41] The behavioral viewpoint, built on the discoveries and teachings of the behavioral sciences, considers free will and moral responsibility to be illusions. Because human behavior is, therefore, causally determined, it should be scientifically studied with the objective of modifying the criminal aspects of the personality.[42] The behavioral position is obviously diametrically opposed to the retributivist position, because the latter incorporates free will and moral responsibility as fundamental principles. According to Orland the great horns of the punishment dilemma are represented by the retributivist-behavioral confrontation. He feels that the criminal justice system will either have to rest on a moral-retributivist foundation, or it will have to abandon ascribing responsibility for criminal behavior.[43]

[39]Ferri's major works are *The Positive School of Criminology* (Chicago: Charles H. Kerr and Co., 1913) and *Criminal Sociology*, trans. Joseph Killey and John Lisle (Boston: Little, Brown & Co., Inc., 1917).

[40]Quoted in Reid, *Crime and Criminology*, p. 126.

[41]Leonard Orland, *Justice, Punishment, Treatment* (New York: The Free Press, 1973), p. 184.

[42]*Ibid.*, p. 185.

[43]*Ibid.*, p. 184.

Determinism, Indeterminism, and "Soft" Determinism

One of the most tantalizing subordinate issues in the punishment–treatment controversy is the question of free will, or indeterminism as it is known in philosophic terms. The question of free will has been the tennis ball in a philosophic match of frustrating proportions. As we have noted, the Classical School accepted free will absolutely, whereas the Positive School rejected indeterminism unequivocally.

To the practitioner in corrections, the question has profound significance. If criminal behavior is predetermined, by what principle do we punish? The positivists evaded a solution by substituting accountability for responsibility, but this is a logical fiction. The classicists attributed absolute free will to everyone. But infants, the mentally disturbed or retarded, and the victims of drug excesses, to give some examples, clearly are incapable of making determinative choices. But what about those of us not so categorized?

The strong adherence of modern behavioral scientists to the hard determinism advocated by the positivists has caused modern criminology to lag behind other disciplines, according to Johnson.[44] Is human behavior so mechanical that it can be predicted like the movements of an automaton? Are we really so inflexibly governed by our external environment? Is there any individual who would be unable to say that he or she never had the opportunity to act self-determinatively?

The Positive School was so science-oriented that hard determinism was a natural philosophic sequel. Science must be precise and, of course, it is characterized by the capacity to predict phenomenal sequences. This was the ideal towards which the behavioral sciences should be directed, according to the positivistic view. But because of the difficulties enumerated in the rhetorical questions posed above, rigid determinism in the behavioral sciences had to bend. "Soft" determinism is a compromise that is gaining adherents. Matza best differentiates "hard" and "soft" determination when he says,

> The difference between hard and soft determinism is that one merely directs the analyst, whereas the other makes a fundamental contention regarding the nature of human action.[45]

In the background is causality, and Matza further qualifies the distinction,

---

[44]Elmer H. Johnson, *Crime, Correction and Society* (Homewood, Ill.: The Dorsey Press, 1978), p. 60.

[45]David Matza, *Delinquency and Drift* (New York: John Wiley & Sons, Inc., 1967), p. 5.

Indeed, soft determinism may be defined as the maintaining of the principle of universal causality as a guide to profound inquiry and an abandoning of universal assumptions regarding the nature of man, criminal or otherwise.[46]

Unwittingly perhaps, Matza comes close to the orthodox theological position on free will: Although God can foresee future actions, the course of a human's action is not causally determined by his foreknowledge but by the determinative choice of the actor. Thus we can accept causality in the universe, without accepting any assumptions about how man, caught in the vortex of that causality, will react.

Before any individual presumes to become involved in professional corrections, he or she should have some familiarity with the issues and dilemmas which we have discussed up to now. The further presumption is that each individual so involved will continue to ponder and probe these critical issues, so that the correctional effort will be increasingly illuminated by defensible truths.

The Rise of Neo-Classicism

Despite the optimism expressed by Zimring and Hawkins that "a cloud of doubt" had settled upon the retributive theory, the fact is that the retributive persuasion experienced a revival in the nineteen-seventies, and an influential segment of the theoreticians in the correctional field began to openly espouse what came to be known variously as the Justice Model, the Equity Model, or the Punishment Model. Because the emphasis of the new *zeitgeist* is on Kantian concepts of punishment, I will use the term Punishment Model hereafter, with the understanding that it subsumes the Justice and the Equity models where warranted.

At the first congress of the American Prison Association (now the American Correctional Association), which was convened in Cincinnati in 1870, commitment to penal reform was so zealously demonstrated that the congress was likened to a revival meeting. But reform did not come readily. More than half a century after the evangelical first penal congress, barbarism still plagued the American prison system. In a series of articles written for a newspaper, an ex-convict offered trenchant insight into the workings of "corrective" corporal punishment in the Missouri State Penitentiary, which was representative of the nation as a whole: "I have known men to be whipped to death simply because it was a physical impossibility for them to do tasks assigned to them under the outrageous contract labor system."[47] Under this system, convict labor had been contracted out to exploitative entrepreneurs in the community.

[46]*Ibid.*, p. 7.

[47]Harry Elmer Barnes, *The Story of Punishment: A Record of Man's Inhumanity to Man,* 2nd ed. (Montclair, N.J.: Patterson Smith, 1972), p. 153.

FIGURE 1-1
Prisoners on Georgia road gang during World War II

Nevertheless, provoked by the awesome history of man's penal inhumanity to his fellow man, and stirred by such works as George Ives' *History of Penal Methods* and John Mitchell's *Jail Journal,* attacks were mounting on the arcane notion that extreme physical punishment in or out of the prison setting was reformative.

In time, standard textbooks on criminology and related disciplines were able to declare, with monotonous regularity, that treatment should dominate the penal process, and that the penal rationale had progressed from retributive revenge to rehabilitation. Rehabilitation became the correctional watchword, and prisons began to be viewed as potential correctional treatment vessels. In the 1950s milieu therapy, pioneered by Dr. Maxwell Jones in an English mental hospital, was introduced into the American prison. In milieu therapy, every staff member and every "patient" is viewed as part of the treatment process.

But mounting evidence called into question the prison's ability to contribute to reformation of the criminal. Increasing cynicism regarding rehabilitation in general began to infiltrate the prose of the correctional philosophers. The new mood was orchestrated by four major works which, remarkably, were all published in the same year. They etched the new ideology in compelling terms. Because the principles of the "new" persuasion largely parallel those enunciated in the Classical School of criminology, the new mood can be termed neo-Classicism. It is not possible to discourse exhaustively on the major tenets and thinking of the leading progenitors of the Punishment Model, but it is necessary to open a door to the new thinking to gain perspective.

The Punishment Model

Dr. Martinson and his associates undertook the monumental task of surveying the outcomes of 231 correctional programs operating in different parts of the country during the period 1945 to 1967. Their doleful conclusion was that

> . . . it still must be concluded that the field of corrections has not as yet found satisfactory ways to reduce recidivism by significant amounts. . . . corrections has yet to sort out from current treatment programs or their components those techniques that are effective.[48]

Harvard's Professor Wilson, calling Martinson's work "unique in its comprehensiveness," nevertheless declared that the findings had been already well documented, and "Studies done since 1967 do not provide grounds for altering that conclusion significantly."[49] David Fogel, whose name is associated with the origin of the Justice Model, described the criminal law as the "command of the sovereign," and declared that "The threat of punishment is necessary to implement the law."[50] And the incisive Ernest van den Haag, one of the principal ideological architects of the modern punishment model, succinctly expressed the new philosophy by resorting to an ancient legal dictum, *pacta sunt servanda* ("a pact must be observed, a treaty must be honored"). As van den Haag precisely expressed it, "Laws threaten, or promise, punishment for crimes. Society has obligated itself by threatening. It owes the carrying out of its threats. Society pays its debts by punishing the offender, however unwilling he is to accept payment."[51]

As might be expected, the emergence—or resurgence—of the so-called Punishment Model has drawn a mixed reaction. In some instances it has polarized practitioners and theoreticians in the field. But it has also had a profound influence on law and philosophy in some areas. Connecticut, for example, repudiated the rehabilitation philosophy in its correc-

---

[48]Douglas Lipton, Robert Martinson, and Judith Wilks, *The Effectiveness of Correctional Treatment: A Survey of Treatment Evaluation Studies* (New York: Praeger Publishers, 1975), p. 627.

[49]James Q. Wilson, *Thinking About Crime* (New York: Basic Books, Inc., 1975), p. 169.

[50]David Fogel, ". . . We Are The Living Proof . . ." (Cincinnati, Ohio: The W. H. Anderson Co., 1975), p. 183.

[51]Ernest Van den Haag, *Punishing Criminals*, p. 15.

tional system in 1976, as evidenced by the statement of its Commissioner of Corrections: "Rehabilitation as a goal for all our inmates has never been attained and probably is not attainable. . . .our goals are now purely safe and humane confinement."[52] In 1977, California abolished the indeterminate sentence, and its new Determinate Sentencing Act (Senate Bill 42) unequivocally announced the changed penal philosophy of the state that once led the nation in correctional treatment innovations: "The legislature finds and declares that the purpose of imprisonment for crime is punishment."[53]

A Rational View of Punishment in Corrections

In 1910, in an address to the House of Commons, Winston Churchill made his memorable statement on the relationship between civilization and the treatment of criminals. He said, "The mood and temper of the public with regard to the treatment of crime and criminals is one of the unfailing tests of the civilization of any country." It is still an unfailing test.

As the pendulum swings back and forth between the permissive libertarians and the punitively vengeful, the baby is regularly thrown out with the bath water. What corrections need is a balanced and rational view of its mission, and that includes a balanced and rational view of the place of punishment in the correctional endeavor. Part of the problem is that punishment is generally equated with physical pain. It does not have to be. As we have stated earlier, deprivation in which the sanction penalizes but does not brutalize, is a valid mode of punishment.

Of course imprisonment constitutes punishment, and it should. The punishing element, however, should be the deprivation of liberty, not physical or spiritual degradation. The correctional philosophy of punishment should be based on restraint of liberty. In exceptionally serious cases, and those for whom rehabilitation cannot be safely predicated, restraint would be total and institutional. Such cases would constitute a small minority. For serious cases with a positive prognosis, there could be a period of institutional restraint, with qualified restraint upon release. For moderate or innocuous offenses, limited restraint would be the rule in community-based correctional programs. This philosophy of punishment would be based not on soft determinism, but on soft indeterminism. A man without options is not a free man, nor can he demonstrate free will. Culpability, philosophically, would be based on the presence or absence of options. Adverse circumstances could always be introduced in mitigation of culpability. It is interesting to note that choice is implicit in Dr. William

[52]John R. Manson, quoted in *Criminal Justice Newsletter*, 7, No. 12 (June 7, 1976), 7.

[53]Sec. 1170, *Deering's California Penal Code*, 1978 ed. An excellent distillation of this important law can be found in *Criminal Justice Newsletter*, 7, No. 18 (Sept. 13, 1976), p. 1.

Glasser's reality therapy, which we shall discuss in greater detail in Chapter 6. In Glasser's theory, the offender must choose to adopt the rules governing the conforming majority as the *quid pro quo* of his reintegration.

We have talked about the philosophy of punishment, although the corrections worker would normally be more involved with the practical aspects of punishment. Nevertheless, there is theory behind every practice. As an adjunct of the theory we have lightly touched upon, a practical system of (penal) penalties could be developed. Menninger made a useful distinction between *punishment* and *penalty,* using "punishment" in the narrower, non-philosophic sense. He called the former, "pain inflicted over the years for the sake of inflicting pain." The latter he defined as "a predetermined price levied automatically, invariably, and categorically in direct relation to a violation or infraction of a pre-set rule or " 'law.' "[54] To consciously inflict pain is to cater to the vengeful and sadistic impulses in man. To establish rational penalties, and to impose them without discrimination and invariably, is to place emphasis upon both the individual's personal responsibility and the law's impartiality. "Penalty," of course, would cover a range of sanctions and would not necessarily imply incarceration. A fine or service to the community epitomizes both deprivation (of money in one instance, and time in the other) and penalty.

Seriously "outrageous" criminals must be neutralized. In the absence of therapeutic magic, neutralization will have to take place in an institutional setting. Nor should release take place until such time as the behavioral sciences have reached a stage where the outrageous criminal's pathology can be rectified, and the public's safety can be reasonably assured. In some instances permanent custodial security would be indicated. The majority of offenders, however, present a different picture.

There is a well-worn truth in corrections that about 95 percent of all institutionalized offenders eventually are released and return to the community. Society has a vested interest in their reintegration. It is not treatment or rehabilitation that has failed; it is ineffectual rehabilitative tactics and strategies that have failed. They must be replaced with more effective modes of reconstruction. Redemption, after all, is intrinsically meritorious.

SYNOPSIS

There is a great deal of philosophic dispute over the nature of punishment, and an equal amount of controversy as to the place of punishment in the criminal justice process. On the one extreme, punishment is viewed

[54]Karl Menninger, *The Crime of Punishment* (New York: The Viking Press, 1968), p. 202.

as an essential element in social control; at the other extreme, it has been called "the application of force to another person against his or her will."

In the classic view, expressed so well by Hart, punishment must involve an unpleasant consequence such as pain, be for an act against legal rules, and be intentionally administered by the duly constituted authority against which the offense was committed. For a succinct definition, one might consider van den Haag's concept: Punishment is "a deprivation or suffering imposed by law."

Theories of punishment are generally based upon concepts of retribution, deterrence, or reformation. Retributivists teach that punishment is deserved, and whether or not it deters is of no consequence. Those who see a deterrent element in punishment, view punishment as emendatory. And humanists generally decry punishment as a barbarism.

The philosophy undergirding the American criminal justice system basically derives from the Classical-Utilitarian viewpoint, which supports deterrence, tactily endorses free will, is motivated by utility, and holds the belief that the punishment should fit the crime.

Historically, the advent of the scientific era brought in positivism and a general repudiation of free will. Accountability was substituted for responsibility. But the inability of this frame of reference to deal with self-determination resulted in the rise of "soft determinism," and a resurgence of the Classical point of view or neo-Classicism. In contemporary times, this culminated in the emergence of the so-called Punishment Model.

Corrections needs a balanced and rational philosophy of punishment, in which deprivation is seen as effective punishment and through which provision is made for differential punishment. The "outrageous offender," for example, might have to be indefinitely immobilized, whereas the nonserious offender would need minimal incapacitation. Menninger says that predetermined penalties, rather than capricious sanctions, would do much to restore justice in the imposition of punishment.

2 Treatment in Perspective

The public will grow increasingly ashamed of its cry for retaliation, its persistent demand to punish. This is its crime, our crime against criminals—and incidentally our crime against ourselves. For before we can diminish our sufferings from the ill-controlled aggressive assaults of fellow citizens, we must renounce the philosophy of punishment, the obsolete, vengeful penal attitude. In its place we would seek a comprehensive, constructive social attitude—therapeutic in some instances, restraining in some instances, but preventive in its total social impact.

Karl Menninger
The Crime of Punishment

Chicago has had more than its fair share of sensational crimes, including such notables as the St. Valentine's Day Massacre in 1929, and the William Heirens case. Earlier, in 1924, that city was stunned by the senseless, wanton murder of ten-year-old Bobbie Frank by two brilliant, wealthy profligates, Richard Loeb and Nathan Leopold. Because it was a "perfect crime" thrill-killing, with no apparent mitigation, the passions of the citizens were inflamed, and it was a foregone conclusion that the two young murderers would be convicted and subsequently executed. The defense attorney was the celebrated Clarence Darrow. With conviction a certitude, it would require every ounce of his legal skill to forestall execution. The trial, without a jury, lasted almost three months. The wily Darrow had encouraged his clients to waive their right to a jury trial, thus permitting the attorney to concentrate the full powers of his forensic skills upon the presiding judge alone.

In an eloquent summation, Darrow pointed out the perplexion that he faced when "officers of justice" plotted and planned for months to take the lives of individuals who were themselves on trial for *plotting and planning* to take the life of an individual. He then asked:

> What is my friend's [the prosecutor's] idea of justice? He says to this court, "Give them the same mercy that they gave Bobbie Frank."
>
> If the state in which I live is not kinder, more humane, more considerate than the mad act of these two boys, I am sorry that I have lived so long.

Addressing the court further, Darrow continued,

> I am pleading that we overcome cruelty with kindness and hatred with love. Your Honor stands between the past and the future. You may hang these boys, but in doing it you will turn your face toward the past. In doing it you would make it harder for every other boy who in ignorance and darkness must grope his way through the mazes which only childhood knows. . . .I am pleading for the future; I am pleading for a time when we can learn by reason and judgment and understanding and faith that all life is worth saving, and that mercy is the highest attribute of man.

It is of historical interest to note that Darrow's eloquence and wily strategy saved his clients from execution. They were both sentenced to life imprisonment. Of greater significance is the fact that "The Loeb-Leopold case has long been pointed to as the entering wedge which permitted psychiatry to be recognized in criminal court."[1] Darrow had employed several outstanding psychiatrists in an effort to mitigate the sentence, rather than to establish a defense of insanity. The prosecution had its experts, who offered contrary opinions. While the defense was not materially benefited by the psychiatric testimony, the fact that so many expert psychiatric witnesses testified for such an appreciable amount of time enhanced the stature of psychiatry in the courts of law. It signalled the beginning of judicial respect for forensic psychiatry. The battle to define and defend treatment in corrections has been relentlessly waged ever since.

TREATMENT: NATURE AND OBJECTIVES

In Chapter One we learned that punishment has been broadly conceptualized in terms of retribution, deterrence, and treatment. According to

---

[1]Harry Elmer Barnes and Negley K. Teeters, *New Horizons in Criminology* (Englewood Cliffs, N.J.: Prentice-Hall, Inc., 1950), p. 322.

the retributivist frame of reference, punishment is inflicted because it is deserved. In the Classical-Utilitarian philosophy, it is imposed to deter the offender and others from further criminality. But as the rehabilitative thrust began to influence corrections, punishment began to be thought of as a means toward the end of reformation.

As far back as the turn of the present century, the humane, reform-minded writer, Frederick Wines, had stated, "Reasonable punishment (we are now using the word in a physical sense) has an undoubted place in criminal therapy, for the contemplation of discomfort is a strong deterrent, especially for the man who possesses fair intelligence and foresight."[2] While the influence of deterrence is evident in Wines' statement, it still pays tribute to the reformative potential of "reasonable" punishment.

Deterrence, so deeply rooted in the Classical tradition, was based on the implicit belief that punishment *per se* diverted offenders from recidivistic behavior. As the rehabilitative ideal flowered, the feeling developed that punishment could be transmogrified into treatment. Packer phrased it well when he said that in this view "punishment is an instrumental use of one man for the benefit of other men." He adds, "After all, the goal sought by the rehabilitative ideal is not reform for its own sake or even for the sake of enabling its object to live a better and happier life. We hope that he will do so, but the justification is a social one; we want to reform him so that he will cease to offend."[3] The real importance of such a philosophy is that it is offender-oriented. The emphasis is on the offender rather than on the offense or the retributive process of the criminal justice system. While such an emphasis is laudable, it can be criticized if it becomes inordinate and omits a proper concern for the safety of society. Before it retreated from a rehabilitative philosophy in the mid-seventies, the California parole system had carried the offender-oriented approach to such an extreme that it was chided formally by an attorney general's task force.[4]

The need for a balanced correctional philosophy is evident. The common good and the offender's transformation must be holistically approached. Reformative efforts must be rational and treatment methods must be effective. Before we can examine the rational and effective efforts of corrections, it is desirable to more precisely enumerate what we mean by treatment.

[2] Frederick Howard Wines, *Punishment and Reformation,* rev. ed. (New York: Thomas Y. Crowell Company, Publishers, 1910), p. 350.

[3] Herbert L. Packer, "The Justification for Punishment," in Leonard Orland (ed.), *Justice, Punishment, Treatment* (New York: The Free Press, 1973), p. 188.

[4] *Report to Attorney General Evelle J. Younger, from the Task Force on Probation and Parole* (Sacramento: Office of the Attorney General, undated, but issued May 18, 1971).

Defining Treatment

Sometimes the terms *treatment* and *rehabilitation* are used interchangeably, but the precise distinction between the two should not be lost sight of. Rehabilitation literally means the restoration to a former capacity. It can be facetiously observed that an unsuccessful burglar, restored to a former capacity, might emerge as a reconstituted burglar! I have previously commented[5] that habilitation might be the preferred term, for it comes from the Latin root, *habilitas,* which means aptitude. Habilitation, therefore, would indicate the act of acquiring aptitude or enhancing one's qualifications.

Rehabilitation has been defined in diverse ways. A popular definition is that it consists of "returning 'independently functioning' individuals to society."[6] But this poses a dilemma, as Wilmot astutely noted:

> Individuals commit deviant acts in response to "system strains and stresses," yet the stated outcome of rehabilitation is to cause individuals to plug back into the same system thereby perpetuating it.[7]

An English writer with uncommon insight has defined rehabilitation as "being sentenced to receive help."[8] For our purpose rehabilitation may be considered as the broad, generic term for the philosophy as well as the activity of human reconstruction. This will serve as a basic working definition. The vulnerable aspects of rehabilitation definition and theory will be touched upon throughout this text, where appropriate.

In contradistinction, treatment broadly refers to those strategies and techniques which are aimed at the alleviation of a state of disability. In this context, criminality constitutes the (social) disability, and correctional treatment would be concerned with terminating, or attempting to terminate, the criminal predisposition.

One commentator asserts that treatment "for correctional 'clients' consists of explicit procedures deliberately instituted to alter those conditions believed to be responsible for unlawful behavior. Treatment implies some rationale which interprets the criminal behavior of the individual as deriving from some particular set of intrapsychic and/or environmentally lodged set of factors or conditions."[9]

[5]Louis P. Carney, *Introduction to Correctional Science* (New York: McGraw-Hill Book Company, 1974), footnote 37.

[6]Richard Wilmot, "What Is Rehabilitation?," *International Journal of Offender Therapy and Comparative Criminology,* 20, No. 3 (1976), 246.

[7]*Ibid.,* p. 247.

[8]Philip Bean, *Rehabilitation and Deviance* (London: Routledge & Kegan Paul, 1976), p. 1.

[9]Sheldon Salsberg, "Treating Offenders: Some Suggestions for Improving Efforts of Change Agents," in Edward Sagarin and Donal E. J. MacNamara, *Corrections: Problems of Punishment and Rehabilitation* (New York: Praeger Publishers, 1973), p. 19.

In the field of corrections, as one authority has observed, treatment is commonly referred to as "correctional intervention."[10] Johnson integates this concept in his definition of treatment, which he describes as "any organized and deliberate intervention, regardless of the particular image held of human nature and of the particular strategy employed."[11] The emphasis in this definition is on the functional and not the philosophical, which gives it practical appeal. The correctional treatment approach is an *intervention approach,* the stated objective of which is to improve the adaptive condition of the individual and, in the long run, the harmony in society. It should not be mistakenly thought, however, that because the practical is emphasized for convenience, the philosophic is unimportant. Paul Tillich once observed that no therapeutic theory "can be developed without an implicit or explicit image of man."[12]

In the medical arts, a treatment strategy or technique might be accompanied by a medicinal substance, but there are no magic pills to hand out in correctional treatment. In lieu of a substance, there are elements of humanistic philosophy, confidence in the efficacy of intervention, a variety of programs designed to facilitate reintegration of the offender into the community and, above all else, a belief that change is possible. To reach that state of affairs, penal philosophy and practice had to endure a long and painful parturition.

The Objectives of Treatment

Earlier in this chapter we quoted Bean's definition of rehabilitation: "being sentenced to receive help." In that broad context, treatment represents all programs, tactics, strategies, and manipulations designed to carry out the helping intent of rehabilitation. This is a very pragmatic definition of treatment. The abstract concept of correctional treatment is characterized by endless controversy. As we have noted, the very efficacy of correctional treatment has been seriously questioned, resulting in what Fairchild calls an "emergent sense of futility. . . ."[13] It is relatively easy to discern the

---

[10]Ted Palmer, "Martinson Revisited," *Journal of Research in Crime and Delinquency,* Vol. 12, No. 2 (July 1975), p. 133.

[11]Elmer H. Johnson, *Crime, Correction, and Society,* 4th ed. (Homewood, Ill.: The Dorsey Press, 1978), p. 61.

[12]Cited in C. H. Patterson, *Theories of Counseling and Psychotherapy* (New York: Harper & Row, Publishers, 1966), p. x.

[13]Erika S.Fairchild, "New Perspectives on Corrections Policy," in John A. Gardiner and Michael A. Mulkey (eds.), *Crime and Criminal Justice* (Lexington, Mass: D. C. Heath and Company, 1975), p. 195.

modes of help that are proferred to ex-offenders, but measuring the treatment potential qualitatively is another issue entirely.

Many see the rehabilitation model as being summarily dismissed, and without serious support from contemporary theoreticians and practitioners. That is only partially true. A sufficient number of promising correctional efforts will be covered in this text to dispel rampant cynicism. A significant amount of pessimism concerning rehabilitation does exist, however, and warrants concern. Two views appear to dominate in corrections, in the wake of the floundering rehabilitation model. One, which Fairchild dubs the "counsel of despair,"[14] might almost be termed the purely retributive stance. The essence of this view is captured in Wilson's dispassionate statement: "Wicked people exist. Nothing avails except to set them apart from innocent people."[15] And they are to be set aside in prisons, the purpose of which is punishment.

A second major view is the haven of those, among others, who are persuaded that the rehabilitation model is dead, but who remain "treatment oriented." The position of this school of thought is that crime and delinquency are the resultants of inequitable or dysfunctional social institutions. Therefore we ought to be attacking the root causes, because the prospect of rehabilitating offenders is remote if societal institutions do not provide the individual with fulfillment. The student should be reminded of Wilmot's statement, quoted earlier in this chapter, that rehabilitation causes offenders to be plugged back into the system which precipitated the delinquent act in the first place. This epitomizes the "dysfunctional view."

This is also a controversial view, despite the seeming logic associated with it, namely, that crime and delinquency actually represent society's failure—through defective institutions—to facilitate personal fulfillment. The controversy centers on the legitimate parameters of corrections. Fairchild feels that "a basic reevaluation of all American society . . . goes much beyond consideration of corrections, which is essentially a small part of the major social change that is called for."[16] That is, corrections is outside of its domain when it becomes an advocate of social change. An opposite viewpoint is implanted in the correctional system of Minnesota, which categorically adopts the position that the correctional agency has an obligation to advocate social change. It has, in fact, made this premise a matter of official philosophy:

[14]*Ibid.*
[15]James Q. Wilson, *Thinking about Crime* (New York: Basic Books, Inc., Publishers, 1975), p. 209.
[16]Fairchild, "New Perspectives on Corrections Policy," p. 196.

The Minnesota Department of Corrections believes that crime and delinquency are symptoms of failure and disorganization, not only of the offender but also of society. All too frequently, the person convicted of a crime has had limited contact with the positive forces that develop law abiding conduct (i.e., good schools, gainful employment, adequate housing, and rewarding leisure time activities). The Department supports the expenditure of staff time and subsidy money for the advocacy of social change, whenever such change is designed to impact on those conditions which are conducive to the commission of crime.[17]

The student can readily sense that corrections is in a state of indecision. This has been brought about by two principal factors: (1) the philosophical, and (2) the political. Corrections is guilty of failing to develop what Culbertson refers to as "a goal structure,"[18] basically because of the philosophic problem centered in the retributive-utilitarian controversy, which we discussed in Chapter One. A lack of consensus as to the purpose of punishment has effectively blockaded corrections in its efforts to define clearly its goals and objectives. Meanwhile, scholars and politicians, for very different reasons, continue the battle to establish the primacy of one view over another.

The political factor is of equal importance. While philosophers take the problem into the realm of the abstract, the politically motivated more often remain in the arena of hard-headed practicality. Reasons and Kaplan have pointed out, for example, that the function of the prison isn't merely to carry out the intent of idealized correction. They contend that the "latent functions" of the prison, borrowing Merton's concept, include providing employment for over "70,000 persons, many of whom would find it difficult to procure jobs elsewhere."[19] Anyone who has worked in the correctional system, particularly in the prison system, can attest to the truth of the qualifying phrase in this statement. The prison also performs the following less obvious latent functions, according to Reasons and Kaplan:

1. Slave labor for prison industries
2. Psychic satisfaction for authoritarian employees
3. Reduction of unemployment
4. Subjects for laboratory testing

[17]Minnesota Department of Corrections, *Report to the 1977 Minnesota Legislature, Summary Report,* p. 3.

[18]Robert C. Culbertson, "Corrections: The State of the Art," *Journal of Criminal Justice,* Vol. 5, No. 1 (Spring 1977), 39.

[19]C. E. Reasons and R. L. Kaplan, "Tear Down the Walls? Some Functions of Prisons," *Crime and Delinquency,* Vol. 21, No. 4 (October 1975), 367.

5. A safety valve for racial tensions in the community by virtue of the incarceration of the minority and the poor
6. Birth control

It is clear that these and other "latent" factors effectively impede the establishment of clearcut correctional goals. For instance, the system provides not only routine jobs, but also many opportunities for political patronage and political payoff. This practice is so deep-seated that it would be a folly to expect that it would be eliminated in the forseeable future. The correctional system, like any other large bureaucracy, is a pork-barreling enterprise and, as such, is a constant source of distress to the idealist in corrections. The idealized objective of corrections should not be abandoned, but they have to be tempered by practicality. Goals should be reasonably attainable.

It is true that social institutions are defective, and defective institutions often precipitate delinquent patterns of behavior. But it is also true that the criminality of many individuals is not so readily attributable to defective social institutions. Crime is coeval with society. The eminent theorist, Emile Durkheim, considered it a normal attribute of society.[20] Society does not have to set as its goal the absolute (and unrealizable) elimination of crime. But it must delimit crime and control it. While scholars pursue the elusive theoretical frame of reference that has been missing in corrections, practitioners can accept as the functional objective of corrections the reintegration of offenders into society. Rational redemption should be the principal objective of corrections, and that equates with maximal diversion of individuals from the criminal justice system, by whatever legitimate means.

Is Rehabilitation Dead?

The contemporary controversy surrounding correctional rehabilitation, which ignited in the mid-seventies, is a strident one, but one that promotes over-simplification. Arrayed at one extreme are the inflexible iconoclasts, committed to an unmitigated punishment philosophy. They attack the penal code for not being sufficiently punitive; prosecutors for not being acceptably vigorous; judges for being "soft-headed"; and probation and parole for unwarranted indulgence. At the other end of the spectrum are the "treatment" zealots, who have such an invincible faith in rehabilitation that they refuse to consider anyone unresponsive to "treatment" medi-

---

[20]Emile Durkheim, *The Rules of Sociological Method*, 8th ed., trans. Sarah A. Solvang and John H. Mueller (New York: Free Press, 1950), esp. pp. 65–66.

ation. Reason dictates a middle ground. It is not simply a case of punishment versus treatment. It is a case of what kind of punishment and what kind of treatment.

A rational view of corrections accepts punishment and treatment as compatible reconstructive elements. Punishment in this context refers to reasonable restraint, deprivation, or incapacitation, not to physical abuse. Rehabilitation presumes the application of influential modes of activity aimed at the redirection of behavior. The one must follow the other. As I have commented in another source, the necessity of punishment equally affirms the necessity of redemption.[21]

Philosophers use the term "meliorism" to indicate a reasonable middle ground between hopeless despair and Pollyanna optimism, with its boundless hope. Meliorists believe in the human capacity to improve conditions of life. They neither despair piteously nor are they blind to the impediments of reality. The motto of a meliorist might well be "Improvement *is* possible." Unmitigated punishment is an affront to reason. Blind optimism is an affront to reality. Meliorism is the ignition of hope and the promise of progress. In an editorial comment on the confusing misinterpretation that has plagued the term *rehabilitation,* Mary G. Almore, of the University of Texas Institute of Urban Studies, stated: "Perhaps it is indeed time to throw out the *word,* to find a new and more meaningful term permitting new and more meaningful programs . . . before confusion leads to the ultimate detriment of corrections and, indeed, to the detriment of the total criminal justice system and the society it seeks to protect."[22] I submit that the new term should be *correctional meliorism,* or, simply, *meliorism.*

Correctional treatment tactics do not have to fit any particular formula, but must submit to empirical examination. Martinson's[23] seemingly devastating attack on scores of correctional treatment programs deserves another inspection. First, assuming the validity of his findings, the worst that could be concluded is that the *strategies,* not the *philosophy,* have failed. This suggests the need for a re-examination of tactic rather than a repudiation of philosophy. Second, the argument in favor of a punishment model will be proportionately weakened as Martinson's findings are contradicted or refuted.[24]

[21]Louis P. Carney, *Introduction to Correctional Science,* 2nd ed. (New York: McGraw-Hill Book Company, 1979), p. 372.

[22]Mary G. Almore, Editorial, "Rehabilitation: The 'Fudge Factor' of Corrections," *Criminology,* Vol. 15, No. 2 (August 1977), 147.

[23]As mentioned in Chapter One, although Martinson had two very competent co-authors, and he is actually the second listed author in the title credits, I refer to the study at hand as "the Martinson study" because it is generally acknowledged that he is the prime theoretician.

[24]Because few studies—or "efforts" as Martinson prefers to call his evaluative

In the space of a little over two years, two articles appeared in reputable sources, each of which was entitled, "Is Rehabilitation Dead?" The first article appeared as the Punishment Model was surfacing, and when the full sound and fury was being directed against correctional rehabilitation.[25] The second had the benefit of two years of sound and fury to look back upon.[26] Both gave convincing arguments that rehabilitation is not dead. *Corrections Magazine* conducted a survey of influential correctional administrators and made these significant statements:

> The overwhelming majority of America's top prison administrators reject the argument that rehabilitation programs don't work.
>
> In a national survey . . . 63 per cent of the prison officials say that some rehabilitation programs can change inmate behavior for the better. An additional 14 per cent maintain that there is not enough evidence to justify scrapping the idea of rehabilitation.[27]

The internationally respected psychiatrist, Seymour Halleck, attributes the attack on correctional rehabilitation to three major trends: (1) the rising crime rates, (2) the "streams of academic research," which have supported the effectiveness of punishment and challenged the efficacy of rehabilitation, and (3) the attacks of civil libertarians, particularly on the indeterminate sentence.[28]

According to Halleck and White, the well-to-do have begun to feel a sense of powerlessness in the face of increasing economic crime, and they have begun to renege on their traditional support of rehabilitation. In addition, academic research has been critically zoning in on rehabilitation and drawing increasingly negative inferences. Martinson is again cited, with his oft-quoted comment, after evaluating 231 rehabilitation programs: "With few and isolated exceptions, the rehabilitative efforts that have been reported so far have had no appreciable effect on recidivism."[29]

---

endeavors—have generated such emotional and polarizing controversy, numerous critical articles have been appearing on the subject. Among the more substantive are the following: Ted Palmer, "Martinson Revisited," *Journal of Research in Crime and Delinquency* (July 1975); Sol Chaneles, "A Look at Martinson's Report," *Fortune News* (November 1975); Stuart Adams, "Evaluating Research in Corrections: A Practical Guide" (National Institute of Law Enforcement and Criminal Justice, 1975). In addition, James O. Robison has undertaken a lengthy review of Martinson's book in *Crime and Delinquency*, Vol. 22, No. 4 (October 1976), 483–86.

[25]Michael S. Serrill, "Is Rehabilitation Dead?" *Corrections Magazine*, Vol. 1, No. 5 (May-June 1975), 3–13, 21–36.

[26]Seymour L. Halleck and Ann D. White, "Is Rehabilitation Dead?," *Crime and Delinquency*, 23, No. 4 (October 1977), 372–82.

[27]Serrill, "Is Rehabilitation Dead?" p. 3.

[28]Halleck and White, "Is Rehabilitation Dead?," 372–74.

[29]Robert Martinson, "What Works?—Questions and Answers about Prison Reforms," *The Public Interest* (Spring 1974), 25.

Finally, "civil liberties workers" are attacking the system from another vantage point. They reason that if rehabilitation is not working, and if the indeterminate sentence requires custodial incapacitation while rehabilitation is taking place, then individuals are being incarcerated without due process.

Halleck and White take the position that "a careful assessment of the evidence" would suggest "that supporting a shift in emphasis from rehabilitation to retribution and deterrence is a major error."[30] They point out that almost all the critical evaluations of rehabilitation have focused on "personality-changing" programs to the neglect of those with an emphasis on "opportunity-changing," and it is hardly valid to draw negative inferences from programs that have generally been "perfunctory, underfunded, understaffed, and carried out in settings certainly not ideal."[31]

Another flaw in the negative evaluations is that they use gross data to determine success. That is, the deterrent potential of rehabilitation is measured in terms of how many *of the total number* of a given treatment cohort recidivate. Halleck and White incisively point out, "The major methodological grounds on which research on deterrence can be criticized is its use of *aggregate data* to test a theory of *individual motivation*."[32] (Italics added). This is the fallacy of the medical model, which sees rehabilitation as engaged in "curing" the aggregate "disease" of crime instead of being concerned with individual uniquenesses. The retributive approach cannot be justified on the basis of conclusions drawn from this type of data. Furthermore, an unmitigated philosophy of retribution in corrections would turn prisons into warehouses, benign though they might be. "What kind of person would want to work in an institution devoted primarily to benign warehousing?"[33]

TRENDS AND ISSUES
IN CORRECTIONAL TREATMENT

The emperor Justinian I (483-565) is fittingly best known for his greatest accomplishment, the codification of the Roman Law. Because this code prohibited the punishing of an imprisoned man, and stipulated the purpose of imprisonment to be solely detention, Barr and Zunin feel that the concept of rehabilitation originated in the Justinian Code.[34] Conceptually

---

[30]Halleck and White, "Is Rehabilitation Dead?," p. 374.

[31]*Ibid.,* p. 375.

[32]*Ibid.,* p. 377.

[33]*Ibid.,* p. 379.

[34]Norman I. Barr and Leonard M. Zunin, "Community Involvement, Judicial Administration and Campus Prisons," *International Journal of Social Psychiatry,* 21, No. 2 (Summer 1975), 94. Both authors, interestingly, are medical doctors.

and historically this may be true, but the shift from a repressive and punitive penal posture to one emphasizing reformation and reconstruction is a relatively recent development. While a veritable potpourri of influences were responsible for the shifting philosophy, it is possible to pinpoint some milestones. For centuries punishment for offenses against the commonweal was purely vengeful and retributive. The purpose of a sentence was the infliction of punishment. The criminal got what he deserved. But some major developments and upheavals in the eighteenth and nineteenth centuries eventually led concerned people to scrutinize the intent of punishment. Values had been changing dramatically as a result of the Age of Enlightenment, the Industrial Revolution, and the emergence of the Scientific Method.

The Wellsprings of Correctional Treatment

The first individual to suggest that "task sentences" would be preferable to "time sentences" was Archbishop Whately, who did so in Dublin, Ireland in 1832. Whately said that a convict "instead of being imprisoned for a certain length of time, should be sentenced to perform a certain amount of work...."[35] This view was shared by Captain Alexander Maconochie, Governor of Norfolk Island and administrator of the infamous penal colony at Van Diemen's Land in Australia. It was Maconochie, celebrated as one of the most distinguished names associated with the development of parole, who introduced the "marks system," through which a convict, by diligent labor and good behavior, could hasten his release from incarceration. The importance of the viewpoint shared by Whately and Maconochie is that it introduced the concept that reformation is the purpose of the penal sentence.

If any one particular event heralded the advent of the reformation era, it was the founding of the Hospice of San Michel by Pope Clement XI, in Rome in 1704. This was the first institution ever established for juvenile offenders. Although it was run by strict monastic rule, with firm discipline and hard work, it was the founding philosophy which impressed observers. Pope Clement XI had placed an inscription above the door which read, *Parum est coercere improbos poena nisi probos efficias discipline* ("It is insufficient to restrain the wicked by punishment unless you render them virtuous by corrective discipline"). According to Wines, this

> was a formal and official admission, by the highest authority, that the entire system of retribution and repression had proved a practical failure. The erection of this juvenile reformatory institution, therefore, is the landmark which divides two civilizations or two historical epochs.[36]

[35]Wines, *Punishment and Reformation,* p. 192.
[36]*Ibid.,* pp. 122-23.

I have earlier made reference to the first congress of the American Prison Association (1870), which was characterized by great reformative zeal. In fact, that congress took the position that the principal aim of punishment was reformation. The nineteenth century was notable for the development of the rehabilitation philosophy. Psychiatry was flexing its prepubertal muscles and taking greater interest in the criminal law. The writings of such influential individuals as Sigmund Freud gave impetus to what Wolfgang called "the psychiatrization of the criminal law."[37] Another force responsible for the rehabilitation model, according to Fogel, was "the ascendancy of democracy with its new hopeful view of the nature of man. . . ."[38]

After centuries of ignorance about criminal behavior and centuries of brutalization of the offender, the rehabilitation model was a natural counterpoint, and the growth of the behavioral sciences was its nutrient. Some would say that it received its first practical application in the Chicago Area Project.

The Chicago Area Project

In the first quarter of this century, the University of Chicago dominated the fledgling discipline of sociology, and was the major influence in this developing field. It sometimes seems as if every one of the giant pioneers in American sociology was, at one time, on the faculty at the University of Chicago. Among the prominent names associated with this faculty during that embryonic period were Florian Znaniecki, W. I. Thomas, Louis Wirth, Frederic Thrasher, Ellsworth Faris, E. Franklin Frazer, George Herbert Mead, Ernest W. Burgess, Robert Park, Henry D. McKay, and Clifford R. Shaw. Clifford R. Shaw, in association with Ernest Burgess and Henry D. McKay, is memorable for instituting a program of delinquency prevention that has come to be known as the Chicago Area Project.

The Chicago Area Project had several distinctive characteristics. First, it was designed to be compatible with the findings in sociological literature pertaining to juvenile delinquency. Second, it placed a heavy emphasis on the relationship of the younger generation to the older generation in terms of delinquency development, and as such the Chicago Area Project could well have been designated as one of the pioneer studies in reference group theory. Third, it gave pioneer emphasis to ecological factors in delinquency causation. Fourth, it was a socio-psychological study, because its main focus was on social control. As Kobrin noted, "the theory on which

---

[37]Marvin E. Wolfgang, "Real and Perceived Changes of Crime and Punishment," *Daedalus,* 107, No. 1 (Winter 1978), 152.

[38]David Fogel, ". . . *We Are the Living Proof . . .*" (Cincinnati: The W. H. Anderson Company, 1975), p. 50.

the Area Project program is based is that, taken in its most general aspect, delinquency as a problem in the modern metropolis is principally a product of the breakdown of the machinery of spontaneous social control."[39]

The Chicago researchers discovered that delinquency was relatively concentrated in specific areas. These were also the areas in which immigrant groups lived. The first filial generation (first born of the foreign-born) was classically experiencing culture conflict, torn between the values of the new world and the old world. One result was that the controlling influence of the older traditions diminished. This resulted in a breakdown in cross-generational control, and delinquency was the frequent end product. For the research people, the inference was obvious: "A delinquency prevention program could hardly hope to be effective unless and until the aims of such a program became the aims of the local populations."[40]

Since delinquency was seen as an adaptive mechanism, in which the male child struggled to find a meaningful adult role, "delinquency prevention activities must somehow first become activities of the adults constituting the natural world of the youngster."[41] And that was what the Chicago Area Project fundamentally sought to do, to develop community action programs which involved the adult community in the preventive battle against delinquency. This was based on the soicological postulate that people will support endeavors only if they have a meaningful role in them. The problem of delinquency was a problem of the wider community. Delinquents were the children of that wider community. Therefore the residents of the wider community should take collective action because the problem was one affecting the whole community, and because the socialization process is so vitally a part of that local community.

Clifford R. Shaw and his associates, in pursuit of these objectives, organized a series of projects in Chicago communities in the 1930s, which were designed to enhance the interaction between adolescents and adults and result in a reduction of delinquency. Indigenous committees were formed in a dozen communities using local citizens, particularly those with perceptive awareness of the important cultural values and institutions of the local residents. While formally trained social workers took exception to the level of competence of such recruits,[42] the fact is that the Chicago researchers were nurturing what has subsequently become a heralded technique—indigenous paraprofessionalism. The thrust of the

[39]Solomon Kobrin, "The Chicago Area Project," in Norman Johnston, Leonard Savitz, and Marvin E. Wolfgang (eds.), *The Sociology of Punishment and Correction*, 2nd. ed. (New York: John Wiley and Sons, Inc., 1970), p. 579.

[40]*Ibid.*

[41]*Ibid.*

[42]*Ibid.*, p. 581.

programs was three-fold: (1) Community pride and coherence was induced by campaigns for community improvement, (2) recreational activities were developed for youngsters, and (3) concern was directed toward
the adjudicated delinquent by the creation of fulfilling activities on his
behalf.

The Chicago Area Project has usually been viewed from two perspectives, that of community organization and that of delinquency reduction.
In the first context, the question is, can communities be effectively organized in such projects, and will they endure? Martin answered this question with a "definitely affirmative."[43] Similar conclusions had been
reached, in earlier evaluations, by Witmar and Tufts, by Sorrentino, and
by Short.[44]

With respect to reduction in delinquency, Martin is less resoundingly
affirmative, but says that the evidence tends to suggest an affirmative
also.[45] He is less definitive merely because of the absence of certain controls which limit the conclusions that may be drawn. For instance, in one
project, only one parolee out of a total of forty-one worked with, in a
nine-year period, was recommitted to an institution.[46] But no comparable
control group was utilized. Witmer and Tufts, however, pointed out that
delinquency rates declined in three-quarters of the communities in which
the projects were operative,[47] and Bartollas and Miller have stated that
"The Chicago Area Project has the most impressive evidence of success."[48]

Although the Chicago Area Project remains operative as an independent, private agency, it can be concluded that it was the impelling influence for the passage of the 1975 Illinois Commission on Delinquency Prevention Act. The philosophy of the Chicago Area Project is embodied in
that Act:

[43]John M. Martin, "Three Approaches to Delinquency Prevention: A Critique," *Crime
and Delinquency*, 7, No. 1 (January 1961), 23.

[44]H. L. Witmer and E. Tufts, *The Effectiveness of Delinquency Prevention Programs*, Chil-
dren's Bureau, U.S. Department of Health, Education, and Welfare, Publication 350
(Washington, D.C.: U.S. Government Printing Office, 1954); Anthony Sorrentino, "The
Chicago Area Project after 25 Years," *Federal Probation*, 23, No. 2 (June 1959), 40-45; An-
thony Sorrentino, "The Chicago Area Project after Forty Years," paper presented at the
Midwest Sociological Society Meeting in Chicago, April 10, 1975; James F. Short, Jr., "The
Chicago Area Project as a Social Movement," excerpt from Introduction to *Juvenile Delin-
quency and Urban Areas*, rev. ed., by Clifford B. Shaw and Henry D. McKay, University of
Chicago Press, 1969, compiled by Illinois Commission on Delinquency Prevention.

[45]Martin, "Three Approaches to Delinquency Prevention," p. 23.

[46]*Ibid.*

[47]Witmer and Tufts, *The Effectiveness of Delinquency Prevention*, p. 16.

[48]Clemens Bartollas and Stuart J. Miller, *The Juvenile Offender: Control, Correctior. and
Treatment* (Boston: Holbrook Press, 1978), p. 186.

The purpose of this Act is to conserve the human resources represented by the youth of the State and to protect society more effectively by providing a program looking toward the prevention of delinquency and crime and by assisting communities in establishing and operating youth welfare and delinquency prevention programs designed to divert children away from the criminal justice system, and by coordinating these programs. Since conditions contributing to delinquency exist in the community where the delinquent child is raised and in the circumstances and associations which effect his early development, it is, therefore, declared that the prevention of delinquency is a matter of public concern and that the State shall encourage the development of local community organizations for effective action on this problem. The enlistment of local people individually and in organized groups in cooperative efforts to attack the problem of delinquency in their immediate neighborhood shall be a basic purpose of the Commission.[49]

Coercive Treatment

In the analysis of treatment in corrections, crucial issues sometimes do not get the emphasis they deserve. There has been a tendency to evaluate correctional treatment from only one point of view, that of the system. The coercive nature of that treatment, and the offender's view of the process, as a result, suffer neglect. The recidivism index, the traditional measure of success or failure, is also a most unsatisfactory instrument, because it is an agregate measure and does not take into account the important dimension of the individual offender's response to the treatment tactics.

The System and Coercion

Treatment is imposed by the authoritative might of the sovereignty behind the criminal justice system, the state. Efforts at reconstruction are initiated *after* the offender becomes a legal ward of the correctional system, and the offender is not ordinarily consulted in terms of the mode of treatment, or concerning his participation. Correctional treatment is coercive treatment. Forced compliance may secure situational conformity, but it denies the individual freedom of choice and the opportunity to become self-motivated. The National Advisory Committee lucidly expressed the inimical features of coercion: "The typical response to coercion is alienation, which may take the form of active hostility to all social controls or later a passive withdrawal into alcoholism, drug addiction, or dependency."[50]

---

[49]Sec. 2, Public Act 79-944, House Bill 199.
[50]National Advisory Commission on Criminal Justice Standards and Goals, *Task Force Report: Corrections* (Washington, D.C.: U.S. Government Printing Office, 1973), p. 223.

Is reformation possible under coercive treatment?

The obvious answer is that not enough is currently known about the effectiveness of various types of treatment to answer this rhetorical question with any degree of certitude. It has been stated that "reformation should be secured through *persuasion* rather than *compulsion*," because the internalization of socially desirable norms is facilitated by volition, whereas coercion produces alienation and further anti-social behavior.[51] Warren introduces an interesting aspect in the analysis of coercion. She states that a request from a loved one is a form of coercion, as are peer demands, and the importunings from those we respect or with whom we identify.[52] The power balance is on the side of the coercer, not on the side of the one coerced. In the criminal justice system, the prospective misuse of coercive power is a clear and present danger, especially with respect to those individuals who are particularly susceptible to pressure. Further research in needed, but it can be speculated that while voluntary treatment participation is overwhelmingly preferable, coercive treatment may not preclude beneficial end results.

Evidence to support this conclusion is suggested in a monumental if highly controversial 16-year study, conducted by psychiatrist Dr. Samuel Yochelson and clinical psychologist Dr. Stanton E. Samenow at St. Elizabeths Hospital, a federal mental institution in Washington, D.C.[53] The senior researcher, Dr. Yochelson, originally sought to determine the difference between criminals who were mentally ill and those who were not. After four years of research he came to the conclusion that there was no difference. The overall study, which was concluded by Dr. Samenow after the death of Dr. Yochelson in 1976, involved an in-depth analysis of over 250 male criminals and collateral contact with their relatives and friends. One dramatic claim made by these researchers is that criminal predispositions are deep-seated and often trace back to very early childhood.

Yochelson and Samenow also instituted a treatment program for these intensively criminalized inmates. Although they drew generally negative conclusions about the recidivistic criminal epitomized in the cohort studied, they estimated that 10 to 20 percent were reformable. Treatment was conducted in the coercive institutional setting, and was pronouncedly moralistic, but was voluntary. Participants were encour-

[51]Louis P. Carney, *Corrections and the Community* (Englewood Cliffs, N.J.: Prentice-Hall, Inc., 1977), p. 31.

[52]Marguerite Q. Warren, "Correctional Treatment and Coercion," *Criminal Justice and Behavior*, 4, No. 4 (December 1977), 357.

[53]Samuel Yochelson and Stanton E. Samenow, *The Criminal Personality. Volume 1: A Profile for Change* (New York: Jason Aronson, Inc., 1976). Two additional volumes complete the published study.

aged to analyze their thinking patterns and were required to keep daily, detailed records of their thoughts. It is too early to make definitive judgments about this study, which has already divided forces, but the important thing is that it indicates the possibility of productive treatment in a penal institution. This study will be discussed in further detail in Chapter Three.

It is clear that the corrections field has been less than dramatically successful in mobilizing definitive answers to the challenging problems of crime and its treatment. Martinson, indeed, likened the history of corrections to "a graveyard of abandoned fads."[54] One of the more enduring fads has been the Medical Model, the obsequies for which have only recently been instituted. Fogel very adequately describes a model as "a conceptualization of a problem and an accompanying strategy to deal with it."[55] The medical model conceptualizes crime as a "social sickness" and the coping strategy is the analogous development of a doctor-patient relationship between the client and the correctional practitioner. With the strong upsurge in social work in the middle decades of this century, and under the hypnotic impetus of Freudian psychoanalysis, the medical model flourished. The battle cry of the social workers was "Study, Diagnosis and Treatment." The unequivocal use of medical terminology, and the medical model paradigm, are evident in this quote from an earlier "bible" of social workers: "Diagnosis is never made for its own sake . . . diagnosis is always for the purpose of treatment."[56]

The most insidious defect in the medical model is that it exempts the offender from responsibility for his or her criminal actions. We normally do not blame an individual for catching a cold, or for contracting cancer. In the medical model, the offender is implicitly exonerated because of the crime–disease analogy.

Satisfying answers just simply are not profusive in the world of corrections. Part of the problem is political, of course. Whether prisons are built or not built is more often a question of politics than it is a question of progressive correctional theory. The fear of crime and the criminal is ordinarily communicated to the politician as a need for control. As Carlson phrased it, "In a climate of fear, crime control is a very potent political issue."[57]

[54]Robert Martinson, "California Research at the Crossroads," *Crime and Delinquency,* 22, No. 2 (April 1976), 181.

[55]David Fogel, ". . . *We Are the Living Proof . . .*" (Cincinnati: The W. H. Anderson Company, 1975), p. 50.

[56]Gordon Hamilton, *Principles of Social Case Recording* (New York: Columbia University Press, 1947), p. 78.

[57]Rick J. Carlson, *The Dilemmas of Corrections* (Lexington, Mass.: D. C. Heath and Company, 1976), p. 11.

Another part of the problem is the correctional paradigm. A paradigm is a conceptual frame of reference, or the blueprint by which a system is understood and presumably operates. Scholars in the field who are critical of corrections tend to see corrections as resistant to "paradigm shift," to use Carlson's term.[58] That is, it has stuck with traditional but unworkable goals and objectives, and old explanations which no longer have validity. New ways of looking at old problems must be devised if corrections is to make progress.

The Offender's Point of View

One helpful impetus to growth, at least in the area of correctional treatment, might be a greater emphasis on what is known as the ethnomethodological approach. Ethnomethodology is a sociological or psycho-sociological frame of reference which accepts interaction as the key factor in human experience.[59] In this frame of reference the actor in the interactional transaction is the ultimate interpreter of the nature of that experience. For instance, suppose that a high rate of divorce and economic depression were concomitant happenings. The traditional, scientific method approach would be to posit a cause and effect relationship between the economic depression and the family breakup, with depression the independent variable and divorce the dependent variable. The ethnomethodologist would, instead, ask how each individual family had reacted to the catastrophe, because despite a high rate of divorce at the time of economic depression, it would not be a universal phenomenon, and some families would remain intact. The key is not a presumed cause and effect relationship, but how *each individual* family reacted to the phenomenon of economic depression.

In the correctional world the key interactor is the inmate, juvenile delinquent, probationer, or parolee, and how each defines the correctional experience should be the first street traversed by the treatment specialist in corrections. Correctional treatment might be fruitfully enhanced if the architects of treatment utilized more of an ethnomethodological emphasis. There is a plethora of information available to indicate how correctional theorists and practitioners feel about treatment of the offender. But how does the offender feel? How does he or she perceive

[58]*Ibid.*, p. 9.

[59]The reader interested in further explorations of ethnomethodology might consult the works of such eminent representatives of variations of this school of thought as Herbert Blumer, Tamotsu Shibutani, Manford H. Kuhn, and Harold Garfinkel. The depression–divorce example employed above, as a matter of fact, was used by Herbert Blumer in a lecture when the author was his student. For a very helpful overview of ethnomethodology, the reader could profitably consult David C. Thorns (ed.), *New Directions in Sociology* (Totowa, N.J.: Rowman and Littlefield, 1976).

correctional treatment? And how is that perception negatively influenced by the presuppositions of correctional staff? The most fundamental objective of the treatment staff in corrections is restoration. It is one thing to have an academic and intellectual appreciation of the dimensions of crime, criminality, and correctional theory, but an empathic ear must be added for effectiveness in the art of correction. You may have a clinical understanding of hurt, but who can best translate my hurt?

Paul Tillich once observed that "only a concern about what is ultimate can animate a healing passion."[60] Perhaps the ultimate rationale for a restorative, compassionate, healing philosophy of corrections is that it is expressive rather than repressive; it is holistic rather than separatist; it is designed to impel man towards his fullness, and not his emptiness. Above all, it values hope above despair.

Dante recorded the ultimate in despair in his desolate invitation to the Inferno. We need no more sepulchral inscriptions over the arches of our prisons. It is time not to abandon, but to renew the effort to put man together, so that the whole world will fall into place.

SYNOPSIS

The nature of treatment is as much a source of controversy as is the nature of punishment. In the correctional context, treatment can be defined as the philosophy and the action of human restoration. It has alternately been defined as "correctional intervention," and as "being sentenced to receive help."

The so-called Rehabilitation Model has been under attack by many correctional theorists in recent years. Two views have dominated in the wake of the criticism. The "counsel of despair" has it that wicked people exist and must be set apart from innocent people for punishment, which is a retributivist viewpoint. The disenchanted who remain treatment-oriented have turned the blame on society, faulting its social institutions for the failure of rehabilitation. Whether or not corrections should be an advocate for social change is a matter of debate, although it is a formal plank in the correctional philosophy of Minnesota.

Despite the cry that rehabilitation is dead, most correctional adminstrators believe in rehabilitation. Rational punishment and treatment are seen as compatible elements based on a philosophy of meliorism.

Even Martinson, whose formidable study seemed to have represented a major blow against correctional rehabilitation, has modified his position.

---

[60]Cited in Sam Keen, "Chasing the Blahs Away: Boredom and How to Beat It," *Psychology Today* (May 1977), p. 83.

In the historic evolution of correctional treatment, its origin is generally traced to the Chicago Area Project, a program designed to organize the community in the effort to reduce delinquency.

Treatment in the criminal justice system is largely coercive, and it is imperative that the offender's perception of the process be added to our research intelligence.

3 Criminal Deviance

To the highest type of philosophic minds it is the usual and the ordinary that demand investigation and explanation. But even to such, no less than to the most naive-minded, the strange and exceptional is of absorbing interest, and it is often through the extraordinary that the philosopher gets the most searching glimpses into the heart of the mystery of the ordinary.

George M. Gould and Walter L. Pyle
***Anomalies and Curiosities of Medicine* (1896)**

DEFINING AND DELIMITING CRIMINAL DEVIANCE

In an actual incident, a woman who had gone to the market to do some shopping returned to find that her apartment had been broken into by a would-be burglar, whom she found asleep in her bed. The burglar's shoes had been placed neatly at the side of the bed. In one of the shoes the intruder had deposited his "outfit," the term addicts use to denote the paraphernalia used to inject the opiate derivative heroin. If the behavior manifested by the interloper in this true situation was not abnormal, it was at least atypical—for a non-addict, non-burglar, that is. But for an addict-burglar it might be considered completely normal behavior. Still, most people would readily describe this behavior as deviant. To deviate means to depart from the normal. But what is normal, and what is abnormal?

Normal or Abnormal?

The norm(al) ordinarily implies that there is conformity to a given standard or principle. It also implies average performance. In civil law, notably in tort actions, the rule governing negligent action is often phrased in terms of what the "average" or "reasonably prudent" individual would do in a similar situation. Culpability, in effect, derives from what the average person would do, not on the basis of the minority that marches to a different drummer. Obviously, if the norm is defined in this manner, a brilliant man such as Louis Pasteur would be abnormal in terms of the norm on an intelligence scale.

There are additional complexities in attempting to differentiate between the "normal" and the "abnormal." I have known individuals to have been imprisoned, and not too long ago, for the possession of *one* marijuana *seed*. Marijuana offenses were subsequently extensively decriminalized, and it would be unthinkable that an individual would go to prison today for the mere possession of a marijuana seed. Sociologists would give this phenomenon the fancy title of cultural relativity. In practical terms, it merely means that norms have changed—and are constantly changing.

It might be helpful to make a distinction, at this stage, between "normal" and "natural." *Normal* refers to the prevailing standard, the dominant mode or average. If, for instance, everyone favored the killing of one's enemies through immediate retaliation, and this practice prevailed in a given society, then it could be said that homicide was normal behavior for that society. *Natural,* on the other hand, refers to the very essence of the being or entity under discussion. Man's nature is rational. If he acts irrationally, he contravenes his nature. Using the same philosophic concept, we might say that a comb's nature is combability, that is, the capacity to facilitate the arrangement of hair. When the comb is used to arrange one's hair, it is a natural act, wholly in accord with the nature of the comb. A comb, however, can be readily used to scratch one's arm, or to stir a cup of coffee. But this would contravene its fundamental nature, and the purpose for which it was created. It would, in effect, be un-natural.

Stirring a cup of coffee with a comb might be considered an amusing act, but it would not constitute an immoral act. A comb and a cup are inanimate objects. When humans interact, morality enters the picture, and the contravention of human nature could have pernicious results. Sexual intercourse, for instance, whether for procreative or companionate purposes, is an activity that requires the volitional participation of both parties to the act. Rape would contravene the nature of this act because it would substitute force for volition. In a philosophic sense, then, rape could be called an unnatural activity.

Defining Criminal Deviance

When it comes to very serious misbehavior, it is not too difficult to distinguish the abnormal from the normal, but a great deal of human behavior vacillates between those parameters of the behavioral continuum. In the legal profession the distinction is sometimes made between crimes that are intrinsically evil and those that are designated crimes simply because the behavior is prohibited and punished by law. The former are called *mala in se.* At English common law all designated offenses were considered *mala in se* crimes, because under the prevailing theory the English common law did not impose punishment for any act that was not wrong in itself. In contemporary times, we might consider crimes such as murder and rape as intrinsically wrong. The "merely prohibited" offenses, that is, crimes so designated merely because society prohibits the particular behavior, are said to be *mala prohibitum.* Included in this category are such offenses as the possession of alcohol during Prohibition, and the infraction of various traffic ordinances. The extremes in each category are relatively easy to agree upon. It is the wide breach between that causes the difficulty. The same may be said of the abnormal and the normal.

There is an extended normal-abnormal continuum, which resembles a kaleidoscope, since the values of society are imprinted in constantly changing patterns. It simply is not possible, except in rare cases, to definitively separate the normal from the abnormal with respect to criminal behavior. Clinard took note of this when he stated,

> There is no question but that one of the principal difficulties in thinking now blocking a meaningful analysis of crime and delinquency, as well as other problems of disorganization, is the tendency to draw a sharp distinction between the normal and the abnormal, between the deviant and the nondeviant.[1]

Quite apart from the fact that deviant behavior is not so easily codified, a companion danger is the temptation to readily stereotype or label behavior. Stereotyping does violence to individualization. It can be scientifically said, for example, that all robbers share only one trait with certitude (aside from their humanness), and that is robbery. The hows and whys

[1]Marshall B. Clinard, quoted in Elmer H. Johnson, "A Basic Error: Dealing with Inmates as Though They Were Abnormal," *Federal Probation,* 25, No. 1 (March 1971), 44.

have to be individually traced to each robber, because motivation is a very individual proposition. Stereotyping, according to Schur, accomplishes two things: It enables the stereotyper to deal with complex interactions in a way that will permit him to predict the actions of others, and it enhances the possibility of inaccurate assessments of human behavior.[2]

Deviant behavior covers a wide spectrum of human activity, and criminal behavior is but a fragment of that spectrum. In a work-ethic society, refusing to work is a form of deviancy. Mental illness is deviancy. Alcoholism, mental retardation, chronic illness, and hermaphroditism are deviances, not one of which necessarily implies criminality. Our concern is with the fragment of criminal deviance. Every human being has the potential for criminal deviancy. Criminologists are concerned with why some individuals criminally deviate and others do not. In correctional treatment, we are not concerned with the etiology of criminal behavior but with the modes of therapeutic redemption.

It is practically a psychological truism that murder mysteries, and assorted violence on television and in the movies, are mechanisms thought which the "normal" citizen vicariously acts out his or her criminal proclivities. As Bromberg noted in his classic work, "The unconscious participation of law-abiding individuals in criminal activity confers on every civilized person a degree of familiarity with the psychological aspects of wrong-doing."[3] The sociology of deviant behavior may be less well perceived by "every civilized person," but it is profoundly important for the student of correctional treatment. Crime, after all, is basically defined in a sociological context.

The oldest known forms of criminal deviance are murder, incest, and sorcery. As civilization developed, crime diversified, and the categories of behavior deemed criminally deviant expanded. Most contemporary crimes were unknown to the primitives, nor could they come into being without technological and cultural developments in society. Armed robbery of a gas station, for example, would be impossible without the invention of gunpowder and the discovery of oil. Technology, in effect, helped to create the definition of armed robbery. Removing all of one's clothing in public on a stifling hot day would be a rational way to counter the discomfort of heat, but it might also result in arrest for indecent exposure or disturbing the peace, because contemporary cultural dictates proscribe this type of behavior. Nudity, obviously, was much less of a problem for tribal primitives.

Sociologists and criminologists have many theories about the origin of the criminal law. According to one theory, the criminal law reflects a crys-

---

[2]Edwin M. Schur, *Labeling Deviant Behavior* (New York: Harper & Row, Publishers, Inc., 1971), p. 41.

[3]Walter Bromberg, *Crime and the Mind,* reprinted. (Westport, Conn.: Greenwood Press Publishers, 1973), p. v.

talization of the mores. *Mores* is the plural form of *mos*, a Latin word that means "custom." As society evolved, so goes the theory, customs which developed as regulatory mechanisms in a given society ultimately crystalized into statutory or codified law. While this theory can be criticized for obvious deficiencies, it can be said, from a sociological perspective, that criminal deviance, by definition, will fluctuate and metamorphose according to the whims and dictates of the culture or society under scrutiny.

Social Control of Deviance

It is said that science knows what it is, but not what it ought to be. The same comment could be made about deviance theory. It is a sophisticated body of conceptual knowledge, from multiple frames of reference, which aspires to describe the etiology of deviance. What it ought to be is clouded by the imprecision and the constantly changing nature that is characteristic of deviance. In Chapter Four we will examine some of the major conceptual frames of reference in deviance theory, to better observe the state of the art, but at this point we are more concerned with the practical rather than the theoretical aspects of deviance.

In a very concrete sense, deviance is a violation of standards established by the power structure. In any society, whether capitalist or communist, whether tribal or monarchical, there is an influential group with the power "to define a society's operational structure," as Schafer and Knudten have described it.[4] It has been asserted, particularly in modern times, that the standards set by the power elite are intended to benefit primarily the power elite, and that is incontrovertible. But rules and standards are also intended to produce maximal harmony in the social body. Conformity and nonconformity, therefore, become the criteria by which the degree of harmony is measured.

Criminal deviance also represents an attack on the prevailing value system. While a degree of criminal behavior is "normal," to the extent that it is coeval with man, if crime and delinquency were to become utterly pervasive it would indicate a mass repudiation of existing values. Ironically, one of the methods of social control in contemporary society is decriminalization. This means that certain behavior that was once dealt with severely is dealt with less severely, or exempted from criminal sanction. The possession of alcohol was decriminalized when Prohibition was repealed. In recent times, the penalties for many drug offenses have been reduced or eliminated. Customs and attendant values constantly change, as we have noted. Heroin *addiction*, for example, was once considered

[4]Stephen Schafer, Mary S. Knudten and Richard D. Knudten, *Social Problems in a Changing Society* (Reston, Va.: Reston Publishing Company, Inc., 1975), p. 5.

criminal behavior. Decriminalization in other instances reflects a decrease in emotional reaction on the part of the public to the behavior in question. Abortion, for instance, was once considered a felony.

In a very broad sense, social control of deviance includes any activity, from vengeance to rehabilitation, that is designed to diminish deviance. Those control activities which are socially defined Cohen calls "the culturally organized structure of control."[5] As culture dictates the value system and what constitutes a breach thereof, so culture will dictate the responses to the breach. That is what Cohen meant by the term "culturally organized structure on control." Society's reaction to deviance is the critical boundary of deviance. Among the Shoshonean people, the Comanche society considered the seduction of women and the theft of horses as noble pursuits. In our society seduction has a negative connotation, and horse theft is a felony. The difference lies in the way the respective societies view the particular behavior. A modern writer based his theory of deviance on this principle, as can be observed in his statement, pertaining to a study of homosexuality: "[I]f the subject observes an individual's behavior and defines it as deviant but does not accord him differential treatment as a consequence of that definition, the individual is not sociologically deviant."[6] Deviance, like beauty, is in the eye of the beholder—in a sociological context, at least.

There is another aspect of social control that is relevant to the concept of deviance. Humans tend to institutionalize their interactions. A football team, for instance, is not composed of eleven disparate individuals who come together at unscheduled times to play a game of football. They are part of the institution of football, a *team,* that has rubrics, behavioral expectations, and sophisticated organization (leagues and divisions). To maintain membership in this institution, certain behavior must be exhibited, and there are clearcut penalties, up to exclusion from the organization, for nonconformity. In like manner, procreative and mating interactions are institutionalized in marriage; fraternal activities are institutionalized in clubs and lodges; spiritual and reverential interactions are institutionalized in churches and synagogues; learning endeavors are institutionalized in the educational system, and so on.

Institutional relations give rise to what Buckner called "the social control of relations."[7] That is, the institution, whether a *sub rosa* institution like a juvenile gang, or a *pro forma* instituion like an industrial corporation

---

[5] Albert K. Cohen, *Deviance and Control* (Englewood Cliffs, N.J.: Prentice-Hall, Inc., 1966), p. 39.

[6] John I. Kitsuse, "Societal Reaction to Deviant Behavior: Problems of Theory and Method," in Howard S. Becker (ed.), *The Other Side* (New York: The Free Press, 1964), p. 97.

[7] H. Taylor Buckner, *Deviance, Reality, and Change* (New York: Random House, Inc., 1971), p. 13.

or an established church, governs the behavior of its member-participants. Exclusion from the group, as we have stated above, can be the ultimate end result of nonconformity. Institutional membership fulfills certain needs, but faithful adherence to the values which are institutionalized is also assured by the imposition of sanctions for unacceptable behavior. Deviance is the institution's branding iron. Erikson said it well: "Deviance is not a property *inherent* in certain forms of behavior; it is a property conferred upon these forms by the audiences which directly or indirectly witness them."[8]

Self-Identity and Labeling

It is a common sociological truism that no social system can exist without some form of organization. Society is basically organized around the division of labor and the fulfillment of social roles. Social roles permit the realization of goals and ideals, but they also limit the behavior that can be performed in a given role. A doctor, for example, would be severely censured by the medical association if he regularly saw his patients in his office while clad only in swimming trunks. It is obvious that wearing apparel has no significant correlation with medical skill, but it is equally plain, from the example given above, that a doctor's role precludes him from wearing certain styles of clothing at certain times. The institutionalized medical profession, in other words, is intimately involved in "the social control of relations." In this instance, the doctor who would breach the protocol of wearing apparel would be a deviant. But what of the avant-garde individual who does not consider his "advanced" behavior deviant? The nudist who fights for public nude beaches? The nurse who discards her white uniform to break down another barrier in patient care, feeling that a closer bond would ensue if she wore civilian clothing?

These questions bring up another important dynamic in deviance, the dynamic of self-identity. If, as Erikson said, deviance is a status conferred by society, we might reasonably wonder about the impact of that conferred status on a given individual, both positively and negatively. To what extent, for instance, is self-identity (as a deviant) necessary for the status to be meaningful? Or, from another point, what are the dynamics involved in the assumption of the status of deviant? The school of thought known as symbolic interactionism or interactionism heavily emphasizes the importance of the interpersonal interaction and the interpretations placed upon those transactions by the "actors." As the pre-eminent sym-

[8]Kai Erikson, "Notes on the Sociology of Deviance," in Howard S. Becker (ed.), *The Other Side* (New York: The Free Press, 1964), p. 11.

bolic interactionist, Herbert Blumer, said, "Society *exists in action* and must be seen in terms of action."[9] The importance of self-perception probably received its main impetus from the writings of Carl Rogers on personality theory.[10]

The process of labeling is also intimately linked with the factor of identity. There are many writers, particularly in the field of juvenile delinquency, who feel that giving a youngster the status or label of "juvenile delinquent" impels the child to identify with the status and role of delinquent and, in fact, reinforces delinquent self-concepts.[11] In other words, if I *am* a juvenile delinquent I ought to act the part.

In an interesting, longtitudinal study, Kaplan hypothesized that "antecedent negative self-attitudes" would be positively correlated with future deviancy, that is, that subjects with more negative self-attitudes would be more likely to become involved in deviant behavior in the future, as a result of prior conditioning in deviant response patterns.[12] The subjects of the study were almost 5,000 seventh-grade students in half of the 36 junior high schools in Houston. They were surveyed at the beginning and end of an approximate one-year period to determine their degree of participation in any of a series of deviant acts, primarily including drug, theft, and assaultive misbehavior. Self-attitude was measured by a standard self-derogation scale which portrayed the individual's sense of self-esteem as well as his sense of self-derogation.

In testing his hypothesis, that antecedent negative response patterns would correlate highly with future deviance, Kaplan found a "consistency of the pattern of associations by which antecedent self-derogation was observed to be related to subsequent reports of each of a range of essentially uncorrelated deviant acts, thus lending strong support to the hypothesis."[13] One clear inference from such a study is that correctional rehabilitation should be largely involved in diversionary strategies designed to prevent the development of deviant response patterns, which lead to recidivism.

Labeling also has a distinctive significance in the interactionist frame of reference. It has been asserted, in this frame of reference, that those who are labeled deviant are merely "a biased selection from among the

---

[9]Herbert Blumer, *Symbolic Interactionism: Perspective and Method* (Englewood Cliffs, N.J.: Prentice-Hall, Inc., 1969), p. 6.

[10]See especially, Carl R. Rogers, *Client-Centered Therapy* (Boston: Houghton Mifflin Company, 1951).

[11]See, for example, Stanton Wheeler and Leonard S. Cottrell, "The Labeling Process," in Harwin S. Voss (ed.), *Society, Delinquency, and Delinquent Behavior* (Boston: Little, Brown & Company, 1970).

[12]Howard B. Kaplan, "Self-Attitudes and Deviant Responses," *Social Forces*, Vol. 54, No. 4 (June 1976), pp. 788-801.

[13]*Ibid.*, p. 799.

group of rule-violators."[14] This is indisputable in view of the fact that only a microscopic portion of the total number of criminals are ever "brought to justice." In the so-called "Radical Criminology" which is a contemporary development, it is contended that the state liberally creates deviant categories as part of its control mechanisms. Quinney, for example, sees the whole criminal justice system as the state's apparatus to justify control.[15] An individual can also be labeled a deviant even where no substantive deviancy has occurred. Children who run away from intolerable home conditions come under the jurisdiction of the juvenile court, and can be placed in juvenile hall "for their own protection." But what impression is later given by the child, *incarcerated* for its own protection, who must acknowledge that he or she has been in juvenile hall? The child will obviously be considered deviant.

Connor speaks of "manufactured deviance" in a study which "may point to a need to rethink some contemporary ideas about deviance."[16] While dealing specifically with the Stalinist purge of 1936–1938, he points out that such phenomena as witchcraft are forms of deviance literally manufactured by "social control agencies" who "largely shaped and sustained the epidemics of deviance they purportedly strove to suppress."[17] Prohibition was a classic example of manufactured deviance. The importance of self-perception, labeling, and manufactured deviance cannot be over-emphasized in any study of deviance. Nor can they be overemphasized by the treatment practitioner in corrections who must dispose of every stereotype.

The Psychological Factor in Criminal Deviance

In a popular work, fittingly titled *Crime Pays!*, a journalist with entry to the world of the professional criminal, eschewed sophisticated psychological concepts and bluntly stated, "Professional crime is the deliberately illegal pursuit of money along well-defined lines. The cause of professional crime is not just the criminal's desire for money, but also the surfeit of it in society. It is not the lack of financial and material resources that is behind professional crime in the United States; it is the visible presence of it."[18] That is an impelling proposition, and it is a wholly reasonable proposition

---

[14]Robert H. Lauer and Warren H. Handel, *Social Psychology: The Theory and Application of Symbolic Interactionism* (Boston: Houghton Mifflin Company, 1977), p. 213.

[15]Richard Quinney, *Class, State, and Crime* (New York: David McKay Co. Inc., 1977).

[16]Walter D. Connor, "The Manufacture of Deviance: The Case of the Soviet Purge, 1936–1938," in F. James Davis and Richard Stivers, *The Collective Definition of Deviance* (New York: The Free Press, 1975), pp. 241-55.

[17]*Ibid.*, p. 241.

[18]Thomas Plate, *Crime Pays!* (New York: Ballantine Books, 1975), p. 2.

that crime can be a rationally calculated mode of activity, simply reflecting greed, whether professional or amateur.

The psychologist, preoccupied with psychological "sets," "motivation," "ego-involvement," and similar stock-in-trade phrases, would ask the journalist, "But what are the precipitating psychodynamics that launched the individual into a criminal career?" In the case of "manufactured" deviance, the dynamics would obviously be different than for those involved in calculated deviance. The group-oriented sociologist would probably inquire, "If there is a surfeit of money in society, and professional crime is the deliberate pursuit of it, why isn't everyone a professional criminal in this gregarious and materialistic society?"

Whereas psychology and psychiatry once held "dominion over palm and pine" in the United States, these behavioral disciplines have come under increasing, critical attack in recent times. Some of the more incisive of the critics have actually been members of the fraternity itself.[19] When a psychologist at the influential National Institute of Mental Health can predict "universal madness as a statistical certainty,"[20] criticism is, indeed, warranted. Real madness consists of labeling a child a delinquent because she ran away from intolerable home conditions.

Social scientists commonly display the variations in human behavior on either a *J-curve* or a *bell-shaped curve*. These instruments depict the behavioral spectrum from extreme underconformity to extreme overconformity, with the great bulk of the "normals" occupying the intervening territory (see Figure 3-1). Cavan, in fact, built her well-known definition of juvenile delinquency around a bell-shaped curve. She portrayed juvenile delinquency as behavior that was "part of a continuum ranging from extremely antisocial actions to extremely conforming behavior...."[21] With respect to both juvenile delinquency and criminality, a bell-shaped curve literally encompasses a range of behavior from psychopathy (extreme underconformity) to sanctity (extreme conformity).

Although a strict parallel cannot be drawn, an interesting comparison can be made when certain psychological traits are depicted on the bell-shaped curve. In one study, overcautiousness was plotted as the left extreme of the graph, and impulsivity as the right extreme. Spontaneity was designated as the central norm. It was determined that while both over-

---

[19]Dr. Thomas S. Szasz, himself a psychiatrist of reputable standing, is, perhaps, the leading "mental health" iconoclast. He contends that the well-being and dignity of individuals is threatened by mental health practices. See his book, *Law, Liberty and Psychiatry* (New York: Macmillan, Inc., 1965).

[20]Martin L. Gross, *The Psychological Society* (New York: Random House, Inc., 1978), p. 6.

[21]Ruth Shonle Cavan and Theodore N. Ferdinand, *Juvenile Delinquency,* 3rd ed., (Philadephia: J. B. Lippincott Company, 1975), p. 29.

FIGURE 3.1

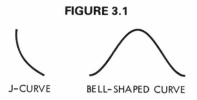

J-CURVE   BELL-SHAPED CURVE

cautiousness and impulsivity were deviations from the central norm, the left side of the curve is more often interpreted as the abnormal side.[22] Several inferences can be drawn from this interesting fact. First, an inherent defect is suggested in depicting data on a curved continuum. Secondly, deviance is not readily susceptible to iron-clad classification. Who, after all, has met the truly "normal" person? Mindful of this qualification, McMahon claims that the only rational division of deviances, at least from the psychiatric-psychologic viewpoint, is between the categories of neurosis and psychosis.[23] Distinctions beyond this are perilous.

From the point of view of corrections, distinctions between the criminal and the non-criminal have to be more generally defined. When P. T. Barnum spoke of a sucker being born every minute, he was also talking indirectly about the large amount of larceny in the human heart. The fact that so insignificant a percentage of the criminals are actually caught makes it almost an obscenity to separate the caught from the uncaught on the basis of the former's "criminality." Qualified in this manner, the most useful approach to crime is *sui generis,* that is, observing crime typologically, or in terms of differentiating traits. Are there unique characteristics that set off the rapist, for example? Are caught criminals notably different from noncriminals? Psychological factors are always operative, but that does not justify a cause and effect relationship between some isolated psychological trait and criminality. It can be said, for instance, that mentally retarded people are highly suggestible and can, therefore, be more readily enticed into criminal behavior. But all mentally retarded people are not criminals, or vice versa, obviously. Social experiences are clearly of greater influence in the etiology of criminal and delinquent behavior, but sociological and psychological dynamics are both involved.

Social scientists are divided on the question of whether or not there is a positive correlation between attitudes and behavior. An attitude may be defined as an emotional predisposition to act in a certain way towards a given stimulus, whether thing or person. This prospective correlation is important in the field of crime and its correction because conformity or

[22]Frank B. McMahon, *Abnormal Behavior: Psychology's View* (Englewood Cliffs, N.J.: Prentice-Hall, Inc., 1976), p. 9.
[23]*Ibid.,* p. 88.

compliance with society's norms obviously reflects one type of attitude, whereas nonconformity obviously represents another type. More important, if a correlation could be developed between attitude and behavior, it might be possible to predict criminal behavior more precisely than at present. While much research has yet to be done in this area, some important findings are already available. In an analysis of research studies in the area, for example, Janeksela has found that deviants are more likely than nondeviants to have negative attitudes towards the legal system and to feel socially alienated.[24]

A considerable body of research in specific crimes exists, spurred by Sutherland's classic work on the professional thief.[25] In a California study 100 rapists were compared with adult males in the general population and with adult male offenders who had not been convicted of sex offenses. When compared to "normal" males, rapists tend "to be less aggressive, less independent and self-motivated, and less self-assured and dominant. They demonstrate a greater heterosexual need, a greater propensity to analyze introspectively their own and others' motives, to be more self-critical, and to have a greater need to endure."[26] When compared to adult offenders, rapists "tend to be less achievement-oriented, less self-assured and aggressive, less independent and self-directed, to have less need for change and a greater need to endure, a lower heterosexual drive, a greater self-criticism, and a greater need to nurture others and to be dependent upon others."[27]

The importance of this and similar studies is that they uncover areas where treatment can be focused. The rapist, as a case in point, is seen as an inadequate, insecure, dependent individual whose hostility indicates defective development in heterosexual relating. Instead of seeing criminals in a sterotypical fashion, the intelligent correctionalist will observe distinguishing characteristics, and concentrate his or her therapeutic energies accordingly.

Absolute and Relative Views of Deviance

Earlier we differentiated between the legal concepts of *mala in se* and *mala prohibitum*. The student may have logically drawn the inference that this is really a distinction between the absolute and the relative, and sensed that theorists also approach deviance in this way. Scholars in the field distin-

[24]Galan M. Janeksela, "Deviants Have Bad Attitudes," *International Journal of Criminology and Penology*, 5, No. 4 (November 1977), 337-47.

[25]Edwin H. Sutherland, *The Professional Thief* (Chicago: University of Chicago Press, 1937).

[26]Gary Fisher and Ephraim Rivlin, "Psychological Needs of Rapists," in William Lloyd McCraney, *Readings in Criminal Psychology* (New York: MSS Information Corporation, 1972), p. 84.

[27]*Ibid.*

guish the two approaches as Absolutist and Relativist. In the former, the position is taken, more from a philosophical than a sociological frame of reference, that certain acts are inherently wrong in all times and in all cultures based on the nature of man. The absolutist would take the position that, since life is the driving force in the universe, it would be intrinsically wrong to perform any act or ingest any substance that would impair the full unfolding of one's life and the full development of one's human potential. The abuse of drugs, including alcohol, and taking one's own life would, in this frame of reference, be inherently deviant.

Relativists, on the other hand, take what Lofland describes as "a somewhat more existential stance."[28] Whereas the absolutist relates to an objective standard by which he can determine what others ought to do, relativists see deviance as "being in large measure a matter of human evaluation and differential power."[29] Philosophy has long endured the division of objectivism and subjectivism, and it is this division that colors the absolutist-relativist dichotomy in deviance theory. The absolutist has his objective standard by which to make evaluative judgment, but "the relativist questions *his* right to interfere. He may well hold strong beliefs and standards by which he judges himself, but he is hesitant to impose these beliefs and standards on others who view the world quite differently."[30] Instead of an objective standard with which he can reconcile moral problems, the relativist sees a world of numerous and often conflicting standards, and he abstains from an absolute position of judgment.

As Lofland commented, both of these positions "proceed from primitive *value premises* regarding the nature and meaning of human life and the relations that should obtain between people."[31] This calls to mind the comment of Paul Tillich, whom we cited earlier, that all treatment is based on some image of man. What is your concept of the image of man? How would you apply the concept of deviance to the Nazi attempt to subject the Jews to genocide?

SOME SPECIAL CONCERNS
IN CRIMINAL DEVIANCE

It should be crystal clear by now that the periphery of deviance is far from precisely drawn. That boundary, on the contrary, is like the pseudopodium in the protoplasm of a cell, constantly expanding and retracting as defini-

---

[28]John Lofland, *Deviance and Identity* (Englewood Cliffs, N.J.: Prentice-Hall, Inc., 1969), p. 24.
[29]Stuart L. Hills, "Mystification of Social Deviance," *Crime and Delinquency,* 23, No. 4 (October 1977), 418.
[30]Lofland, *Deviance and Identity,* p. 24.
[31]*Ibid.*

tions, the power structure, and cultural dictates change. This is one major dilemma confronting the student of deviance. There are others.

Although we have used the analogy of protoplasm in a cell, projecting *and* retracting, the emphasis, with respect to deviance, would be on the projecting aspect. It is rather rare for decriminalization to take place on an extensive basis. The normal course of events is for definitions of deviance to expand. Schafer feels that when criminology extended to include deviance it did not constitute an extension of the scientific analysis of behavior but, instead, constituted an enlarging of the data to which the traditional concept of deviance could be applied. The result has been "to increase the size and variety of the population subject to 'Tagging,' 'Labelling' or 'Stigmatising' according to which school one belongs."[32] Professionals in the criminal justice system should be committed to reducing the metastatic growth of expanding definitions of criminal deviancy. There is an awful lot of dead wood in our penal codes.

Influence of Stratification

Students of sociology are familiar with the fact that all societies are stratified with different classes. In a simple society there may be only two classes, the upper class and the lower class. In a complex society such as the United States, there can be as many as six separate classes. When people are stratified, they tend to become segregated, particularly from the more remote classes in the social system. Above and beyond the separation that derives from stratification, our society is characterized by other separations. There is the so-called gap between the youth and the older generations, the racial insulations, and, of course, there is the disparate relationship between the deviants and the nondeviants.

Proponents of the so-called "radical criminology" attribute the etiology of deviance to such institutional factors as stratification and consequent segregation. One writer, perhaps taking this viewpoint to an extreme but without sacrificing perception, stated that

> this process of segregation has very real consequences in terms of society's reaction to its so-called deviants. For it limits drastically the quality of the information we receive as to the motivation, attitudes, behaviour and humanity of these individuals. And it is because of the distorted information that we are bombarded with, because of the demented caricatures that are presented to us, that we—like the 1940s German inundated by anti-Semitic propaganda—lash out blindly at these scapegoats, support organized violence against them in our name, lament the passing of the hangman.[33]

[32]Stephen Schafer, *Readings in Contemporary Criminology* (Reston, Va.: Reston Publishing Company, Inc., 1976), p. 256.

[33]Jock Young, "The Zoo-Keepers of Deviancy," *Catalyst* (Summer 1970), pp. 38-39.

One implication from the foregoing quote is that one class or stratum infrequently consorts with another, on an intimate level. The correctional practitioner, who is typically a product of the middle class, should realize that most individuals labeled criminal or delinquent come from a different socioeconomic stratum, or cultural milieu, and hold many values that are not consonant with those of the middle class.

Dinitz and his colleagues touched the nucleus of deviance in three rhetorical questions: "What behaviors are to be included as deviant and how are these to be defined? How is society to control these behaviors? And what shall be public policy towards deviation?"[34] Some insight should have been gained by now with respect to the first and second questions. The answer to the third will be largely determined by the success or failure of the treatment tactics in corrections. But it will take more than correctional treatment, on a public policy level, to resolve the relationship between pornography, abortion, drug abuse, insurrection, gambling, homosexuality, and similar behavior, and deviance. The task will be far greater for the relativist than for the absolutist.

Aggravated Pathology

One of the most baffling forms of human deviance involves aggravated pathology, such as is evidenced in widespread or multiple acts of violence. While behavior of this nature is largely unpredictable— or we would abort it—the public quickly reaches consensus on this issue. The violent act is a highly visible, dramatic challenge to the social order, and it must be neutralized. Scholars still furiously debate the nature of human aggression and cannot decisively agree whether it is a natural disposition, a learned response, or an adaptive mechanism. The last-named was the fundamental premise to Lorenz's noted work.[35] Although he shared the Nobel prize for this work, his basic principle is flawed. Lorenz saw the aggressive drive as an instinct preserving the species, just one instinct in "a great parliament of instincts," a stabilizing force. But it is hazardous to analogize from lower forms of life to *homo sapiens*. How can genocide, a human pastime, be considered a stabilizing force—without dehumanizing the human? Montagu was severe in his criticism of Lorenz's position:

> Lorenz knows a great deal about the behavior of animals, but with respect to man he apparently knows very little else that is not in the realm of nineteenth-century desk anthropology. Like Ardrey, he extrapolates his

[34]Simon Dinitz, Russell R. Dynes and Alfred C. Clarke, *Deviance* (New York: Oxford University Press, 1969), p. 527.

[35]Konrad Lorenz, *On Aggression*, trans. Marjorie Kerr Wilson (New York: Harcourt, Brace & World, 1966).

dubious interpretations of animal behavior to still more dubious conclusions concerning man.[36]

The point is that human behavior is largely learned behavior, and aggression has not been decisively established as a human instinct.

The scientific thrust in criminology and corrections, to the extent that either can be scientific, is towards predictability. If (criminal) behavior could be predicted, it would be a major breakthrough for those engaged in correctional diversion or reconstruction. But it would also pose a major headache for the philosopher who did not subscribe to "Big Brother" controls. The resolution of this dilemma would necessarily involve what Lofland called a "value premise." In any event, we know little about the implosive forces that lead some individuals to aggravated pathology.

If this type of behavior was predictable to any degree whatever, we would obviously have aborted the bloody violence of our sensationally violent deviants. Would we not have forestalled the bloody carnage that took place in California in 1969? In that year, the nation was stunned by the murderous orgy of the Charles Manson "family," which resulted in the savage slaying of seven individuals, including the pregnant Sharon Tate and the heiress to a coffee fortune, Abigail Folger. Consider, further, the Richard Speck case. Speck methodologically slaughtered eight nurses in Illinois in 1966. Spared execution when the United States Supreme Court abrogated capital punishment, he is currently serving sentences cumulatively exceeding 400 years. Even more bestial was the cannibalism of Albert Fish, at 66 the oldest man ever executed in Sing Sing's electric chair. Admitting a sordid history of molestation of more than 400 children, and at least six murders, Fish actually carved up one of his victims and made a stew out of the 12-year-old child. Psychiatrists described Fish as the most perverted individual they had ever met. For twenty undetected years, from 1917 until 1936, he was engaged in predatory violence.

The tragic fact is that if we wished to continue to describe mass murder, sufficient material exists to go on endlessly. Whether or not human aggression is an innate instinct, sociologists would agree with the statement made in one pertinent study of violence:

> Violent behavior reflects the social and cultural environment of a society. Who commits the assault, who gets taken to a hospital or a morgue, who witnessed the event, and the reaction of the community reflect in part how a society is socially structured and what that society considers important.[37]

[36]M. F. Ashley Montagu (ed.), *Man and Aggression* (New York: Oxford University Press, 1968), p. 13.

[37]Samuel E. Wallace, "Patterns of Violence in San Juan," in Simon Dinitz, Russell R. Dynes, and Alfred C. Clarke, *Deviance* (New York: Oxford University Press, 1969), p. 62.

In our materialistic, competitive, sensate culture, violence is a natural by-product. The pressure to acquire material symbols of status, and the dehumanizing isolation imposed on so many by a highly stratified and technological society, provoke abrasive conflicts and trigger the acting out of violent proclivities. There is, of course, the inexplicable violence that results purely from psychically warped personalities. How this type of violence is generically related to the wider spectrum of situational violence is academic, at least in terms of etiology. It is clearly generic as violence. It has been stated that "Many believe that the key to building a realistic general theory of deviance lies in first understanding component microsystems."[38] A microsystemic study of criminality would be similar to a typological approach to criminals, that is, the focus would be on the dynamics of specific forms of deviant behavior. In homicide, for example, a trend has developed in which the emphasis is on the offender-victim relationship, following pioneer work by Mendelsohn, von Hentig, Amir, Wolfgang and others.

In 1967, a national survey was conducted of the violent crimes of criminal homicide, robbery, forcible rape, and aggravated assault in 17 major cities in the United States. This was a companion endeavor to research conducted by the National Commission on the Causes and Prevention of Violence during 1968-1969. The results of that research were published in the useful work that is cited in footnote 38. It contains a great deal of rich source material on violence, from which it may be hoped additional research of a definitive nature may be forthcoming. Impressive data have been collected. The challenge now is to relate these data to causal precipitants.[39]

We must reiterate, however, that crime, whether directed against person or property, "reflects the social and cultural environment of a society." If violence is to be curtailed, social institutions will have to be changed. In one volume of a series of works which focus on the reconstruction of society, the position is taken that the elimination of violence will not come about until our children are raised and educated differently. We will also have to "prepare for the national defense differently, to change the ways in which we view the police, the courts, the prisons, the business community, politicians, and ourselves."[40] Correctional treatment, in this context, is literally band-aid therapy, but the Dutch boy with his finger in the hole in the dike could be similarly described.

[38]Lynn A. Curtis, *Criminal Violence* (Lexington, Mass.: D. C. Heath & Co., 1974), p. 2.
[39]The student interested in theoretical aspects of aggression and violence will find a valuable resource in Edwin I Megargee and Jack E. Hokanson, *The Dynamics of Aggression* (New York: Harper & Row, Publishers, Inc., 1970).
[40]Jeffrey H. Goldstein, *Aggression and Crimes of Violence* (New York: Oxford University Press, 1975), p. 145.

The Career Criminal

One enduring, major correctional challenge has been the recidivistic, career criminal, who seems immune to correction. This is the individual who has adopted a criminal life style, usually involving some form of larceny. In the past, traditional correctional strategies were applied, but every professional in the field can buttress the dismal prognosis with countless case histories. There are notorious cases such as that of Floyd Hamilton, Public Enemy No. 1 in 1938. He was released from the federal penitentiary at Leavenworth, Kansas in 1971, after 32 years of incarceration. A short time later he was shot to death by a Texas Ranger as he held 3 hostages. In New York, police arrested a pickpocket for the 130th time, in 1978. Peter Dimitri was 65 at the time, and about 42 years of that life had been spent behind bars, basically because of his pickpocketing.

While recidivism is a general term for repeated criminality, the concept of career criminal is relatively new, and pertains not to mere recidivism, but to long-term persistent recidivism. The district attorney of Los Angeles County, John Van de Kamp, established a special, state-funded unit in 1978 to vigorously prosecute the career criminal. He expressed the philosophy behind it by saying: ". . . now when we speak of 'career criminals,' we are really identifying an entirely different attitude. We are taking the approach that there are people as committed to a career of crime as you may be to a career in law."[41]

Two important studies in the late nineteen-seventies dealt with the habitual criminal. A Rand Corporation study supported the philosophy subsequently behind the District Attorney's program in Los Angeles, with the conclusion that the "intensive" habitual criminal should be identified early and incarcerated during his or her active years. This should occur irrespective of gender, for gender was not a significant variable. The study maintained that this would do more for crime reduction than rehabilitation or prevention.[42] The subjects of this research were incarcerated at the time of the interviews, and were all felons. One immediate criticism of this study is that it involved only 49 subjects, not a very significant sample.

A much more extensive study was conducted at St. Elizabeths Hospital in Washington D.C., a federal mental facility used by the Bureau of Prisons. In this particular study, as we discussed in Chapter Two, over 250 hard-core criminals were studied in-depth over a 16-year period. The program was inaugurated in 1961 by a distinguished but traditional psy-

---

[41]Quoted in Los Angeles *Times,* January 30, 1978.
[42]J. R. Petersilia, *Criminal Careers of Habitual Felons: A Summary Report,* August 1977. Rand Report No. P-5972.

chiatrist steeped in psychoanalysis, Dr. Samuel Yochelson. Dr. Stanton Samenow, a clinical psychologist, joined the research project in 1970, and, upon Dr. Yochelson's untimely death in 1976, brought the voluminous findings to publication.

After fruitlessly trying the traditional approaches of orthodox and Freudian psychiatry, and relying on standard sociological and psychological theories about criminal behavior, Yochelson introduced a new, "phenomenologic" technique. He asked the inmate subjects to make detailed "stream of thinking" reports of their daily thought processes. Previously the inmates had been playing games with the therapists. Under this new technique they appeared incapable of appreciably faking the "phenomenologic" material. The researchers were astounded by some of their findings. First of all, the subjects admitted vast amounts of criminal activity, with hundreds, sometimes thousands, of criminal acts occurring before the first arrest. Criminality was frequent and wide-ranging, and much more pervasive than was indicated by the official records. Second, the subjects possessed a "criminal personality" and this frequently traced back to early childhood, and was *not* attributable to "bad homes" and other standard behavioral rationales. Third, the researchers discovered that those inmates who had effectively used a defense of insanity in court, and committed as such, were far from psychotic: "We have studied at length more than 100 patients of Saint Elizabeths Hospital who have been adjudicated 'not guilty by reason of insanity.' *From our frame of reference,* their diagnoses do not stand up."[43]

Significant changes were made in the research design as the research progressed. Eventually Yochelson and Samenow "abandoned the search for causes, discarded mental illness as a factor in criminality, [threw] out psychologic and sociologic excuses, and assumed a firm, directive stance based on a considerable body of knowledge about the criminal mind."[44]

During the course of the study, Yochelson and Samenow saw themselves less therapists than teachers, and in fact began to refer to themselves as the latter. To reorganize the life of a hard-core criminal, they decided, was an educational process, not a therapeutic one. The word "change" was considered an ineffective word in the context of this reorganization. The appropriate word was "metamorphosis."

The "program for total change" devised by Yochelson and Samenow consisted of reality confrontation, and dealing with the criminal when he was most vulnerable. "A criminal is most vulnerable to change when he is locked up or is about to face a period of confinement, when his options in

---

[43]Samuel Yochelson and Stanton E. Samenow, *The Criminal Personality, Volume I: A Profile For Change* (New York: Jason Aronson, Inc., 1976), p. 235.
[44]*Ibid.,* p. 35.

life are considerably reduced and he is more likely to reflect on his past."[45] At that point the "teacher" confronts him with the character of his past life and begins the education of what his life could be like in the future. Speaking of the research subjects, Yochelson and Samenow said, "We reminded them of the three options open to a criminal: crime, suicide, and change. It was clearly up to them. We knew that we could not persuade them to make a particular choice, but we could help to clarify the issues."[46] The re-education stance went from an amoral one, to an emphasis on morality, finally accenting responsibility. It was felt that the meaning of responsibility could be broadened "so that it could be taught and then implemented as a *set of mental processes.*"[47]

It is not possible to do justice to all of the ramifications of this project in the limited space available here. The controversy surrounding the study will, however, necessarily cause its findings to be subjected to continuing, critical scrutiny. Already the battle lines have formed. The study has been both hailed as a breakthrough and damned for its lack of scientific methodology. Symptomatic of the divided viewpoints, the study has been called "a blueprint to begin the serious work of rehabilitation,"[48] and the published work has been condemned as "a dangerous book that can be used in the same fashion Robert Martinson's materials have been used by haters and hard-liners."[49]

The Neglected Female Deviant

In the past the female offender was not only largely ignored, she was also significantly misunderstood. Recent events, however, have led to a new concern about the facts and etiology of female deviancy. With dramatic role shifts, and the impetus of women's liberation, the profile of the female offender has radically altered. Deviancy (crime) is becoming less dominantly a male prerogative. No longer is the protected, domestic role the only one available to the female. In fact, in 1978 approximately 8 million (11%) of the 76 million households in the United States were

[45] *Ibid.,* p. 36.
[46] *Ibid.*
[47] *Ibid.,* p. 37.
[48] University of Cincinnati (Criminal Justice Program) Professor Robert B. Mills, quoted in Eugene H. Methvin, "The Criminal Mind: A Startling New Look," *The Reader's Digest* (May 1978).
[49] Comment made by O. J. Keller, past president of the American Correctional Association, to the Salvation Army annual breakfast at the 107th Congress of Correction, Milwaukee. See *American Journal of Corrections,* Vol. 39, No. 5 (September-October 1977), p. 32 for excerpted remarks. The Robert Martinson alluded to is the central author of the controversial work that evaluated over 200 correctional treatment programs and found them wanting: Douglas Lipton, Robert Martinson, and Judith Wilks, *The Effectiveness of Correctional Treatment* (New York: Praeger Publishers, 1975).

headed by a woman, an increase of 2.5 million in the eight-year period from 1970. This is but one measure of the changing female role.

Of greater significance is the increasing female involvement in the world of commerce, in a wide variety of non-domestic vocational pursuits. As Pollak pointed out some time ago, criminologists have long believed that "the entrance of women into ever wider fields of economic pursuits would lead to an increase in the volume of female crime."[50] The male has been the socially dominant sex in our Western culture for a long, long time. Dominance has extended to all spheres, including that of criminal deviance. As the so-called women's movement has grown, it has "served to reinforce what many have always believed: that there is a close relationship between societally dominant *gender roles* and *patterns of misconduct*," as two observers of the phenomenon have noted.[51]

From a correctional treatment point of view, the new approach to the female offender is an encouraging development. Accurate insights about the specialized needs of the female offender must be obtained, with the collateral destruction of the unscientific and discriminatory myths that have too long embellished the distaff criminal. Lombroso, for example, described women as physiologically immobile and psychologically conservative.[52]

Freud, as is well known, accused women of penis-envy, alleging that the female child, upon first observing a young boy's genital apparatus, felt short-changed. Why, one might muse, didn't Freud teach that the male felt envy for the female because of his superfluity! After a fairly comprehensive review of the literature on the female offender, Klein concluded that "a good deal of the writing on women and crime" by contemporary writers continues an ignorant tradition, and the writings are "sexist, racist and classist...."[53] Fortunately, there is enlightened research and writing, too.

Again from the correctional treatment point of view, greater attention must be paid to the female in the context of her contemporary role. Correctional institutions must diversify their training programs to recognize the needs and the latent talents of the female inmate. Following a long tradition, most female institutions train their inmates—where training occurs—in the purely domestic function. Variations, based on pre-

[50]Otto Pollak, *The Criminality of Women* (Philadelphia: University of Pennsylvania Press, 1950), p. 58.
[51]Stephen Norland and Neal Shover, "Gender Roles and Female Criminality," *Criminology*, 15, No. 1 (May 1977), 88.
[52]Caesar Lombroso and William Ferrero, *The Female Offender* (New York: D. Appleton and Company, 1898).
[53]Dorie Klein, "The Etiology of Female Crime: A Review of the Literature," in *The Aldine Crime & Justice Annual 1973* (Chicago: Aldine Publishing Co., 1974), p. 58.

sumed female roles, include training in cosmetology, typing, nursing, and clerical work. The narrow vocational role assigned to the female is epitomized in the fact that "the average number of vocational programs in male institutions is 10; for women, the average is 2.7 . . . "[54]

From the theoretical point of view, contemporary scholars are debating the etiology of the rapid increase in female criminal deviance. One point of view holds that the increase is clearly a result of the changing female role.[55] Another view contends that the increase is the result of "sex-role determined opportunity."[56] As I have stated in another source, "women's crime is being *discovered* through her changing role, but it is yet to be established that it is being *caused* by it."[57]

Once more from the correctional treatment point of view, it is not so important that this academic dispute be settled as it is that the correctionalist be adequately equipped to assist the female offender. This requisite adequacy must come from a sensitive approach, and should be based on an authentic knowledge of the modern female (offender) and her specialized needs. Oscar Wilde once remarked of the female that she was the decorative sex. She said nothing, but she said it so charmingly. The modern woman is saying a lot. The effective correctional treatment specialist will have very attentive ears.

SYNOPSIS

On the continuum of human behavior, it is impossible to make a sharp demarcation between the normal and the abnormal. Many factors enter into the definition of deviant behavior, not the least of which is society's level of tolerance for the behavior in question. In fact, it has been said that one of the major difficulties blocking a meaningful assessment of crime and delinquency is the tendency to seek a sharp distinction between the normal and the abnormal.

Deviance can be described as a violation of standards established by the power structure. But theorists, especially symbolic interactionists, in-

---

[54]Severa L. Austin, "Women's Corrections: Old Myths, New Directions," *Proceedings of the One Hundred and Seventh Annual Congress of Correction of the American Correctional Association,* Milwaukee, Wisc. (August 21-25, 1977), pp. 260-61.

[55]Freda Adler, *Sisters in Crime* (New York: McGraw-Hill Book Company, 1975); see also her article, "The Interaction Between Women's Emancipation and Female Criminality: A Cross-Cultural Perspective," *International Journal of Criminology and Penology,* Vol. 5, No. 2 (May 1977).

[56]See, for example, Joseph G. Weis, "Liberation and Crime: The Invention of the New Female Criminal," *Crime and Social Justice,* Vol. 6 (Fall-Winter 1976), pp. 17-27.

[57]Louis P. Carney, *Introduction to Correctional Science,* 2nd ed. (New York: McGraw-Hill Book Company, 1979), p. 309.

sist that self-identity is a key factor in the acceptance of the label of deviant. Absolutists maintain that certain acts are inherently wrong (*mala in se*) at all times and in all places, and relativists see deviance more as a matter of evaluation and differential power. It has also been asserted that "deviance" may not be an acceptable synonym for "criminality," and its use as such constitutes an unscientific disservice to criminology, needlessly proliferating definitions of deviance. The school of Radical Criminology attributes deviance to the factors of social stratification and segregation.

Special areas of concern include the individual who becomes involved in aggravated, pathological behavior and the career criminal. The former continues to baffle behavioral scientists, and the latter is the center of high controversy concerning whether or not (career) criminals and non-criminals are distinctly different personality types. The controversy has been fueled by the Yochelson-Samenow study, which has been hailed and damned, but mostly damned.

The neglect of the female deviant is also a matter of concern, because less is known about her due to benign neglect in past research.

4 Theories of Deviant Behavior

How oft the sight of means to do ill deeds
Makes deeds ill done!

William Shakespeare
King John, **Act IV. Scene 2.**

The most invulnerable profession has to be that of meteorologist. The meteorologist is almost universally expected to be wrong, most of the time, in his weather forecasts. A prediction of snow in August in Arizona, which failed to materialize, would most likely draw an indulgent chuckle from the average listener, or a comment to the effect that "old whatsisname blew it again." An individual seeking job security certainly ought to give due deliberation to becoming a meteorologist. The behavioral sciences, however, might provide some stiff competition. Behavioral scientists have made so many conjectural theories about human nature and human behavior, that the general public seems predisposed to indulge the implacable traditionalist and the avant-garde speculator with equal tolerance. From the often bizarre, and scientifically unverifiable tenets of psychoanalysis, to the thoroughly fallacious, monistic theories of crime causation, nothing appears to have shaken the public's tolerance.

Literally hundreds of theories and interpretations of human behavior and its diverse manifestations have been produced by behavioral scientists. Some are impressive and compelling. Others are less so. We have already discussed the position of Yochelson and Samenow, who have absolved society of culpability for criminality because its genesis lies in the individual. Orthodox sociologists, on the other hand, attribute the origin of deviance to defective group or socialization processes. Sociologists traditionally emphasize the group factor, psychologists accent the mental factor, and social psychologists put the stress on the influence of group phenomena on the individual's mental faculty. How do we explain the shortcomings of so much deviance theory? It might be said that a theory is deficient to the extent that it neglects or does not adequately account for one or the other of the two fundamental metaphysical principles that must be dealt with in explaining all human phenomena. The two principles are the *telic* and the *causal*. *Telic* is a word of Greek origin, deriving from *telos* which means end, or purpose. A teleological philosophy is one which holds a purposive view of life. In the present context, as a fundamental metaphysical principle, the *telic* aspect is concerned with *the purpose of* (deviant) *action*. The *causal* principle, on the other hand, is related to the energizing relationships among phenomena, or to *the antecedents of action or change*. According to Bruyn, "Both principles are basic to the full explanation of man as he exists in society."[1]

Perhaps the only way to draw consolation from the plentitude of theories is to assume that they all contribute to the fund of knowledge that will ultimately help to develop a more definitive understanding of humankind. In viewing the plethora of clinical persuasions on psychotherapy, Cohen once suggested that they were characterized by "a common core of reality."[2] Perhaps we can muster the same optimism in examining some of the major theories of criminal deviance, seeing them as also sharing a common core—of sociological reality.

In his work on theoretical criminology, which was published more than two decades ago, Vold stated

> It must of necessity be admitted that with the best intentions, and despite much industry and effort applied to the problem, human behavior still is not

[1]Severyn T. Bruyn, *The Human Perspective in Sociology* (Englewood Cliffs, N.J.: Prentice-Hall, Inc., 1966), p. 41.

[2]Sidney Cohen, *The Beyond Within* (New York: Athenenum Publishers, 1966), p. 182. Cohen was paraphrasing Judd Marmour's thesis delivered at the Academy of Psychoanalysis, Chicago, May 1961.

completely understood. No present scheme of theoretical concepts is entirely valid or entirely sufficient to account for the full range and complexity of human behavior.[3]

Vold's appraisal remains as valid today as when it was first uttered. The full range and complexity of human behavior remains uncircumscribed by the behavioral scientist, and the narrower field of criminal deviance is no exception. In this context, the following review of deviance theory is admittedly limited. Instead of an exhaustive assessment, we will undertake a representative sampling of some basic tenets of the more influential theoretical positions. The individual engaged in correctional treatment should be at least minimally exposed to the thinking of scholars in this critical and relevant area.

FROM SOCIAL PATHOLOGY TO THE NATURALISTIC VIEWPOINT

The sociology of deviance is one of the younger offspring of sociology. It did not really develop general respectability until the 1950s, but it had an honorable ancestry despite the fact that "it has long been subject to isolating strains which attempt to transform it into a curiously bastardized and multi-disciplinary enterprise or into a correctional aid."[4] In the infancy of sociology, stability characterized the sociological view of deviance. The macrocosmic universe reflected the operation of orderly laws. It followed that the microcosmic society should be ruled by law and characterized by order. Furthermore, as Scott and Douglas have pointed out, "the relation between rules and social order was also seen as absolute: 'Law and Order' were necessary, desirable, and moral, and the goal of sociology was to help attain and preserve them."[5] This led to a naturalistic, if absolutist, view of deviance by sociologists. It is generally conceded that the studies conducted by the so-called Chicago school constituted the first significant contributions to the naturalistic viewpoint, at least in the United States. Matza, in fact, categorically says that "it was the Chicagoans who inspired the naturalistic study of deviant phenomena. . . ."[6]

Early American sociologists described deviation as social pathology. Alcoholism, divorce, delinquency, and similar phenomena were so desig-

[3]George B. Vold, *Theoretical Criminology* (New York: Oxford University Press, 1958), pp. 3-4.

[4]Paul Rock and Mary McIntosh, *Deviance and Social Control* (London: Tavistock Publications, 1974), p. xi.

[5]Robert A. Scott and Jack D. Douglas, *Theoretical Perspectives on Deviance* (New York: Basic Books, 1972), p. 4.

[6]David Matza, *Becoming Deviant* (Englewood Cliffs, N.J.: Prentice-Hall, Inc., 1969), p. 24.

nated. The early emphasis in sociology was on a common-sense and reformative approach to social pathology. The early sociologists were also zealous for reform. With the advent of the Chicago school, this zeal was tempered, and the emphasis shifted to social organizations. Deviance was seen as social disorganization. According to Matza, the main effort of the naturalists, namely, the Chicago school, "was to rid the study of man of the conception of pathology."[7] And, in the context of envisioning deviancy as social disorganization, "[e]ntering deviant worlds was the major contribution of the Chicago school to emergent naturalism."[8]

Sociologists of the Chicago persuasion felt impelled to understand deviance from the point of view of the deviant, and considered the city the primary laboratory for research. Since man is a group animal, he is most productively studied in the great urban group concentrations. The city of Chicago was lanced and examined to an impressive degree. Classic studies were made of conditions in the urban center. Between 1925 and 1931 Louis Wirth produced *The Ghetto;* Paul G. Cressey wrote on *The Taxi-Dance Hall: A Sociological Study of Commercialized Recreation and City Life;* Frederic Thrasher made his incomparable study of the delinquent gang, published as *The Gang;* Nels Anderson examined *The Hobo: The Sociology of the Homeless Man;* Harvey W. Zorbaugh recounted *Gold Coast and Slum;* Robert E. Park, Ernest W. Burgess, and R. D. McKenzie studied the metropolis itself, culminating in *The City;* Clifford R. Shaw contributed *The Jack-Roller* and *The Natural History of a Delinquent Career,* and there were many more.

The Chicago school could be criticized for its rigid separation of the deviant and the non-deviant worlds. The deviant, whether taxi-dance hall girl or criminal, was studied *qua* deviant. The tendency was described by Merton in this fashion: "Our primary aim is to discover how some social structures exert a definite pressure upon certain persons in the society to engage in nonconformist rather than conformist conduct."[9] The shortcoming in this view is that the deviant is *a part of* the larger society, and not a separate culture or society. The Chicago school's view was obviously static; it ignored the considerable movement that constantly takes place to and from the deviant world.

Abandoning the speculative, doctrinal approach of the early sociologists, the Chicago school adopted a pragmatic, academic stance instead. It looked upon urban conditions in the context of natural phenomena. The metropolis was like an iceberg whose hidden mass was pathological and corrupting. The city, in short, was an ambivalence. The

[7] *Ibid.,* p. 44.
[8] *Ibid.,* p. 70.
[9] Mark Lefton, James K. Skipper, Jr., Charles H. McCaghy, *Approaches to Deviance: Theories, Concepts, and Research Findings* (New York: Appleton-Century-Crofts, 1968), p. 57.

serious deficit in this view is that it missed the symbiosis in the city between deviant and non-deviant.

The Chicago school deserves considerable credit for spotlighting the complex nature of urban existence, and especially for turning the focus on deviance away from social pathology and toward social institutions and organizations. It also paved the way for redirecting thinking in functionalism and interactionism, which we shall discuss later in this chapter. The many studies undertaken by the Chicago school, however, provided no unifying theory of deviance. As Davis incisively comments, "Entering deviant worlds, and taking the subjective viewpoint, produced a sociological portfolio of unique urban groupings and happenings. The Chicagoans were not successful, however, in tying these disparate pictures together."[10]

Conflict Theory or Social Crisis Theory

Deviance theories based on social conflict or social crisis seem particularly reasonable, because conflict and crisis are so evidently an integral part of human life. It should be kept in mind, however, that conflict theory, in its broadest sense, involves a total view of society. Sociological theorists who espouse a conflict theory of society do not take an organismic view; that is, they do not see society as an evolutionary entity moving toward stability. Conflict theorists are preoccupied with change, which they see as much more properly the characteristic of social organizations than stability. The Marxist view of society is a classic conflict theory. Appelbaum, indeed, has asserted that "Conflict theories constitute the legacy of Karl Marx...."[11]

The student is probably familiar with the term "dialectical materialism" as it applies to Marxist philosophy. Karl Marx was a student of Georg Hegel, who was a philosophic idealist, that is, one who gave primacy to ideas. Hegel considered matter the least important aspect of existence. Marx inverted Hegel's view, and gave supremacy to matter. But he also borrowed the dialectic from his mentor. According to Hegel, everything is constantly in the process of change, and these changes proceed from thesis (affirmation) through antithesis (denial) to synthesis (integration). This is known as the Hegelian triad, and it is the basis for the conflict theory of Karl Marx. Interestingly, this theory of deviance has been gaining renewed support from numerous scholars since the emergence of the school of "radical criminology" in the 1960s and 1970s.

---

[10]Nanette J. Davis, *Sociological Constructions of Deviance* (Dubuque, Iowa: Wm. C. Brown Co., Publishers, 1975), pp. 60-61.

[11]Richard P. Appelbaum, *Theories of Social Change* (Chicago: Markham Publishing Company, 1970), p. 81.

In other versions, conflict theory points the finger at power-seeking or competition between interest groups as the basis for conflict. The theory of deviance that rests on social conflict or social crisis is a social-psychological orientation. It is also fundamentally based on the concept of man as a group-living, gregarious animal. Society is seen as a network of groups interacting, often frictional because of opposing interests. This is a dynamic theory which emphasizes social process.

Conflict, far from being a negative thing, "is viewed . . . as one of the principal and essential social processes upon which the continuing ongoing of society depends."[12] It is a recurring sociological theme that society consists of competing interests (groups), and that rules and laws frequently represent the concrete manifestation of the dominant group's value system. The law is a central issue in conflict theories. There is a criminological theory, in fact, which maintains that the criminal law originated in the conflict between special interest groups.

A variation of the social crisis theory can be seen in the Bloch-Prince social disorganization concept. The capacity to adapt to social crisis is the key to the concept of deviance in this model. The authors were clearly impressed with social crisis data. Pointing to the doubling of the population since 1880, juxtaposed with a tripling of the marriage rate and a thousandfold increase in the divorce rate, as well as "the appalling increase in psychoneurotic disorders,"[13] they conclude: "All such forms of disorder seem to be part of a general pattern of violent struggle and change, stemming from certain fundamental disorders in the social structure itself."[14] We are confusing symptom with "fundamental dislocations," they insist, and failing to see that "The clue to personal and social pathologies may no longer be sought only in the individual problems themselves."[15] A good example would be drug addiction. According to the Bloch-Prince formulation, an individual's addiction problem should not receive the primary emphasis. It is but a symptom. It is "the pattern of the age" that such influences as migration and mobility produce this and other forms of deviancy.

Describing human behavior as "essentially *contingent* and dependent," Bloch and Prince saw the disorganizational social forces as so overwhelming as to justify absolution for much deviance: " . . . the basic fact is this: The individual may not be held entirely accountable for the types of difficulties or problem situations in which he finds himself. These diffi-

---

[12]Vold, *Theoretical Criminology,* p. 204.

[13]Herbert A. Bloch and Melvin Prince, *Social Crisis and Deviance* (New York: Random House, Inc., 1967), p. 4.

[14]*Ibid.,* p. 5.

[15]*Ibid.*

culties are parts of complicated and intricate process-situations."[16] This is a deterministic point of view, which once again introduces the controversial issue of the degree of human self-determination.

The criticisms usually directed against conflict theories of deviance are the following:

1. The class conflict implicit in this type of theory presumes that more crime will be committed by the so-called lower classes. This is because, in the competition of interests, the ruling class will naturally more frequently define as crime the unpalatable behavior of the lower classes. Contemporary criminology is discovering, on the contrary, that crime is pervasive and regular among all classes.

2. A conflict theory of deviance loses perspective by its narrow focus on class-versus-class conflict, for it overlooks intra-class conflict which is just as real.

3. A theory that depends exclusively on a foundation of human conflict ignores the great body of law that is directed towards the reduction of conflict and the instituting of harmony.

Functionalism

The approach to deviance known as functionalism is an outgrowth of the naturalistic posture espoused by the Chicago school. It is also a very theoretical approach. Whereas the Chicago school was preoccupied with participant-observer field research, the functionalists were more abstract than concrete, more subjective than objective. But they were also utilitarian. Functionalists believed that patterns of social activity which persisted did so because they serve a functional need. Robert Merton, who is considered one of the leading sociological theoreticians, was a functionalist, as was the distinguished sociologist, Kingsley Davis. As the devotees of the Chicago school felt the necessity of invading the world of the deviant and looking at deviance from the inside, so to speak, the functionalists felt compelled to stand outside of the system in order to observe the patterns of activity.

Functionalists take a unified view of the world. Davis calls this belief "the single, overarching conviction" of functionalism.[17] Social order is the watchword of the functionalist perspective. Where the conflict theorists see an abrasive interaction as the hallmark of society, the functionalists

[16] *Ibid.*, p. 138.
[17] Davis, *Sociological Constructions of Deviance,* p. 80.

consider equilibrium the normal state of affairs. This does not mean that functionalists deny change. It is simply that they see dysfunctional activities as temporary phases in society's readjustment to the ideal state of harmony or equilibrium. The very term *functionalism* pragmatically indicates that social developments are evaluated on the basis of their capacity to promote or to negate societal harmony. Sociologists who espouse the functional approach are usually described as *structural-functionalists* because they are committed to the belief that social institutions must be reduced to their constituent elements and functions if the mechanics of social order are to be discovered. Structural-functionalism was dominating American sociology as the decade of the fifties came to a close.

Although there are several variations on the theme of functionalism, it basically takes a benevolent view of deviance. Several functional studies are noted for taking the position that deviance has a latent function, which makes it actually supportive of conforming behavior. One of the works usually cited in this regard is Kingsley Davis' study of prostitution. In this study, Davis makes the point that prostitution protects the institution of the family because it restricts sexual deviance on the part of mothers and wives. Furthermore, when prostitution, and its concomitant, promiscuity, are officially condemned because they fulfill no *approved* social need, the positive nature of the institution of marriage is affirmed.[18]

Emile Durkheim, one of the theoretical giants in sociology, was early identified with this type of thinking. According to Durkheim, crime is an inevitable and even necessary product of social life. Crime establishes the moral boundaries of the community,[19] and it "brings together upright consciences and concentrates them."[20] Durkheim's hypothesis, that crime contributes to moral cohesion, was systematically applied to a Puritan settlement by Erikson. Although his method and conclusions are suspect, he affirmatively stated that crime

> may actually perform a needed service to society by drawing people together in a common posture of anger and indignation. The deviant individual violates rules of conduct which the rest of the community holds in high respect; and when these people come together to express their outrage over the offense and to bear witness against the offender, they develop a tighter bond of solidarity than existed earlier.[21]

[18]Kingsley Davis, "Prostitution," in Robert K. Merton and Robert Nisbet (eds.), *Contemporary Social Problems,* 3rd ed. (New York: Harcourt Brace Jovanovich, Inc., 1971).
[19]Emile Durkheim, *The Division of Labor in Society* (New York: The Free Press, 1949), p. 102.
[20]*Ibid.,* p. 127.
[21]Kai T. Erikson, *Wayward Puritans: A Study in the Sociology of Deviance* (New York: John Wiley & Sons, Inc., 1966), p. 4.

The works of Durkheim, Davis, Erikson, and others, demonstrate the fundamental position of the functionalists, that conventional behavior cannot be understood without reference to unconventional behavior. As Tacitus said, *Vitia erunt, donec homines* ("As long as men live, there will be vices").

The major criticisms of the functionalist position are these:

1. The functionalist contention that the body of the criminal law reflects a "moral consensus," which is the unifying element in society, is challengeable. It is only necessary to mention Prohibition to clarify the criticism. Prohibition was a criminal law which was manipulated into the Constitution of the United States by a small vested interest, and it did not come close to representing the national "consensus." Further, with the vast amount of law violations that take place in this country, a good case might be made for the fact that law violation represents the consensus! As far back as 1926, the gangster Al Capone, reflecting on his criminal occupation, commented: "The funny part of the whole thing is that a man in this line of business has so much company."[22]

2. By assuming societal stability *a priori,* functionalists exempt themselves from considering the very real possibility that society, or power groups in society, may actually cause deviance.

3. Because functionalists take a global view of society, and an overly abstract view of deviance, they detach themselves from concrete research and fail to deal with the realities of social institutions.

4. Functionalists have not demonstrated how the process of unification takes place in society.

5. Because they have minimized its importance, functionalists have neglected the element of conflict in human relations. Conflict is very real and very significant.

Labeling Theory

We have stated that *structural-functionalism* dominated American sociology as the 1950s came to a close. But during the decade of the fifties, its successor, *labeling theory,* was germinating, especially in the writings of Edwin Lemert and Howard Becker. The shifting scene in deviance theory had gone from social pathology and reform, through social problems and social and personal disorganization, to conflict and functionalism, and finally to labeling theory. Labeling theory, indeed, had evolved out of a general dissatisfaction with prevailing theories of deviance. Specifically, it

---

[22]Quoted in Christopher Hibbert, *The Roots of Evil* (Boston: Little, Brown & Company, 1963), p. 331.

was being increasingly felt that existing theories did not pay a great deal of attention to the process of becoming deviant, nor to the institutional responses to deviancy.

The dissatisfaction was implicit in the address of Herbert Blumer to the American Sociological Society in 1953. Blumer, the *spiritus rector* of *symbolic interactionism,* could have had the functionalists in mind as he passionately spoke of the need to perfect social theory. Social theory, he said, must be brought "into a close and self-correcting relation with its empirical world so that its proposals about that world can be tested, refined and enriched by the data of that world."[23]

Although the emphasis in this section is nominally on labeling theory, it must be kept in mind that labeling theory interpenetrates with interactionism and is heavily influenced by the theorizing of the symbolic interactionists. According to symbolic interaction, man depends upon his group interactions for the very definition of his social existence. He is the product of endless processual dynamics, but whether conforming or nonconforming, *he translates* the play of process upon his being. The interactionist is preeminently concerned with the meanings that individuals give to things. Blumer clearly elucidated this principle when he stated:

> The first premise is that human beings act toward things on the basis of the meanings that the things have for them. . . .The second premise is that the meaning of such things is derived from, or arises out of, the social interaction that one has with one's fellows. The third premise is that these meanings are handled in, and modified through, an interpretative process used by the person in dealing with the things he encounters.[24]

It can be said without contradiction that interactionism is the heartbeat of labeling theory. Labeling theorists see deviance as resultant of group interaction. They are critical of existing theories for failing to regard deviance as a process, and for failing to consider the institutional or organizational response (or adaptation) to deviance. Becker's definition of deviance will make this point clearer. He maintains that

> . . . social groups create deviance by making the rules whose infractions constitute deviance, and by *applying those rules to particular people* and labeling them as outsiders. From this point of view, deviance is not a quality of the act the person commits, but rather a consequence of the application by others of rules and sanctions to an *offender.*[25]

[23]Herbert Blumer, "What Is Wrong with Social Theory?" *American Sociological Review,* 19, No. 1 (February 1954), 9.

[24]Herbert Blumer, *Symbolic Interactionism: Perspective and Method* (Englewood Cliffs, N.J.: Prentice-Hall, Inc., 1969), p. 2.

[25]Howard S. Becker, *Outsiders: Studies in the Sociology of Deviance* (New York: The Free Press, 1963), p. 9.

Although the birth of labeling theory is usually traced to the 1960s, the concept of deviant labeling had appeared earlier. As far back as 1938, Tannenbaum had shown rare insight when he pointed out that

> In the conflict between the young delinquent and the community there develop two opposing definitions of the situation. . . . This conflict over the situation is one that arises out of a divergence of values. . . . The young delinquent becomes bad because he is defined as bad and because he is not believed if he is good. . . . The community cannot deal with people it cannot define.[26]

Tannenbaum was stating what later became a canon of the labeling theorists, namely, that the social structure itself can spawn deviant behavior. A little over a decade later, Lemert developed this concept further in a work of great importance.[27] He drew attention to the fact that rules which are ostensibly intended for social control sometimes actually precipitate rule infraction. In the criminal justice system, a good example could be found in parole. In those jurisdictions which impose total abstinence as one of the conditions of parole, it can certainly be said that the vast majority of parolees, who do not have a problem with alcoholic beverages, would be placed in a position with high incentive for infraction by virtue of this rule.

The basic premise of labeling theory is that deviance is a status imposed upon an individual, for specific behavior, by a social group that finds that behavior unpalatable. When Becker asserted that social groups create deviance by making the rules and by labeling rule-breakers as outsiders, his implication was clear and intended. Deviance imposes an inferior status on the deviant, separating him from the rule-making group which imposed the label of deviant. Even a limited familiarity with the system of criminal justice would provide verification of the fact that people are treated differently for similar offenses, and that the imposition of sanctions is a very inequitable and inconsistent process. As two contemporary symbolic interactionists observed, those who are labeled deviant are merely "a biased selection from among the group of rule-violators."[28]

Labeling theorists do not limit their theoretical and practical concerns solely to the process by which deviancy is established. A collateral concern has been to draw attention to the potential for recidivism as a result of deviant labeling. According to Becker:

> . . . one of the most important contributions of this approach [labeling theory] has been to focus attention on the way labelling places the actor in circum-

---

[26]Frank Tannenbaum, *Crimes and the Community* (Boston: Ginn & Company, 1938), pp. 17-18.

[27]Edwin M. Lemert, *Social Pathology* (New York: McGraw-Hill Book Company, 1951).

[28]Robert H. Lauer and Warren H. Handel, *Social Psychology: The Theory and Application of Symbolic Interactionism* (Boston: Houghton Mifflin Co., 1977), p. 213.

stances which make it harder for him to continue the normal routines of everyday life and thus provoke him to "abnormal" actions (as when a prison record makes it harder to earn a living at a conventional occupation and so dispose its possessor to move into an illegal one).[29]

In labeling theory, a distinction is made between *primary* deviation and *secondary* deviation. It was Lemert who "proposed the concept of secondary deviation to call attention to the importance of the societal reaction in the etiology of deviance, the forms it takes, and its stabilization in the deviant social roles or behavior systems."[30] When we speak of recidivism precipitated by deviant labeling, we are speaking of secondary deviation. In this type of deviance, the role of deviant is adopted *ex post facto* by the person so labeled. In other words, *because of* society's disapproval and stigmatizing, the individual redirects himself towards illegitimate norms and endeavors. This type of situation is familiar to people who work in the criminal justice system, particularly in the correctional components of probation and parole. The barriers (stigmata) facing the ex-offender when he attempts reintegration can, indeed, become precipitants of further deviancy.

Lemert devised his concept of secondary deviation to distinguish it from primary deviation, those "*original* and *effective* causes of deviant attributes and actions which are associated with physical defects and incapacity, crime, prostitution, alcoholism, drug addiction, and mental disorders."[31] Even labeling theorists have to recognize that there are some forms of "deviant" behavior which are clearly not induced by labeling.

Labeling theory was the reigning sovereign of deviance theory in the 1970s, but it has shortcomings. The principal criticisms that can be directed against the labeling theory position are:

1. Labeling theory has only partial applicability to crime phenomena. It is obvious that much crime is not precipitated by labeling.
2. The cause and effect relationship between labeling and deviation is vulnerable. If we stop labeling, would secondary deviance go away?
3. The concept of secondary deviance, while impressive, is largely descriptive. Labeling theorists have not shown how the labeled deviants use the labeling concept in their daily existences.
4. As Scott and Douglas have pointed out, "although the labeling theorists adopt the rhetoric of participant observation and understanding of the subject's worlds, they actually use their own theory as the starting point for the analysis of what deviance is, rather than

[29]Howard S. Becker, "Labelling Theory Reconsidered," in Paul Rock and Mary McIntosh (eds), *Deviance and Social Control* (London: Tavistock Publications, 1974), p. 42.

[30]Edwin M. Lemert, *Human Deviance, Social Problems, and Social Control* (Englewood Cliffs, N.J.: Prentice-Hall, Inc., 1967), p. 40.

[31]*Ibid.*

empirically investigating the construction of deviance . . . in everyday interaction."[32]

5. It has been alleged that labeling theorists are preoccupied with obfuscatory rhetoric at the expense of dealing with society's core values, and while they condemn the traditional theories of deviance, they yet retain the "traditional categories of deviance, the use of sociologists to locate and diagnose deviance in society, and, more generally, the taking of an official perspective on deviance."[33]

Anomie and Some Other Theories

In reviewing the naturalistic, conflict–crisis, functional, and labeling approaches to deviance, the student will have been introduced to what have been the more influential and pervasive of deviance theories. But there are many others, ranging from the esoteric to those with substantial followings. We will conclude this chapter by briefly touching upon some of the more notable of these remaining deviance theories, culminting with a description of "The New Criminology."

A popular vehicle for explaining deviant behavior has been the concept of *anomie*.[34] "Anomie" derives from the Greek. It original meaning was lawlessness, but sociologists use the word, in deviance theory, to indicate normlessness. The two names most frequently associated with the development of the concept of anomie are Emile Durkheim and Robert K. Merton. With respect to deviance theory, anomie is almost purely a sociological approach. That is, it does not lean on the psychological or biological disciplines for adjunctive support. Basically, deviation is seen as the end result of a basic conflict between cultural and institutional society. In our society, for example, the culture is heavily success oriented, but the institutional part of society does not provide the means for all to accomplish the goal. This imbalance necessarily constitutes a pressure towards deviation, particularly among the lower socioeconomic groups. Anomie theory could be called disjunctive theory, because it rests on the basic premise that the uneven access to goals by various members of our society results in structural strain in society, which constitutes an impetus to deviation.

Speaking specifically of criminal deviance, sociologists have never been satisfied with purely legal definitions, because the concrete perspective of the law is at variance with the sociologist's processual view of the

---

[32]Robert A. Scott and Jack D. Douglas, *Theoretical Perspective on Deviance* (New York: Basic Books, 1972), pp. 89-90.

[33]*Ibid.*, p. 89.

[34]A good source for deeper development of this position is Marshall B. Clinard, (ed.), *Anomie and Deviant Behavior* (New York: The Free Press, 1964).

social universe. Even where mitigants have tempered the severity of the law, there are sociological nuances and cultural imperatives which influence the behavior of individuals, and which are not recognized in the pragmatic body of law. Hence, the proliferation of sociological theory to account for criminal deviance.

Cohen, for instance, speaks of reaction-formation in theorizing about the delinquency of "lower-class" youth, seeing their delinquency as a repudiation of middle-class values.[35] Reckless talks of internal and external constraints or inhibitory factors in his containment model.[36] Cavan, in addressing juvenile delinquency, reintroduces the concept of public tolerance as an integral element in the definition of deviancy.[37] Mathematical probabilism is offered an important role in the definition of deviance, as witnessed by this comment: "Individual or group behavior is deviant if it falls within a class of behavior for which there is a probability of negative sanctions subsequent to its detection."[38] Edwin H. Sutherland is noted for his differential association theory, which is both a learning and an interactionist theory. In Sutherland's view, "*A person becomes delinquent because of an excess of definitions favorable to violation of law over definitions unfavorable to violation of law.*"[39] (Italics in the original). This means that criminal deviance is the result of "contacts with criminal patterns and also . . . isolation from anti-criminal patterns."[40] Cloward and Ohlin, with a variation on the Sutherland theme, offer a concept of differential *opportunity*, in which criminal deviance is viewed in the context of blocked avenues to legitimate satisfaction of needs, with consequent diversion to illegitimate avenues of fulfillment.

The field of criminal deviance theory is a prolific one. The correctional treatment practitioner, or embryonic practitioner, should approach it eclectically!

The New Criminology

Although we have indicated that labeling theory seemed to be the most strongly supported, especially in the early seventies, a "new" or "radical"

[35]Albert K. Cohen, *Deviance and Social Control* (Englewood Cliffs, N.J.: Prentice-Hall, Inc., 1966), pp. 65-66.

[36]Walter C. Reckless, *The Crime Problem* (New York: Appleton-Century-Crofts, 1973), pp. 55-57.

[37]Ruth Shonle Cavan, *Juvenile Delinquency* (Philadelphia: J. B. Lippincott Company, 1973), p. 28.

[38]Donald J. Black and Albert J. Reiss, Jr., "Police Control of Juveniles," *American Sociological Review*, 35, No. 1 (February 1970), 63.

[39]Edwin H. Sutherland, *Principles of Criminology*, 4th ed. (Philadelphia: J. B. Lippincott Company, 1947), p. 6.

[40]Richard A. Cloward and Lloyd E. Ohlin, *Delinquency and Opportunity* (New York: The Free Press, 1960).

theory was incubating in the 1960s and 1970s, which has become popularly referred to as "The New Criminology." In essence, the New Criminology repudiates all pre-existing theories (although conflict is a central theme in its philosophy) because "Our social theories, based on old sensibilities, have done little else than support the established order."[41] Neo-Marxism flavors the new philosophy.

The widespread protests of the sixties and seventies did not have a transitory impact. The depths of human feelings had been sounded in rebellion against the deprivation of civil rights, the mistreatment of the imprisoned, the degradation of the poor and the handicapped, the exploitation of minorities, and the horror and meaningnessless of war in the far-off jungles of Viet Nam. The attack was on the military-industrial power complex, and on misdirected power in general. Abusive power and economic inequity were at the base of the protest by angry idealists. So it followed that Marxist-oriented thinking would emerge against the backdrop of the power-economic exploitation of "the masses." Quinney is a prominent, if not the leading exponent of this new posture.[42] Of greater significance than the resuscitation of a dormant philosophy is the actual development of the "New Criminology," of which Quinney is considered a principal theoretician. As Gilbert Geis says of Quinney's definitive work: "It calls forcefully for a dramatic shift in the kind of work sociologists have been doing, and predicts, indeed, that under the new order sociology itself may become an anachronistic and counter-revolutionary enterprise. . . ."[43] One of Quinney's fundamental principles is as revelatory as his entire thesis: "The criminal justice movement is thus understood as a state-initiated and state-supported effort to rationalize mechanisms of social control."[44]

Quinney maintains that deviance theory heretofore has had but one objective, and that is to preserve the established social order, and these theories have been as repressive as the social order has been oppressive. He then states:

> But we are entering a new age, one based on liberation as opposed to repression. Our theories and our lives must be appropriate to the new age. No longer can we rely on obsolete ideas, inhertied from a former age. Existing social theory—especially that pertaining to "deviance"—must be recognized for what it is and replaced by ideas that are relevant to the world we are

[41]Richard Quinney, "From Repression to Liberation: Social Theory in a Radical Age," in Robert A. Scott and Jack D. Douglas, *Theoretical Perspectives on Deviance* (New York: Basic Books, Inc., Publishers, 1972), p. 317.

[42]See Richard Quinney, *The Social Reality of Crime* (Boston: Little, Brown & Company, 1970), and particularly his *Class, State and Crime* (New York: David McKay Company, Inc., 1977).

[43]Geis' critique was imprinted on the jacket of Quinney's book, identified below.

[44]Richard Quinney, *Class, State and Crime*, p. 10.

creating. The only thing we have to lose is our captivity; what we will gain is our liberation.[45]

Reading this quoted material, without the definitive reference, would lead the reader to suspect that he or she was reading an excerpt from the writings of Karl Marx, but it actually is an expression of the philosophic position of the new criminology. Quinney traces the history of the social sciences as one of subservience to the establishment. Sociology's goal, in its infancy, was to discover the immutable laws of society, and thereby introduce tranquillity in the social universe. As we have noted in discussing earlier theories, order in the societal universe was the sociological watchword. Quinney repudiates this, opting for a conflict model:

> Order will not be taken as the ideal of social existence. Disorder and change, rather than consensus and stability, will be recognized, and therefore will be an integral part of social theory. Society will be understood in terms of its power structures. The segments of society will be viewed according to their conflicts.[46]

The New Criminology is actually a groundswell repudiation of traditional criminological and social theory doctrines. In the first place, these doctrines and theories have never given completely compelling explanations of social process and social deviance. Secondly, the theoreticians have incestuously supported the establishment, that is, theories have been tailored to conform with traditional presuppositions. Over and above these "principles," the adherents of the New Criminology have become increasingly sensitized to the inherent inequities of the criminal justice system. For them, only a radical redirection of thought and philosophy offers promise for the future. There are theories galore on white-collar crime, rape, poverty, abuse of police power, sentencing inequities, and so forth. But no sociological theorist has brought the legions of white-collar criminals to the bar of justice; none has recognized the role of the cult of male dominance in rape; none has freed the inmates from the prison of poverty; none has offered definitive insights into the increased killing of citizens by policemen; and none has brought justice to the courts of justice.

The New Criminologists put the establishment of justice above the creation of a theory.

> In this sense, the growth of our new approach to understanding crime requires us to participate in struggles for social justice. Moreover, we must never presume to speak for those who have not selected us to do so. Ideally,

[45]Quinney, "From Repression to Liberation," pp. 317-18.
[46]*Ibid.*, p. 319.

out of the dialogue and dialectic of ongoing struggles for social change will come the fresh insights, the clues for theory construction, and the priorities for research and practice.[47]

What criticisms should be brought against the New Criminology, aside from the traditional criticisms leveled at monistic Marxism? Krisberg said, "The New Criminology is in the process of becoming, and at this point we can only speculate as to future developments."[48] That which is in the process of becoming should not be criticized until it has become. Therefore, we will leave the final criticism to the reader.

SYNOPSIS

The sociology of deviance is an infant discipline, not really developing general respectability until the 1950s. Early sociologists viewed society as governed by orderly laws, and the goal of sociology was seen as the preservation of that order. Deviance, as such, was considered social pathology, illustrated in divorce, alcoholism, crime, poverty and similar phenomena. The development of the Chicago School led to a definition of deviance as social disorganization. The city became the laboratory, and the city of Chicago was explored to an astounding degree. The Chicago School, however, made the mistake of rigidly dichotomizing the deviant and the non-deviant worlds, for a great deal of interpenetration of these worlds takes place.

The Marxian imprint is seen in the development of conflict or social crisis theories of deviance. These theories see conflict, rather than stability, as the fundamental characteristic of social organization, and tend to emphasize power-seeking and competition in their interpretations. A variant of the social crisis theory is contained in the Bloch-Prince concept of social disorganization, in which the capacity to adapt to social crisis is seen as the key to understanding deviance.

The functional school developed the premise that patterns of social activity persist because they serve a functional need. The functionalist stands outside the system, as it were, to observe patterns of activity. The norm for the functionalist is the opposite of that for the conflict theorists, namely, that equilibrium is the normal state of affairs.

In modern times, labeling theorists have dominated the sociological effort to understand deviance. The labeling theorist, dissatisfied with existing theories, feels that the process of becoming deviant has been ne-

---

[47]Barry Krisberg, *Crime and Privilege* (Englewood Cliffs, N.J.: Prentice-Hall, Inc., 1975), pp. 168-69.
[48]*Ibid.,* p. 168.

glected. Labeling theorists have a close affinity with symbolic interactionists. Blumer accented this when he said that "human beings act toward things on the basis of the meaning that things have for them."

Other modern theories, such as anomie theory, see deviance resulting from cultural conflict and the inaccessibility of the means to fulfill needs.

5 Correctional Models

Each correctional agency should immediately develop and implement policies, procedures, and practices to fulfill the right of offenders to rehabilitation programs. A rehabilitative purpose is or ought to be implicit in every sentence of an offender. . . .

National Advisory Commission on Criminal Justice Standards and Goals, 1973

In primitive times, offenders were banished from the tribe. It was a very severe form of punishment because it was tantamount to a death sentence. Outside of the safety and security of one's own tribe, death almost certainly awaited from hostile enemies. It might be suspected that this ancient form of punishment had passed into history, but it would be an inaccurate supposition. Italy still banishes "undesirables" to remote islands for penal exile. Death is not an almost certain sequel, as in primitive times, but the "out of sight, out of mind" philosophy of banishment endures. While Italy banishes, Saudi Arabia performs public decapitation, and the United States still imposes sentences exceeding life. Why does the severe punishment sentiment endure, particularly in cultures whose folk music throbs with love and brotherhood?

THE PUNISHMENT SENTIMENT

Garfinkel describes punishment as "a public degradation ceremony,"[1] but the absolute elimination of punishment is neither likely nor reasonable. If some form of sanction is not imposed for serious threats to the commonweal, then justice would no longer remain among the virtues. Reasonable deprivations and restraints can be effective sanctions. The offender does not have to be debased or physically brutalized to be convinced of society's dissatisfaction with his behavior. When punishment is criticized in this text, it is inordinate, brutalizing, and unduly severe punishment that is being criticized.

How, then, is the retaliatory impulse in the human to be explained, for man has endeavored to exact his pound of flesh since time immemorial? A number of distinguished sociologists have written about reciprocity as a social process. This refers to the universal practice of reciprocity when a kindness or a service has been bestowed, or what Gouldner has called the "norm of reciprocity."[2] He points out that Howard Becker has even gone so far as to call man *Homo reciprocus,* indicating how important and generic he thinks this process is. It may be that reciprocation characterizes not only benevolent actions, but also malevolent ones.

Victims are emotionally reactive with respect to their assailants. In the more personal types of offenses, such as physical assaults, it is reasonable to suspect that the victim would bear animosity for the perpetrator of the offense. Furthermore, the victim is usually not alone in experiencing this feeling. There are wives and husbands, and other relatives, as well as friends and neighbors, to share the animus for the offender, because they become vicarious victims. The norm of reciprocity is, therefore, an inevitable part of human interaction.

The shortcoming in the theory of reciprocity is that not all offenses would precipitate feelings of hostility. A thief who steals two dollars from a millionaire will scarcely cause the victim to experience annoyance, let alone hostility. Again, not all crimes have an identified offender, and for those that do there would be a dramatic difference in the hostility experienced by the victims. More emotion would be felt as a result of rape, for

[1] Harold Garfinkel, "Conditions of Successful Degradation Ceremonies," *American Journal of Sociology,* 61, No. 5 (March 1956), 420-24.
[2] Alvin W. Gouldner, "The Norm of Reciprocity: A Preliminary Statement," *American Sociological Review,* 25, No. 2 (April 1960), 161-78.

FIGURE 5-1
Joliet Prison, late 1800s

Courtesy of CONtact, Inc.

example, than would be for petty theft. Reciprocity may, therefore, be more of a collective than an individual norm. Irrespective of the source of the norm, whatever sanction is imposed on an offender must ultimately stand the test of rationality.

The prevalence of severe punishment calls into question the claims made in many textbooks that the criminal justice system is being dramatically humanized. Particularly brutal punishment is ill-designed to inspire regenerative sentiments in the offender. Revenge would be a more likely response. Seven centuries ago, St. Thomas Aquinas taught that to be effective and advance the purpose of rehabilitation, punishment must be accepted by the one punished.[3] And seven centuries later it has been asserted that:

> The belief that society serves the common and individual good by a system of rigid punishment has never been fully justified by history, and its persistence looks more and more like superstition than a conviction based on fact.[4]

The reality therapist, William Glasser, adds a specific psychodynamic, wrapped in a crime statistic, to illustrate the inefficacy of punishment. Pointing out that 60 percent of those in custody have been in custody previously, Glasser states that

> ... when a man who identifies himself as a failure is punished, his failure identity is reinforced. He will tend to behave in the same way that led to his initial incarceration and usually spend more and more time in custody as he grows older. Therefore, the assumption that punishment will cause a person to change his behavior and become rehabilitated is completely wrong.[5]

Punishment must be placed in perspective. In the so-called administration of justice, the ultimate objective is to *redirect* individuals away from criminal behavior and to *deter* prospective criminals from acting out. Treatment and punishment, in the correctional system, are inextricably linked. Redirection is the challenge of treatment and rehabilitation; deterrence is the function assigned to punishment. As von Hirsch said, speaking for the Committee for the Study of Incarceration, "It seems almost a truism that criminals should be punished so there will be less crime."[6] He also said that "general deterrence, never forsaken by law-enforcement officials, is again a topic of interest to scholars."[7]

Although the question of the deterrent potential of punishment is a vexing one, there is a growing belief, based on relevant research, that there may, indeed, be a deterrent factor in punishment. Deterrence, it must be remembered, has a dual mission: to dissuade the offender from renewed criminality, and to encourage the compliance of others. Even if only one of these objectives was accomplished, it would be testimony in favor of the efficacy of deterrence.

---

[3]*Summa theol.*, Vol. 2 (Pegis ed.), Question 87, Article 6.

[4]Gregory Zilboorg, *The Psychology of the Criminal Act and Punishment* (New York: Greenwood Press, 1968), p. 97.

[5]William Glasser, *The Identity Society*, rev. ed. (New York: Harper & Row, Publishers, Inc., 1976), p. 189.

[6]Andrew von Hirsch, *Doing Justice* (New York: Hill and Wang, 1976), p. 37. This is the official report of the Committee for the Study of Incarceration, a Field Foundation study commissioned in 1971 because of the "growing disenchantment with prisons, and with the disparities and irrationalities of the sentencing process" (p. xv).

[7]*Ibid.*, p. 37.

Still, it must be obvious that deterrence alone is insufficient to diminish criminal behavior significantly. Recidivism data will clearly support this contention. As two experimenters in the field sagely asserted, "while punishment may indeed suppress behavior, it can, by itself, have no such therapeutic or beneficial consequences because its effects are usually transient and depend on continuous and repeated applications."[8]

It should be pointed out that the Committee for the Study of Incarceration does not advocate increased punishment although it speaks of punishment being deserved. Nor does it espouse retribution. It appears to reflect a philosophy that has shifted from a concept of the collective good to a renewed reverence for the individual. This philosophic shift can be ascertained in the following statement of the Committee:

> Both in tone and content, the recommendations of the Committee represent a departure from tradition. Permeating this report is a determination to do less rather than more—an insistence on not doing harm. The quality of heady optimism and confidence of reformers in the past, and their belief that they could solve the problem of crime and eradicate the presence of deviancy, will not be found in this document. Instead, we have here a crucial shift in perspective from a commitment to do good to a commitment to do as little mischief as possible.[9]

The Committee was gravely influenced by the disparities and inequities that characterize sentencing in this country. It was also impressed with the fact that the deterrence concept cannot stand alone. It needs a "moral" claim—that punishment is deserved. In this "new" philosophy, it is accepted that those who violate the rights of others deserve to be punished. But it is also a principle that punishment should not be deliberately added to the reservoir of human suffering. Consequently, punishment must be justified—and is—on the basis of the efficacy of deterrence, which will actually prevent more misery than it occasions:

> When one seeks to justify the criminal sanction by reference to its deterrent utility, desert is called for to explain why that utility may justly be pursued at offenders' expense. When one seeks to justify punishment as deserved, deterrence is needed to deal with the countervailing concern about the suffering inflicted. The interdependence of these two concepts suggests that the criminal sanction rests, ultimately, on *both.*[10]

Just as theory is the tool by which data is consistently applied to particular situations, so philosophy controls one's approach to the concept of

---

[8]James B. Appel and Neil J. Peterson, "What's Wrong with Punishment?" *The Journal of Criminal Law, Criminology and Police Science,* 55, No. 4 (December 1965), 450.

[9]Von Hirsch, *Doing Justice,* p. xxxiv.

[10]*Ibid.,* p. 55.

punishment. The range is wide: from pure retributive vengeance, to pure treatment, with many variations. The American Friends Service Committee report on crime and punishment described punishment as "the application of force to another person against his or her will," and criminal law as "the sanctioned official use of force."[11] And the Committee for the Study of Incarceration, an equally distinguished group of talented and concerned individuals, says the criminal law can "do justice" and is a deterrent. And so the ideological battle continues. In the collision of ideas, the constant hope is that we will be propelled ever closer to the truth.

THE REHABILITATIVE SENTIMENT

The controversy over rehabilitation or treatment in corrections largely involves the attitude toward change. If behavior is to be modified, which is the treatment intent, change must be induced on the basis of knowledge about the offender, particularly knowledge about his or her motivation. The why of deviant behavior is crucial to its modification. The difficulty is that we are not really too knowledgeable about methods for inducing enduring behavioral changes. On top of that, as Kalmanoff pointed out, "many offenders ... learn to exploit rehabilitation as a 'con game.'"[12] Every practitioner in corrections is familiar with this situation. Most offenders feel that the system consists of "games" to be played. A state prison inmate once told me that "doing time" consisted of jumping through hoops held by the staff, the last hoop being the gate to the outside world. I encountered the same sentiment repeatedly during some extensive interviewing of federal parolees. Almost exclusively, they expressed the opinion that getting out of prison, or succeeding on parole, depended on "playing the game." These opinions to the contrary, every practitioner in the field is also familiar with the fact that people can and do change, and that significant modifications in life styles have frequently been observed during the time an offender was in the correctional system or under supervision in the field.

If the offender's behavior is going to have to change, then so is the correctional system. If sufficiently compelling attacks can be made on the effectiveness of correctional rehabilitation, and if the recidivism rate is truly dismal, then deficiencies in the correctional system can be legitimately assumed. Part of the problem is that corrections tends to succumb to inertia, and goes with outmoded traditions and practices. Furthermore, the adherents of the various schools of thought often maintain their views

[11]American Friends Service Committee, *Struggle for Justice* (New York: Hill and Wang, 1971), p. 22.

[12]Alan Kalmanoff, *Criminal Justice: Enforcement and Administration* (Boston: Little, Brown & Company, 1976), p. 319.

in logic-tight compartments, incestuously refusing to indulge in eclectic interaction. The proponents of the various persuasions also tend to defend their respective positions implacably, and to feel that they alone have the correctional panacea. For example, treatment-oriented correctionalists tend to unrealistically assume that everyone can be rehabilitated, wrongfully believing that the present state of knowledge in the behavioral sciences is sufficient to justify that assumption.

Corrections could start its own correction by refining the classification procedures to ensure that those most responsive to treatment strategies will be selectively screened into treatment programs. There are too many unresponsive sociopaths on traditional probation and parole caseloads, contributing to a skewed recidivism rate, and concealing the true scope of correctional treatment. Uehling, who spent 37 years as a psychologist in a correctional setting, makes a reinforcing comment as he speaks of certain conclusions that must be confronted, if any meaning is to be attached to the correctional treatment process: "First of all, it is important to recognize that an adequate screening process in our dealings with the criminal offender is one of paramount importance."[13] In the light of the mounting criticism of correctional rehabilitation, additional innovations and changes must take place to restore the vitality and promise of correctional treatment. The gauntlet was thrown down in 1974.

In 1974, the arch-critic of correctional rehabilitation, Robert Martinson, published an article that had the same power as Paul Revere to stir up the countryside.[14] His basic premise, that correctional treatment was an exercise in futility, was the opening shot heard round the correctional world. His "almost nothing works" became the battle cry of the cynics. His influence was magnetic, and punishment and deterrence again became prominent in the lingua franca of corrections. Martinson fueled the controversy by later suggesting that each released prisoner be assigned an official surveillant, "his own private policeman," who would constantly monitor the activities of the ex-offender in order to protect the public.[15] This suggestion has been jocularly referred to as the "cop-a-con" concept. As the voice of the pessimists became louder and more insistent, Adams was led to comment that "it appeared that programmed rehabilitation of criminal offenders was about to become an extinct process—a type of social action without a future."[16]

[13]Harold F. Uehling, *Correction of a Correctional Psychologist in Treatment of the Criminal Offender* (Springfield, Ill.: Charles C Thomas, Publisher, 1973), p. 179.

[14]Robert M. Martinson, "What Works—Questions and Answers about Prison Reform," *Public Interest,* No. 35 (Spring 1974), pp. 22-54.

[15]Judith Wilks and Robert M. Martinson, "Is the Treatment of Criminal Offenders Really Necessary?" *Federal Probation,* 40, No. 1 (March 1976), 6.

[16]Stuart Adams, "Evaluating Correctional Treatments: Towards a New Perspective," *Criminal Justice and Behavior,* 4, No. 4 (December 1977), 323.

But Martinson tempered his apparent cynicism (he calls it "realism"), and the cause of correctional treatment was capably defended by a number of influential and impressive scholars and professionals. Palmer had sifted through Martinson's controversial article (see footnote 14) and found innumerable admissions on the part of Martinson that various treatment programs *did* work.[17] He also pointed out that Martinson made no allowance for the success of subgroups within the larger correctional treatment programs which he evaluated and condemned. The tendency to take a global view of a program, and to focus on the gross recidivism rate, is a common one in correctional evaluation. But it is a defective approach because it obscures the success that may have been obtained with segments within the larger group. As Adams said, in his critical comments on Martinson's position, if "we ask what treatments show effects with at least some types of offenders, the result is different. We are struck by the apparent evidence that a wide variety of treatments seems to work, at least with some people, in some places, and perhaps under some practitioner types."[18]

It is almost a truism that corrections is not so much unsuccessful as untried. MacDougall put this concept in an appealing literary style when he said, "Corrections, like Christianity, has not been tried and found wanting, it has been found difficult and not tried."[19] The President's Task Force on Prisoner Rehabilitation opened with the statement that, "The voluminous literature on the subject [rehabilitation] overflows with excellent ideas that never have been implemented, nor, in many cases, even tested."[20] If corrections has not really been tried, it can scarcely be dismissed as a failure. While treatment and rehabilitation efforts have been legitimately questioned, and punishment seeks to dethrone rehabilitation, it is obvious that we cannot warehouse our offenders without being concerned about them as individuals with futures. Despite our imperfect understanding of the etiology of crime, we simply cannot ignore the end product, and we do have knowledge to bring to bear upon the problem. As one sensitive and perceptive writer stated:

> In spite of our lack of understanding, ignorance and misconceptions there are certain solid facts we do know—when people fail to develop good feelings about themselves and good feelings about other people, when their needs to love and be loved and accepted are thwarted, when their early experiences

[17]Ted Palmer, "Martinson Revisited," *Journal of Research in Crime and Delinquency,* 12 (1975), 133-52.

[18]Adams, "Evaluating Correctional Treatment," 329.

[19]Ellis C. MacDougall, "Corrections Has Not Been Tried," *Criminal Justice Review,* 1, No. 1 (Spring 1976), 63.

[20]*The Criminal Offender—What Should Be Done?,* the report of the President's Task Force on Prisoner Rehabilitation, April 1970.

engender mistrust and doubts rather than trust and confidence, when their desires to be recognized and relate happily never materialize and when their ability to communicate is stifled, substitutes are often sought and accepted.[21]

Crime is one of the substitutes. It is the responsibility of correctional treatment to reopen avenues of positive experience so that the negative life experiences can be effectively counteracted.

GENERIC CORRECTIONAL MODELS

A model is a conceptual representation of how something works or should work. It can be a description of what is or the ideal expression of what ought to be. In systems analysis, models are created of existing systems, and the components are then experimentally manipulated to facilitate the development of ways to improve the efficiency of the system. In addition to the descriptive aspects, a model also implies a philosophy. When the Gemini model was on the drawing board, for instance, a philosophic commitment to space exploration was also there. Correctional models also contain philosophical implications. They tell us of a philosophic disposition toward the criminal, as well as conceptualizing the mission of corrections. Three major models have typified correctional philosophy in the present century.

The Custodial Model

This model, obviously, was the pioneer, a heritage from the primitive days of penology. Prior to the nineteenth century, imprisonment, for the purpose of punishment, was not conventionally employed. In fact, it was not until the nineteenth century that sentencing, as we understand it today, and imprisonment came into wide use. The penitentiary was America's contribution to penology, and its philosophy was rooted in an odd mixture of militaristic control and the Quaker theology of introspection. It was confidently believed that reformation would result if prisoners were given the opportunity of solitary contemplation of their misdeeds. So the first prison (penitentiary) was characterized by silence and complete segregation of the inmates. It should also be noted that the prison resulted basically from humanitarian rather than punitive impulses. It was to be the correctional instrument that would bypass severe physical punishments, which pre-existed in the "administration of justice." But that was before the barbarisms generated by the prison itself were manifested.

---

[21]Florence L. Nichols, "Release and Community Co-operation," *International Journal of Offender Therapy and Comparative Criminology,* 20, No. 3 (1976), 217-18.

Through the persuasion of the custodial model, well over 400 major penal institutions were built in this country, typified in the fortress prisons at Sing Sing, New York; Jackson, Michigan; and Stateville, Illinois. These fortresses, built of granite, steel, and concrete, epitomized the custodial philosophy in their very structure. They were formidable and implacable, and the message of control and restraint was not lost upon either the inmates or the community: Dangerous people (criminals) should be securely held, and the community collaboratively protected. This was the philosophy embedded in the fortress prisons of America, and their names became legends in American folklore. Folsom, San Quentin, Leavenworth, Alcatraz, Auburn, the Eastern Penitentiary, the Territorial Prison at Yuma, Joliet, and many others in addition to those already mentioned. It was not until recently that correctionalists began to recognize the influence of architecture on the prison philosophy, and the negative influence of the prison on rehabilitation. In 1973 the National Advisory Commission on Criminal Justice Standards and Goals recommended a moratorium on the building of new prisons. Ironically, the attacks on the rehabilitation model began shortly after that time.

The Rehabilitation Model

The almost simultaneous development of probation and parole in the mid-nineteenth century was the influential boost needed for redirected thinking in the field of corrections. Still, it took almost a century for these correctional devices to become sophisticated, and the rehabilitation model itself took almost a century to develop, following the emergence of probation and parole. Many feel that the first practical application of the rehabilitation model took place with the Chicago Area Project, which we discussed in Chapter Two.

The development of the rehabilitation model, however, like most developments of this nature, reflected a great many influences. The rapid growth of the behavioral sciences was a prime force. A growing recognition that there were more negatives than positives in long-term incarceration was another. An imperious social work profession added its mark. Armed with "insights" from Freudian psychoanalysis, it moved toward the correctional field confident that the behavioral sciences (especially psychiatric social work) had the medicine for the sickness of crime. In the previous chapter, we spoke of the zeal for reform that inflamed the sociologists in the early part of this century. This zeal was also an impetus to the rehabilitation model. The offender was to be recovered from his misdirected life, not abandoned.

Ironically, the indeterminate sentence, which developed with parole, became a plank in the foundation of the rehabilitation model. It dovetailed with the medical model approach, because the professionals were now able to "treat the patient" and release him or her when appropriate response to the "correctional medication" had been made. The irony is that the indeterminate sentence was included in the indictment brought against correctional rehabilitation in the 1970s. The objection to the indeterminate sentence is based on the fact that no one is capable of determining the precise moment at which a person is rehabilitated, and the indeterminate sentence, therefore, merely imposes unwarranted psychological anguish up on an inmate.

Most of the "treatment" programs and adjunctive devices familiar to the reader were introduced under the aegis of the rehabilitation model. These included diagnostic centers, halfway houses, work and education furloughs from prison, and such institutional programs as Narcotics Anonymous, Alcoholics Anonymous, Toastmasters International, and similar groups. Psychiatric, psychologic, and sociologic professionals were added to prison staffs, and psychotherapy became accessible to inmates.

Several criticisms have been directed against the rehabilitation model. In particular, as I have noted elsewhere, to convince an offender that he is ill, and that crime is a sickness, is to encourage him to ignore his personal responsibility for his behavior. We do not blame sick people for becoming ill, but we do for becoming criminal. Furthermore, to posit some sort of psychiatric, quasi-psychiatric, or emotional problem for all criminal behavior leads to the presumption that crime cannot be rational and deliberate, and nonpsychiatric. As Cole said, "For a poor man to steal may be quite rational behavior."[22] As time passed, the feeling that prisons were ill-designed to facilitate rehabilitation or treatment increased. Community-based corrections and diversion became correctional watchwords. A new model appeared.

The Reintegration Model

In 1973, Professor Newman stated, with respect to probation and parole, that the emphasis was shifting from an unproductive clinical approach to what he termed "a reintegrationist focus."[23] The prison is not conducive to treatment or rehabilitation, a fact which is accepted by the majority of people in the field. In fact,

> Few persons in correctional administration really believe that effective rehabilitation can take place in a situation of total repression, degradation, and

[22]George F. Cole, *The American System of Criminal Justice* (North Scituate, Mass.: Duxbury Press, 1975), p. 401.

[23]Donald J. Newman, "Legal Model For Parole: Future Developments," in Benjamin Frank (ed.), *Contemporary Corrections* (Reston, Va.: Reston Publishing Company, 1973), p. 244.

control. . . .[I]mprisonment is seen as useful for diagnosis or cooling-off, if it is useful at all, but not for treatment.[24]

The unreal nature of the prison is one of the most acute barriers to treatment. For example, in the "free world" workers in the construction trades are expected to frame so many houses, or construct so many fireplaces, or sheath so many roofs in a given day. In the prison, where idleness is ever-present, the vocational trade training programs simply do not train the neophytes to accommodate to the speed and pressures which are part of outside industrial and technological life. Inmates (and their keepers) have nothing but time, and so the pace is much slower, and in some trades the training simply cannot be given at all.

Implicit in the reintegration model is the belief that if individuals are allowed to participate in the basic and social institutions, they will find fulfillment and be disposed towards conformity. The premise is that when an individual has no significant ties to the community, no meaningful work, no family ties, and no spiritual guidance, he is free to engage in criminal behavior. The alert student will see the hint of anomic theory in this position. Social and community ties are the fabric of conformity; when these ties are severed, the individual drifts into nonconformity— which often means crime.

Also implicit in the reintegration model is a de-emphasis on incarceration. It logically follows, from the principles enunciated in the preceding paragraph, that protracted absence from the community and its nurturing ties would be a countermilitant to reintegration. As Newman said, prisons are seen as useful for diagnosis, and for "cooling-off," but not for rehabilitative treatment. Community-based corrections is the preferred mode in the reintegration model. Probation and parole, community correctional centers, halfway houses, diversion from the system, and similar emphases are supported as proper correctional endeavors. The role of the probation officer and the parole officer, however, will be different from the traditional roles. These individuals will become what I have previously defined as "community resource brokers."[25] If reintegration is the functions of corrections, then the correctionalist's function must be to mobilize the resources of the community on behalf of the offender, to plug the client back into the nurturing tributaries of the community.

The models which we have just reviewed are the generic models, which depict the full spectrum of philosophy towards the offender, and the role of corrections. As a classification system of correctional philoso-

---

[24]*Ibid.*, p. 250.
[25]Louis P. Carney, *Probation and Parole* (New York: McGraw-Hill Book Company, 1977), p. 317.

phy, containment-rehabilitation-reintegration is almost as exhaustive as Aristotle's categories. Most models could be subsumed in this broad classification. The punishment model, for example, would come under "containment." There are variations on the major theme, however.

THE O'LEARY-DUFFEE SCHEMATIC

Vincent O'Leary and David Duffee made a comparative analysis of correctional organizations to determine the relative degree of emphasis placed upon the community vis-á-vis the offender.[26] From this analysis they devised a schematic, or "Models of Correctional Policies," for classifying correctional organizations. The classification consists of four basic types or models:

1. Restraint model
2. Reform model
3. Rehabilitation model
4. Reintegration model

It can be seen that this classification approximates the generic classification given above, with a reform model added. After reading the description of the O'Leary-Duffee reform model below, the student should be able to determine if this is truly a new model, or one that can be subsumed in the Containment-Rehabilitation-Reintegration trilogy.

The Restraint Model

The restraint model is characterized by little concern for the offender and little conern for the community. This is the classic don't-rock-the-boat philosophy. People will change only if *they* want to, so correctional staff are not expected to be "change agents." When offenders are committed to prison, it is in the interest of control, which is the purpose of punishment, but punishment, *per se,* is not a goal in the restraint model. Containment is.

The parole board is super-sensitive to public opinion, to such an extent that the public's disfavor would be sufficient to block an individual's release on parole. The status quo is to be maintained, and even parole should be revoked to protect the agency from criticism. Due process and

---

[26]Vincent O'Leary and David Duffee, "Correctional Policy: A Classification of Goals Designed for Change," *Crime and Delinquency,* 17, No. 4 (October 1971), 373-86.

legal redress for inmates is discouraged, because they "rock the boat." The effective agency in this model is the one that does not make waves.

The Reform Model

The reform model places great emphasis on the standards of the community, and little emphasis on the offender, who is conceded limited rights. The objective of the correctional agency in this model is to maintain the safety of the community, and to reduce the injury done to society by offenders. In prison, therefore, control is stressed and conformity to the prison rules is expected of inmates. In an authoritarian atmosphere, compliance with the rules is secured by a system of rewards and punishments. The overall goal of the prison, aside from isolation and control, is to inculcate the inmate with suitable habits, particularly vocational skills, so that he can return to society as a minimal threat. Staff is not required to have particular skill in the behavioral disciplines, but they are expected to be effective managers, since they have absolute discretion.

The Rehabilitation Model

The rehabilitation model is identified as one in which inordinate emphasis is placed on the offender, and low emphasis placed on the community. This is a system in which the inmate or offender is the center of the correctional universe. He is the patient, and the correctional social worker carries the little black bag with the curatives. Medical and hospital terminology adorn the language in this model. Within the more broadly conceptualized rehabilitation model, the medical model is operative. The program at the California Medical Facility (even the title of this *prison* was apropos) at Terminal Island, California in the 1950s is a classic example. Although it was actually a maximum security state prison, it was headed by a medical doctor, and hospital terminology was mandatory for staff. Inmates were "patients," barracks were "wards," and "treatment" was the umbrella over the institution. If the one-eyed man was king in the kingdom of the blind, the therapist was king in the kingdom of the rehabilitation model, and there are those who think that this was a form of blindness.

Staff, in the rehabilitation model, is expected to help the offender gain insight, with consequent growth and maturation. Therapy—and punishment is also considered "therapy"—is the bridge to self-understanding, as well as the ladder to freedom. Where the rehabilitation model is operative in a prison, it results almost inevitably in an abrasive dichotomy of staff into "custody" and "treatment." The treatment staff views the custodial staff as the nonprofessionals. Custody staff is obviously affronted because their importance, they feel, is evident in the fact that the fundamental purpose of a prison is custody.

The Reintegration Model

The reintegration model gives high emphasis to both the offender and the community. Because reintegration of the offender into the community is the objective in this model, the stress is on reaching this goal as soon as possible. It follows that extended incarceration is disparaged. Programs that facilitate return to the community are encouraged. This would include work furlough, conjugal visiting, education furlough, home furlough and similar activities. The correctional mission is seen as a joint venture between correctional staff and clientele. The offender is given options and alternative programming in the operational model, to permit him or her to develop an appreciation of more appropriate forms of behavior.

The therapeutic community concept colors this model. Ordinarily, the thinking behind the therapeutic community, which was introduced in a mental hospital in England, is that every member of the staff has a treatment potential. The reintegration model, instead of giving an exalted status to the therapist, considers all staff members on "the team," and capable of contributing skills which can induce change.

In this model, community-based corrections is preferable to the traditional, institutional system, because the prime objective is to minimize the offender's community dislocation. Correctional institutions should be located in urban areas, to permit continued contact with family and other members of the community. It is interesting to parenthetically note that the Federal Bureau of Prisons, in its *Handbook of Correctional Institution Design and Construction,* specifically criticized the Ohio State Penitentiary for its "unfortunate location in [the] midst of urban area."[27]

It might be said that the reintegration model is a very democratic model. Offenders and staff work cooperatively with the mutual goal of facilitating the reintegration of the offender into the community. In 1975, "justice" became the watchword.

THE JUSTICE MODEL

The protest mood of the 1960s finally caught up with the criminal justice system in the 1970s, as the deficiencies of the latter became the target of

---

[27]*Handbook of Correctional Institution Design and Construction* (Washington, D.C.: U.S. Bureau of Prisons, 1949), p. 5.

critical attack. Inequitable sentencing, plea bargaining, the frightening autocratic power wielded by parole boards, differential class access to justice, and the deprivation of the legal and constitutional rights of prisoners were prominent issues in the bill of particulars. The irony is that the clarion call of the critics was not for more scientific precision, but for the appearance of a virtue—justice.

The so-called justice model was articulated by Dr. David Fogel, executive director of the Illinois Law Enforcement Commission, in 1975.[28] Basically, the justice model operates on the assumption that the present system must be replaced because it is so obviously ineffective. The vast and increasing amount of crime in this country, the apparent ineffectiveness of correctional tactics, and other dissatisfactions including those listed above, support this assumption in the eyes of Fogel. Although he criticizes corrections for its failures, he does not espouse a punitive or pure punishment model as an alternative. As Ohlin noted in the foreword to this important work, Fogel "is not . . . proposing a new model for the rehabilitation of individual offenders so much as a set of principles for the rehabilitation of the correctional system itself."[29] He also envisions a humane system.

Fogel proposes the following twelve basic principles upon which "the model of justice in corrections can be operationalized."[30] They are as follows:[31]

1. Criminal law is the "command of the sovereign."
2. The threat of punishment is necessary to implement the law.
3. The powerful manipulate the chief motivators of human behavior— fear and hope—through rewards and punishments to retain power.
4. Socialization (the manipulation of fear and hope through rewards and punishments) of individuals, however imperfect, occurs in response to the commands and expectations of the ruling social-political power.
5. Criminal law protects the dominant prescribed morality (a system of rules said to be in the common and best interest of all) reflecting the endorsement aspect "of the failure of socialization."
6. In the absence of an absolute system of justice or a "natural law," no accurate etiological theory of crime is possible nor is the definition of crime stable.

[28]David Fogel, ". . . We Are the Living Proof . . ." (Cincinnati: The W. H. Anderson Company, 1975).

[29]Ibid., p. xii.

[30]Ibid., p. 183.

[31]David Fogel," . . .We Are the Living Proof . . ." (The Justice Model for Corrections), 2nd ed. copyright 1979, The W. H. Anderson Publishing Co., Cincinnati, Ohio. Reprinted with permission of the publisher. (Citation is from pp. 183-84).

7.   Although free will may not exist perfectly, the criminal law is largely based upon its presumed vitality and forms the only foundation for penal sanctions.

8.   A prison sentence represents a punishment sanctioned by a legislature and meted out through the official legal system within a process of justice against a person adjudged responsible for his behavior. Although the purpose of such a punishment may be deterrence, it is specifically the deprivation of liberty for a fixed period of time.

9.   The entire process of the criminal law must be played out in a milieu of justice. Justice-as-fairness represents the superordinate goal of all agencies of the criminal law.

10. When corrections becomes mired in the dismal swamp of preaching, exhorting, and treating ("resocialization"), it becomes dysfunctional as an agency of justice. Correctional agencies should engage prisoners as the law otherwise dictates—as responsible, volitional, and aspiring human beings.

11. Justice-as-fairness is not a *program;* it is a process that insists the prisons (and all agencies of the criminal law) perform their assigned tasks with non-law-abiders lawfully. No more should be expected, no less should be tolerated by correctional administrators.

12. William Pitt said: "Where the law ends tyranny begins"; so does the exercise of discretion. Discretion "may mean either beneficence or tyranny, either justice or injustice, either reasonableness or arbitrariness." Discretion cannot be eliminated, but the justice perspective seeks to narrow, control, and make it reviewable.

Reducing Fogel's "model" to its essence, the following key ingredients emerge:

a.   The ruling social-political power group (sometimes referred to as an "elite" in the literature) implements the dominant prescribed morality" by manipulating fear and hope in the citizenry. The mechanism for this manipulation is a system of rewards and punishments.

b.   There is an implied deterrent property in punishment.

c.   It is not possible to determine the cause of crime, and the definition of crime is characterized by instability.

d.   Freedom of the will is the criminal law's justifying principle for penal sanctions.

e.   The punishment of imprisonment is the deprivation of liberty for a specified time, whether or not the purpose of the sanction was deterrence.

f.   Justice, which is equated with fairness, must be the overriding objective of criminal law.

g.   When corrections becomes hortatory instead of treating prisoners as the law intends, and as justice dictates, then corrections is dysfunctional.

h. All agencies of the criminal justice system should "perform their assigned tasks with non-law-abiders lawfully."

i. The use of discretion in the criminal justice system should be severely diminished.

Fogel said that the "justice approach [is] necessary to free corrections from its rhetoric of godliness and practice of devilishness."[32] He maintains that a "consumer perspective" rather than an official perspective must be taken of corrections. "The justice perspective involves a shift of focus from the processor to the consumer."[33] The official position is hidebound by rhetoric and tradition and self-fulfilling prophecy. When Thomas Murton, in the 1960s, publicized the tortures being practiced in the Arkansas correctional system, and then dug up from the prison grounds the skeletons of three decapitated prisoners, impliedly murdered by staff, his reward was to be fired by Governor Winthrop Rockefeller. Winthrop's brother, Nelson, then Governor of New York, would later refuse to go to Attica during the notorious uprising at that lamented institution.

Exemplifying the "rhetoric of godliness and the practice of devilishness," Fogel pointed out that a resolution was introduced at the Annual Conference of the American Correctional Association (ACA), in Miami, in 1971, urging an investigation of the report that 200 prisoners were missing from the Arkansas prison system, and were presumably dead. The ACA was also importuned to condemn the unnecessary use of force against inmates. The resolution was rejected. The chairman of the resolutions committee was Walter Dunbar, former director of the California Department of Corrections. A short time later he was to have a prominent role in the onslaught at Attica. According to Fogel, this series of events epitomizes the "official perspective," which does not help the taxpayer, the victim, or the potential victim—the consumer—in the context of the justice model.[34]

The usual critical comments can be made about the justice model. (1) It is obviously impossible to transform the entire system in one fell swoop. Given this fact, how would uneven changes, in various components of the system, affect the whole system? (2) The emphasis on justice and fairness is highly commendable, but it pertains to human *interaction,* not human *regeneration.* How is regeneration of the individual offender to be accomplished through the justice model? (3) If we have an essentially unjust

---

[32]*Ibid.,* p. 188.
[33]*Ibid.,* p. 190.
[34]*Ibid.,* pp. 187-89.

criminal justice system, and one that literally deals with but a microscopic minority of the lawbreakers in this society, how does justice applied to a microscopic minority assure the integrity of the total system?

Of course, any impetus towards justice and fairness is laudable. Furthermore, for the millions who have always "known" that they are in command of their destinies, Fogel's positive emphasis of free will is a welcome doctrine. Although free will is obviously not absolute, it can no more be put in a scientific test tube than justice or fairness. They are moral issues, and Fogel is detailing the moral framework of the criminal justice system.

THE POLITICS OF CORRECTIONAL TREATMENT

In dealing with the criminal justice system, or any part of it, one necessarily encounters the political element. This refers both to outside politics and to inside politics. As we have indicated elsewhere in this text, correctional programs must pass the test of compatibility with public sentiment. That test is administered by the representatives of the people in their legislative role. Politicians are not idealistic academicians. They are pragmatists. They are sensitively attuned to public opinion. If an unenlightened public calls for an unenlightened correctional measure, the politicians will be strongly influenced by the sentiment of the public. At least where the issue is not an obviously outrageous one, the politicians will frequently opt for expediency (and reelection) over idealism. Suppose, for example, that a given politician had a personal belief that prison furloughs would expedite the reintegration of offenders, but a poll showed that 97 percent of his constituency vociferously opposed such a practice. How would he vote on a bill to implement furloughs from prison?

But politics in corrections also refers to internal operation of the system. With an Orwellian look at corrections in 1986, MacDougall spoke of the need for qualified and capable professional staff to carry out the correctional mission and to sustain the treatment philosophy. People who are unqualified and unenthused can sabotage a program. But MacDougall also said, "Following closely behind the problem [of unqualified staff] is the one of promotion systems. Another sign of illness found in too many correctional agencies is that of unfair, political, senseless promotion policies."[35] It is plain that managerial and organizational factors are intimately related to the progress made in corrections. When treatment programs are operated in inimical organizational structures, or with less than

[35]Ellis MacDougall, "Corrections Has Not Been Tried," *Criminal Justice Review*, 1, No. 1 (Spring 1976), 73.

adequately trained and enthusiastic staff, the prognosis for success is obviously diminished.

In the prison setting, the endless custody–treatment confrontation continues the dimension of "politics." The custody staff is suspicious of the treatment staff, and the treatment staff often assumes that it represents the only element of professionalism in the prison. The inmate becomes the ball in the ping-pong game. The inmate is also the manipulating fulcrum, because he knows that he is on the side of the "angels" when the treatment staff member becomes his ally. As two qualified observers declared,

> All actions within a correctional setting reflect the values and judgments of the doer. Because there is an ongoing adversary process between the have-nots—the prisoners, and those designated to keep them as have-nots—the staff, every decision and interaction by a counselor or any staff member can be evaluated on this scale of "whose side are you on?"[36]

> For a treator to be effective, it is critical that he knows how these perceptions affect him and how to deal with them. If he gains the confidence of one group, it may alienate him from the other [custodial, administrative] groups.[37]

SYNOPSIS

It has been suggested that the retaliatory impulse in the human can be explained on the basis of the norm of reciprocity, but the rational human must also put punishment in perspective. Treatment and punishment (rational deprivation) are inextricable, but senseless, brutal, physical punishment contravenes treatment.

The three major correctional models under which most particular models can be subsumed are: (1) custodial, (2) rehabilitative, and (3) reintegrative. O'Leary and Duffee have developed a schematic that enlarges this classification to include (4) reform model. All models will reflect a primary emphasis on protecting the public, a primary emphasis on rehabilitating the offender, or a shared emphasis. These are the broad approaches to the correctional mission.

Justice, determinate sentencing, equity in the operation of the criminal justice system, crime-producing factors in the capitalist system, and similar issues have become the foci of correctional theorists. Many of them

---

[36]Stanley L. Brodsky and Charles L. Horn, "The Politics of Correctional Treatment," in Albert R. Roberts (ed.), *Correctional Treatment of the Offender* (Springfield, Ill.: Charles C Thomas, Publisher, 1974), p. 72.

[37]*Ibid.*

feel that the entire system will have to be changed in a revolutionary manner before justice can truly come into the justice system. Proponents of the New Criminology are the most revolutionary in this regard. A moderate "revolutionary" position is epitomized in the justice model, which also calls for a radical reorganization in the criminal justice system, but without being ideologically Marxist. It emphasizes justice through fairness, to the victim, to the taxpayer, and to the offender.

Variations on the major themes (custody, rehabilitation, reintegration) have resulted in models with special emphases. The punishment model, for instance, insists that certitude of punishment will more readily advance the correctional mission than rehabilitation programs, which allegedly have not worked. Certitude of punishment is an essential and commendable goal for the criminal justice system, but it only guarantees the occupation of our penal institutions. It is not a recipe for human regeneration. That is the mission of correctional treatment.

It is evident that contemporary corrections is afflicted with a great deal of ambivalence. Rehabilitation has been subjected to relentless criticism, radical theorists are cannonading cherished traditions and traditional beliefs, and the punishment model has reared its mournful head. But it is also a time of promise. The American Correctional Association feels that "corrections is entering a promising new era."[38] Certainly there is a unique opportunity to develop new ideas by positively responding to the criticism. If society declines to support correctional progress and opts, instead, to build more prisons and to impose longer sentences, it would soon have an increasing "burden of criminals." According to the American Correctional Association, "It would deserve to ... as a penalty for its abandonment of a defensible philosophy with respect to crime."[39] Comparing the punitive and the rehabilitative correctional philosophies, the American Correctional Association further said "that whatever validity the punitive philosophy may have in this country and century is so far out-weighed by the merits of the philosophy of rehabilitation that the latter should take unquestioned precedence in current penal thought."[40]

To abstain from regenerative efforts is to reject the redemptive impulse that is consistent with our higher faculties, and rooted in the very nature of things human.

[38]American Correctional Association, *Correctional Classification and Treatment* (Cincinnati: The W. H. Anderson Company, 1975), p. 1.
[39]*Manual of Correctional Standards* (College Park, Md.: American Correctional Association, 1975), p. 7.
[40]*Ibid.,* pp. 7-8.

6 Psychotherapeutic Strategies

Here man is revealed as a being in search of meaning—a search whose futility seems to account for many of the ills of our age. How then can a psychotherapist who refuses a priori to listen to the "unheard cry for meaning" come to grips with the mass neurosis of today?

Viktor Frankl
The Unheard Cry for Meaning

Psychotherapy literally means treatment of the mind, soul, or immaterial aspect of the human. The term, however, has metamorphosed many times in its evolution. In modern times it might be best described as an intimate professional relationship, involving a therapist and a patient, ordinarily conducted on a verbal level, which seeks to enhance the patient's psychological and social adjustment by engaging the patient in a pursuit of his or her authenticity. That is a rather general definition. The student will probably be overwhelmed by the endless types of psychotherapy that are prevalent—and mushrooming. That is why a basic definition must necessarily cover the generic thrust of psychotherapy, which will always be towards maximizing the client's adjustment to himself and to his world. In becoming acquainted with various subspecies, the student will find himself or herself drawn to a particular philosophy, or to an eclectic combination of philosophies.

INTERPERSONAL FUNCTIONING

Psychotherapy, essentially, seeks to repair defective interpersonal interaction. Carkhuff and Berenson have conceptualized "interpersonal functioning" in terms of levels of facilitative communication.[1] As one proceeds through these levels, communication becomes more meaningful, authentic, and reciprocal. The ultimate level consists of communication that is spontaneous, open, relevant, and constructive for those engaged in the process. Without going into the sophisticated intricacies of this theory, we can draw some important insights from an examination of the distinguishing characteristics of its first three levels.

Level 1.   This is the "severely disabled person who is out of contact with his world and is unable to engage in constructive human encounters."[2] We ordinarily call this state *psychosis*.

Level 2.   At this level, the individual is functioning "relatively well by societal standards," but her assumptions about the world are largely erroneous, causing distortions in her meaningful relationships.

Level 3.   This is the level of counseling, rather than therapy, in which the client is relatively well-adjusted. She needs short-term rather than long-term assistance, and is quite able to get effectively involved in the helping relationship. The counselor's role in this type of case is largely one of providing appropriate information in alternative decision-making situations.

It is important to note that the Carkhuff-Berenson frame of reference is equally applicable to therapist as to patient, and to counselor as to client. It is too often incorrectly assumed that the recipient of the therapeutic service is the only one who contributes to the blocking of communication. Ill-trained treatment functionaries can retard or impede progress by failing to be sufficiently perceptive or knowledgeable.

A cogent reason for directing attention to these three levels of behavioral adaptation is that they tend to indicate the distinctive areas in

---

[1]Robert R. Carkhuff and Bernard G. Berenson, *Beyond Counseling and Therapy* (New York: Holt, Rinehart & Winston, Inc., 1967).

[2]*Ibid.,* p. 55

which clinical and non-clinical therapy is applicable. The qualifications necessary to do given types of psychotherapy is a matter of on-going controversy. When it comes to an organic psychotic condition, this is usually considered to be the province of psychiatry. Conversely, clinical training is not prerequisite to giving out uncomplicated, factual information. But in between there are many gray areas. Usually some governmental body certifies the level of clinical competence but, in the behavioral sciences, this would normally include only such professionals as psychiatrists; clinical psychologists; marriage, family, and child counselors; and clinical social workers. While the level of skill and clinical competence of probation and parole officers, and of correctional counselors in the prison setting, is increasing every day, the great bulk of these correctionalists are not clinicians. But they are charged with a primary responsibility for correctional therapeutics. Are they fish or fowl?

THE PSYCHOTHERAPIST

The answer to that question depends on the answer to another question. What is a psychotherapist? Definitions range from the very restrictive to the rather general. *The Dictionary of Psychology* formally defines psychotherapy as:

> ... the application of specialized techniques to the treatment of mental disorders or to the problems of everyday adjustment. In its strictest sense, the term includes only those techniques (psychoanalysis, nondirective or directive counseling, psychodrama, etc.) which are utilized by specialists.[3]

According to this definition, the individual who is professionally engaged in the fashion described qualifies as a psychotherapist.

On the other side of the spectrum, a more general and flexible definition is provided by an academic psychologist: "Psychotherapists include anyone (though usually with some sort of degree) who treats people with psychological problems. This is a rather broad term: a psychotherapist might be a clinical psychologist, social worker, psychiatrist, or even a layman with minimal training."[4] This *is* a broad definition, and it plainly includes correctional social workers. If we go back to our opening definition of psychotherapy, and focus on the largest body of treatment professionals in corrections—the probation and parole officers—it is apparant that these individuals do, indeed, maintain an intimate, professional rela-

---

[3]J. P. Chaplin, *Dictionary of Psychology,* new rev. ed. (New York: Dell Publishing Co., Inc., 1975), p. 432.
[4]Frank B. McMahon, *Abnormal Behavior: Psychology's View* (Englewood Cliffs, N.J.: Prentice Hall, Inc., 1976), p. 31.

tionship with their clients. Furthermore, the professional relationship is usually conducted on a verbal level, and its objective is to enhance the social adjustment of the probationer or parolee. In this context, assuming adequate training in the behavioral sciences, psychotherapy is taking place.

THE MENTAL HEALTH INFLUENCE IN CORRECTIONS

The mental health movement was late coming to corrections, and even yet, in the institutional setting in particular, it cannot be said to have secured an influential beachhead. For some obvious reasons, the prison system has been unresponsive to the idea that at least some criminal behavior is the result of emotional pathology, and that behavioral scientists have a contribution to make to corrections. The historical dominance of punishment in the penal philosophy has been a major barrier. Prisons, it has been historically insisted, exist to punish criminals for their wrongdoing. The prison is not a mental institution. Punishment and treatment are not compatible. Even today, this philosophy permeates the thinking of many penal systems, and colors the feelings of many individuals engaged in correctional work.

Writing on the issue of treatment in corrections, a clinical psychologist and a psychiatrist underscored another barrier:

> Criminals as a group are threatening and offensive; when herded together in a locked fortress and goaded by regulations that ignore the individual, they tend to become even more so. Many correctional workers throw up defenses against their fears by believing that the inmate is something less than a man— "humanoid" rather than human. They can tolerate his antics and behavior only so long as they view him as different from themselves.[5]

This means that one of the barriers blocking treatment efforts in the institution (and to a lesser degree in the field) results from the impaired perceptions of staff, a defect which, itself, falls within the purview of mental health. New employees in a prison system have to deal not only with the forbidding, treatment-thwarting architecture of the average prison, but also with its folklore. A serious effort should be made, in pre-employment in-service training, to disabuse the neophyte correctionalist of the misperceptions embedded in the prison folklore. Altering the climate of a prison to make it receptive to treatment endeavors is admittedly a most difficult task, but it is an essential one.

[5]Asher R. Pacht and Seymour L. Halleck, "Development of Mental Health Programs in Correction," *Crime and Delinquency*, 12, No. 1 (January 1966), 3.

Critics of correctional treatment are predisposed to enumerate the past failures of correctional rehabilitation. Von Hirsch reviewed the history of organizations created to reform corrections, as far back as the pioneering Philadelphia Society for Alleviating the Miseries of Public Prisons (which was founded in 1776). He concluded, "Invariably, the results of such efforts were meager, at best promoting reform without change."[6] We are bound to the future, not chained to the past. The need to work with individuals who have a lessened capacity for social adjustment or personal fulfillment is beyond question. The emphasis ought to be on discovering more effective treatment strategies, rather than becoming discouraged by what is admittedly a very brief history.

AN OVERVIEW OF PSYCHOTHERAPY

Using the broad definition of psychotherapy given earlier in this chapter, it has to be acknowledged that there is ample justification for criticism of correctional psychotherapy, on all levels. First, there is not really a great deal of scientific precision in the field of psychotherapy. How does one, for instance, empirically prove the (scientifically outrageous) claim of the Freudians that a male infant considers his father a competitor for the sexual favors of his mother—the so-called Oedipus complex? Although ideas and feelings obviously cannot be captured in a test tube, empirical data, validating the effectiveness of therapy, ought to be pursued with greater vigor. Instead we see an endless proliferation of systems, so that it becomes very difficult to establish a solid, empirical foundation for psychotherapy.

While it may be true that the proliferation is "a dynamic and creative quality in a field where inadequate methods have prevailed too long,"[7] the proliferation itself is bewildering. Where once it was comforting to know that the domain of psychotherapy scarcely extended beyond Freud, Jung, and Adler, we now have implosive therapy, the primal scream, illumination method, radical therapy, multiple impact therapy, autogenic therapy, and numerous other "modalities." In fact, we have even reached the point where computers have been effectively "programmed to function as therapists"![8]

Second, ethics is another grave issue in therapy. In a therapeutic or treatment relationship, one individual (the therapist) exercises an enor-

---

[6] Andrew von Hirsch, *Doing Justice* (New York: Hill and Wang, 1976), p. xxi.
[7] Allen E. Bergin, "An Empirical Analysis of Therapeutic Issues," in Dugald S. Arbuckle (ed.), *Counseling and Psychotherapy: An Overview* (New York: McGraw-Hill Book Company, 1967), p. 175.
[8] George Alexander, "Terminal Therapy," *Psychology Today*, 12, No. 4 (September 1978), 50–60.

mous amount of power and influence over the life of another (the client). When the client is a captive one, such as an inmate, it is not too difficult to see how ethical obligations could be readily contravened by an abuse of the power that is inherent in custodial control. Effective therapy requires the willing assent of the patient or client.

The custodial status, like the military status, brings with it a certain predisposition to submit to authority without question. The other side of the coin is that some therapists or treatment people, dealing with a captive subject with limited rights, will be tempted to a level of experimentation beyond ethical propriety. In recent years, the Alabama and California correctional systems have been accused of unethical medical experimentation with prisoners. Professional ethics demands that the rights and dignity of the correctional client be protected to the fullest extent possible, whether the issue is radical medical therapy or intrusive psychotherapy.

Third, considerable controversy centers on the question of what constitutes an adequate standard of education and/or professional training for the individual who aspires to a treatment career in corrections. It is obviously necessary to have an adequate foundation in the behavioral sciences, but in view of the scientific imprecision that characterizes psychotherapy, and the multitude of therapeutic persuasions which abound, it is not easy to set educational requirements on the lower levels of treatment. Certainly a bachelor's degree in a behavioral science, hopefully with some degree of supervised internship, should constitute a minimal requirements for counseling competence. Graduate study would be preferable for more sophisticated treatment endeavors, and clinical certification would be the ultimate.

But education, of course, is not the sole qualification. There are many highly educated therapists who exert a destructive rather than a constructive influence. How effective is the counsel of an obese, role model psychiatrist to an obese patient, whom he/she encourages to go on a diet? The requisite education of which we spoke should be superimposed on a warm, caring, people-oriented individual, who is committed to be of service to humanity. One overlooked advantage possessed by the treatment person in corrections is that the venal commercialism which characterizes much "free world" psychotherapy is, *ipso facto*, aborted in the correctional setting. Conversely, the prison treatment staff is not always the most professionally competent.

Fourth, the most critical issue is probably the question of the effectiveness of psychotherapy. As Bergin precisely states:

> Most controlled studies of psychotherapy reveal no significant effect of treatment. The contradiction between such research studies demonstrating the ineffectiveness of therapy and the experience of practitioners who claim to observe personality changes in their cases has been difficult to resolve. This

issue has probably divided practitioners and researchers more than any other.[9]

It is obviously desirable to have scientific validation of positive treatment outcomes, but treatment itself is an art, or, perhaps, a combined art and science, and it may transcend the empirical boundaries that confine science. Whether art or science, however, scrupulosity should be the guiding spirit in both research and practice. There is also an economic factor to consider, for costly psychotherapy has to be justified on the basis of effectiveness.

It is important for the person who aspires to a career in correctional rehabilitation to have a working knowledge of the major psychotherapies, for several reasons. First, correctional treatment constitutes the practical application of the fruits of research in the behavioral sciences. Second, increasing this type of knowledge will assist the correctionalist in obtaining a clearer perspective on troubled humanity. Third, techniques and skills can be learned for use in the treatment setting. Over and above these basic reasons, a grounding in the major psychotherapies will prepare the practitioner to effectively assist his clients in managing life's crises, and it will at least guarantee that neither the client *nor the practitioner* will, during their professional relationship, live what Socrates called the unexamined life.

As we have indicated, there has been a veritable proliferation of systems of psychotherapy, causing the distinguished clinical psychologist, Harold Greenwald, to say that "it is almost impossible for even the most nimble of researchers in the field to keep up with the almost infinite variety of new approaches and new techniques."[10] It is unnecessary, for our purpose, to attempt to develop an exhaustive classification system, with branches and subbranches. But an eclectic overview will be indispensable for the neophyte student of correctional treatment.

All the different schools of thought have persuasive doctrines. Why an individual turns in one direction rather than another is a result of more than the sheer fact of intellectual assent. The individual brings to the study of treatment modalities certain philosophic predispositions, which have been shaped by his or her personal life experiences. Those predispositions will be further shaped as he or she is attracted to or repelled by the fundamental premises of a given psychotherapeutic persuasion. It is safe to assume that no given modality has exhausted the restorative potential of treatment, and the student is encouraged to sample broadly the wares in the marketplace of psychotherapy.

[9]Bergin, "An Empirical Analysis of Therapeutic Issues," p. 177.
[10]Harold Greenwald, *Active Psychotherapy* (New York: Jason Aronson, Inc., 1974), p. ix.

All forms of psychotherapy have one clearcut common objective, and that is to help the individual resolve personal conflicts that impede growth or adjustment. Additional shared features, according to Frank, include "an intense, emotionally charged, confiding relationship," and "facilitation of emotional arousal" in the anticipation of change.[11] How they go about doing this, and by what fundamental principles they operate, vary immensely. Several different approaches have been used in attempting to develop a classification of psychotherapies. They can be simply divided on the basis of whether or not they emphasize the rational (cognitive) processes, or the emotional (affective). Another, more extensive approach is to classify psychotherapies as deriving from a rational frame of reference, learning theory, psychoanalysis, existentialism, phenomenology, or eclecticism. Broader classifications will include such categories as "cognitive restructuring," "will therapy," "character analysis," "interpersonal psychotherapy," and peripheral modalities.

Instead of providing an exhaustive classification of psychotherapeutic systems, we will instead examine an arbitrary but representative selection of major approaches with a conscious purpose in mind. The cross-section selected will fulfill several objectives. First, it will give examples of all the major persuasions, identifying the generic classification of each at the same time. Second, the selection will range from the patriarchal psychoanalytic school to major contemporary developments, thus providing a representative overview. Third, those systems which have particular utility for correctional treatment will be included.

Psychoanalysis

Sigmund Freud (1856–1939), the originator of psychoanalysis, had pursued a medical degree with a specialization in physiology. Upon completion of his studies, he became a practicing neurologist, specializing in the treatment of nervous disorders. Freud was particularly interested in the hysterical patient, and fascinated by the admittedly limited developments in the areas of suggestion and hypnosis. Dr. Friedrich Anton Mesmer (1733?–1815), for instance, had earlier spoken of "animal magnetism," and had personally exercised a remarkable influence over people. (The term "mesmerism" derives from Mesmer, who is actually considered something of a charlatan.)

But Dr. Jean Charcot (1867–1936) was of more substance; he attracted Freud with his theories about hysterical behavior. Charcot operated a neurological clinic in Paris, and specialized in hysterical patients.

[11]Jerome D. Frank, "Therapeutic Factors in Psychotherapy," *American Journal of Psychotherapy*, 25, no. 3 (July 1971), 355, 357.

The leader of the so-called Parisian school, he felt that because these patients could be easily hypnotized, the ability to be hypnotized was a symptom of hysteria. That is, Charcot felt that only individuals who were potentially hysterical could be hypnotized.

Freud was also impressed with Bernheim and Liebault, leaders of the opposing Nancy school, who maintained that practically everybody could be hypnotized. This ultimately proved to be the correct view. Cameron said that the most important result of the controversy between the two schools of thought was that "it focused the attention of the chief contestants and their associates upon behavior pathology, its origins, characteristics and treatment."[12] One of the "associates" was to have a bigger impact on psychotherapy than all the others combined. His name was Sigmund Freud.

It was during this time that Freud began conceptualizing what later came to be psychoanalysis. He was leaning to the belief that the psyche had an unconscious as well as a conscious realm, and felt that unresolved conflicts, buried deeply in the unconscious, were the cause of hysteria, and other neurotic behavior manifestations. His first paper, published in 1893, dealt with the mechanics of hysteria. In developing his views, Freud was more heavily influenced by Charles Darwin than is generally recognized. Freud was envisioning man as a creature with several strata to his personality. Darwin's theory of evolution, which saw the species improving as it evolved, allowed Freud to explain the baser aspects of man as being atavistic on the evolutionary scale.

Freud developed psychoanalysis to deal with neuroses; it is not designed to deal with psychoses. In his view, neuroses are the result of unsatisfactory libidinal (sexual) development, with resultant repression. The purpose of psychoanalysis is to break through the inhibitory resistances set up by the maldevelopment, releasing every repressed thought that has been buried in the subconscious. This is ordinarily done by free association. The recall process in psychoanalysis is known as *anamnesis;* the intense emotional feelings that are released are called *abreactions;* and the rapport that is established by the patient with the therapist is known as *transference,* a love-like feeling which is supposed to be the original love that the patient had, as an infant, for his or her mother.

According to Freud, the psychosexual development of an individual is a matter of evolutionary stages, with normal heterosexuality the culminating stage. The first stage is the *oral stage,* from birth to approximately two years of age. It is characterized by oral gratification; that is, the child's mouth becomes the primary source of sensual satisfaction. The

---

[12]Norman Cameron, *The Psychology of Behavior Disorders* (Boston: Houghton Mifflin Company, 1947), p. 319.

second stage is the *anal stage,* from two to three years of age, when the sensual gratification shifts to the excretory function and the control of the sphincter muscles. The third stage is the *phallic stage,* when the attention shifts to the genitalia, and they become the source of sensual satisfaction. This occurs from ages 3 to 5; this is the stage of the Oedipus complex, the castration complex, and the penis-envy complex. Unresolved conflicts during the phallic stage lead to most neuroses, including hysteria. In the *latency stage,* from age five to puberty, there are no sexual conflicts, because sexual feelings are dormant. From puberty on is the *genital stage,* and there will be a smooth transition to mature adulthood providing that the first three phases are successfully handled.

The nucleus or core of our being, according to Freud, is the *id,* the reservoir of our conflictual instincts, basically consisting of sexual and aggressive strivings. The *ego* is that part of the psychic being that attempts to contain, or constructively channel, the strivings of the id. It is absorbed in self-preservation and in reality-testing. The *superego* is Freud's synonym for conscience. It is the idealized self. If there is harmony between the ego and the superego, it is difficult to differentiate the two, but if there is not, then superego is like the reproachful conscience.

Psychoanalysis is usually classified as a separate category, and not as part of some group. Sometimes it is termed an analytical therapy, and when this is done it encompasses neo-Freudian schools of thought as well as those of Jung and Adler, who broke early with the maestro. Psychoanalysis can also be considered a dynamic psychology theory. It can be inferred that psychoanalysis offers a conflictive view of man, and philosophically is rather grim. Dynamically, psychoanalysis is accomplished over a lengthy period of time, and essentially consists of abreaction and catharsis. While psychoanalysis is a form of psychotherapy, one distinguished psychoanalyst points out that, "The literal meaning of psychoanalysis is the analysis of the psyche, while psychotherapy denotes the therapy of the psyche."[13] He then goes on to derogate those who eschew the long-term involvement required by psychoanalysis: "Patients who seek psychotherapy as distinct from psychoanalysis are on the whole more interested in their therapy as a means of problem-solving. They are usually in a hurry, they want quick results, have little or no patience, and also often find it difficult to commit themselves to any psychotherapeutic process of long duration."[14]

Psychoanalysis was the dominant influence in American psychotherapy, and in the behavioral disciplines in general, for the better part of the first half of this century. Although it has been increasingly criticized

---

[13]Hendrik M. Ruitenbeek, *Psychotherapy: What It's All About* (New York: Avon Books, 1976), p. 23.
[14]*Ibid.,* p. 25.

in recent years, it is far from moribund. But the criticism is mounting. For one thing, the current trend is toward short-term therapy; long-term psychoanalysis is not only excessively lengthy but also excessively costly. A most serious criticism is that the basic tenets of psychoanalysis are utterly beyond scientific validation and come close to being psycho-therapeutic dogmas. In fact, one medical critic said, "The psychoanalyst can best be portrayed as someone with dictatorial dogmatism totally wrapped around the symbolism of sex."[15] In any event, the psychoanal-ytic approach is ill-designed for correctional treatment, for obvious reasons.

Transactional Analysis

Stewart Alsop once said, "There are mysteries, above all the mystery of the relationship of mind and body, that will never be explained, not by the most brilliant doctors, the wisest of scientists or philosophers."[16] He surprisingly left out psychotherapists, because they are undaunted in their "infinite variety" of explanations. Transactional analysis grew out of a psychoanalyst's dissatisfaction with psychoanalysis. Eric Berne (1910–1970), a psychiatrist and member in good standing of the San Francisco Psychoanalytic Institute, found himself uncomfortable with the tradition that required therapists to impose their will on patients. Insights in psychotherapy, according to this tradition, derived from the wisdom of teachers, rather than from the "script" of the patients themselves. As Berne recounted, "The theory and practice of transactional analysis began to develop after I received permission (to use a transactional ex-pression) to reverse this trend and listen to patients rather than to teachers."[17]

Berne developed his basic theories between 1954 and 1958, originally stimulated by a lawyer-patient's comment that he was a little boy rather than a lawyer. Transactional analysis peaked in popularity after his book, *Games People Play*, made the best-seller list in 1964, a most unusual feat for a work of non-fiction. Because of his long association with the psychoanalytic school of thought, it is understandable that transactional analysis is usually classified as a derivative of this school. Steiner, for in-stance, unequivocally asserts that "transactional analysis can be seen to be a branch, rather close to the roots, on the tree of psychoanalytic personal-

[15]Edward R. Pinckney, *The Fallacy of Freud and Psychoanalysis* (Englewood Cliffs, N.J.: Prentice-Hall, Inc., 1965), p. 9.
[16]Quoted in Adam Smith, *Powers of Mind* (New York: Ballantine Books, 1975), p. 19.
[17]Eric Berne, Claude M. Steiner, and John M. Dusay, "Transactional Analysis," in Ratibor-Ray M. Jurjevich (ed.), *Direct Psychotherapy*, Vol. 1 (Coral Gables, Fla.: University of Miami Press, 1973), p. 371.

ity theory."[18] In contrast, Patterson scarcely mentions transactional analysis in his survey of theories, except to say that it is not "a theoretically systematic attempt to apply the transactional viewpoint to counseling or psychotherapy. . . . "[19] Because transactional analysis is basically a group process, it is also subclassified as a form of group psychotherapy. Thomas A. Harris, Berne's best known disciple, said that transactional analysis "works at its best in groups. It is a teaching and learning device rather than a confessional or archeological exploration of the psychic cellars."[20] Harold Greenwald, an internationally distinguished psychotherapist in his own right, says that transactional analysis also "has the virtue of greater simplicity and comprehensibility."[21]

The essence of transactional analysis is that human encounters (social intercourse) constitute transactions, a concept which occurred to Berne as he observed the dynamics of a group. The first person to speak in an encounter sends out a *transactional stimulus*. The individual retorting creates a *transactional response*. Berne noted that there were some conversations in which the covert meaning and the content of the conversation differed. In other words, manipulations were taking place, which Berne termed *games*. Furthermore, feeling changes, experienced by the participants, could be visibly observed, and were thus indicative of changes in what Berne called *ego states*. Blushing, trembling, a stony countenance, and the like are some of the observable symptoms.

According to the founder of transactional analysis, each individual is possessed of three ego states: the Parent, the Adult, and the Child. These stages are not parallels of Freud's id, ego, and superego. Berne considers them "phenomenological realities," as opposed to the Freudian *concepts*.[22] *Structural analysis* of the ego states must precede transactional analysis in order "to establish the predominance of reality-testing ego states and free them from contamination by archaic and foreign elements."[23] In Berne's words, "An ego state may be described phenomenologically as a coherent system of feelings related to a given subject. . . . "[24]

The patient in transactional analysis proceeds through five stages:

1. Structural analysis
2. Transactional analysis

[18]*Ibid.*, p. 374.

[19]C. H. Patterson, *Theories of Counseling and Psychotherapy*, 2nd ed. (New York: Harper & Row, Publishers, Inc., 1973), p. 282.

[20]Thomas A. Harris, "Transactional Analysis: An Introduction," in Virginia Binder, Arnold Binder and Bernard Rimland (eds.), *Modern Therapies* (Englewood Cliffs, N.J.: Prentice-Hall, Inc., 1976), p. 35.

[21]Greenwald, *Active Psychotherapy*, p. 119.

[22]Eric Berne, *Transactional Analysis in Psychotherapy* (Secaucus, N.J.: Castle Books, 1961), p. 24.

[23]*Ibid.*, p. 22.

[24]*Ibid.*, p. 17.

3.   Game analysis
4.   Script analysis
5.   Social control

We have already described structural analysis as the phase in which the ego states, as they are operative in the individual, are analyzed. *The Parent state* is the one in which the person's behavior is identifiable with that of his parents. *The Adult state* is that reflecting mature, reality-oriented behavior. *The Child state* is characterized by evidence of fixated or residual child-like behavior in the adult.

All three states are involved in the individual's adaptive functioning, sometimes appropriately and sometimes inappropriately. For example, it would be all right for a man to receive *maternal* solicitude from his wife in the privacy of his conjugal life, but it would be inappropriate for him to be dominated by the Child state in the daily world of his occupational activities. The objective of transactional psychotherapeutics is obviously to assist the individual to learn to recognize and understand the influence of these three interactional states.

Transactional analysis, in the five-stage schematic above, deals with the transactions that engage interacting individuals, which are either *complementary* or *crossed transactions.* For Berne, the transaction is the unit of social intercourse. In fact, he terms his system, "the theory of social intercourse."[25]

The game stage is "an ongoing series of complementary ulterior transactions progressing to a well-defined, predictable outcome."[26] Games are undertaken in order to dominate the relationships with others, so that those others may be manipulated. Games are also considered segments of scripts. *Script analysis* involves the exploration of one's entire human life drama.

The final phase is *social control,* which is the ultimate objective of psychoanalysis. As Berne phrased it, "The aim of transactional analysis is *social control,* in which the Adult retains the executive in dealings with other people who may be consciously attempting to activate the patient's Child or Parent."[27]

Transactional analysis has made a very favorable impression on correctional workers for apparent reasons. First of all, it is relatively easy to grasp. Secondly, it is a short-term approach, unlike psychoanalysis, and is adaptable to the prison setting. Furthermore, Berne himself said that the principles of transactional analysis "are easier to teach effectively than most other clinical approaches. The principles can be grasped in ten

[25]Eric Berne, *Games People Play* (New York: Grove Press, Inc., 1964), p. 13.
[26]*Ibid.,* p. 48.
[27]Eric Berne, "Transactional Analysis Psychotherapy," in William S. Sahakian (ed.), *Psychotherapy and Counseling* (Chicago: Rand McNally & Company, 1976), p. 478.

weeks, and with a year of supervision an otherwise well-qualified clinician or research worker can become quite adept in theory and practice."[28] Critics disparage transactional analysis for being simplistic and insubstantial. Despite criticism, transactional analysis has developed remarkably, with professional organizations throughout the world.

Behaviorism

Theories and techniques of psychotherapy which fall under the collective umbrella of behaviorism are distinguished by their emphasis on learning theory. *Behavior* is considered a process of learning in interaction with one's environment. Consequently, behavioral problems or emotional problems are viewed as the result of faulty learning. Somewhere along the line, the individual has learned maladaptive rather than adaptive responses. Behaviorists feel that what is learned can be unlearned, and adaptive behavior substituted. Another characteristic of behaviorism is that it emphasizes the present and does not, like psychoanalysis, see the etiology of emotional problems as residing in some deep-seated part of the psyche. This is, of course, a simplified encapsulation.

Major systems of psychotherapy have similar objectives, and all have the improvement of the patient as the primary goal. Where they differ is in theoretical orientation. Behaviorists tend to be mechanists and determinists, and draw the ire of humanistic psychotherapists for mechanizing humanity. They also tend to be more empirical, treating in the here and now for redirection in the future, and with less concern for the past. Behavioristic therapy largely involves conditioning, induced externally, as opposed to the cognitive approaches, such as transactional analysis. The so-called "rat men," those researchers who relentlessly studied behavior patterns by observing rats, were (and are) largely behaviorists. The best known of these is undoubtedly Harvard's scholarly psychologist, B. F. Skinner (1904–).

Burrhus Frederic Skinner, who is always referred to and known as "B. F." Skinner, seems to have leaped into especial prominence in the late 1960s and early 1970s, although he had been a notable behavioral psychologist for more than three decades. The measure of his importance can be seen in the fact that his disciples have their own special section in the American Psychological Association, and their own journal, *The Journal of the Experimental Analysis of Behavior.*

Skinner is a stimulus-response theorist, in the general tradition of Pavlov, Watson, Thorndike, and Guthrie. Behaviorists subscribe to the belief that learning is a conditioned response. They stress the importance of external variables and the recency of stimuli, deny introspective or sub-

---

[28]Berne, *Transactional Analysis in Psychotherapy,* p. 22.

jective explanations of behavior, and believe that behavior is more properly interpreted in terms of stimulus than in terms of effect. Because behaviorists tend to denigrate the rational component, those with opposing views are normally referred to as cognitive theorists. Jourard feels that Skinner and his fellow behaviorists are so mechanistically dogmatic that they tend to fail to respond to people as persons, and their manipulations may actually harm man.[29]

Skinner is associated with the "Skinner Box," a device which he created for conditioning the behavior of rats and other creatures. He also developed a comparable box, or "air crib," in which infants were supposed to experience the ideal developmental environment. He proposed a formulation of behavior which he developed from observing animal performance in the "Skinner Box." In this noise-insulated dark box, white rats were rewarded with pellets of food when a brass lever was tripped, which they learned to do by conditioning. In the conventional view of stimulus-response, it is axiomatic that if there is no stimulus there will be no response. Skinner goes beyond this view, by holding that there are two classes of responses, *elicited* responses and *emitted* responses. Responses which are elicited by known stimuli (such as the knee jerk) are classified as *respondents*. Responses not correlated with any known stimuli are designated as *operants*. Driving an automobile would be an example of this type.

Responses are not measured in terms of the strength of the stimulus, but by the rate of response; this is what Skinner calls *the measure of operant strength*. The importance of this concept of operant strength can be adduced from the fact that Skinner considers most human behavior to be operant in character, that is, resulting from emitted responses or operants. When an operant is regularly reinforced, the rate of emitted response is increased. The increase in rate is an indicator of increased probability of response, which is an appropriate measure of operant strength. When an operant develops a relationship to a prior stimulation, it becomes a *discriminated operant*. Symbolic behavior has no place in the Skinnerian perspective. The response of an organism is infinitely more important than the provocative stimulus. Behavior can be conditioned (controlled) by a system of positive reinforcements, and positive reinforcements are always superior to negative reinforcements.

In *Walden Two*[30], Skinner outlined a utopian world in which behavior was strictly controlled and conditioned, albeit in a benevolent, caring environment. In a later work of more than ordinary importance, he repeated his plea for the control of behavior, saying that our culture must

---

[29]Sidney M. Jourard, *The Transparent Self,* rev. ed. (New York: D. Van Nostrand Company, 1971), p. 137.

[30]B. F. Skinner, *Walden Two* (New York: Macmillan, Inc. 1969).

shape and design the kind of behavior which will assure survival. In particular he complained that we were being impeded in this objective by adhering to outmoded concepts of personal freedom and human dignity.[31] Skinner feels that we are excessively concerned with the introspective pursuit of knowledge, instead of facing the imperative need to control communal behavior, before it leads us to perish in the face of some unregulated catastrophe. The question that naturally comes to mind is: Who is going to design the utopian plan of behavior control?

While Skinner represents the mechanistic and deterministic extreme of behaviorism, and there are more moderate forms of behaviorism. Albert Bandura (1925–   ) expresses much more hope than Skinner in the ability of the individual to manage his environment. He also stresses *social* learning theory and is, more properly, a neo-behaviorist. Sahakian terms Bandura's brand of behaviorism "humanistic behaviorism." Behaviorists are, of course, determinists, but Bandura opts for what is being commonly called "soft determinism." As he observed, "theorists who exclude the capacity for self-direction from their view of human potentialities restrict their research to external sources of influence."[32] He does not see the human as a free agent, but neither does he see him as a powerless object in a controlling environment.

Bandura's social learning theory has three main features: (1) It "emphasizes the prominent roles played by vicarious, symbolic, and self-regulatory processes in psychological functioning." In other words, "human thought, affect, and behavior can be markedly influenced by observation, as well as by direct experience. . . . "[33] This has led to the development of models for studying "socially mediated experience." (2) Because of the "extraordinary capacity" that humans possess to utilize symbols, there is a renewed emphasis placed on the symbolic function. (3) A central role is given to the self-regulatory process. This is the heart of the break with Skinner, for Bandura rejects the view of the human as an organism manipulated by external stimuli.

Behavior modification, in this theory, is based on the power of *modeling as a vicarious experience.* According to the social learning theory, learning experiences which are gained by direct participation can also be gained by observing the behavior of others and its consequences. Adequate evidence exists to substantiate this principle. Three results can obtain from modeling influences: (1) the subject observer may acquire new patterns of response which were not previously in his repertoire. (2)

---

[31]B. F. Skinner, *Beyond Freedom and Dignity* (New York: Alfred A. Knopf, Inc., 1971).
[32]Albert Bandura, *Social Learning Theory* (Englewood Cliffs, N.J.: Prentice-Hall, Inc., 1977), p. vi.
[33]*Ibid.*, p. vii.

Inhibitory responses in the observer may be weakened or strengthened by the modeled behavior. (3) The behavior of the model may provoke a *response facilitation effect*, such as when passers-by look towards the sky because an individual (model) is standing on the sidewalk looking towards the sky. While new patterns of response can result from modeling influences, the emotional response to modeled behavior can also be extinguished vicariously. Induced awareness, for example, has been shown in experiments to eliminate the arousal of fear. It can be seen that social learning theory, as exemplified in Bandura's humanistic behaviorism, could have some practical implications for correctional treatment.

This has been but a brief discussion of the highlights of the polar views in behaviorism. It should be pointed out, in concluding this section, that the practical application of behaviorism, known as behavior modification, which has been described as "a family of techniques,"[34] has made a big impact on correctional treatment. Behavior modification programs, with built-in deprivation and reward systems, have caught on in many juvenile institutions. The "token economy" approach to correctional treatment is an evolution in behavior modification. In this type program, tokens are earned for prescribed behavior, and relinquished for negative performance. The acquisition of so many tokens permits the individual to purchase comforts. The nonconformist, deprived of these creature comforts, purportedly will be stimulated to emulate his more fortunate peers. In the California Youth Authority, this system has been jocularly referred to as "jelly bean therapy," the implication being that it is analogous to giving candy to children to induce tractable behavior, a sort of bribe.

The central question, in the correctional setting, is this: Are the rewards given to assure a smooth-running ship, a highly desirable objective to correctional administrators, or is behavioral reformation (modification) actually taking place? There is no question but that behavior can be conditioned, but the critical issue is not conditioning, it is reinforcement. Modified behavior requires reinforcement if it is to endure. What happens after the institutionalized inmate or ward is released from custody?

Existentialism and phenomenology are the polar opposites of behaviorism. Those therapies that are existentially or phenomenologically oriented are sometimes collectively labeled humanistic psychotherapy. Modern existentialism is usually traced to philosophers such as Soren Kierkegaard and Martin Heidegger, and is reflected in the literary field in the work of such writers as Albert Camus and Jean-Paul Sartre. *Existen-*

---

[34]Bertram S. Brown, Louis A. Wienckowski, and Stephanie B. Stolz, *Behavior Modification: Perspectives on a Current Issue* (Washington, D.C.: U.S. Government Printing Office, 1975), p. 4.

tialism is a philosophy that emphasizes the importance of man's existence and self-determinative faculty, and the meaning that life has for him. *Phenomenology* focuses on the study of phenomena as they occur immediately in human experience, without the necessity of interpretation. The subjective experience is considered the transcendental experience. A large number of distinguished psychotherapists are identified with the existential and phenomenological posture, although they may differ substantially in their specific systems. Included are such luminaries as Carl Rogers, Rollo May, Friedrich S. Perls, George A. Kelly, Roy R. Grinker, and the remarkable survivor of Auschwitz, whose existential philosophy was leavened in the concentration camps of World War II, Viktor Frankl.

Logotherapy

Viktor E. Frankl is noted for, among other things, his publication of *Man's Search for Meaning*.[35] As Distinguished Professor, he also taught a course with this same title at United States International University in San Diego, California. The original title of this book was profoundly significant. It was *From Death-Camp To Existentialism*. A victim of the Nazi persecution, Frankl was imprisoned at Auschwitz. A professor of psychiatry and neurology at the University of Vienna, he was to experience the epitome of degradation in the concentration camp. His circumstances were desolate. He lost his wife and almost all his family to the executioners, and he suffered almost unendurable privation. He was reduced to what he, himself, called his "ridiculously naked life." He emerged from this ghastly experience a man of philosophic beauty, possessed of superlative compassion. He did not surrender to oppressive suffering, but found that to understand the meaning of suffering is to understand the meaning of life.

Although he had begun to think existentially as early as 1938, when he first used the terms *Existenz-Analyse* and logotherapy, he really nurtured the seeds of logotherapy in the sorrowful soil of Auschwitz. The greater part of his book is, as a matter of fact, a tempered account of his experiences in the concentration camp.

Logotherapy is fundamentally an existential psychotherapy, important enough to be considered the third Viennese school of psychotherapy, the other two being those of Freud and Adler. Frankl categorically condemns the "nothing-butness" view of man, that is

> the theory that man is nothing but the results of biological, psychological and sociological conditions, or the product of heredity and environment. Such a

[35]Viktor E. Frankl, *Man's Search for Meaning: An Introduction to Logotherapy* (New York: Pocket Books, 1973).

view of man makes him a robot, not a human being. This neurotic fatalism is fostered and strengthened by a psychotherapy that denies that man is free.[36]

The logotherapeutic view sees life as a very individual prospect, differing from man to man, and not susceptible to sweeping generalizations. Thus the sufferer must see his suffering as his unique and singular task, a task that cannot be delegated, and from which he cannot be relieved. "His unique opportunity lies in the way in which he bears his burden."[37] The essential challenge of life is for each man to discover the meaning for his own existence.

Frankl points out that the Greek word *logos* not only signifies *meaning*, it also signifies *spirit*, and his psychotherapeutic rationale contains substantive spiritual overtones. He maintains that many difficulties of man, such as depression, are by no means diseases, but evidence of spiritual distress, an offshoot of existential frustration. Existential frustration is frustration of the will to meaning, which is essentially boredom. It is interesting to note that prisoners constantly complain of boredom.

In attempting to clarify logotherapy, Frankl uses an analogy in which he points out that whereas a painter portrays the world to the viewer, the opthalmologist (logotherapist) *helps the viewer to see* the world as it really is, to widen and broaden "the visual field of the patient so that the whole spectrum of meaning and values becomes conscious and visible to him."[38] Freud accented the pleasure principle; Adler stressed the will to power; Frankl offers the will to meaning.

Frankl takes exception to the position of Sartre, who maintains that man invents himself. On the contrary, Frankl holds that "the meaning of our existence is not invented by ourselves but rather detected."[39] Nor is he enamored of the self-actualizing concept popularized by Maslow. In this regard, Frankl was incisive:

> ... the true meaning of life is to be found in the world rather than within man or his own *psyche*.... By the same token, the real aim of human existence cannot be found in what is called self-actualization. Human existence is essentially self-transcendence rather than self-actualization. Self-actualization is not a possible aim at all, for the simple reason that the more a man would strive for it, the more he would miss it. For only to the extent to which man commits himself to the fulfillment of his life's meaning, to this extent he also actualizes himself. In other words, self-actualization cannot be attained if it is made an end in itself, but only as a side effect of self-transcendence.[40]

[36]*Ibid.*, p. 205.
[37]*Ibid.*, p. 124.
[38]*Ibid.*, p. 174.
[39]*Ibid.*, p. 157.
[40]*Ibid.*, p. 175.

Frankl cites examples from the concentration camp to prove the existence of free will, specifically illustrated in the fact that heroic acts of abnegation, or charity for others, occurred in a milieu that would speculatively destroy everything but a primitive urge for survival. As he phrased it, "everything can be taken from a man but one thing: the last of the human freedoms—to choose one's attitude in any given set of circumstances, to choose one's way."[41] He is fond of citing Nietzsche: "He who has a *why* to live for can bear with almost any *how*."[42]

Logotherapy endeavors to help the patient feel that he or she has a responsibility toward life, and that meaningful goals give meaning to life. It is based on the "will to meaning," the insistent human striving for the ultimate meaning of life. Frankl makes it a point to draw a distinction between logotherapy and psychotherapy (although the former is undoubtedly related to the latter), frequently stating that "logotherapy is not meant to substitute for psychotherapy but, rather, to supplement it."[43] Or, as he explained in another context, "Psychotherapy endeavors to bring instinctual facts to consciousness. Logotherapy, on the other hand, seeks to bring to awareness the spiritual realities. As existential analysis, it is particularly concerned with making men conscious of their responsibility—since being responsible is one of the essential grounds of human existence."[44]

Logotherapy contains a number of techniques, including the search for meaning, self-detachment, logodrama, humor, dereflection, and paradoxical intention. Because of the limitations of space and purpose, we will restrict our discussion to Frankl's best-known technique, *paradoxical intention*. Frankl had used paradoxical intention since 1929, although he did not formally publish a description of it until 1939.[45] To understand how paradoxical intention is applied, it will be helpful to understand the mechanism known as *anticipatory anxiety*. This is the apprehensive state of an individual when he fears that a symptom, which relates to his behavioral disorder, will recur. In the words of Frankl, "Thus a self-sustaining vicious circle is established: a symptom evokes a phobia; the phobia provokes the symptom; and the recurrence of the symptom reinforces the phobia."[46]

---

[41]*Ibid.*, p. 104.

[42]*Ibid.*, p. 164.

[43]Viktor E. Frankl, *The Unconscious God* (New York: Simon & Schuster, Inc., 1975), p. 73.

[44]Viktor E. Frankl, *The Doctor and the Soul* (New York: Alfred A. Knopf, Inc., 1972), p. 25.

[45]Viktor E. Frankl, *The Unheard Cry for Meaning* (New York: Simon & Schuster, Inc., 1978), pp. 114–115. (See also Viktor E. Frankl, "Paradoxical Intention and Dereflection," *Psychotherapy: Theory, Research and Practice*, 12, No. 3 (Fall, 1975), 226–37).

[46]Frankl, *The Unheard Cry for Meaning*, p. 115.

The patient will ordinarily attempt to flee from his fear by avoiding those situations which provoke the arousal of his anxiety. This, according to Frankl, is "the starting point of anxiety neurosis."[47] How is the phobia-reinforcing feedback mechanism to be neutralized? According to Frankl, "this is precisely the business to accomplish by paradoxical intention, which may be defined as a process by which *the patient is encouraged to do, or to wish to happen, the very thing he fears* (the former applying to the phobic patient, the latter to the obsessive-compulsive)."[48] (Italics in the original).

To give an example, a patient in Dr. Frankl's clinic in Vienna was suffering from a coronary infarct. As a result he became so extremely anxious that his anxiety became his major complaint. He began to withdraw from contacts in both professional and social areas, and became very reluctant to leave the hospital. Treatment consisted of encouraging the patient to try to make his heart beat faster and to increase the pain and fear that he was experiencing, while his doctor briefly left the room. The patient attempted to do so and was surprised to discover that not only was he unable to, but that his pain and fear had disappeared. For the first time in six months, the patient was able to leave the hospital for a walk on the streets outside. Entering a store, he felt a slight palpitation, but immediately employed the technique of trying to feel even more anxiety. The patient was discharged from the hospital and, six months later returned for a visit, when it was determined that he was free of the negative symptoms.[49] It should be noted that logotherapy has applicability only to phobias and neuroses.

There is a touch of humor in this therapy and, indeed, Frankl says that "it is essential in practicing paradoxical intention to . . . mobilze and utilize the exclusively human capacity for humor."[50] The use of humor in combatting disabilities is not new. The Greek orator, Demosthenes, had a speech impediment. To overcome it, he practiced talking with a mouth full of pebbles, in a sense humorously attacking his impediment.

There are, to be sure, critics as well as defenders of existential logotherapy. It is not palatable to the mechanists and behaviorists. But Frankl speaks of rehumanizing psychiatry and freeing it from the delimiting and mechanistic view which has imprisoned it for half a century.[51] The charge is made, and it is a valid one, that logotherapy is a philosophy of life rather than a scientific system of psychotherapy. One observer said that she saw Frankl

---

[47]*Ibid.,* p. 116.
[48]*Ibid.,* p. 117.
[49]Viktor E. Frankl, *Psychotherapy and Existentialism* (New York: Simon & Schuster, Inc., 1967), p. 150.
[50]Frankl, *The Unheard Cry for Meaning,* p. 121.
[51]Frankl, *Man's Search for Meaning,* p. 212.

. . . as a mixture of prophet, guru and preacher disguised as a psychiatrist who disseminates his message in a language to which men and women of the twentieth century are likely to listen, the language of psychology. But the world, and perhaps the man himself, has taken the disguise too seriously and has become oblivious to the prophetic person who stands behind the psychiatric cloak.[52]

Reality Therapy

One of the more practical therapeutic approaches to arrive on the recent scene is the cognitive system of William Glasser (1925–   ) known as reality therapy. Cognitive systems are those which give priority to cognitive or rational processes in learning, as opposed to stimulus-response systems, which emphasize reinforced responses. In cognitive approaches, personal responsibility is stressed because the cognitive faculty of an individual enables him to be aware, contemplative, judgmental, recollective, analytical, and predictive. He has the capacity to plan and to decide in choosing courses of action and, consequently, must be responsible.

Like Berne's break with orthodox psychoanalysis, Glasser's reality therapy was also a break with conventional psychotherapy: "Dissatisfied with traditional therapy as early as my last year of training, I was groping for a better way to treat people than what was being taught."[53] His feelings crystallized into action when an obnoxious, acting-out eleven-year-old child came to him for treatment. Aaron was the son of an overly intellectualizing, emotionally cold divorcée, who was employed as a mathematician in a space laboratory. The boy was extremely intelligent and extremely manipulative. In the established tradition, his previous therapists had dealt with him permissively and uncritically, constantly interpreting his behavior to him. To quote Glasser, "Regardless of how he behaved, no one had ever attempted to put a value judgment on his behavior, no one had ever told him he was doing wrong. Everything he did was accepted as something to be explained or, in psychiatric terms, "interpreted" ad nauseam."[54]

Play therapy had previously been employed, with the therapist translating Aaron's activities with toys. Violence towards a doll, for example, would be interpreted as hostility toward his mother. Aaron was impulsive and inconsistent in his behavior, at times cajoling and seductive, and at others detached and withdrawn. He was actually desperately striving for someone to set limits. Instead, everyone, therapists and mother, had been treating him like an object, rather than a person, to be permissively en-

---

[52]Edith Weisskopf-Joelson, "Logotherapy: Science or Faith?" *Psychotherapy: Theory, Research and Practice*, 12, No. 3 (Fall 1975), 240.

[53]William Glasser, "Reality Therapy," in Ratibor-Ray M. Jurjevich (ed.), *Direct Psychotherapy*, Vol. 2 (Coral Gables, Fla.: University of Miami Press, 1973), pp. 562–63.

[54]*Ibid.*, p. 564.

dured. At this time, Glasser had not formulated a definite concept of reality therapy, but he said that "it was with Aaron that I first discovered the dramatic force of confronting a child with present reality."[55] He further commented, "I realized dimly that in following the principles of orthodox therapy, I was contributing to Aaron's present desperation rather than relieving it, and I made up my mind to change my approach."[56] From that point on, Glasser emphasized present behavior and reality. Reality therapy had been born.

Glasser communicated to the young lad that his obnoxious behavior was repelling, and that he would have to change dramatically before anyone could care for him. He then instituted a confronting relationship in which Aaron was praised for his progress and criticized for his shortcomings. Firmly, but kindly, Glasser stood athwart the boy's path, blocking wrong turns, and holding him responsible for his performance. The dramatic changes that took place in the patient's behavior reinforced Glasser's concept of a reality approach to therapy.

Reality therapy's fundamental distinction is that it "departs from traditional one-to-one and group treatment techniques along two theoretical lines."[57] First, a premium is placed on conventional morality and responsible behavior. Second, the therapist does not remain clinically detached, but deliberately establishes an involved, caring relationship with the patient. The central foundation of reality therapy is *personal responsibility*. Glasser defined responsibility "as the ability to fulfill one's needs, and to do so *in a way that does not deprive others of the ability to fulfill their needs*."[58] (Italics in original). As Glasser said in addressing a Canadian corrections institute, "regardless of what the young offender has done, how he feels, where he comes from, his size, shape, mental ability, physical condition or heredity, he suffers from a universal malady: he is unwilling to take responsibility for his behavior to himself and to his community."[59]

According to Glasser, there are two basic psychological needs, "the need to love and be loved and the need to feel worthwhile to oneself and to others."[60] Those who fail to have these needs fulfilled he calls irresponsible rather than mentally ill. It is a basic premise of reality therapy that we must become involved with other people, and everyone should have a close, caring relationship with at least one person. Without this essential

[55] *Ibid.*, p. 565.

[56] *Ibid.*, p. 566.

[57] Allen E. Bergin and Sol L. Garfield, (eds.), *Handbook of Psychotherapy and Behavior Change* (New York: John Wiley & Sons, Inc., 1971), p. 483.

[58] William Glasser, *Reality Therapy* (New York: Harper & Row, Publishers, Inc., 1965), p. 13.

[59] William Glasser, "Reality Therapy: A Realistic Approach to the Young Offender," address given to the Fall Institute of the British Columbia Corrections Association, Vancouver, British Columbia, November 3, 1962.

[60] William Glasser, "Reality Therapy," in Binder, Binder, and Rimland (eds.), *Modern Therapies*, p. 52.

person, needs cannot be fulfilled. The reality therapist fills this need, transiently, with his patients. This "essential person" does not have to be in close proximity, but must be one who has a strong feeling and concern for our existence.

In taking strong issue with the premises of conventional psychiatry, Glasser puts forth the definitive characteristics of the reality therapy approach as follows (here paraphrased):[61]

1. The concept of mental illness has no validity in reality therapy because personal responsibility must be asserted.
2. The past is not as consequential as the present and the future, so past history, because it cannot be changed, is unimportant.
3. The therapist relates to the patient as a person, not as a transference figure.
4. A patient cannot use unconscious motivation as an excuse for present behavior.
5. Behavior must be moral, and the issue of right and wrong must be confronted.
6. Teaching new ways to fulfill needs, which is not a part of conventional therapy, is a central part of reality therapy.

Punishment is not imposed in the reality therapy system because it is considered largely ineffective as an inducement for responsible behavior and because the patient will automatically experience the natural consequences of his or her irresponsible behavior.

Reality therapy has had a very favorable reception in correctional treatment circles, because it comports with the "gut feeling" sentiments of so many individuals in the field of corrections. It is also a reasonable, practical, and morally definitive system. Its principles are easy to absorb and to apply because reality therapy is essentially a pedagogic endeavor. It also has appeal because it stands in direct opposition to classic Freudian psychoanalysts, the "arch-critics of our mores, morals, and values. . . . "[62] The sentiment of many was expressed in the newspaper editorial which commented, "We find it quite refreshing to hear the theory advanced that emotions and a sense of responsibility can exist within the same person."[63]

THE LAST WORD IN PSYCHOTHERAPY

We have made a very arbitrary, but hopefully representative, selection of contemporary psychotherapeutic tactics. The student will have to pursue

---

[61]Glasser, *Reality Therapy,* pp. 44–45.
[62]*Ibid.,* from the foreword by O. Hobart Mowrer, p. xv.
[63]Long Beach, California *Press-Telegram,* July 26, 1962.

the subject further on the basis of his or her own brand of tropism. There is a bewildering array of dispositions to choose among, both conventional and revolutionary. There is network therapy, conjoint family therapy, crisis intervention, various modes of sex therapy, transcendental modalities, Morita therapy, encounter and sensitivity groups, implosive and art therapies, systems of assertiveness, integrative approaches, biofeedback, regressive, and total approaches, *ad infinitum.*

Among the more important of the conventional psychotherapies, which space limitations preclude from inclusion, are the rational-emotive psychotherapy of Albert Ellis, a directive psychotherapy extremely committed to logic and reason; the client-centered approach of the patriarch of counseling, Carl R. Rogers, from whom the importance of self-perception probably received its main impetus; and the influential gestalt approach of Friedrich S. Perls, which is holistic and neo-psychoanalytical. But each of these is inclusive in one or another of the broad classifications which we have reviewed.

One incontestable conclusion can be drawn: There is no last word in psychotherapy.

SYNOPSIS

There is a wide range of psychotherapeutic strategies in practice today, yet esoteric proliferation seems to be the order of the day. Not every strategy is particularly suitable in correctional treatment. Psychotherapy is, essentially, an effort to repair defective interpersonal interaction. Carkhuff and Berenson conceptualize interpersonal functioning in terms of five levels of "facilitative communication." As one proceeds towards the fifth level, one advances toward the ultimate in communication: open, reciprocal, and authentic.

The psychotherapist can be seen in the narrower clinical perspective, or in the broader context of anyone "who treats people with psychological problems."

In corrections, the mental health influence is a recent one. The prison system strenuously resists the belief that some crime and delinquency result from emotional disorder and, hence, behavioral scientists have a contribution to make in corrections. On the other hand, there is not really a great deal of scientific precision in psychotherapy, nor any substantial track record of success, such as would justify confidence.

A selective review of some of the major psychotherapeutic persuasions indicates that psychoanalysis, which Freud developed for the treatment of neuroses, is too protracted to have much utility in the correctional endeavor. Transactional analysis, on the contrary, developed by the former psychoanalyst, Eric Berne, has been enthusiastically adopted.

Criticized for being insubstantial, transactional analysis is easy to learn and to apply in the correctional setting.

Psychotherapies which are based on learning theory come under the general classification of behaviorism. B. F. Skinner's concept of operant conditioning, and his behavior modification approach to human behavior (and misbehavior) is a prime example, and unashamedly deterministic. Behavior modification has had conspicuous popularity in corrections, particularly in the juvenile field. The polar opposite of behaviorism is existentialism or humanism. A classic example is found in Viktor Frankl's *logotherapy*, which essentially teaches that deviance results from an existential vacuum. It has not been seriously introduced into correctional therapy so far.

Reality therapy, developed by the psychiatrist, William Glasser, is particularly popular with correctionalists, basically because it is rational and emphasizes personal responsibility and self-determination, and because it appeals to the "gut-level" feeling of many in corrections.

7 The Practitioner's Basic Treatment Tools

. . . of two who suffer evil either in body or soul, which is the more wretched, the man who submits to treatment and gets rid of the evil, or he who is not treated but still retains it?

Socrates to Polus

A certain judge, who was never known to have driven an automobile, was once asked how he managed to sit in judgment on automobile accident cases which came up for trial in his court. The judge replied, "It's really no handicap. I also try rape cases." The same analogy can be used with critics who claim that the non-criminal mind cannot adequately understand and deal with the criminal mind. But it is a highly qualified analogy. It can only be applied by the correctional worker who is sufficiently grounded in prerequisite knowledge and skills. A doctor does not have to have had tuberculosis in order to treat it successfully in a patient, but he must have competent medical knowledge. Similarly, the correctional treatment specialist, with competent behavioral knowledge, can engage in effective rehabilitation efforts. Part of his competence will come from knowing when he *cannot* effectively accomplish rehabilitation. What basic qualifications, in addition, should the correctional caseworker possess?

THE PRACTITIONER

The modern correctionalist has to be a very special breed of person. With correctional philosophy shifting like sand before the winds of revolutionary change, there is more to this profession than the mere acquisition of platitudes from psychology, sociology, and criminology. In the endless confrontation between "hard-liners" and those who are treatment oriented, the luxury of what Johnson calls an "unexamined faith"[1] in rehabilitation cannot be indulged. The correctional professional must relentlessly examine the critical issues which face him and his profession.

What really works in correctional treatment? Does the criminal actually differ from the non-criminal? How is the punishment–treatment conflict to be resolved? Does the client have free will? If he does, to what extent is the treatment prerogative infringing upon his self-determinative capacity? What deviance theory, what correctional model, and what psychotherapeutic persuasion holds the most promise for effective correctional work? Does any? Who should be treated and who are untreatable? How do you justify treating a minority of amateur criminals when a majority of syndicate and white-collar criminals remain inviolate in the community? These are just some of the vexing issues which merit the continuous concern of the person who would adopt corrections as a career.

In addition to formal academic training, the practitioner must have a keen awareness of self. If change or redirection is to be initiated in the correctional context, it will be accomplished through the medium of a human relationship. The professional must know himself well in order to understand his impact on the client.[2] In general terms, he should be a well balanced individual, able to maintain objectivity, who genuinely appreciates the opportunity of service to the community through the vehicle of correctional social work. It is vital to be able to relate to the client with what Carl Rogers called non-possessive warmth, and to be able to deal

---

[1]Elmer H. Johnson, *Crime, Correction, and Society,* 4th ed., (Homewood, Ill.: The Dorsey Press, 1978), p. 13.

[2]Because the practitioner profile is usually given in detail in introductory correctional texts, I will refrain from an exhaustive enumeration of the desirable qualifications which a practitioner should possess. It is suggested that the reader consult, for elaboration, Chapter 12, "The Practitioner," in Louis P. Carney, *Introduction to Correctional Science* (New York: McGraw-Hill Book Company, 1979).

effectively with client hostility, the use of authority, over-identification, subconscious bias, ethnic diversity, and similar issues.

It is also imperative to recognize that correctional treatment is far from maturity, in terms of both theory and practice, and the practitioner should remain open and searching for ways to enhance and validate his treatment efforts. It will also take courage, in the face of episodic attacks by "hard-line" iconoclasts, to defend the redemptive philosophy in corrections. Fortunately, there are countless models to demonstrate the infinite capacity for change possessed by the human spirit. St. Augustine was a recidivistic profligate, yet lived to completely reverse his life pattern, producing the literary masterpiece, *Confessions,* in which he repented his wild youth at Carthage. Centuries later, in a distant land, a member of the Detroit Tigers, Ron LeFlore, was picked to play in the All-Star game, and his life was made into a television special. Five years earlier he had been a convict in a Michigan prison. Human redemption is, fortunately, an endless chronicle.

Among the critical issues which the correctionalist must face are certain ethical and moral problems associated with rehabilitation. One of these we touched upon in our opening comments. It is this: How does the correctional rehabilitator, as society's representative, provide a model of rectitude when that rectitude is clearly absent in society? On what grounds does he supplicate the client to reach a state of sanctity that is patently absent in the official echelons of society, a fact which the client knows well? Shoham calls this "the personal dilemma of the treatment man," and he is forceful in explaining it:

> To the offender he is the representative of "legitimate society." He personifies everything and everybody on the other side of the legal barricade. In this capacity the treatment man is in a peculiarly weak position. He is supposed to speak for an acquisitive, money-hungry, "cut-throat," competitive, morally confused and patently dishonest "affluent" society.[3]

The client well knows the character of "legitimate society." Al Capone, in fact, once described white-collar crime as "the legitimate rackets." The professional in corrections, if he cannot represent society *in toto,* must certainly represent the idealized society. He is a role model; he must maintain a high standard of personal integrity.

Another critical issue concerns the use of authority. The correctional treatment person always works under the color of authority, for he represents a component of the criminal justice system. For this reason, correc-

---

[3]Shlomo Shoham, "Moral Dilemmas in Rehabilitation," in Rudolph J. Gerber and Patrick D. McAnany, *Contemporary Punishment* (Notre Dame: University of Notre Dame Press, 1972), p. 201.

tional treatment is often called coercive treatment, because the full weight and power of "the system" is the imprimatur for all endeavors undertaken in its name, including treatment. But authority can be abused, or misused. It is essential that the professional convey to the client that he represents legitimate authority and not oppressive authority. Inevitably, because of his cloak of authority, the practitioner will tend to induce submission rather than constructive participation in the treatment plan. As Max Weber stated: "A criterion of every true relation of imperative control . . . is a certain minimum of voluntary submission. . . . "[4]

But we are all subject to authority—the authority of moral and civil law, of parental and governmental restraint. Authority which is designed to perpetuate justice and induce communal harmony is legitimate authority, and no one can live beyond its realm. Authority, therefore, should be a very constructive part of the treatment endeavor.

There are other important issues which we shall touch upon throughout this text. The very nature of the treatment relationship is, perhaps, the most critical issue of all. Is it possible that a certain offender, by the time the correctional treatment relationship is instituted, has already internalized a value system that satisfies his or her needs in such a way as to be beyond retraction? Is it really possible to influence an individual, through a so-called treatment relationship, to alter his or her behavior? There are many other questions that must be pondered as we engage our fellow humans in the battle of recovery. Before we can attempt to formulate definitive answers, we must have adequate knowledge of human behavior and the academic disciplines that regulate our involvement in correctional treatment.

THE KNOWLEDGE BASE

The term "knowledge base" has a specific meaning for researchers. It refers to the fund of knowledge available about a given subject. The knowledge base in corrections, for example, would consist of all the practical and theoretical knowledge available concerning the cause of criminal behavior, the methods of coping with it, the efficacy of treatment, and so forth. Obviously, the greater the knowledge base, the greater the ability to make valid generalizations. It is plain that the correctional knowledge base is unfortunately limited and restricting.

In this section we will use the term "knowledge base" in a narrower sense, restricting it to mean the factual foundation which is prerequisite

[4]Max Weber, "Authority and Legitimacy," in Eric A. Nordlinger (ed.), *Politics and Society* (Englewood Cliffs, N.J.: Prentice-Hall, Inc., 1970), p. 35.

for effective correctional treatment. One of the difficulties with the rehabilitation model is that its disciples blindly and zealously act on the assumption that all offenders are in need of treatment. But, as Weihofen warned, "Any attempt to make rehabilitation a primary objective for *all* offenders creates certain difficulties. Not every person whose conduct is deemed criminal is in need of rehabilitation."[5] The modern practitioner in correctional treatment must beware of panaceas, as well as the indiscriminate imposition of coercive treatment upon those for whom it has no efficacy. The failure of a great number of rehabilitation programs can undoubtedly be traced to the failure to exclude from the programs those subjects unresponsive to treatment methods.

A related and insidious problem concerns the tendency to view all criminal behavior as a form of pathology. "Pathology" is a medical term, which indicates the presence of disease. Criminals are not sick. Criminality is not a disease. There are, of course, cases in which deviant behavior is positively linked with organic pathology, such as alcoholism, drug addiction and, indirectly, mental retardation, where suggestibility is a factor. But the Freudian term "criminosis," which implies a universal link between crime and disease, is insupportable. The research of Yochelson and Samenow, and others, is increasingly suggesting that criminal deviance is more often a calculated lifestyle, or the result of a socialization process influenced by defective social values and social institutions, than it is a result of mythical sickness.

In order to engage in an effective treatment relationship it is, of course, necessary to have a working knowledge of correctional treatment tactics, the limitations inherent in correctional treatment, and the myths surrounding correctional therapy. But before that stage is reached, it is necessary to have a great deal of specific knowledge about human nature. In discussing the various psychotherapeutic strategies in Chapter Six, we should have learned that, despite the different nuances in the various theories, two basic models of man were being proposed. These two basic models, incidentally, have persistently divided theorists not only in psychotherapy and in the various behavioral sciences, but also in philosophy. The two models are the behavioristic and the phenomenological.

The Image of Man and His Needs

Every treatment approach rests upon an image of man. It is impossible to relate to another human being, or to help him, without some philosophic

---

[5]Henry Weihofen, "Punishment and Treatment: Rehabilitation," in Stanley E. Grupp (ed.), *Theories of Punishment* (Bloomington: University of Indiana Press, 1971), p. 257.

concept of humanity. In the behavioristic approach, man is seen as a passive respondent to stimuli emanating in his external environment. Man's behavior can be controlled by controlling these stimuli. The phenomenological view, on the other hand, sees man as essentially free, his freedom deriving from his consciousness and awareness. Behavior is, therefore, only an expression of being. *Response* is the key to behaviorism, while *experience* is the hallmark of phenomenology. The practitioner will, of necessity, subscribe to one or another of these views. It is not difficult to determine that the present text has a phenomenological bias. The important thing to remember is that the dignity of the client must be preserved, and that philosophic persuasions are intended to facilitate the helping process, and not to superimpose an alien philosophy.

In addition to philosophic knowledge of man, the individual who would engage in correctional treatment must have knowledge concerning basic human needs, the process of forming a self-concept, and the manner in which the objects of treatment perceive the treatment process. First, what basic needs do human beings possess? If we can understand these, we might get closer to explaining why these needs are sometimes fulfilled through deviant behavior. Earlier sociologists and psychologists spoke of needs as biological and instinctual, and in a very structured way. Where a need (sex, food, sleep) was unfulfilled, psychic or psycho-physiologic tension resulted. But modern psychology is providing a much more expansive analysis of human nature, and speaks "of those other motives which we sense but which we cannot always name—those vague yearnings and desires to explore something new, or to understand something now only dimly perceived, or to achieve a new level of consciousness, or to create some new thing under the sun."[6]

Maslow's Hierarchy of Needs

Abraham Maslow is well known for his hierarchy of human needs. According to Maslow, there are ascending levels of human needs. First, there are the *physiological* needs which demand satisfaction. These are insistent needs because survival is at stake, and include food, water, air, sex, shelter, elimination, and the like. Next in the order of ascendancy are the *safety* needs, such as security, order, freedom from fear and anxiety, protection, and general stability. Above these needs are the needs for *belongingness and love*. Love, communal identification, family ties, friendship, group and clan organizations, and the feeling of belongingness are

---

[6]Vincent O'Connell and April O'Connell, *Choice and Change* (Englewood Cliffs, N.J.: Prentice-Hall, Inc., 1974), p. 185.

included. Next are the needs for *esteem*. This category includes not only self-esteem, but the esteem of others, confidence in one's self, recognition, mastery of the environment, achievement, and similar need fulfillment. At the top of the hierarchy, according to Maslow, is the need for *self-actualization*.

Maslow defined the process of self-actualization as a state

> in which the powers of the person come together in a particularly efficient and intensely enjoyable way, and in which he is more integrated and less split, more open for experience, more idiosyncratic, more perfectly expressive or spontaneous, or more fully functioning, more creative, more humorous, more ego transcending, more independent of his lower needs . . . closer to the core of his Being.[7]

The self-actualized person is the utterly developed and self-satisfied individual who is in touch with and in command of his or her own destiny. Life is meaningful and the person has achieved total humanness and integration of the self. (The student will recall that Viktor Frankl took exception to Maslow's concept of self-actualization, maintaining that it cannot be an end in itself). The basic concept is that the person has developed the full human potential, and has achieved the greatest inner harmony. Self-actualization is akin to what Teilhard de Chardin called "the Omega Point." It is clearly a state that few have achieved, but which all are directed toward. The importance of this, or any other hierarchal value concept, is that it gives the professional a base from which to attempt to understand the client. Atypical behavior, for example, may be interpreted in terms of need frustration and need satisfaction. It can also be dealt with on the basis of the level of the need in question. Concrete remediation steps can then be taken in the treatment context.

Maslow also taught that an individual develops his values within himself. They are intrinsic to him. This concept is very significant because, as Van Hoose and Kottler state, "Therapy is a search for values, an attempt to unroot the deepest, most intrinsic values in the client."[8] There are many variants when it comes to value systems, but it is not a matter of consequence. The important thing for the correctional therapist to remember is that the human has a great many needs, and when these needs are thwarted or frustrated, dysfunction can occur. It must also be remembered that all needs must be satisfied, from the biological to the psycholog-

---

[7]Abraham H. Maslow, *Towards a Psychology of Being* (New York: D. Van Nostrand Company, Inc., 1962), p. 91.

[8]William H. Van Hoose and Jeffrey A. Kottler, *Ethical and Legal Issues in Counseling and Psychotherapy* (San Francisco: Jossey-Bass, Inc., Publishers, 1977), p. 29.

ical, from the material to the spiritual. When a harmonious fulfillment of needs is engineered, the healing process has been introduced.

The Client's Perception of His Own Universe

It is also important for the correctional worker to understand that individuals rarely perceive situations in the same fashion. As we have noted, traditional psychotherapy has been predisposed to provide the recipe for improvement from its reservoir of theory. Modern therapies, particularly the encounter varieties and the phenomenologically oriented, have begun to listen to the client in order to develop insights. How people perceive their worlds is important to know if we are to invade those worlds with a helping service.

Even the criminal justice system is not perceived with unanimity, which has obvious implications for the treatment process. Research sponsored by the Kerner Commission, for instance, revealed that blacks complained much more frequently about police behavior than did whites.[9] This finding was supported by a study undertaken in Milwaukee, Wisconsin in 1969, in which three different socioeconomic groups, two white and one black, were surveyed to ascertain their perceptions of the police (and other legal agencies). A total of 224 respondents constituted the almost equally-numbered groups. An extensive series of attitudinal tests were administered to the participants to determine their perceptual evaluations. While a degree of overlap was found among the groups, and within each group, it was categorically stated that "Blacks perceive the police as more corrupt, more unfair, more excitable, more harsh, tougher, weaker, lazier, less intelligent, less friendly, more cruel, and more on the bad than good side than white respondents in either of the two other neighborhoods."[10] Without debating whether or not this perception is valid, we must be concerned with the authenticity of the feeling in any treatment context involving criminal *justice*.

The importance of understanding how another perceives his universe lies in what Gage called "the simple idea that the better you understand people the better you can get along with them."[11] Any effort to treat people with emotional or social adjustment problems presumes a deep understanding of the clients to be treated. Psychotherapy is, after all, fundamentally an act of understanding.

[9]Angus Campbell and Howard Schuman, "Racial Attitudes in Fifteen American Cities," *Supplemental Studies for the National Advisory Commission on Civil Disorders* [The Kerner Commission] (Washington, D.C.: U.S. Government Printing Office, 1968).

[10]Herbert Jacob, "Black and White Perceptions of Justice in the City," *Law and Society Review*, 6, No. 1 (August 1971), 73.

[11]N. L. Gage, "Accuracy of Social Perception and Effectiveness in Interpersonal Relationships, *Journal of Personality*, 22, No. 1 (September 1953), 128.

The Client's Perception of Self

In addition to an understanding of how the client perceives the world, it is essential to discover how the client perceives himself. It is a truism in correctional work that offenders tend to have a very poor self image. If an individual has an attitude of self-deprecation, it would follow that he would be less than motivated to improve his circumstances. An understanding of the dynamics of an individual's self-derogation would provide clues for the remotivation of that person. Furthermore, it has long been held that there is a positive correlation between the acceptance of self and the acceptance of others. Carl Rogers, for example, taught that interpersonal relations are enhanced when a person accepts himself,[12] and Karen Horney insisted that a person is incapable of loving others who cannot love the self.[13] This basic premise has been frequently affirmed experimentally.[14]

Because man is a social animal, his adaptations are basically to his social world. A great deal of research has been undertaken in the area of what social psychologists call "self–social constructs," that is, the ways in which individuals perceive themselves in relation to their social world and significant others. These constructs mediate the way in which a person adapts to his world. The importance of this concept was stressed by two researchers who said "the first step toward the understanding of individual behavior and *particularly nonadaptive individual behavior* is the description of the self–other orientations. . . ."[15] (Italics added).

On another front, it will surprise most readers to learn that the majority of criminals do not consider themselves to be deviant. In Bromberg's classic work, it is stated that there are as many differences within nonconforming groups as there are in conforming groups. "More remarkable is the discovery that the individual criminal is not generally cognizant of the essential antisociality of his attitude toward society."[16] In the controversial

[12]Carl R. Rogers, *Client-Centered Therapy* (Boston: Houghton Mifflin Company, 1951). Later, Rogers categorically stated that, "As a client moves towards being able to accept his own experience, he also moves toward the acceptance of the experience of others." From *On Becoming a Person* (Boston: Houghton Mifflin Company, 1961).

[13]Karen Horney, *New Ways in Psychoanalysis* (New York: W. W. Norton & Company, Inc., 1939).

[14]For representative time comparison studies see Robert C. Ziller and others, "Self-Esteem: A Self-Social Construct," *Journal of Consulting and Clinical Psychology*, 33, No. 1 (February 1969), 84–95; and Katharine T. Omwake, "The Relation Between Acceptance of Self and Acceptance of Others Shown By Three Personality Inventories," *Journal of Consulting Psychology*, 18, No. 6 (December 1954), 443–46.

[15]Robert C. Ziller and Searles A. Grossman, "A Developmental Study of the Self-Social Constructs of Normals and the Neurotic Personality," *Journal of Clinical Psychology*, 23, No. 1 (January 1967), 15.

[16]Walter Bromberg, *Crime and the Mind* (Westport, Conn.: Greenwood Press, Publishers, 1948), p. 1.

research of Yochelson and Samenow, which took place thirty years later, Bromberg's basic premise was reaffirmed. Yochelson and Samenow asserted that the criminal feels that the consummate injustice is getting caught. "Broadly speaking, the injustice lies in the offender's belief that he is a good person, helpful to society, not a criminal; now, here he is, in the hands of the law; what greater injustice could there be!"[17]

It is not possible to indicate all the crucial areas in which the aspiring correctional therapist should possess a priori knowledge, but we have given sufficient indication of the essential ones. There must be a fundamental understanding of human nature and the makeup of the offender. The student must be able to disabuse himself of the lingering myths that criminal behavior is pure pathology, that criminals perceive themselves as antisocial, that the criminal and the non-criminal are in a polar relationship, that all offenders are responsive to therapeutic endeavors, and that change can be imposed from the outside, without an inner commitment from the client.

Furthermore, the aspiring practitioner of the healing art in corrections should dwell thoughtfully on the offender's self-concept and manner of perceiving his social world, and should have a healthy and ennobling image of humanity. More, the discriminatory manner in which justice is dispensed in the criminal justice system should provoke the correctional practitioner to be particularly sensitive and fair in dealing with society's *caught* miscreants.

CORRECTIONAL SOCIAL WORK

Very simply, correctional social work refers to the application of social work principles to the field of corrections. Although the terms are not technically synonymous, "social work" and "social casework" are almost universally used interchangeably. Social work "is the general term for the combined art and science which has as its objective the remediation of social problems."[18] Essentially, that includes preventing social dysfunction as well as restoring those with impaired capacity for adjustment. Social casework, on the other hand, is a particular social work persuasion, which has long and unfortunately been identified with the now discredited medical model. The indications are, however, that common usage is obliterating the distinction.

Most individuals who are performing a therapeutic or quasi-therapeutic function in corrections, such as probation and parole officers,

---

[17]Samuel Yochelson and Stanton E. Samenow, *The Criminal Personality, Volume 1: A Profile for Change* (New York: Jason Aronson, Inc., 1976), p. 436.
[18]Louis P. Carney, *Probation and Parole: Legal and Social Dimensions* (New York: McGraw-Hill Book Company, 1977), p. 314.

and institutional counselors, are operating under the umbrella of correctional social work. But it is not to be assumed that social work has an established beachhead in corrections. There have been barriers. In the administration of justice, a rehabilitative approach to the offender has not been consistently popular. Moreover, the lack of dramatic success in correctional treatment efforts has not enhanced the popularity of a treatment approach. The recent development of the so-called punishment model also reflects a growing sentiment against correctional "indulgence." The hardened attitude of the public towards the offender reflects the continuation of myths, such as we have described above, and constitutes another barrier to treatment programming. And the enduring belief that behavior can be modified by coercive punishment also militates against treatment advances.

There are, however, countermilitating forces. If anything, the increasing involvement of individuals, particularly juveniles, in the criminal justice system, and the soaring cost of maintaining that system, will have to lead to alternative thinking. It averages over $10,000 per year to institutionalize a juvenile or adult offender, and that is merely a maintenance cost. The national cost of corrections in 1975 was over $2 billion, and for the entire criminal justice system it was a staggering $17 billion.[19] And the cost mounts daily. The fiscal burden of corrections—the institutionalized version—will be intolerable at some proximate point in the future. It is imperative that correctional social work, and alternative correctional programming, be vigorously implemented as a rational effort to lessen the public's burden. One writer optimistically sees a time in the future when "the distinction between the correctional and the social service systems will become blurred."[20] The particular challenge of rational corrections is to pave the way for that eventuality.

The social work approach in corrections implies a philosophy as well as the application of techniques for problem solving. We will discuss techniques at various locations in this text, particularly later in this chapter. It has been suggested that the operational philosophy of social work in corrections rests upon three specific premises, here paraphrased. The student will be able to grasp the core of the correctional social work approach from these premises.

1. The function of intervention is to target on a problem in social functioning.

2. Social work conceives problem-solving as a partnership activity (between social worker and client).

---

[19]U.S. Department of Justice/U.S. Department of Commerce, *Expenditure and Employment Data for the Criminal Justice System, 1975,* March 1977, p. 271.
[20]Charles H. Shireman, "The Justice System and the Practice of Social Work," *Social Work* (September 1974), 563.

3. Response to the client means most, and equilibrium is best restored, at the point of crisis, so crisis-related social work should be emphasized.[21]

Exception could be taken to the third statement, as some scholars would feel that anticipatory social work should be emphasized. Still, correctional social work has been classically characterized by crisis-intervention.

The role of contemporary correctionalists, particularly probation and parole officers, is being increasingly seen as that of "manager of resources,"[22] or broker of community resources. The Federal Probation Officers Association envisions the probation officer as being called upon "to provide a more explicit evaluation of the needs of the individual offender and to recommend the best available alternatives for meeting those needs. . . ."[23] This comports with the reintegration model. In this model, the correctional effort is seen as a partnership between the professional and the client, a partnership which seeks to mobilize those resources which are needed to meet and fulfill the client's legitimate and unmet needs. This partnership, or relationship, is ordinarily initiated during the first encounter.

Insight and Empathy

Two of the more common terms associated with counseling and therapy are "insight" and "empathy." Insight might be described as perceptive understanding. Naturally, insight should be acquired both by the client (in terms of his behavioral dynamics) and by the counselor (in terms of directing the treatment process). The primary meaning of insight in the therapeutic sense, however, is the process of discovery experienced by the client. It has been defined by Carl Rogers as "the perception of new meaning in the individual's own experience."[24]

It is not quite so easy to define empathy correctly, but it is a critical ingredient in the therapeutic process. The developer of psychosynthesis (which emphasizes will as a constructive force in the mastery of life), Roberto Assagioli, described empathy as "the projection of one's consciousness into that of another being."[25] In his model, empathy represents the operation of the law of synthesis. Carl Rogers was speaking of empathy when he said that, "it is the counselor's function to assume, in so far

---

[21] *Ibid.*, 563–64.

[22] Louis P. Carney, *Corrections and the Community* (Englewood Cliffs, N.J.: Prentice-Hall, Inc., 1977), p. 220.

[23] Federal Probation Officers Association, "Goals of Federal Probation Service" (mimeographed), October 1972, p. v.

[24] Carl R. Rogers, *Counseling and Psychotherapy*, (Boston: Houghton Mifflin Company, 1942), p. 174.

[25] Roberto Assagioli, *The Act of Will* (New York: Penguin Books, 1974), p. 88.

as he is able, the internal frame of reference of the client, to perceive the world as the client sees it, to perceive the client himself as he is seen by himself, to lay aside all perceptions from the external frame of reference while doing so, and to communicate something of this . . . understanding to the client."[26]

In a word, empathy means getting inside of the other person and sensitively experiencing how that other person feels. The reader would probably be able to name some of his or her friends who seem particularly capable of doing this. The question then arises: Is empathy something that can be learned? In view of the fact that some people are more empathic than others, the argument can be advanced that the sense of empathy is charismatic, perhaps a mysteriously inborn talent. On the other hand, as empathy represents heightened social sensitivity, a cogent argument can also be made for the fact that it can be learned. It has to be kept in mind, however, that empathy is still "hazily conceptualized," more than two decades after a similar assessment was made.[27] But the haze will disappear as our perceptions are perfected, and as accuracy colors the data drawn from our interpersonal relationships. Pending that state of affairs, the counselor would be well advised to work constantly on developing empathic sensitivity.

Interviewing

In defining psychotherapy, we discovered that it consists of an activity that is almost always conducted on a verbal level. The heart of *positive* human interaction is effective communication, whether it takes place in a simple, information-gathering interview, or in an intense psychotherapy session. Since the interview is the fundamental tool at the disposal of the correctional professional, it should be characterized by fluid communication. An interview is not merely a "rap session" but rather what Garrett called "professional conversation."[28] It is a skilled and complex tactic for gaining meaningful information and insight, as well as being the vehicle for counseling and subsequent treatment.

Cross employs a "working definition" of the interview, seeing it essentially in terms of its constituent elements:

first, the persons who are participating in the interview; second, the inherent role expectations which the participants attach to each other and which define[s] the obligations of each participant; third, the actual communication

[26]Rogers, *Client-Centered Therapy*, p. 29.

[27]N. L. Gage and Lee J. Cronbach, "Conceptual and Methodological Problems in Interpersonal Perception," *Psychological Review*, 62, No. 6 (November 1955), 4ll.

[28]Annette Garrett, *Interviewing*, 2nd ed. (New York: Family Service Association of America, 1972), p. 5.

which takes place . . . and, fourth, the social and cultural pressures acting on all participants which subtly pressure them to react in specific ways according to the cultural background. . . . [29]

In the correctional setting, these elements take on a particular meaning. The client, to begin with, is not necessarily predisposed toward fruitful participation in the interview. Furthermore, an inmate or a parolee may quite naturally feel coerced to participate because of his status as a convicted felon. The cultural element obviously can be a crucial factor. In fact, ignorance of cultural imperatives can effectively impede any meaningful communication.

The problems raised in the foregoing paragraph clearly suggest why interviewing is a skillful strategy (whose skills can be learned). It must be kept in mind, at all times, that the interview is an act of social intercourse. The observation of Goode and Hatt is germane: "Neither reliability nor depth can be achieved, however, unless it is kept clearly in mind that interviewing is fundamentally a process of social interaction."[30] The interviewer, therefore, should be grounded in knowledge of human behavior, and well versed in non-verbal communication. Individuals participating in interviews are constantly giving clues to their behavior and feelings, frequently through non-verbal "body language." These clues should be observed and can be translated. For example, in an interview involving a married couple, the husband can induce silence in his wife through threatening looks or nuances in his behavioral gestures. In my practice, I sometimes counter this obstructive tactic by placing the couple in chairs which are placed back to back. This neutralizes the husband's non-verbal control and permits free expression by his wife. Non-verbal behavior, or the "verbal-intuitive split in consciousness," as it has been termed, is given great importance in gestalt therapy. During gestalt therapy the patient is frequently asked, "What is your body telling you?"[31]

The good interviewer is a trained observer, alert to the substance of the "messages" being sent by the person interviewed, and capable of sensing and appropriately responding to the emotional feelings of the client. He is also a role model and a facilitator. As a role model, the interviewer's behavior will tend to be taken as the model to be emulated. As a facilitator, the interviewer will act as a catalyst for change, and not as the cause of change in the client. It is important for the interviewer, in situations where the interviews (counseling sessions) are relatively continuous, to make

[29]C. P. Cross, "Interviewing and Communication," in Crispin P. Cross (ed.), *Interviewing and Communication in Social Work* (London: Routledge & Kegan Paul, 1974), p. 12.

[30]William J. Goode and Paul K. Hatt, *Methods in Social Research* (New York: McGraw-Hill Book Company, 1952), p. 186.

[31]Robert E. Ornstein, *The Psychology of Consciousness* (San Francisco: W. H. Freeman and Company, 1972), p. 219.

predictions about the course of the client's actions. This will enable the facilitator of change (the interviewer) not only to measure changes in the client's behavior, but also to test his own competence and awareness. It is also important to remember that the skill of interviewing, and the success of particular interviews, can always be improved upon. The key to improvement is the constant acquisition of new knowledge about the process. And the greater the understanding that one has of himself, the greater his ability to understand the whys and wherefores of others' behavior.

The basic objective of an interview can be the mere acquisition of information, as in specific purpose, non-therapeutic interviews. But with the type of interview that is ongoing and psychotherapeutic, and which is part of correctional social work, the objective is a trifle more sophisticated. Social work's motto could well be: "Through problem-solving to self-realization." It has been wisely said that "the only satisfactory means of evaluating social work is to consider whether it is directed towards enabling the client to manage without the assistance of a social worker."[32] We have stated that the interview is the most fundamental tool in the repertoire of the correctional social worker. In counseling, it is honed and refined and sometimes very sophisticated. As interviewing is the basic tool of correctional treatment, counseling is its epitome.

Counseling

In Chapter Six we discovered that there are myriad systems of psychotherapy. There is also a panoply of counseling approaches based on the spectrum of therapeutic philosophy. It should not be presumed that counseling or psychotherapy is always a constructive endeavor. I recall the case of a professional individual who was obviously manifesting symptoms of mental ill health. His therapist, committed to "uncovering," relentlessly bore in until the patient had a frank psychotic break. The patient later told me that he simply could not handle the aggressive attack therapy of his therapist. The defense is often offered that such an individual was pre-psychotic, and the break was inevitable. That sort of a presumption throws ethics out the window, and removes responsibility from the therapist. The *Manual of Correctional Standards* defines counseling as

> a relationship in which one endeavors to help another understand and solve his problems of adjustment. It is distinguished from advice or admonition in that it implies *mutual* consent. As the term has come to be used in working with offenders, counseling encompasses the personal and group relationships undertaken by staff. It has as its goals either the immediate solution of a

---

[32]Robert Bessell, *Interviewing and Counseling* (London: B. T. Basford, Ltd., 1971), p. 16.

specific personal problem or a long-range effort to develop increased self-understanding and maturity within the offender. Counseling may be part of the activity of professional casework or psychiatric staff, but is also the proper province of the teacher, the work supervisor, and the group supervisor.[33]

The Captive Client

The counselor in corrections has a captive clientele, and the dynamics of the counseling process will differ to the extent that the client's liberty is constrained. This qualification must be kept in mind when reading some of the broad generalizations expressed in this section. The client, however, whether captive or free—or conditionally free—"is saying whether explicitly or implicitly, "I am simply not living effectively." When the counselor or therapist indicates his involvement, he is saying, "I can help you to live effectively."[34] And the reason that the therapist or counselor can, is because *he* is living effectively. If he is not, he cannot be an effective counselor.

It has been said that, "There is no profession more potentially useful or devastating than the psychological helping sciences."[35] Counseling comes within that purview. With the therapist's implied capacity to control the destiny of the patient, the vulnerability of the client is obvious. The ethical dimension is ever-present in the counseling or therapy situation. The practitioner must realize that he or she is possessed of feelings just as is the client. "There are those clients who are personally attractive and others who we would never care to be around in anything other than a professional encounter. It is crucial for therapists to exercise restraint and sound judgment, and to honor moral obligations for the persons to whom they are entrusted."[36]

There are other ethical responsibilities that devolve on the counselor or therapist. He must avoid creating dependency in the client; he must not breach the confidences that are implicit in a therapeutic relationship; he must not become personally involved with his clients, because it is counterproductive to the aims of therapy to do so; he must be honest with his clients at all times; he must not superimpose his own moral values on the client; and, above all, he must bring an acceptable degree of competence to the counseling relationship.

---

[33]*Manual of Correctional Standards* (College Park, Md.: The American Correctional Association, 1975), p. 422.

[34]Robert R. Carkhuff and Bernard G. Berenson, *Beyond Counseling and Therapy* (New York: Holt, Rinehart and Winston, Inc., 1967), p. 227.

[35]Van Hoose and Kottler, *Ethical and Legal Issues in Counseling and Psychotherapy*, p. 50.

[36]*Ibid.*, p. 54.

G. K. Chesterton once commented that it was natural to take oneself gravely. It is easier to be grave than light-hearted, he intimated, pointing out that Satan fell by the force of gravity. Counseling is, above all, a human relationship, in which one party to the relationship is particularly in need of help. The very fact that there is a need for help would suggest that the client is disposed toward gravity, rather than *joie de vivre*. The counselor, quite plainly, should exude positive and joyous qualities, for gravity begets gravity and procreates depression. (Chesterton also said that laughter was a leap.)

For a seeming eternity, therapists have been dredging up unconscious material from the past, obliging the patient to deal with his dead past in the living present. There have been countervailing developments. In reality therapy, for instance, the patient is not confronted with his past because it is of little benefit in helping him to adjust to present reality. As the popular psychologist–author, Wayne Dyer, vigorously stated

> the most obvious thing about which you can do nothing now is your past behavior. Everything that you ever did is simply over. . . . Since you can only live in the present moment, it is preposterous and self-negating to let yourself be hurt about what used to be.[37]

In correctional counseling, the so-called "now therapies" are popular because the correctional setting is usually more conducive to that mode of approach, and because it is obviously desirable to have the offender–client come to believe that it is "self-negating to let yourself be hurt about what used to be."

The patriarch of counseling, Carl Rogers, first articulated his "basic hypothesis" in 1942: *"Effective counseling consists of a definitely structured, permissive relationship which allows the client to gain an understanding of himself to a degree which enables him to take positive steps in the light of his new orientation."*[38] (Italics in the original). He emphasized specific techniques, which had developed out of his own practice. But before a decade had passed, the maestro had shifted his emphasis, and instead of technique was stressing the importance of the attitude of the counselor or therapist. He began to use "implementation" instead of "technique," teaching that the counselor must have an hypothesis about his client. "The client is apt to be quick to discern when the counselor is using a 'method,' an intellectually

---

[37]Wayne W. Dyer, *Pulling Your Own Strings* (New York: Thomas Y. Crowell Company, 1978), p. 52.
[38]Rogers, *Counseling and Psychotherapy,* p. 18.

chosen tool which he has selected for a purpose. On the other hand, the counselor is always implementing, both in conscious and nonconscious ways, the attitudes which he holds towards the client."[39]

In Rogers's view, a counselor cannot perform client-centered counseling if he cannot respect the worth of the individual. The desired attitude of the counselor consists of this, that "the counselor must perceive the internal frame of reference of the individual as accurately and completely as possible, and then feed his perceptions back to the client."[40] The purpose of this approach is to enable the client to see himself as he is reflected by the counselor, so that he obtains an objective view of his own attitudes and perceptions in a non-judgmental milieu. Rogers explains:

> Psychotherapy deals primarily with the organization and functioning of the self. There are many elements of experience which the self cannot face, cannot clearly perceive, because to face them or admit them would be inconsistent with and threatening to the current organization of self. In client-centered therapy the client finds in the counselor a genuine alter ego . . . a self which has temporarily divested itself (so far as possible) of its own selfhood, except for the one quality of endeavoring to understand.[41]

The shift from technique to the relationship between the therapist and the client has attracted a growing number of theorists in the field of counseling. While specific techniques, such as role reversal, hypnotherapy, and encounter are extensively used, the fundamental nature of counseling inheres in the relationship and not in the technique. As a modern text on the subject expressed it,

> Technique has become less stringent in order to allow concentration on the relationship between the counselor and client. *Counseling is a process of establishing a cooperative relationship* and then using that interpersonal interaction to help the client learn his or her desired appropriate behavior.[42] (Italics added).

Counseling, therefore, is initiated with the establishment of this relationship.

In Rogerian counseling, the main responsibility for the relationship belongs to the client, because it is he or she that has come seeking help. In the correctional setting, the client is most often a captive, and the responsibility is necessarily shared. It is not impossible to develop an effective and productive relationship with a captive client, assuming a modicum of

---

[39]Rogers, *Client-Centered Therapy,* pp. 25–26.
[40]James G. Hansen, Richard R. Stevic, and Richard W. Warner, Jr., *Counseling: Theory and Process* (Boston: Allyn and Bacon, Inc., 1972), p. 91.
[41]Rogers, *Client-Centered Therapy,* p. 40.
[42]Hansen, Stevic, and Warner, *Counseling: Theory and Process,* 2nd ed., p. 239.

cooperation on his part. It just means that there is a more difficult challenge facing the therapist, but the client and not the problem *per se* remains the center of the counseling universe.

The Counselor as a Change Agent

It has become popular in the helping services, in modern times, to refer to the counselor or social worker as a change agent. This is basically because, broadly speaking, counseling is seen as an effort to change individuals' behavior patterns and attitudes. A therapeutic relationship is not instituted in order to maintain the status quo. The client is supposed to emerge from therapy in a changed condition. But, as Arbuckle noted,

> While there is general agreement that the broad goal of counseling and psychotherapy is change of behavior, there is by no means similar agreement on the question of changes to what kind of behavior, and who is the one who is in control of the changing of behavior.[43]

"Change agent" is not a satisfactory term, despite its optimistic implication, yet change remains the counseling objective. The dilemma can be solved by applying a term that takes due cognizance of the generally accepted objectives of therapy, and which recognizes the fact that change cannot take place without initiation by the client. Counselors, instead of being referred to as change agents, should be referred to as *change facilitators*.

In order to fulfill this function, counselors and therapists must have power to offset the powerlessness of the client. Power in this sense is healing power or, as Wolman defined it, "the ability to satisfy needs. . . ."[44] We can understand this concept better if we draw an analogy to Maslow's concept of the hierarchy of needs. Power, in the sense that we use it here, is synonymous with the capacity to control one's destiny, absolute power being equated with complete, self-determinative control of one's being. The counselor brings potency, as it were, to activate the client's potential. As it is actuated, the capacity to direct one's destiny grows.

Stigma Theory and Self-Esteem

While generic principles of treatment are applicable to all types of counseling, the correctional client has to be approached and understood in

---

[43]Dugald S. Arbuckle, *Counseling and Psychotherapy An Existential-Humanistic View,* 3rd ed. (Boston: Allyn and Bacon, Inc., 1975), p. 174.

[44]"The Process of Treatment," in Benjamin B. Wolman (ed.), *The Therapist's Handbook* (New York: Van Nostrand Reinhold Company, 1976), p. 4.

terms of his unique circumstance. On top of emotional dysfunction, the correctional client must endure social stigma. This has led to the development of what is known as *stigma theory*. *Stigma* derives from the Latin, and means a mark or a brand. A stigma was a mark of shame, placed on criminals, in ancient Greece and Rome. Stigma theory

> assumes a predisposing configuration of behaviour, or in another form a predisposing attribute or attributes, which leads the subject to commit his first offence or a child to make his first steps towards delinquency. At this state the subject is reproached, given a derogatory description, identified with a despised or rejected class of person, humiliated, discriminated against, rejected or expelled. His reaction to this treatment results in increasing alienation from the rejecting group and a search for security in a peer group.[45]

Whether or not there is validity to this quoted principle of the stigma theory, the stigma of being an ex-convict is a barrier to rehabilitation.[46] The tragedy is that this blemish is relentlessly imposed by society. An individual, unless pardoned, never really loses the status of ex-convict. The correctional counselor has an exceptionally difficult challenge in dealing with the factor of stigmatism, and must be particularly sensitive to the client's feelings about this "mark of Cain."

We have previously spoken of the importance of the self-concept. The individual's feelings about himself are crucial in terms of the way he reacts to his environment. According to Mossman and Ziller, "the self-concept is a mediating agent between the organism and the environment, and . . . self-esteem is that component of the self-system which is associated with the consistency of the organism's response to the environment.[47] A central objective of correctional counseling or therapy is to restore the client's sense of self-esteem. At one time, "self-esteem" was considered too vague a term to have substantive meaning, but there now exist methods for determining the client's self-perception. Coopersmith's Self-Esteem Inventory is a pioneering example.[48]

A variation on the self-esteem inventory could be used as a counseling technique for the initial interview. The client could be asked to provide

---

[45]D. Chapman, "The Stereotype of the Criminal and the Social Consequences," in Stephen Schafer, *Readings in Contemporary Criminology* (Reston, Va.: Reston Publishing Company, Inc., 1976), p. 257. For further elaboration of this theory, see Erving Goffman, *Stigma* (Englewood Cliffs, N.J.: Prentice-Hall, Inc., 1960).

[46]For another view of the effect of stigma on the offender, see Richard D. Schwartz and Jerome H. Skolnick, "The Stigma of 'Ex-Con' and the Problem of Reintegration," in David M. Peterson and Charles W. Thomas (eds.), *Corrections: Problems and Prospects* (Englewood Cliffs, N.J.: Prentice-Hall, Inc., 1975), pp. 126–38.

[47]Beal Monroe Mossman, III, and Robert C. Ziller, "Self-Esteem and Consistency of Social Behavior," *Journal of Abnormal Psychology*, 73, No. 4 (August 1968), 363.

[48]Stanley Coopersmith, "A Method for Determining Types of Self-Esteem," *Journal of Abnormal and Social Psychology*, 59, No. 1 (July 1959), 87–94.

the counselor with a self-description, a profile of how he saw himself. This would not only reveal a great deal about the client's sense of self-esteem, but it would simultaneously give the counselor clues for the structuring of the counseling thrust. The real importance of such an instrument is that it individualizes the client on the basis of his own perceptions, thus permitting a treatment approach tailored to his specific needs. It can also be used as the standard against which success in the counseling endeavor can be measured.[49]

The Value Problem In Therapy

We cannot leave our discussion of counseling without a word on values. Every individual has a set of values, which are shaped by personal experiences, and which change frequently. The importance of values lies in the fact that they are the guides of behavior. R. B. Perry claims that values have no objectivity: "The silence of a desert is without value until some wanderer finds it lonely and terrifying; the cataract, until some human finds it sublime, or until it is harnessed to satisfy human needs."[50] The nature of the counseling relationship, in theory at least, is such that the dignity and self-determinative capacity of the client are the controlling dimensions. But when the client comes in out of the desert of anonymity, to confront the therapist's moral authority, he may find his value system under siege.

Directing himself to the aspect of the therapist's moral power, Lowe remarked, "Because the therapist is an expert in the social and the behavioral sciences, he is called upon to direct man's moral quest. The spiritual man, who was replaced by a rational individual, is in turn replaced by the social self."[51] Because the modern emphasis is on adjusting to one's environment, the therapist becomes the social theologian. This is a burden that the therapist should not have to bear. Viktor Frankl would say that the modern therapist's clients suffer from an existential vacuum. They are really searching for the meaning of life, not the secular theology of a psychotherapist.

The therapist must use his implicit moral authority to reflect respect for the individual client's ability to take command of his destiny ultimately, and to accept the pertinence of his value system, where it is not pathologically obstructing growth and development. The correctional

[49]An interesting account of the use of a self-description technique can be found in Frank Barron, "Some Personality Correlates of Independence of Judgment," *Journal of Personality,* 21, No. 3 (March 1953), 287–97.

[50]Quoted in Van Hoose and Kottler, *Ethical and Legal Issues in Counseling,* p. 173.

[51]C. Marshall Lowe, *Value Orientations in Counseling and Psychotherapy* (Cranston, R.I.: The Carroll Press Publishers, 1976), p. 31.

therapist, because he operates from a position of coercive authority, must be especially alert to guard against the assumption of unwarranted authority.

Group Counseling

A phenomenon of more than usual significance has been the proliferation of various types of group therapy, although the origin of the phenomenon is in dispute. Corsini, for example, said that the concept of group therapy "was not in the air" prior to the early 1930s.[52] A contrary opinion traces group activity back almost a century, to Jane Addams' Hull House, which was opened in Chicago in 1889, and to religiously supported organizations such as Catholic Charities and Jewish Family Services.[53] Whatever the source, the development of group interactions witnessed a remarkable development in the middle decades of this century, and most scholars in the field "agree that its great proliferation and general acceptance have occurred rather recently."[54] Corrections, desperate for some effective tactics to advance rehabilitation, applied the group "therapy" approach almost indiscriminately.

Criminology, and its bastard child, corrections, has been under the dominance of sociological thought in this country, rather than legal thought, as in Europe. Sociological principles, therefore, have been the formative influences in the development of criminology and corrections. Because sociology is a discipline whose concern is with group activities and group relations, *group* counseling became a highly palatable instrument for correctional treatment. Group counseling is wholly compatible with a sociological theory of deviance: Since man is a social animal, who learns and behaves on the basis of his reference groups, then it follows that deviant behavior, formed in group associations, can be re-formed in nondeviant group associations.

In the California correctional system, in the fifties and sixties, group counseling was practically *de rigueur*. Everyone from institutional carpenters to field parole agents were subtly pressured to conduct group counseling sessions. Even those who felt uncomfortable in the role of group counselor were expected to participate and to conduct groups. One can speculate at the amount of harm done, or at least good left undone, by unwilling, hostile "therapists." It was not surprising, therefore, that a trio

---

[52]Raymond J. Corsini, *Methods of Group Psychotherapy* (New York: McGraw-Hill Book Company, 1957), p. 7.

[53]John B. P. Shaffer and M. David Galinsky, *Models of Group Therapy and Sensitivity Training* (Englewood Cliffs, N.J.: Prentice-Hall, Inc., 1974), p. 1.

[54]Richard M. Stephenson and Frank R. Scarpitti, *Group Interaction as Therapy* (Westport, Conn.: Greenwood Press, 1974), p. 15.

of authorities, zeroing in on the California experience, wrote at length on the negative impact of group counseling on parole violation.[55] As a pertinent study concluded, "poor group counseling is worse than no group counseling at all."[56]

The emergence of group counseling has most frequently been attributed to economic factors; that is, there are not enough therapists available to permit one-on-one therapy for everybody in need. Group counseling or group therapy, therefore, is a sort of bargain package which widened the scope and influence of therapy. Uehling, speaking of the Wisconsin State Prison, said that group psychotherapy "was introduced under pressure of 'treatment needs' within an overburdened psychiatric staff rather than because of any sudden insight into the benefits which might accrue to the individual offender."[57]

Corsini suggests another rationale. Because "at least twenty different people, entirely independently of one another, have discovered group psychotherapy,"[58] we must consider the possibility that it is actually a result of "cultural demand." Irrespective of the origin, group therapy or counseling has been found to be something more than multiplied individual therapy. The internal dynamics are unique to a group structure. For one thing, there is the operation of peer influence; and there is collective reinforcement of members, as well as collective blocking of negative behavior as the occasion demands. The group, in other words, becomes the influential vehicle of change.

The Group Process

The group process, like the single interview process, can be used merely for the imparting of information. It can also be used for "support therapy" or for advanced treatment. Eric Berne used the term "group treatment" to indicate "the treatment of psychiatric patients when the leader meets in a specified place for a specified period of time with a small number of them, usually not exceeding eight or ten."[59] Group counseling could be similarly described, except that the members would not necessarily have to be psychiatric patients. Most group counseling done by correc-

---

[55]Gene Kassebaum, David Ward, and Daniel Wilner, *Prison Treatment and Parole Survival: An Empirical Assessment* (New York: John Wiley & Sons, Inc., 1971), see especially pp. 311–24.

[56]Robert J. Resnick, Frank Lira, and John H. Wallace, "On the Effectiveness of Group Counseling," *Criminal Justice and Behavior,* 4, No. 1 (March 1977), 85.

[57]Harold F. Uehling, *Correction of a Correctional Psychologist in Treatment of the Criminal Offender* (Springfield, Ill.: Charles C Thomas, Publisher, 1973), p. 67.

[58]Corsini, *Methods of Group Psychotherapy,* p. 7.

[59]Eric Berne, *Principles of Group Treatment* (New York: Oxford University Press, 1966), p. 3.

tionalists consists of support therapy. The group provides, at the very least, a forum for ventilation of hostilities, which hopefully offsets acting out.

Group counseling, or guided group interaction as it is sometimes formally described, was first introduced into the correctional world in 1951 in the well-known experiment at the Highfields Group Rehabilitation Center in New Jersey. Twenty teen-age, male juvenile delinquents were involved in this residential program. As part of the program, the boys were required to attend ninety-minute group sessions at least five days per week. The Highfields program was very innovative, especially for it time. Extended visits from relatives were permitted, and furloughs and passes to the community were liberally dispensed, in line with the philosophy that ties to the community were to be nurtured. Highfields was so enthusiastically received that it became a prototype.

An interesting variation was instituted in Newark, New Jersey, known as Essexfields. The hybrid name derived from the fact that it was located in Essex County, and that it also evolved from Highfields. Whereas the boys at Highfields lived at the program site, with cottage parents and other staff, the boys in the Essexfields program did not. They came to the program during the day, but spent the evenings and weekends with their families at home. Essexfields had two major program components, work and group meetings. Highfields and Essexfields were the pioneers of group counseling in American corrections. (In both programs, the recidivism rate was reduced.)

The Group Method

We have mentioned above that one of the unique aspects of group counseling consists of peer influence. As Arnold has pointed out, "A large number of studies demonstrated repeatedly that inmates are extensively controlled by their peers in correctional settings."[60] The core of group counseling, in corrections, consists of efforts to mobilize the therapeutic potential in the offender's peer culture. The ideal number of members for a group is usually spoken of as from eight to twelve. When extremely large groups are conducted, they are usually referred to as therapeutic communities. The group is open to improvisation, and numerous techniques can be applied, some of which are particularly useful in the launching of the group. One technique is to ask each member some question such as: "If you were to die, and could come back to life as some other

---

[60]William R. Arnold, "Group Methods in Correctional Treatment," in Albert R. Roberts (ed.), *Correctional Treatment of the Offender* (Springfield, Ill.: Charles C Thomas, Publisher, 1974), p. 177.

creature, what would you choose to be?" The responses will reflect not only the manner in which each individual views himself or herself, but also how the group reacts to the group member's self-image.

Generally, the group leader gives subtle direction to the group, but not in a didactic or pedagogic sense. It is, after all, a group process, and not a lecture. Most therapists recommend the removal of such items of furniture as conference tables or coffee tables, feeling that they constitute blocks to free communication in the group. The group may be formally structured or informally structured, it may be homogeneous or heterogeneous, and it can be a special purpose or general purpose collectivity. In other words, the group may remain at a nonthreatening conversational level, or it may rise to dynamic therapeutics; it can focus on a specific type of problem, such as sexual deviation or drug addiction, or it can be generally oriented; and it can be composed of individuals of similar backgrounds, or dissimilar backgrounds. With respect to psychotherapy groups, at least, there is a considerable body of opinion that the homogeneous-heterogeneous debate is a spurious one, and that balanced, interactive groups are the ideal.[61] While there is substantial disagreement about the therapeutic potential of group counseling, Trotzer adequately states the case for the affirmative when he says:

> The positive aspects of the helping process are incorporated into the group setting, which facilitates the transfer of learning more readily to the ongoing life of the participant. The group-counseling process if properly constituted and led meets the demands of an effective learning environment. . . . In addition, the process is directed toward self-exploration, encouraging introspection and feedback so that communication can occur and relationships can develop. Therefore, it establishes the fundamental basis needed to make good decisions.[62]

One of the major criticisms of group counseling is that it does not have a model which would provide counselors with a systematic theory to apply. The premise is that functional models are necessary in the behavioral sciences, because they provide the foundation from which theory is converted into practice. An ambitious effort has only recently been made to develop a model of systematic counseling,[63] and it should be con-

---

[61]Arnold P. Goldstein, Lee B. Sechrest, and Kenneth Heller, *Psychotherapy and the Psychology of Behavior Change* (New York: John Wiley & Sons, Inc., 1966), pp. 323–25.

[62]James P. Trotzer, *The Counselor and the Group: Integrating Theory, Training, and Practice* (Monterey, Cal.: Brooks/Cole Publishing Company, Inc., 1977), p. 3. An earlier study found that positive adjustment in group members was related to "leadership, popularity, and total activity rate" in that order. See: Richard D. Mann, "A Review of the Relationship Between Personality and Performance in Small Groups," *Psychological Bulletin*, 56, No. 4 (July 1959), 265.

[63]Norman R. Stewart and others, *Systematic Counseling* (Englewood Cliffs, N.J.: Prentice-Hall, Inc., 1978).

sulted by those individuals who are moving towards professional counseling activity.

SYNOPSIS

We have discovered in this chapter that the practitioner's basic tools include both concrete tactics and some less than concrete pedagogic skills. First, the practitioner must have an awareness of the ethical dimensions of counseling, as well as the constructive use of authority. Correctional treatment also presupposes an adequate fund of knowledge about human behavior. In addition, there must be a familiarity with correctional social work and its objectives. When a professional in the field has the responsibility of a caseload, he or she is obliged to apply the knowledge described above to those cases.

Interviewing and counseling, which merge on a continuum of therapeutic skill, constitute the key tools at the disposal of the practitioner. They should rest on an adequate knowledge base. Group counseling is a treatment option which became very popular in corrections following the experimental work done at Highfields and Essexfields. It is based on the premise that the group has treatment potential because its inherent peer pressure can be manipulated to redirect the behavior of the members. Whether through individual, one-on-one counseling, or in the group setting, the correctional worker with a treatment responsibility has to depend upon his skill in developing a productive relationship with his clientele. He will do this principally through the counseling process.

Adjunctive tools are available. Team treatment, in which a number of professionals collectively manage the therapeutic endeavor, is a popular and useful strategy. Mobilization of community resources is an unappreciated tool in corrections but it is an obvious *quid pro quo*. The probation officer and the parole officer are destined to become the resource brokers in the corrections of tomorrow. It is, therefore, imperative that they become highly skilled in this type of community organization in anticipation of the metamorphosis that will take place in their profession.

In becoming a skilled and competent therapist, or counselor, or correctionalist, or whatever term or station is preferred, the professional in correctional treatment will be able to understand, and savor, the meaning of George Bernard Shaw's wise observation:

> This is the true joy of life—the being used for a purpose recognized by yourself as a mighty one, the being thoroughly worn out before you are thrown to the scrap-heap; the being a force of nature instead of a feverish, selfish clod of ailments and grievances.

8 Corrections and Psychiatry

There are only two kinds of people who never make mistakes: Newborn babies and the dead.

Mao Tse-tung

One of the more remarkable phenomena of the nineteen seventies has been the growing cynicism and irreverence shown towards psychiatry and, to a lesser degree, psychology. Where once the psychiatrist stood midway between God and super-God (with psychologists being, at the very least, seraphim), critics are now vociferously proclaiming that the psychiatrist has feet of clay, and his power, instead of being exercised for the good of humanity, has been wielded to achieve unconscionable control over the defenseless. What is even more embarrassing to the psychiatric profession is that some of the most iconoclastic critics are members of the profession.

PSYCHIATRY UNDER FIRE

There is supporting evidence for the criticisms and, unfortunately, it is plentiful. In 1957, Kenneth Donaldson, having been previously taken into custody by deputy sheriffs, was committed to the State Mental Hospital at Chattahoochie, Florida. His "sickness" consisted of writing a barrage of letters to various government officials, protesting that someone was trying to poison his food. Although the law required a psychiatric examination before commitment to a mental institution, Donaldson did not receive one. At the hospital he was threatened with shock treatments if he did not behave, and was locked in a ward with tubercular patients as punishment because he denied being crazy. He spent fifteen years without treatment in that institution. He was diagnosed as having "delusions" because he expressed an interest in becoming a writer. Because he expressed dissatisfaction with his sporadic occupation as a laborer, he was described as making "a poor adjustment to life."

In 1971, Donaldson was unconditionally released from the institution. The psychiatrist-author, Thomas Szasz, said that Donaldson was released from psychiatric confinement, not because he had suddenly become mentally healthy, nor because he had suddenly become non-dangerous, but because subjecting the legitimacy of his continued psychiatric incarceration to such a test [a class action suit which he had filed] was, under the new circumstances, deemed too risky by the legal-psychiatric authorities in charge of his case.[1]

In 1976, Donaldson became an established writer, his "delusion" notwithstanding, with the publication of his book, *Insanity Inside Out.* In the same year he became another kind of celebrity when the United States Supreme Court, ruling on his case, held that non-violent individuals cannot be kept in a mental institution involuntarily without being provided with treatment. Donaldson also received a generous out-of-court settlement in a civil suit which he brought against two psychiatrists at the Florida hospital.

In 1976, in Montgomery County, Maryland, a nineteen-year-old mother was putting baby oil on her child. At first she massaged him gently, but suddenly she began to hurl imprecations at the infant, punched him fiercely on the abdomen with her clenched fists, and then, hooking a finger in his mouth, she hurtled the baby to its doom. She screamed that she was God, and rebuked the baby for being the "filthy demon" Satan. Arrested, she was charged with murder, and entered a plea of not guilty by reason of insanity, a plea which the judge accepted. Then the psychiatrists brought their expertise to bear upon the issue.

---

[1]Thomas Szasz, *Psychiatric Slavery* (New York: The Free Press, 1977), p. 29.

One psychiatrist at the mental institution in which she was detained pending trial testified that she was psychotic from the time she committed the crime until just before the hospital staff examined her—a psychotic period of approximately one month. Another psychiatrist, whom the court consulted, diagnosed the young woman as a "hysterical personality of the dissociative type" who had a "100-to-one chance" of committing further violence. Still a third psychiatrist testified that he was deeply mystified by the defendant's condition, but as of that moment he could not bring himself to sign a commitment certificate.

The judge was thus placed in a bizarre position. He had a defendant who had pleaded not guilty by reason of insanity, a plea which he had accepted. But the psychiatrists would not certify that the young woman was insane. Since the judge had accepted her plea of insanity, he could not proceed to sentence her for the crime of murder. He handed down the only verdict that seemed appropriate to him. He released the prisoner. Because of the psychiatric impasse, she could not even be required to continue psychiatric treatment. It was later revealed that she had also claimed responsibility for the fire which had burned her mother and her brother to death.

In California, a man who had two previous convictions, and who had served two terms for forcible rape, was psychiatrically cleared for release to the community by the prison psychiatrist because there was "no psychiatric contraindication to release," and because it appeared that he had "reversed his attitude toward conventional behavior." His "reversal" was so superficial that within a short time after his release he raped and savagely beat a thirteen-year-old child with a tire iron, almost killing her. He went back to prison in 1978 for this offense, with a twenty-year sentence. It was his third *known* rape. There was evidence that he had committed at least one other rape which had not been reported to the police.

In the same year, also in California, a convicted rapist was released from the Atascadero State Hospital (where sex offenders are processed under California's sex psychopathy law). A month after he was released from the hospital as "not dangerous to others at this time," the convicted rapist committed three additional rapes within a five-day period. The presiding judge remarked that it had been a waste of time sending this man to the state hospital.

A variety of events have brought psychiatry into disfavor, quite apart from scientific misgivings. Such incidents as the following are obvious contributors: A psychiatrist, co-author of a book on how to handle emotional problems, was arrested for conspiring to murder a fellow physician with whom he had been having an emotional altercation.

A woman, who was intercepted while making her eighth attempt to commit suicide by jumping from the Golden Gate Bridge in San Francisco, had a history of brief hospitalization after each prior attempt. On one occasion she was released so abruptly that she was back on the bridge making another attempt before the patrol car, which had taken her to the hospital, had returned to the bridge. The hospital said that the woman had been carefully evaluated each time and was considered capable of dealing with her suicidal impulses.

In Orange County, California, in 1975, a psychiatrist in a county facility recommended a lobotomy for a 17-year-old boy.

In 1977 two psychiatrists described the use of shock treatment in the California state hospitals as appalling. One of those state hospitals was described by the licensing division of the State Department of Health and the National Institute of Mental Health as bad, or worse, than any they had ever reviewed. Trash was "all over" the condemned hospital, constituting a grave problem in terms of control of infection; the use of obsolete drugs involved a threat to the health and safety of the patients; and the physical therapy department was "a disaster waiting to happen."

Three years before this negative evaluation was given, a group of individuals in San Francisco organized a group called the Network Against Psychiatric Assault, to fight, through the legal system, all forms of involuntary psychiatric "assault." The group was founded on the principle that involuntary psychiatric treatment is an inhumane practice, and psychosurgery, shock treatment, and drug therapy must not be involuntarily administered. As we learned earlier in the Donaldson case, this general principle was eventually upheld by the United States Supreme Court. The concern about psychiatry became more cogent when members of the psychiatric profession themselves began to vocalize criticism, and were joined by other competent professionals.

THE LIMITATIONS OF PSYCHIATRY

It has always been assumed that psychiatry has some method of diagnosing and classifying which renders it easy to distinguish the sane from the insane. The average citizen has a lot of faith in psychiatry. But the imprecision in psychiatric diagnosis is startling. It was demonstrated once in a rather dramatic way. Law and psychology professor, D. L. Rosenhan, described an experiment in which eight sane individuals secretly gained admission to twelve different psychiatric institutions.[2] The "pseudopatients" included three psychologists, a psychiatrist, a pediatrician, a painter, a housewife, and a young graduate student. Three were females. All

[2]D. L. Rosenhan, "On Being Sane in Insane Places," *Science*, 179, No. 4070 (January 1973), 250–58.

adopted fictitious identities, and those in the mental health professions also adopted fictitious occupations. The pseudopatients were admitted to hospitals located in five different east coast and west coast states, eleven of which were public institutions and one a private hospital.

A wide variety in the hospital settings was purposely sought in order to permit generalization of the findings. For instance, they ranged from old to modern facilities, and from research-oriented to those that were not. Some had rich staffing patterns; others were understaffed.

The bogus patients called the respective hospitals for appointments. Each merely stated that he or she had been hearing voices, and described symptoms consistently. When asked about the voices they heard, they said, in each instance, that the voice was of the same sex as the pseudopatient, and did not speak too clearly, but appeared to say "empty," "hollow," and "thud." These words were purposely chosen because they were similar to those expressed in existential symptoms, and because there is no evidence of existential psychosis in the literature. Apart from adopting a fictitious identity and giving spurious symptoms, the pseudopatients gave accurate life history data to the hospital's staff. Further, upon being admitted to the psychiatric ward, each ceased simulating abnormal symptomatology, and acted as he or she would in everyday life. All were labeled schizophrenic, and eventually discharged as schizophrenics in remission. Rosenhan commented that "the evidence is strong that, once labeled schizophrenic, the pseudopatient was stuck with that label. If the pseudopatient was to be discharged, he must naturally be "in remission"; but he was not sane, nor, in the institution's view, had he ever been sane."[3]

Perhaps the most disturbing thing that surfaced in this experimental study was the fact that *sanity* could not be recognized in a psychiatric hospital. This renders the atmosphere of such a hospital counterproductive because of the irrational bias. As Rosenhan express it,

> The hospital itself imposes a special environment in which the meanings of behavior can easily be misunderstood. The consequences to patients hospitalized in such an environment—the powerlessnes, depersonalization, segregation, mortification, and self-labeling—seem undoubtedly counter-therapeutic.[4]

When psychiatric inferences are drawn about criminals, a distinctive limitation is added. In the words of a psychiatrist of considerable stature,

> Psychiatric investigations of criminals have generally suffered from psychiatric bias in the selection of subjects and from the absence of specific diagnostic criteria. An additional important limitation has been the absence of psychiat-

[3]*Ibid.*, p. 252.
[4]*Ibid.*, p. 257.

ric follow-up and family studies to validate the psychiatric diagnoses and evaluations.[5]

In the absence of these elements, competent conclusions about criminal behavior simply cannot be drawn. We have made earlier reference to Yochelson and Samenow's criticism of insanity as a defense in criminal proceedings. They maintained that they were unable to substantiate a legitimate case of mental disorder among those committed as insane. When the trial of notorious David Berkowitz, alias "Son of Sam," was being conducted, Dr. Samenow was interviewed and his opinion solicited concerning the defense of insanity in criminal proceedings. He replied, "It is a charade participated in by the courts, some psychiatrists, and criminals."[6]

The issue of the power of psychiatrists surfaced during the interview of an authority in the field, psychiatrist-lawyer Dr. Jonas Robitscher. The concern that psychiatry may be overstepping its bounds is revealed in this abstracted interchange:

Q. Dr. Robitscher, are many people who don't really need a psychiatrist consulting one because of minor emotional or mental problems?

A. For some people, minor problems are experienced as acute, so I don't think we can say flatly that a psychiatrist isn't always needed.

But psychiatry certainly is spreading into new fields, and that's a trend that bears watching. We have gotten into the habit of defining such things as marriage difficulties, job tensions and even school truancy as needing psychiatric attention. In many instances, there are ways of dealing with those conditions that don't require psychiatry.[7]

A psychologist, commenting recently on forensic psychiatry, made this tart observation:

The participation of psychiatrists in legal matters can probably be described as a catastrophe. Forensic psychiatry has been a burden to the taxpayers and an encumbrance on the legal system. Unfortunately, psychiatry rode into the courtroom on the coattails of medicine without ever being subjected to the kind of rigorous scrutiny the courts have applied in the case of other kinds of expert evidence.[8]

---

[5]Samuel B. Guze, *Criminality and Psychiatric Disorders* (New York: Oxford University Press, 1976), p. 23.

[6]Quoted in the Los Angeles *Times,* June 9, 1978.

[7]*U.S. News & World Report, Inc.,* Feb. 27, 1978, p. 42.

[8]California District Attorneys Association, *Prosecutor's Brief,* 3 No. 6 (May–June 1978), p. 8.

The implication is that psychiatric expertise should be adjunctive to the court process and not a domineering influence. Expressed in another way, and by a psychiatrist, "The expertise of psychiatry is an ancillary to the implementation of the common law, and not a substitute for it."[9]

In the most recent effort of the American Psychiatric Association to revise its *Diagnostic and Statistical Manual of Mental Disorders* (DSM-III), which is *the* guidebook to mental disorders, controversy was provoked in many quarters. One serious criticism is that the proposed revision "is bloated with a number of new categories that may be human problems but hardly qualify as illnesses."[10] This is the issue of the over-extension of psychiatry addressed by Dr. Robitscher above. But it is given a more sinister interpretation by the former president of the American Psychological Association, who said,

> The advance intelligence on the DSM-III reportedly has it turning every human problem into a disease, in anticipation of the shower of health-plan gold that is over the horizon. . . . The unvarnished fact is that most of the emotional problems of living do not belong in the category of disease.[11]

Heresy in the Profession

The shortcomings of psychiatry are like the shortcomings of medicine. They can be concealed behind the esoteric veil that shrouds each from the inexpert probing of the layman. But when the critic is one who is not only fluent in the mystic language of the discipline, but also a member in good standing of the profession under attack, then the criticism comes with authority and profound impact. Increasing numbers of the "inner council" are voicing their displeasure.

E. Fuller Torrey, a psychiatrist, wrote a book with a portentous title,[12] in which he vigorously castigated the medical model of psychiatry. He is also particularly critical of the established psychotherapies, claiming that they are, for the most part, based on the medical model and are really educative rather than therapeutic endeavors. Backing his contention with numerous case histories, Torrey also advances the position that we introduced earlier in this chapter, namely, that most so-called problems of the mentally ill are problems in social adaptation, and not psychiatric prob-

---

[9]Charles E. Smith, "Psychiatry in Corrections," in John G. Cull and Richard E. Hardy (eds.), *Fundamentals of Criminal Behavior and Correctional Systems* (Springfield, Ill.: Charles C Thomas, Publisher, 1973), p. 283.

[10]Daniel Goleman, "Who's Mentally Ill?", *Psychology Today,* 11, No. 8 (January 1978), 34.

[11]Quoted in *Ibid.*

[12]E. Fuller Torrey, *The Death of Psychiatry* (New York: Penguin Books, 1974).

lems. He bluntly declared, "When psychiatrists go out into the community, they inevitably follow the road to psychiatric fascism."[13]

In 1962, Dr. David Cooper, an English psychiatrist, began an experiment in an English mental hospital, which involved breaking down the artificial staff–patient roles created by conventional psychiatry. His aim was to introduce a greater degree of interactional freedom. He called this an experiment in "anti-psychiatry."[14] Cooper also attacked psychiatry for its submission to the medical model. He said in his book that he would have occasion

> to question the appropriateness of medical or pseudo-medical ways of seeing things. . . . We shall, in fact, have to consider the point of view that psychiatry, over a major area of its whole field of operation, has been co-operating in the systematic invalidation of a wide category of persons.[15]

This is a harsh indictment, but it is being echoed with increasing frequency.

Cooper is distressed by the fact that psychiatry too often deals in "opaque clinical data, that is to say data which may be (at least theoretically) biologically explicable but which are socially unintelligible."[16] And he was particularly concerned with violence:

> Above all, I have been concerned with the question of violence in psychiatry and have concluded that perhaps the most striking form of violence in psychiatry is nothing less than the violence *of* psychiatry in so far as this discipline chooses to refract and condense on to its identified patients the subtle violence of the society it only too often represents to and against these patients.[17]

The key to Cooper's thinking lies in the critical distinctions which he makes. He decries the nosological approach of conventional psychiatry, which consists of classifying behavioral disorders, such as schizophrenia, as diseases. This error results not only from attachment to the inappropriate medical model, but also because we are not making a requisite distinction between physical science and "a science of personal interaction." In the former, the facts under consideration are inert, and they are perceived in a manner that does not disturb the relationship between the observer and the facts being observed. Testing the valdity of $2 + 2 = 4$ would be an example. In Cooper's words, inert facts "are grasped from

---

[13] *Ibid.*, p. 187.
[14] David Cooper, *Psychiatry and Anti-Psychiatry* (New York: Ballantine Books, 1967).
[15] *Ibid.*, p. x.
[16] *Ibid.*, p. xi.
[17] *Ibid.*

the exterior by an observer who is not disturbed by them and does not disturb them by his process of observation."[18]

On the other hand, "In a science of personal interaction . . . mutual disturbance of the observer and the observed is not only inevitable in every case *but it is this mutual disturbance which gives rise to the primary facts on which theory is based,* and not the disturbed or disturbing personal entities."[19] Cooper's position is that schizophrenia, for example, should be dealt with in the context of verbal and non-verbal communicative behavior, principally that conducted with the significant others in one's life. With young patients (and schizophrenics are classically young), the significant others are those in the family constellation. Consequently, he developed a program which was known as "Villa 21." It featured not only observation of the patient in a group interactional situation in the hospital ward, but also observation of the patient in specific interaction with his family. The intent was to determine the family influences that precipitated specific types of ward behavior. According to Cooper's theory, behavior can be much more readily unraveled in terms of these ontological relationships of interiority than through exterior observation and medical model classification.

In the United States, the preeminent iconoclast is the psychiatrist Thomas S. Szasz. In a succession of books he has thrust the deft rapier at his profession. In an important earlier work, written a year after Cooper's work was begun in England, Szasz condemned the unconstitutional tyranny represented by widespread mental health practices, and suggested that "mental health" is a euphemism for "psychiatric despotism."[20] He is scathing in his comments on the American Psychiatric Association and contemporary psychiatry. He bluntly states that "what organized psychiatry wants now is what it has always wanted: more power, more public funds, and less legal accountability;"[21] and he has particular animosity for psychoanalysis with its "lexicon of loathing."[22] Szasz's displeasure with psychoanalysis mirrors a growing dissatisfaction with the tyrannical domination of American psychiatry by Freudian psychoanalysis. The well-known English psychiatrist, William Sargant, said in an interview that he was "bewildered at the way direction and control of American psychiatry has been taken over since World War Two by psychoanalysis."[23]

---

[18]*Ibid.*, p. 5.

[19]*Ibid.*

[20]Thomas S. Szasz, *Law, Liberty and Psychiatry* (New York: Macmillan, Inc., 1963), p. 240.

[21]Szasz, *Psychiatric Slavery*, p. 72.

[22]Thomas S. Szasz, *The Myth of Psychotherapy* (Garden City, N.Y.: Anchor Press/Doubleday, 1978), p. 155.

[23]Quoted in Martin L. Gross, *The Psychological Society* (New York: Random House, 1978), p. 145.

The deficiencies in psychoanalysis do not have to be exhaustively enumerated to make the point. It is sufficient to say that its claims are beyond empirical validation, it is costly, it is ritualistic, and neutralist. On top of that, "analytic dogma does not permit direct repair of the patient's life."[24] Worse, the psychoanalyst's utter preoccupation with sex approaches the absurd. Gross mentions a case written up in the *Journal of the American Analytical Association* in which "an eight-year-old girl's opening and closing her eyes are compared to her 'anal-vaginal contractions.' "[25] In this frame of reference, it is easy to understand what prompted Dr. Torrey to write *The Death of Psychiatry.*

The critical case against psychiatry has been well displayed in the preceding section of this chapter. The indictment is so trenchant that one might doubt the ability of psychiatry to provide any assistance to the correctional world. In the remainder of this chapter, we will endeavor to ascertain if there *are* benefits or contributions that a beleaguered psychiatry can make to the equally beleaguered correctional treatment specialist.

THE DEFENSE OF PSYCHIATRY

Shifting our focus to probe for the positives in psychiatry, we are at once struck by a compelling fact: Most of the important critics whom we have paraded in the foregoing portion of this chapter are themselves psychiatrists. This certainly suggests that there is a palpable degree of sensitivity and concern within the profession, with a consequent effort to improve the art. Guze, Torrey, Cooper, and Szasz are psychiatrists of distinction. There are many others who do not buy into the distressing aspects of psychiatry which we have discussed above, and who do not misuse the power of their office. Karl Menninger, for example, tirelessly works for the betterment of the socially handicapped, and is a very sober and thoughtful student of the human state of affairs. In the preface to Seymour Halleck's pertinent work, Menninger said that we will have more and more victims "unless and until we replace our ignorance, hate, and fear with an intelligent, scientific revision of our whole wretched system."[26] The system which he refers to is the criminal justice system, but the wider implications of his statement are obvious.

Halleck himself said that an "enlightened correctional system" would use psychiatrists for only two purposes, to help in the diagnosis, treatment

[24]*Ibid.*, p. 155
[25]*Ibid.*, p. 163.
[26]Seymour L. Halleck, *Psychiatry and the Dilemmas of Crime* (Berkeley: University of California Press, 1971), p. xi.

and rehabilitation of offenders, and to help with the control of dangerous offenders.[27] He also makes the important observation that psychiatrists should be absolved from the necessity of testifying as to whether or not an offender knew that his behavior was right or wrong. Like other "expert witnesses," psychiatrists should simply provide the court with all of the psychiatric information available. "The judge or jury could then make up their own minds as to whether the offender possessed evil intent and should be punished. In making such decisions, they would be assisted only by psychiatric fact and opinion and would not be influenced by the philosophical speculations of a single professional discipline."[28]

Some Significant Mitigants

In the face of the groundswell of critical opposition to correctional rehabilitation that became prominent in the nineteen seventies, there are some mitigating factors that are too often lost sight of. Frequently the laws of a given state are archaic or obstructive. Equally often, those who implement the law are inexpert in their application when it comes to disturbed individuals. In Hillsborough, California, in the spring of 1978, a charming and personable young man, who was under psychiatric care for paranoia, shot and killed his prominent attorney father, his mother, and himself. Because the young man was "personable and coherent," he was not perceived as dangerous in the community at large. It was, in fact, his psychiatrist who, warning the police of his professional apprehension, led to the discovery of the multiple killing. The doctor said that the family of the boy was victimized by California's mental health legislation, which "doesn't do anything with people who are dangerous and require hospitalization."[29] And attorneys, who should be instrumental in initiating commitment procedures, are too often disarmed and dissuaded by the charm and personality of many dangerous offender-clients.

In Washington, D.C., in 1976, the privately funded Committee for the Study of Incarceration published its four-year study which concluded that most first offenders should be released after a mere scolding by the judge, but violent criminals should be imprisoned because they deserve to be. But how many of the innocuous "first offenders" are human volcanoes? And how many of the violent criminals pose a continuing threat of dangerousness? The problem is that the normal human tendency to react negatively to violence, and to be beguiled by the innocuous, prejudices thinking in the absence of scientific data. Many of the shortcomings attributed to psychiatry are shortcomings in the knowledge base, which

[27]*Ibid.*, p. 224.
[28]*Ibid.*, p. 225.
[29]Quoted in Los Angeles *Times,* May 21, 1978.

may result from official disinterest in the profession, insufficient funding, and lack of official support. Scapegoating invariably follows.

It is a basic premise of the critics of corrections that rehabilitative treatment of the offender does not work particularly well in prison. Martinson's work and statements have been consistently cited to support this proposition. But as we have stated in Chapter 5, Martinson et al. do not give proper credit for successes *within* the programs which have allegedly failed. Furthermore, with respect to the spectrum of treatment efforts in corrections, "'Treatment' in penal institutions generally consists of little more than variations in the conditions of custody, and probation rarely involves more than cursory supervision."[30] In this regard, it has been wisely observed, "If the quality is this poor, the response should not be to abandon treatment altogether but to improve it."[31]

PSYCHIATRY AND CORRECTIONS

The belief that psychiatry can provide a panacea for criminal deviance is an insupportable presumption. To begin with, most criminals are not suffering from the sort of deep-seated pathology that would be susceptible to, or even require, psychiatric intervention. The constant recidivism rate, in addition, is *de facto* proof of the inefficacy of psychiatry in the *general* resolution of criminal deviance. Criminal problems, for the most part, are problems of defective social interactions, and resocialization rather than depth therapy is the prescriptive order of the day. Then what can the correctional worker obtain from psychiatry, in a heuristic sense?

Despite his admission that psychiatry is "an inexact science," and his surprising support of the medical model, a forensic psychiatrist, with more than a quarter of a century of correctional experience, offered a nuclear answer to the question posed. He said that psychiatric "diagnoses carry with them implications of practical significance."[32] Practical application is the key for the correctionalist. There are other positive considerations:

> Psychiatry can also offer lessons of practical importance which it has learned through long experience. Without any claim to infallibility, psychiatrists have learned the main indicators for potential suicide through bitter experience.

[30]Norval Morris and Gordon Hawkins, "Rehabilitation: Rhetoric and Reality," *Federal Probation*, 34, No. 4 (December 1970), 11.

[31]Lois Shawver and Bruce Sanders, "A Look at Four Critical Premises in Correctional Views," *Crime and Delinquency*, 23, No. 4 (October 1977), 431.

[32]Henry L. Hartman, *Basic Psychiatry for Corrections Workers* (Springfield, Ill.: Charles C Thomas, Publisher, 1978), p. 8.

They can help jail or prison leaders pick out those individuals who demand greater attention in this regard than do most. Similarly, the insights of psychiatry can help to pinpoint for the corrections worker those people who are apt to become violent or to express their feelings in impulsive, aggressive ways.[33]

It has also been pointed out that "in separating out the emotionally disordered offender," psychiatry can be particularly helpful with respect to the crime seemingly without motive, bizarre offenses, atypical behavior in an individual, senselessly repetitive criminal behavior, sex and arson offenses, and crimes by individuals with a prior history of mental illness.[34]

Another advantage that is not always perceived is that because psychiatry makes *individual* diagnoses and prognoses, it tends to encourage differential treatment, which is the treatment ideal. Psychiatry, more properly social psychiatry, can also make a significant contribution to correctional treatment endeavors by providing the correctional practitioner with clinical insights about various forms of behavioral disorders. In addition, there is a wealth of information to be derived from pertinent research which has been conducted in the field of social psychiatry. Some of it can be integrated in correctional programming. A classic example is the concept of the therapeutic community, inaugurated by Dr. Maxwell Jones in England's Belmont Hospital.[35] Theoretically designed for a mental hospital, the principle of the therapeutic community has been adapted to correctional institutions, an example being the California Rehabilitation Center at Norco, an institution for the civil commitment of drug addicts administered by the Department of Corrections.

While most correctionalists function as active members of a helping profession, not a great deal has been said about their motivation. Dr. Hartman dedicated his book "to the members of one of the most unrecognized and underacknowledged disciplines in this country, the professional corrections workers." He was more specific in the body of the text:

Certainly, the size of the paycheck is not an adequate explanation as to why people spend their lives in these positions. Admittedly, there are a few people who enter this field out of a need to exercise power [but] . . . the majority of corrections workers have a basic interest in people. They share a belief that behavior can change or be changed.[36]

[33]*Ibid.*, p. xv.

[34]Charles E. Smith, "Psychiatry in Corrections," p. 287.

[35]Maxwell Jones and others, *The Therapeutic Community* (New York: Basic Books, Inc., 1953). For further insight on the historical development of the therapeutic community, see Harry A. Wilmer, *Social Psychiatry in Action* (Springfield, Ill.: Charles C Thomas, Publisher, 1958).

[36]Hartman, *Basic Psychiatry for Corrections Workers*, p. 5.

For this reason they are normally disposed to enhance their skills by adding to their fund of knowledge of criminal deviance and human behavior. Knowledge is needed about a wide range of human disability, organic and functional. In Chapter 13 we will deal with special problems in correctional treatment. Before concluding this section, however, we will briefly examine a uniquely special challenge in corrections, the borderline mentally retarded offender.

The Mentally Retarded Correctional Client

Despite the advanced state of our knowledge concerning borderline mental retardation, the afflicted individual gives no directly observable indication of the presence of this disability, and the correctional worker is thus obliged to exercise particular understanding and sensitivity. Mental retardation is classified in terms of several levels, ranging from borderline to profound.[37] Because our concern is with the level that is likely to be encountered in a correctional client, although not readily perceived, we will eliminate any discussion of the remaining subordinate levels. They are ordinarily characterized by severe disability, at least those with an IQ of 50 or less. Severe disability would be recognizable, and these individuals would rarely be correctional clients.

The borderline mentally retarded have an IQ in the range of 68–85. The causes of this type of retardation are numerous, but organic factors are rarely to blame. The American Psychiatric Association's *Diagnostic and Statistical Manual of Mental Disorders II* classifies the bulk of the borderline retarded as Psychosocial (Environmental) Deprivation, which is subdivided into *Cultural-Familial Mental Retardation* and *Associated with Environmental Deprivation*. The very terms used to describe these disabilities provide the important clues. The first is attributed to the absence of requisite stimulation for full growth, which would occur, for example, if the parents were mentally retarded. In the latter category, an impoverished environment is held responsible, such as the bleak environment in the coal country of Appalachia, or in some of our ghettoes.

For the practitioner in corrections, the important thing to remember is that the professional has a responsibility to individualize and to understand his clients. Treatment may be a generic art, but it is an art of individualized application. Case material should provide the definitive diagnosis, but in the absence of a definitive diagnosis, the practitioner must be

---

[37]Because Dr. Hartman has given this subject such capable treatment in his text (*supra*), heavy reliance will be placed upon his work in the section which follows. It should be emphasized that there is no research proof that the intelligence level plays any role in criminal behavior. We are dealing here with those individuals who come into the criminal justice system and who happen to be retarded.

sufficiently competent to be able to make a tentative diagnosis of retardation himself. Hartman defines mental retardation as "a term which designates those people whose general intellectual functioning is below that considered to be normal."[38] This type of individual will find it difficult to adjust in general to society, will be slow to learn and thus have difficulties in school, and will lack physical dexterity. Because of their inadequacies and many frustrations, they obviously develop an acute lack of self-esteem. In some instances, the endless frustrations provoke outbursts of criminal behavior.

The professional lessons to be learned are these:

1. The retarded individual should not be treated in a fashion that would reinforce the frustrations and pressures noted above.
2. Since this is a problem whose etiology is usually an environmental one, it should be recognized that great improvement can be anticipated with careful, concerned treatment.
3. Since feelings of self-esteem and self-worth are minimal in the retarded person, the professional worker should try to reinforce a feeling of worth in his retarded client. The individual should never be denigrated, and should always be addressed respectfully.
4. An emphasis should be placed on vocational rather than academic training for obvious reasons. As Dr. Hartman commented, "Perhaps nowhere in the whole field of criminology is rehabilitation to gainful employment as important as it is in dealing with the mentally retarded who are apt to form the dregs of the labor market."[39]
5. Because a mentally retarded individual is more than usually susceptible to suggestion, his associates should be carefully scrutinized.
6. Firm structuring should characterize the type of supervision imposed and uncomplicated language should be the medium of communication.
7. The professional relationship should be developed on the basis of the significant aspects enumerated above.

As Hartman said, as a postscript, "The loyalty to those who are seen as genuinely trying to be of help may be the worker's most potent tool."[40]

Conscious of the fact that so many law enforcement and criminal justice personnel do not have sufficient knowledge to handle the developmentally disabled offender, a relevant program was inaugurated in South Carolina in 1978. The South Carolina Statewide Technical Assis-

[38]Hartman, *Basic Psychiatry for Corrections Workers*, p. 15.
[39]*Ibid.*, p. 20.
[40]*Ibid.*

tance and Training Project (STAT), on the campus of the University of South Carolina, and several state agencies, are collaborating in the development of programs to increase the awareness of the developmentally disabled (which includes the autistic, palsied, and epileptic, as well as the mentally retarded, which represents about 10 percent of the prison population).

The retarded victims of pathogenic environments are truly the offspring of pathos. The pathos is compounded when the individual blunders through the criminal justice labyrinth in what, to him, must indeed be Stygian darkness. It should not be further compounded by the ignorance and incompetence of those charged with his reconstruction.

SYNOPSIS

In recent times, psychiatry has come under withering attack, often by members of the profession, and basically because of its track record for imprecise diagnosis and undue exercise of control. In one dramatic experiment in which a number of subjects, including a psychiatrist, feigned psychotic symptoms to gain admittance to various mental hospitals, it was determined that *sanity* could not be recognized by these hospitals. It is a particular concern that psychiatry appears to be extending its jurisdiction far beyond what is appropriate for the discipline.

Although psychiatry is in a state of ferment, and under attack, it may be a healthy sign that its major critics are members of the profession. The real contribution to corrections that psychiatry can make is perhaps didactic rather than curative. The insight of psychiatry with respect to suicidal predispositions, dangerous behavior, and psychotic and psychopathic symptomatology would be most useful to corrections workers. The goal of individualized treatment in corrections is also advanced by the fact that psychiatrists make individual diagnoses.

This chapter concluded with a definitive look at the often overlooked mentally retarded correctional client and urges knowledge and patience in dealing with him or her.

9 Institutional Treatment

We take on a burden when we put a man behind walls, and that burden is to give him a chance to change. If we deny him that, we deny his status as a human being, and to deny him that is to diminish our own humanity, and plant the deeds of future anguish for ourselves.

Chief Justice Warren E. Burger

Senator William Proxmire became so incensed with what he considered the wasteful expenditure of federal funds on worthless research projects, that he instituted a "golden fleece of the month," to be awarded to the governmental agency subsidizing the most useless piece of research. In February 1978 he gave his award to the Law Enforcement Assistance Administration (LEAA) for spending almost $27,000 "to determine why inmates want to escape from prison." The senator presumed that the answer to that question was self-evident!

It then has to be asked: Is there any possibility of treatment taking place in an environment from which the motivation to escape is so insistent?

THE NATURE OF THE PRISON

In recent years an endless litany has been intoned, proclaiming the many negative attributes of the American prison. The indictment is imposing. In 1972, I received the following communication from an individual still in his thirties, and it speaks eloquently of the "treatment climate" in the Texas prison system in the not so long ago:

> At seventeen, I broke men's hands and cut off their toes so that they could get jobs inside walls, away from the steaming hell of Texas' prison farms, a place to rival the worst devil's island on earth.
>
> A thousand times my eyes were blacked, a dozen times my bones were broken. Once, I was attacked by a man called "the mad dog," because I refused to let him take my cigarettes. This man, a murderer just freed from death row, broke my jaw into seven agonizing pieces!! Later, the guards mocked me, making me sit for two burning hours, holding my shattered jaw in my trembling hands, and laughing at my pain.

It costs between $6,000 and $14,000 per annum to keep a man in prison, the cost varying with the jurisdiction and the resources and staffing utilized. For that investment, we have a prison system that has been racked with violence, and which houses a population approximately 65 percent of whom are recidivists. The deficiencies in that system are regularly paraded in the news media. In 1978, two inmates at the Lucasville

FIGURE 9-1
A modern prison—The Coffield Unit, Texas Department of Corrections
Courtesy, Texas Department of Corrections

penitentiary in Ohio cut off the first joint of their little fingers to protest conditions at that institution. One of the prisoners mailed his fingertip to the State Department. Also in the late seventies, in representative disorders: 300 convicts staged an uprising at the Iowa State Penitentiary; inmates took eleven hostages in a protest against intolerable conditions in Washington, D.C.; a guard was held hostage by armed convicts in Brushy Mountain, Tennessee; and more than a hundred inmates held fourteen hostages in a major riot at New York's Eastern Correctional Facility.

Disturbances in prisons were international in scope during the same period. Riots swept prisons in England, Ireland, France, Italy, Holland, Mexico, and Canada most notably. In Canada, a disturbing report to Parliament revealed that, "In the 42 years between 1932 and 1974 there were a total of 65 major incidents in federal [Canadian] penitentiaries. Yet in two years—1975 and 1976—there was a total of 69 major incidents, including 35 hostage-takings involving 92 victims, one of whom (a prison officer) was killed."[1]

Where progressive penal methods should have been evolving, it has been discontent that has been festering. There is discontent outside the prison walls also.

The Federal Bureau of Prisons, which has grown by 500 percent from 1970 to 1978, provoked heated opposition from numerous sources with its plan to convert the 1980 Olympic facility at Lake Placid, New York, into a federal prison at the conclusion of the Olympics. Among the objections raised by the opposition are that this prison will be but another graphic evidence of the fact that the United States, so much more than any other nation, relies on the prison as an instrument of correction. Moreover, "The Olympic games symbolize the unity of humanity. Prisons are the visible symbol of the failure of unity."[2]

In California, the State Fire Marshal asserted that California's twelve prisons are becoming fire traps. Ironically, part of the blame was placed on the liberal attitude of the correctional system, which allows prisoners to accumulate combustible material in their cells. As the State Marshal's office said, "the things which make for a more home-like atmosphere in today's prisons may very well lead to the prisoner's death by fire."[3] Besides fire, the California system was also plagued by violence. From 1974 through June 30, 1977, there were 740 assaults with weapons, by inmates, in the prison system. In the summer of 1977, prison authorities "reluctantly" announced that prisoners were being racially segregated in San

---

[1]The Sub-Committee on the Penitentiary System in Canada, Standing Committee on Justice and Legal Affairs, *Report to Parliament,* Second Session of the Thirtieth Parliament, 1976–77, p. 5.

[2]Quoted in *Justicia,* October, 1978, p. 1.

[3]Quoted in *The California State Employee,* August 17, 1977, p. 7.

FIGURE 9-2
Attica Prison Memorial
The Walter F. Daly, Jr. Collection

Quentin prison to cool down a "serious situation of racial hostility."[4] On top of that, the chairman of the Joint Legislative Audit Committee said that the California prison system is too costly, and should possibly be turned over to the federal government for management.[5] In a sense, that sets the scene. Over 300,000 prisoners were housed in these turbulent penal facilities, across the land, in early 1979. The first barrier confronting correctional treatment in the prison setting is the prison itself.

[4]Los Angeles, California *Times*, July 14, 1977.
[5]Vacaville, California *Reporter*, March 23, 1977.

FIGURE 9-3
San Quentin Prison

SOME NEGATIVE FACTORS
IN THE PRISON EXPERIENCE

The student should have a pretty fair idea by now of the inimical nature of the prison as it relates to correctional treatment. It will be of some benefit to focus on some of the particularly negative aspects at this point.

Overcrowding

The prisons of the United States are woefully overcrowded. The situation is critical. From 1972 to 1976, for instance, the nation's prison population increased 44 percent. By 1978, there was a shortage of more than 20,000 beds in the prisons of the United States.[6] Compounding the felony, "Forty-two percent of all inmates in federal and state prisons are confined in institutions more than 50 years old, and one-third of all maximum security inmates are in prisons more than 100 years old. . . ."[7]

One reason for the overcrowding is that confinement is being increasingly selected as the sentencing option. The criminal justice philosophy

[6]National Institute of Law Enforcement and Criminal Justice, LEAA, *Over-crowding in Correctional Institutions,* Washington, D.C.: February 1978, p. v.
[7]*LEAA Newsletter,* 6, No. 15, November 1977, p. 6.

has been shifting toward the punishment model, and legislators are more and more inclined to add punitive sanctions to the penal code. Orland calls this *overpunishment,* and comments: "To the legislators, and presumably to many of their constituents, prison is the solution to crime: the more serious the crime, the lengthier the appropriate term of punishment."[8] According to Harvard criminologist, Lloyd E. Ohlin, the net effect of overpunishment "is to produce chaos in the prisons."[9]

Idleness has always been the bane of prison existence. Overcrowding strains program resources, exacerbates discontent, worsens tensions, and delimits the participation of inmates in treatment programming. Excessive sentencing, or overpunishment, necessarily brings about congestion in the prison system. In 1977, federal prisons housed over 30,400 prisoners, which was more than 7,000 above their rated capacity. In fiscal 1979, the Bureau of Prisons budget was $360,400,000, an increase of more than $42 million over the preceding year. Over $35 million of the budget was earmarked for the construction of new prisons and the renovation of old ones.

Overcrowding also typifies most state systems. The ten jurisdictions with the *highest level of prisoners* per 100,000 of the population in 1977, in descending order, were:

District of Columbia

North Carolina

South Carolina

Georgia

Florida

Maryland

Texas

Alaska

Nevada

Oklahoma

Those with the *highest levels of commitments* per 100,000 of the population, again in descending order, were:

District of Columbia

North Carolina

Delaware

[8]Leonard Orland, *Prisons: Houses of Darkness* (New York: The Free Press, 1975), p. 111.
[9]Quoted in the New York *Times,* February 18, 1977.

South Carolina

Georgia

Maryland

Vermont

New Mexico

Florida

Arkansas[10]

Irrespective of the density of population, prisons exist, prisoners inhabit them, and the obligation and the challenge to redirect those inhabitants into more satisfying life styles is inextricably tied into the whole penal process.

Prisonization

Donald Clemmer was one of the noteworthy pioneers in the serious study of the prison society and social system. He coined the term "prisonization" to describe the negative socialization process which he claimed so often takes place in the prison culture. Clemmer selected ten inmate "advisors" in the prison under study, and explained his concept of prisonization to them in detail. (Prisonization is the negative socialization that takes place through imprisonment whereby the prison culture, in all its negative aspects, is internalized.) He then asked them to evaluate their four closest associates after applying the prisonization concept. Of the forty subjects assessed, 11 were considered "completely prisonized," and only 2 were deemed to be minimally prisonized. For the group as a whole, more were considered prisonized to a higher degree than to a lower degree. Clemmer was led to conclude: "From the case-sketches illustrating the various ways in which prisonization occurs and from the judgments of the ten inmate advisors, we have enough knowledge, imperfect and inexact as it is, to suggest that most men in penitentiaries have no chance of being salvaged if they become prisonized."[11]

The negative aspects of the prison milieu have been subsequently well chronicled by writers such as Sykes and Irwin. Sykes points out that the prison "custodians . . . can find little comfort in the conflicts and ambiguities of the free community's directives concerning the proper aims of imprisonment. They must somehow take those demands and these limited means and construct a regime—a social order—to which they hope

---

[10]National Clearinghouse for Criminal Justice Planning and Architecture (University of Illinois at Urbana), *United States Incarceration and Commitment Rates*, June 1977.

[11]Donald Clemmer, *The Prison Community* (New York: Holt, Rinehart and Winston, 1966), p. 313. Note that this study was first published in 1940.

they can make their captors conform."[12] In other words, the requirements of custody and conformity are transcendental and catalytic elements in the social world of the prisoner.

On the other hand, as Irwin points out, "The system is able to exist partly because it actually accommodates the official system."[13] It is, in fact, a smug axiom in the convict world that the prison is run by the inmates. If there is to be order in the prison, it is the convicts who will be responsible for it, and the prison administrator deals out privileges and maintains an informant system to facilitate this order (control). Considering the disproportionate ratio of staff to inmates, a great deal of diplomatic negotiation is necessary with the inmate population to keep the boat from rocking.

In a recent study of an English prison by King and Elliot, in which extensive research was undertaken, three conclusions were drawn by the authors about the "sociology of the prison": (1) "There is no simple way of understanding what makes a prison tick." (2) Prisoners "adapt not just to the fact of imprisonment but also, in varying degrees, to the particular prison they are in." (3) The adaptation (to the prison) problem is not solely an inmate problem. Staff also has difficulty in adjusting to the prison regimen. Indeed there are some remarkable parallels between staff and inmates. For example, both substantially complain about working conditions, and the attitudes of both staff and inmates crystallize around core elements in each group.[14]

Although staff and inmates are captives of the same prison world, they also occupy different worlds. In a study of a prison in Connecticut, Duffee reports that staff and inmates not only had different perceptions of correctional goals, "but also felt that they were living in rather dissimilar social environments."[15] The one obvious dissimilarity between the worlds of the "free man" and the "convict" is that the prison code encourages the inmate to consciously resist assimilation in the culture of the custodians.

The lesson for the correctional practitioner is that he or she must be tuned in to the unique character of the prison in which he or she is employed.

Contemporary research has thrown considerable doubt on the "prisonization" concept advanced by Clemmer, and by so many writers since Clemmer. More recently, sociologists have been disposed to explain the

[12]Gresham M. Sykes, *The Society of Captives* (Princeton, N.J.: Princeton University Press, 1972), p. 39.

[13]John Irwin, *The Felon* (Englewood Cliffs, N.J.: Prentice-Hall, Inc., 1970), p. 62.

[14]Roy D. King and Kenneth W. Elliot, *Albany: Birth of a Prison—End of an Era* (London: Routledge & Kegan Paul, 1977), pp. 332, 333, 262.

[15]David Duffee, *Correctional Policy and Prison Organization* (New York: Sage Publications, Inc., 1975), p. 11.

FIGURE 9-4
The "Big Yard" at Green Haven (New York) Prison
The Walter F. Daly, Jr. Collection

character of the prison inmate system by one or the other of two theories known as the *functional model* and the *importation model*. Simply expressed, the functional model stresses the expedient and learned adaptation of the inmates to the prison society in which they have been implanted; whereas the importation model emphasizes the prior experiences of the individual inmate, as they are brought to bear upon his present circumstances.[16] Neither model, however, is sufficient unto itself to fully explain prison behavior. Research by Akers (a functionalist), has shown that the influential factors (associated with prison leadership) are the criminality of the inmate population, the social factors of age and race, and the type of prison (the first two being importations!). He comments: "Our data suggests that a treatment-oriented institution, which provides a more open, less punitive prison environment, is likely to have leaders among its prisoners who lead democratically and relatively benignly. . . . "[17]

The lingering presumption that imprisonment advances the criminalization of the inmate, and that there is a positive correlation be-

[16]For an interesting comparative study of prisonization, which espouses the functional model, see Ronald L. Akers, Norman S. Hayner, and Werner Gruninger, Prisonization in Five Countries," *Criminology,* 14, No. 4 (February 1977), 527–54.

[17]Ronald L. Akers, "Type of Leadership in Prison: A Structural Approach to Testing the Functional and Importation Models," *The Sociological Quarterly,* 18, No. 3 (Summer 1977), 383.

tween length of servitude and criminalization, has been deflated. Hawkins does a creditable job of recapitulating the research data in this area, and his work is commended to the student for its valuable insights.[18] Hawkins reduces the criticism of the prisonization concept to three basic premises, each of which is fully supported by the research which he reviews: First, several substantive studies have resulted in findings which contradict Clemmer's contention regarding prisonization; specifically, that the length of the sentence is positively correlated with the degree of prisonization. A study which was published after Hawkins' work adds further support. A group of researchers, using powerlessness, meaninglessness, normlessness, and social isolation as indices of alienation, surveyed approximately 300 inmates in a medium security midwestern institution. Questionnaires were administered to small (25 to 35) groups of these inmates. The indices used were "variables drawn from the larger society" rather than from the prison, because their validity had already been established in existing research. The researchers discovered, "in contrast to our a priori expectation," that there was an inverse ratio between length of servitude and alienation in prisoners.[19]

The second of Hawkins' premises is that the prisonization concept is defective because it does not allow for the possible effects of changes on the inmates' behavior as a result of "variations in the organization of the institution."[20] An example would be the therapeutic community, which significantly alters the relationship between staff and inmates. We might also consider those programs in juvenile institutions, such as the Highfields experiment, which de-emphasized the formal authority role of staff, resulting in a different interrelationship with the inmates. It is clear that institutions that are run autocratically and those that are run therapeutically will have differing impact on the inhabitants of the respective institutions.

The third point made by Hawkins is that it is a presumption that inmate behavior is bred of the prison culture or the inmate culture. It is common, in the literature, to speak of the inmate culture, not merely as a vestment which the prisoner must wear while incarcerated, but as the genesis of a particular kind of behavior that is associated with the status of prisoner. Pertinent studies "lend support to the view that pre-institutional behavior patterns are the crucial determinants of behavior inside prison."[21] Sociologists have tended to ignore the predominant influence of "behavior that is deeply rooted in the inmate's past," as Hawkins de-

---

[18]Gordon Hawkins, *The Prison* (Chicago: The University of Chicago Press, 1976).
[19]Arthur G. Neal, Eldon E. Snyder, and Joseph K. Balough, "Changing Alienations as Consequences of Imprisonment," *Criminal Justice Review*, 1, No. 2 (Fall 1976), 93–105.
[20]Hawkins, *The Prison*, p. 65.
[21]*Ibid.*, p. 68.

scribed it,[22] because they have been preoccupied with the "prison society." This predisposition, in turn, can be traced to the influence of the structural-functional school of sociological thinking. Structural-functionalism views behavior as a functional end product of the system with which it is associated. Inmate behavior, in this frame of reference, is produced by the system (prison) and has the function of facilitating adaptation to the prison system.

Prison Atmosphere

It might well be said that treatment in prisons is a difficult matter not so much because of prisonization, or because of an inimical inmate culture, but because the prison itself is, in Keve's words, "a severe depressant of the human spirit."[23] The monotony, regimentation, absence of privacy, depersonalization, boredom, lack of opportunity for creativity, official disinterest, staff abuse, and restriction of personal freedom form the conspiracy that depresses the human spirit. But innovative and concerned treatment efforts can provide some respite, because the human imagination, whether of convict or free man, permits creative interaction as well as flight and fantasy, even in the prison.

Violence

A phenomenon that is as old as the prison, but which has gained an unenviable prominence in recent years, is the specter of violence and violent uprisings in the prison. It is the counterpoint to harmony and, as such, a barrier to treatment. Understanding human aggression, particularly as it characterizes the caged human, is prerequisite to controlling it. It is not too well understood, obviously. By violence we mean not only the dramatic uprisings such as occurred at Attica, Soledad, and elsewhere, but also the sexual violence, the gang violence, the aggressive altercations which are a feature of prison existence, and the violence by the system against the captive inmate population. In the early history of the prison, brutalization of the inmate was a *modus vivendi,* but one would think that it would have abated in the face of unfolding knowledge and legal prohibition. Considerable room for improvement remains, as the following events will indicate.

In 1970, United States District Court Judge Herbert W. Christenberry heard a class action suit (*Hamilton* v. *Schiro*) filed on behalf of the inmates of the Orleans (Louisiana) Parish Prison seeking injunctive relief

---

[22]*Ibid.,* p. 69.
[23]Paul W. Keve, *Prison Life and Human Worth* (Minneapolis: The University of Minnesota Press, 1974), p. 16.

from allegedly unconstitutional conditions in that prison. Judge Christenberry ruled in favor of the inmates, finding that "the conditions of . . . confinement in Orleans Parish Prison so shock the conscience as a matter of elemental decency and are so much more cruel than is necessary to achieve a legitimate penal aim that such confinement constitutes cruel and unusual punishment in violation of the Eighth and Fourteenth Amendments of the United States Constitution. . . . "[24]

On January 13, 1976, the U.S. District Court Judge Frank M. Johnson issued the first court order in the history of American corrections imposing specific guidelines for *constitutional* incarceration, in the penal system of Alabama. The previous August, the judge had issued an emergency order closing the Alabama prisons to new admissions, other than parole violators and escapees. This followed a finding that conditions in those prisons were "barbaric and inhumane." Two of Alabama's four major institutions were found to be wholly unfit for human habitation.

On December 29, 1976, the Justice Department filed suits against both the State of Illinois and Cook County officials, alleging unconstitutional conditions in both the state prisons and in the county jail. In the same year, in Philadelphia, a Court of Commons Pleas panel of three judges ordered improvements in health and living conditions in the correctional institutions in Philadelphia County.

In 1977, in a class action suit filed on behalf of prisoners in Rhode Island's adult correctional institutions (and on behalf of pre-trial detainees, as well), a federal court issued a sweeping mandate requiring major improvements in the state's prisons. The court found conditions to be "barbaric" and "shocking," both as to physical conditions and as to the violence which was rampant in the correctional institutions.

In 1978, for the first time in correctional history, a *state* court ruled that an entire state penal system was operating unconstitutionally. Hearing a class action suit filed on behalf of about 7,000 state prisoners, Chancery Court Judge Ben H. Cantrell of Davidson County issued an indictment of the Tennessee penal system, including the charge that it was permeated with violence and the constant fear of assault.

Also in 1978, the United States Supreme Court affirmed a district court's judgment prohibiting the California system from continuing its practice of transferring inmates from the general population into maximum security housing units without certain procedural safeguards. And a federal court ordered the closing of two Mississippi prison units because of "many unconstitutional violations."

[24]Cited in Dudley P. Spiller, Jr., "A Case Study of *Hamilton* v. *Schiro*," in M. Kay Harris and Dudley P. Spiller, Jr., *After Decision: Implementation of Judicial Decrees in Correctional Settings* (Washington, D.C.: U.S. Government Printing Office, 1977), p. 251.

It is plain that treatment overtures will be less than persuasive in a correctional system that is less than constitutional.

Prison Gangs

A relatively modern phenomenon has been the rapid growth of the prison gang—not the fraternal association that would be indigenous to a prison, but the violent, predatory, crime-oriented gang. In recent years, considerable attention has been focused on the "Mexican Mafia" and similar gangs in the California prison system. A popular magazine referred to the Mexican Mafia as "America's Newest Crime Syndicate," and aptly described it as "a sinister new organized-crime syndicate spreading like a cancer throughout California."[25] Ironically, this gang was first established by inmates in a prison cell in the California system in 1957. It is rumored that the narcotics trade in California is controlled by the Mexican Mafia, *from inside the prison system.* Other major gangs in the California prison system include *La Neustra Familia,* the Aryan Brotherhood, and the Black Guerilla Family. According to a report by the California State Board of Corrections, "150 men and women have died in prisons and the streets of California in the three years beginning January 1, 1975, as the result of prison gang activity."[26]

It is interesting to note that during the English prison disorders in the early seventies, notably at the Albany Prison on the Isle of Wight, newspapers asserted that Mafia gangs were directing the disorders, despite disclaimers from prison officials. The prison gang phenomenon is not by any means restricted to California. Since 1969, four street gangs, three black and one Latin, have dominated Stateville prison in Illinois. The Black P Stone Nation (formerly the Blackstone Rangers), The Devil's Disciples, the Conservative Vice Lords and the Latin Kings have "turfs" in the slum districts of Chicago and "because of their great size, the relatively high age of their leaders, and their imperialistic annexation of smaller gangs they might aptly be termed 'supergangs.' "[27] When gang members went to prison, they were supported from the streets and maintained cohesion and leadership in the prison setting. According to Jacobs, it was reliably estimated that, by 1972, "at least 50 percent of the inmate population was affiliated with one of the four gangs."[28]

[25]Nathan M. Adams, "America's Newest Crime Syndicate—the 'Mexican Mafia,' " *The Reader's Digest* (November 1977), pp. 97–102.

[26]State of California, Board of Corrections, *Prison Gangs in the Community*, Sacramento, June 14, 1978, p. 5.

[27]James B. Jacobs, *Stateville* (Chicago: The University of Chicago Press, 1977), p. 139.

[28]*Ibid.*, p. 146.

FIGURE 9-5

Contraband weapons found in a shakedown of a California prison in 1976

Because of the caliber of the prison population, a degree of violence is not considered atypical in the prison system. Violence is still largely destructive behavior, however, and counterproductive of rehabilitation. Researchers continue to probe the aggressive component in man, and a considerable amount of literature is accumulating so that some tentative propositions can be made.

Recent research reveals "increasing evidence that crowding is related to psychological stress and its concomitant physical illness."[29] While a direct causal connection from crowding to violence has not been clearly drawn, ethnologists have done sufficient research to indicate that aggressive behavior is associated with the invasion of one's territory or space.

[29]Arthur Veno and Marilyn J. Davidson, "Prison Violence: Some Different Perspectives," *International Journal of Criminology and Penology,* 5, No. 4 (November 1977), 401.

Territoriality is an operative principle in the animal kingdom, where herds stake out a territory by exuding a distinctive scent, and social psychologists have established that social distance is an operative principle in human interaction. Each person perceives himself or herself as occupying a certain spatial territory, and resists its invasion at a certain point. It is suggested that the basis for a lot of aggression in the prison, and subsequent violence, relates to space infringements, and that is something that an enlightened administrator *can* do something about. Not all prison violence can be traced to issues of territoriality, of course, but anything that would reduce the precipitants of violence in the prison setting should be a priority objective.

THE TOTAL INSTITUTION

Erving Goffman is noted for his concept of the "total institution." He includes prisons in this concept, and says of these institutions that "Their encompassing or total character is symbolized by the barrier to social intercourse with the outside. . . . "[30] The importance of the open prison, which we discussed earlier, is that it undermines the barrier to social intercourse, which is characteristic of the total institution. It is axiomatic that the hope of reconstruction is positively related to the degree to which social intercourse is amplified in any institutional program. The importance of opening this social tributary was stressed in the comment of an observer at the prison when he said, "The absence of contact can create a psychological vacuum; its presence can be a good mood modulator or safety valve."[31]

Institutional treatment will obviously be influenced by the atmosphere and the philosophic climate in the given prison. The utterly closed institution, with its enforced separation from the community, offers a stagnant environment in which to attempt treatment. The prisons upon which judicial censure have descended, which we have cited earlier, degrade human beings and make a mockery of correctional treatment.

In gestalt psychology, the whole is considered more than the sum of its parts. Similarly, the prison is more than a mere aggregation of staff, inmates, and physical plant. While a particular prison shares a general character with other prisons, each prison is a world unto itself and has its own unique identity, resulting from its own, singular gestalt. As Erving Goffman also said, "Every institution captures something of the time and interest of its members and provides something of a world for them; in

[30]Erving Goffman, *Asylums* (New York: Anchor Books, 1961), p. 4.
[31]Hans Toch, *Living in Prison* (New York: The Free Press, 1977), p. 52.

FIGURE 9-6
Sing Sing Prison

brief, every institution has encompassing tendencies."[32] Institutional treatment must be attempted in this frame of reference.

The correctional practitioner must recognize this world. He must in a manner of speaking, penetrate its organizational structure, its sociology, and its contraculture, if he is to be effective. The fact that so many authorities deny the possibility of rehabilitation in the prison setting only enhances the challenge. Thomas Murton cites the cultural attributes of the prison to support his argument that rehabilitation cannot take place in prison, "an environment of fear, aggression, totalitarianism, and exploitation."[33] The convict–author, Lou Torok, said with some feeling, "I am convinced that prisons as they are run today do far more harm than good. Most convicts leave prison in worse shape than when they went in. It is wishful thinking to believe that the system as it operates today can correct, retrain or reform criminals in any meaningful way."[34] Ramsey Clark called prisons "warehouses of human degradation."[35]

When the long-awaited report of The Committee for the Study of Incarceration was finally released, and it turned out to be a discussion of how the prison was to be used as an instrument to provide some offenders with "their deserts," the venerable Karl Menninger was admittedly stunned. Menninger acidly commented, in attacking this report:

[32]Goffman, *Asylums,* p. 4.
[33]Thomas Murton, *The Dilemma of Prison Reform* (New York: Holt, Rinehart and Winston, 1976), p. 60.
[34]Lou Torok, *Straight Talk From Prison* (New York: Human Sciences Press, 1974), p. 88.
[35]Ramsey Clark, *Crime in America* (New York: Pocket Books, 1971), p. 193.

FIGURE 9-7

To refer to jail and prison life as "Unpleasant," . . . is like referring to the Nazi torture of the Jews as "unkind" . . . [I]ncarceration . . . is a particularly horrible, painful, dehumanizing, character-destroying kind of confinement. I don't think any victim ever fully recovers from the experience.[36]

The cynical viewpoint is epitomized in the words of a Canadian law professor:

[36]Karl Menninger, "Doing True Justice," *America*, 137, No. 1 (July 2–9, 1977).

It is clear that the crime industry [the criminal justice system] cannot continue to promise delivery with respect to treatment, prevention and deterrence. It must cut back its operation and continue to offer only what it can deliver: punishment that is at once humane, fair and restrained.[37]

While it is hoped that correctional punishment will, indeed, be "humane, fair and restrained," the cynicism of the above views, if carried to the extreme, would result in an abandonment of treatment endeavors in the institutional setting. The prison well deserves every criticism made, but no barrier should be insurmountable in the effort to reach and reso-cialize the imprisoned offender. Treatment may be extremely difficult in a prison, but to fail to try is to invite despair, a sentiment that has too long been endemic to the American prison.

While the prison is an affront to rational sensibilities, it is not likely to disappear from the "crime industry" in the forseeable future. Consequently, there are only two options that can be considered: The prison can be seen as a purely punitive instrument for the unmitigated punishment and restraint of offenders; or it can be viewed as a facility for the imposition of fair and humane punishment, with human redemption the end objective, and treatment an integral part of that effort.

The total institution can be mitigated to some degree by a reasonable philosophy, and appropriate programming, even when the incarcerated are "high risks." Dr. Sturup, superintendent of the famous Herstedvester Detention Center in Albertslund, Denmark, has said:

> . . . packing convicts together into degrading institutions is responsible for the enormous difficulties of accepting—and being accepted back into—society. . . . Hence it facilitates recidivism.
>
> In any case, we at Herstedvester have demonstrated that humanization of the institutional setting does not result in greater risks of recidivism. On the contrary, it possibly gives a better prognosis in the long perspective for those prisoners with the heaviest odds against them.[38]

The program at Herstedvester, which is for the more serious offender, is based on the belief that the most important thing for the offender is to regain his self-respect. Change in his behavior is based on what he believes others will expect of him. Inner controls are stressed, and the inmate is not permitted to delegate personal responsibility. The inmate is taught to make better use of his personal assets, and to be able to develop the type of social support that will make for continuity in social living. When staff

---

[37]Keith B. Jobson, "Dismantling the System," *Canadian Journal of Criminology and Corrections,* 19, No. 3 (July 1977), 260.

[38]Georg K. Sturup, "Indeterminacy as Individualization," *San Diego Law Review,* 14, No. 5 (July 1977), 1057.

anticipates a serious breach in behavior, they are obliged to intervene at once and to thoroughly discuss, with the inmate(s), the dynamics preceding the confrontation. As Dr. Sturup said, "Only an intellectual and unemotional understanding of what happens in actual situations makes it possible for him to face the results of his own behavior."[39] Group living necessarily curtails individual freedoms, and these necessary limitations on freedom are put in focus in the group encounters, which the inmate is obliged to attend. Reform in the prison is imperative. Reform is obviously represented in the program at Herstedvester.

PRISON REFORM

The long bill of particulars against the prison has been echoed incessantly of late. It need not be repeated here, beyond what we have already said. There is a pressing need for reform. The main impediment to reform is the inertia that has been created by a blind allegiance to a rather rigid penal tradition. Prisons *can* be transformed architecturally, for one thing, to enhance the treatment possibility, without sacrificing security. Fortunately, some momentous efforts are being initiated in this regard.

Canningvale Maximum Security Prison in Western Australia serves as a good example. Those responsible for planning this new prison in 1972 "concentrated on *jointly* optimizing between the goals of security and retention of human responsiveness in the prisoners. Also, they recognized the effects on staff of the task of confining inmates, and specified that they should be able to maintain control but that staff roles should be designed so as to increase the positive satisfactions which could be obtained from their working lives."[40] Shared responsibility is the key to inmate activity. Prisoners live in wings containing eight or ten people whose work and leisure time activities are jointly planned in a task-oriented manner. "The design attempts to increase the opportunities for inmates to develop greater interest in life within the prison itself through the sharing of responsibility for domestic work and leisure objectives."[41]

The group is the core unit. Interpersonal skills are nurtured purposely, as a part of the broad program objectives, through the small groups. Regular contact with the outside world, in some manner, is an obligation imposed on the inmate. Specifically, he is obliged to keep up with changes in that world. That can be accomplished in conversations

---

[39]*Ibid.*, p. 1049.
[40]J. E. Thomas and T. A. Williams, "Change and Conflict in the Evolution of Prison Systems: Old Dilemmas, Emergent Problems and Future Strategies," *International Journal of Criminology and Penology*, 5, No. 4 (November 1977), 358.
[41]*Ibid.*

with staff, recourse to the communication media, or contact with people in the community. While staff is trained for a security role, it is accomplished in an innovative way. The staff must deal with "social islands;" that is, small numbers of individuals in structured groups in specific wings of the prison. Staff, therefore, has much better knowledge of every member of the wing, and can control through knowledge and interaction, rather than with repression. "By allowing small groups of inmates greater autonomy within defined areas, the intention is both to reduce inmate deprivations and make the officer a less central figure of coercion in the inmate's world."[42]

The staff is also organized on a team basis. The "staff team" consists of a group of officers, on the same watch, who are jointly responsible for the decision making in the blocks to which they are assigned. The intent of this team operation is to counteract the negatives of the traditional "individual-based prison hierarchy" which inhibits positive interactions with the inmates. An interesting concept, known as "undermanning," is also applied at Canningvale Prison. This means that a staff is never maintained at a level of excess, the idea being that a busy staff ("undermanned") is less vulnerable to boredom and frictional role relationships with the inmates.

In their classic work on punishment Rusche and Kirchheimer said that "No reform program has been willing to abandon the principle that the living standard of the prisoner must be depressed in order to retain the deterrent effects of punishment."[43] Canningvale has exploded this supposition, and proven demonstrably that alternative strategies are possible and desirable in the modern prison, and that the inimical features of prison life can be neutralized in the interest of rational treatment.

The Open Prison

The open prison concept, that is, the idea of a prison without bars, constitutes an innovative reform of relatively recent origin. While Witzwil Prison in Switzerland, established in 1891, was "almost certainly" the first open prison (although it had secure sections), the idea of the open prison did not seriously develop until the 1930s in the United Kingdom, and the 1940s in the United States.[44] The English are fond of quoting Sir Alexan-

---

[42] *Ibid.*, p. 359.

[43] Georg Rusche and Otto Kirchheimer, *Punishment and Social Structure* (New York: Russell & Russell, 1939; reissued 1968), p. 159.

[44] Howard Jones, Paul Cornes and Richard Stockford, *Open Prisons* (London: Routledge & Kegan Paul, 1977), p. 5. For one version that traces the first attempt to develop an open institution to the Borstal system in 1930, see: Sean McConville, (ed.), *The Use of Imprisonment: Essays in the Changing State of English Penal Policy* (London: Routledge & Kegan Paul, 1975), especially p. 58.

der Patterson, a member of the English Prison Commission from 1922 to 1947, for the philosophic rationale for the open prison: "You cannot train a man for freedom under conditions of captivity." Sir Alexander was instrumental in the establishment of the first open prison in Britain, New Hall Camp, a satellite of Wakefield Prison in Yorkshire, England. "Here there were no walls, and indeed not even a boundary fence—the men sleeping in wooden huts and the bounds designated if at all, by whitewash marks on the trees."[45]

Minimum security prison camps may be considered open prisons within the meaning of the definition used. Such well-known minimum security American prisons as the California Institution for Men and the federal institution, Seagoville, Texas, may be similarly considered. *Most* of the institutional facilities in the Scandinavian correctional systems are open prisons. The major obstruction to an extension of the open prison concept in the United States is the intractable tradition that prisoners *must* be constrained, that somehow criminal behavior must be punished by custodial immobilization and concrete and steel housing. Secure custody will be necessary for some inmates, of course, but the belief that *all* prisoners must be kept in a condition of super-security is an idea that is not supported by reason, and is confounded by the practice in other lands.

The Scandinavian Experience

In examining the penal practices in other nations, it must be kept in mind that unique cultural differences and national temperament shape the evolution of criminal justice programs and institutions. Still, much can be learned from the intercultural perspective. The Swedish penal system is usually thought of as an enlightened, model system. For almost the entire first half of this century, the socialist Social Democrat Party ruled Sweden,[46] and the penal philosophy of that nation reflects the socialist influence of that dominant political party.

The penal philosophy of Sweden can be gleaned from a statement made by Claes Amilon, Deputy Director-General of the Swedish National Correctional Administration: "A Society without slums cannot let its prisoners live under slum conditions; a society which has accepted collective responsibility for the physical and economic welfare of its citizens cannot abuse the rights even of those who transgress its rules. . . . "[47]

A murderer in Sweden can anticipate being released from confinement after serving five years, but a tax dodger (presumably because he

[45] *Ibid.*
[46] The Social Democrat Party was finally defeated in the 1975 election, which could presage significant correctional changes.
[47] Quoted in *Corrections Magazine*, 3, No. 2 (June 1977), 11.

threatens the collectivity) faces a mandatory six months in jail, and could be imprisoned for up to six years. In addition, he would have to pay his back taxes with interest added. The vast majority of offenders, however, serve less than four months.

Sweden places most of its committed offenders in small, minimum security type institutions, where the inmate has a great deal of freedom. Only 15 percent of Sweden's offenders are sent to prison. Conjugal visitation and liberal furloughs to the community are standard Swedish practices, and all inmates are employed while imprisoned, and adequately paid for their labor (.60 to $1.00 per hour). Following a reform of the Penal Code in 1966, which put the emphasis on prison alternatives, the prison population of Sweden drastically declined. Sweden has a rate of imprisonment of 39.7 per 100,000 of the population, compared to the 200 rate of the United States.[48]

In Denmark, the correctional system rivals that of Sweden for idyllic conditions. Sentences are precisely fixed, so that the anguish of the indeterminate sentence is obviated, and most sentences are for less than one year but, as in Sweden, the actual time served in the majority of cases is less than four months. The prisons are small, none holding more than 200 inmates, and most holding about half that number. The staffing pattern in the prison system is rich, and professionals give maximal attention to the needs of the imprisoned. Inmates who fall in love in the co-educational prison at Ringe are permitted to live together in the prison. Open prisons dominate the Danish system, and at these institutions the prisoners have rights and privileges that would be considered remarkable in the United States. Frequent furloughs home, for example, are considered a right in the Danish correctional system, and not an earned privilege as in the United States.[49]

The Netherlands

The foreign system that has attracted the greatest interest among would-be American prison reformers has been that of Holland. Holland has the lowest incarceration rate in the Western world; at 24 per 100,000 of the population it is substantially lower than even that of Sweden. In order to probe the reasons for the low incarceration rate, and to simultaneously determine what Dutch practices could enhance the American effort, a group of people concerned with prison reform made an on-site study of

[48]Michael S. Serrill, "Profile/Sweden," *Corrections Magazine*, 3, No. 2 (June 1977), 14. According to the National Council on Crime and Delinquency, the American commitment rate is actually 250 per 100,000 of the population.

[49]For a comprehensive overview of the Danish system, see: Michael S. Serrill, "Profile/ Denmark," *Corrections Magazine*, 3, No. 1 (March 1977), 23–43.

the Dutch system through the medium of a seminar. The two-week seminar was administered by a number of organizations, including the American Foundation Institute of Corrections. The participants included "prison reformers and abolitionists, ex-prisoners, representatives of the religious community, justice system administrators, a White House staff member, minority group members, and representatives of non-profit action and service agencies."[50] From such a diversity, a balanced examination was anticipated.

The major characteristics of the Dutch criminal justice system are these:

1. Sentences are inordinately short, the average being about 35 days.
2. There is a consensus among criminal justice officials that imprisonment does not control crime.
3. Officials in the criminal justice system have considerable discretion.
4. The system relies extensively on fines and short sentences.
5. There is a limited bed capacity in the Dutch prisons.

The investigating group also drew attention to the influence of the great Dutch tradition of tolerance for individual liberty, the highly developed level of social services in the Netherlands, and the relatively balanced distribution of wealth in the nation. It was also signally impressed "by one often repeated view: *Prisons are damaging institutions and should not be heavily relied upon.*"[51] (Italics in the original). One Netherlands official was quoted as saying, "It is almost hypocritical to think a person in prison can be made better . . . so we try to limit the damage."[52]

Instead of the heavy reliance that Americans place on the criminal justice system, the Dutch invoke the system only when all others have failed. The Dutch also feel that social problems require collective community action to resolve, and the rugged individualism that is so characteristically American is not evident in the Netherlands. Furthermore, while the American system is punctuated with violence, there is a low incidence of violence and a low tolerance for it in the Dutch culture. "There is no death penalty, and in most prisons there are virtually no reported incidences of physical violence. By resolving disputes at the earliest possible time and with minimal official intervention, the criminal justice system itself plays a role in curtailing violence."[53]

[50] *How Holland Supports Its Low Incarceration Rate: The Lessons for Us,* Netherlands Criminal Justice Investigative Seminar, April 13–28, 1978 (Philadelphia: American Foundation, mimeographed).
[51] *Ibid.,* p. 6.
[52] *Ibid.*
[53] *Ibid.,* p. 5.

In the Netherlands, officials, at practically every point in the system, are empowered to exercise discretion in minimizing the individual's involvement in the system. Dutch police, for example, can impose fines at the scene of a crime, or act as arbiter between disputants. Less than half of the cases referred by the prosecutor are sentenced, and more than half of those sentenced are diverted. The limited number of bed spaces available in the prisons is limited by conscious design. The thinking is that buliding more beds merely assures more prison occupants. If no bed is available, the offender is put on a waiting list. If he waits long enough, he has an excellent prospect for amnesty.

The on-site investigators did not give blanket endorsement to the Dutch system; they were more concerned with identifying those practices that might have utility in American criminal justice agencies. They were also careful to note that "it would be a mistake to expect that simple importation of Dutch practices would produce similar results" in the United States. However, "a cross-cultural exchange helps us to see what we are accustomed to do is not sacrosanct—that there are other posible "norms." Such an exchange stimulates creative thinking as to how one country can learn from another's experience."[54]

The following are the elements which the visitors to Holland felt could be integrated in the American system of criminal justice:

1. Shorter sentences.
2. The "subsidiary principle," namely that prison should only be used as a last resort, and that the criminal justice system should do as little harm as possible.
3. Reduced incarceration through extensive use of alternatives such as fines and suspended sentences.

REHABILITATION PROBLEMS IN THE U.S.

It is interesting to note that in the Scandinavian and Dutch systems rehabilitation has long been considered a right of the offender, whereas, in the United States this right has not yet been universally conceded. Generally, the thinking is that the right of an inmate to rehabilitation will evolve from the recently developing judicial disposition to hold that mental patients have a constitutional right to treatment. On July 1, 1977, the U.S. District Court of New Hampshire held that imprisoned inmates do have the "right to rehabilitation" (*Laaman* v. *Helgemue*), thus suggesting that the transition is underway. Specifically, the court held that prison condi-

[54]*Ibid.,* p. 1.

tions could not threaten the sanity or mental well-being of inmates or countermilitate against the inmates' efforts to rehabilitate themselves. Further, every inmate has to be given the opportunity "to work at a useful job" and to learn marketable skills. Where these rights do not exist, the court held, there is a violation of the Eighth Amendment to the Constitution, which prohibits cruel and unusual punishment.

While the correctional treatment professional would instinctively support the idea that the inmate has a right to rehabilitation, an interesting caveat was made by a member of the legal profession:

> We must ask whether, in pursuing the goal of helping people, we may force conformity with average middle-class, middle-American ideals upon all those who come within the grasp of the law. In striving to achieve the right to rehabilitation, the attorney in correctional law must vehemently and totally deny the concept of a duty on the part of the inmate to be rehabilitated.[55]

The student is called upon to recognize the subtle distinction between "right" and "duty" in the resolution of this seeming dilemma. A right may impose a collateral duty, but a right exists independent of a duty, inhering in the very nature of things (such as the right to procreate or parent), or decreed by constitutional fiat (such as the right of free assembly).

The Female Offender

The female offender suffers some unique penalties because of her presence in the criminal justice system. First of all, she represents only about 5 percent of all institutionalized offenders, and this naturally results in limited attention. The estimate is that approximately 16,000 women are in penal custody on any given day, with 8,000 in jails, 7,000 in state prisons, and the remaining 1,000 in the federal prison system.[56] Correctional budgets are not characterized by liberality, and when it comes to that portion allocated for the female in the system, they are penurious. This, in turn, means that programming is insufficiently supported. A 1973 survey by the *Yale Law Review* revealed that an average of 2.7 vocational training programs were offered in women's prisons, whereas there was an average of 10 in male prisons.[57]

One distaff commentator said that the female prisoner derives "little or no advantage from her term of incarceration because few if any meaningful efforts are made to prepare her with alternatives, legal options

---

[55]Richard Singer, "The Coming Right to Rehabilitation," in Michele G. Hermann and Marilyn G. Haft (eds.), *Prisoners' Rights Sourcebook* (New York: Clark Boardman Company, Ltd., 1973), p. 196.
[56]*OAR-NEWS*, 2, No. 2, January 1978, p. 5.
[57]*Ibid.*

FIGURE 9-8
Female prisoners in Georgia

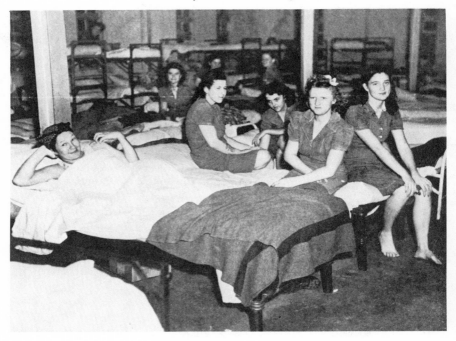

when released."[58] The problem was put most succinctly by the National Advisory Commission:

> Women's institutions, owing to their relatively small population and lack of influence, have been considered an undifferentiated part of the general institutional system and therefore have been subjected to male-oriented facilities and programming. Special requirements of the female offender have been totally ignored. Male domination often extends to administration of the institution.[59]

The most widespread problem for female offenders is coping with the separation from their children, which is enforced in the American correctional system. It is estimated that from 60 to 80 percent of incarcerated women have dependent children.[60] Several important studies have

[58]Laura Crites, *The Female Offender* (Lexington, Mass.: D.C. Heath and Company, 1976), p. 91.

[59]National Advisory Commission on Criminal Justice Standards and Goals, *Task Force Report: Corrections* (Washington, D.C.: U.S. Government Printing Office, 1973), p. 379.

[60]"Planning For the Female Offender," in Annette M. Brodsky (ed.), *The Female Offender* (Beverly Hills: Sage Publications, 1975), p. 102.

pointed out that it is a particularly traumatic experience for the female offender to be separated from her child.[61] The male offender does not experience a similar distress.

Cultural factors have been largely responsible for the neglect of the female offender. For one thing, the prisons have been, heretofore, largely dominated by the male, and the bulk of the funds and energies of the criminal justice system have gone to the male offender. The neglect of the female offender was epitomized in the numerous task force reports completed by the President's Commission on Law Enforcement and Administration of Justice, which were published in 1967. Not one contained a single paragraph on the female in the criminal justice system!

The women's movement, and the increasing involvement of the female in criminal activity are responsible for an accelerated interest in the female offender. It is to be anticipated that this increased attention will also mean increased understanding and extended programming. Some important developments are already underway. In Minnesota, for example, an advisory task force has been set up on the Future of Women Offenders, which will study the status and needs of the female in the correctional system.

Emotional Repression

Whether male or female, an unhealthy part of incarceration is the artificial repression of the emotional needs of the offenders. Not only is it unfortunate that inmates cannot legitimately express their emotional needs, it is equally unfortuante that a large percentage of institutional staff, including the treatment cadre, are ignorant of the defense mechanisms employed by the prisoners to compensate for their anxious frustrations. Harold F. Uehling, after a career of thirty-seven years as a correctional psychologist in a penal setting, poignantly depolored the "colossal tragedy" of the "unexpressed emotional needs" of the inmate population in the *treatment-oriented* prison in which he worked.[62]

If the program in that prison was, indeed, "treatment-oriented," how could there possibly be such a colossal tragedy? According to Uehling, it is because there is a distressing lack of understanding about the self-punishing incentives which inmates employ to relieve their anxieties.[63] Prison treatment people tend to standardize their wares, and dispense them according to a particular psychotherapeutic bias. The medical

[61]See expecially Rose Giallombardo, *Society of Women: A Study of a Women's Prison* (New York: John Wiley & Sons, Inc., 1966); and David A. Ward and Gene G. Kassebaum, *Women's Prison* (Chicago: Aldine Publishing Company, 1965).
[62]Harold F. Uehling, *Correction of a Correctional Psychologist in Treatment of the Criminal Offender* (Springfield, Ill.: Charles C Thomas, Publisher, 1973), p. vii.
[63]*Ibid.*, p. 179.

model has been too often followed in the effort to get the "sick" prisoner "well." The ironic part of it is that when an individual acts out emotionally in the prison, the end result is usually punitive discipline rather than prescriptive treatment.

Consider the relatively common event in which an inmate, who is about to be paroled, gets involved in some disciplinary action and has his parole date rescinded. What are the precipitating dynamics behind such seemingly irrational behavior? How often does staff relate the dynamics to the inmate's poor self-image and fears associated with the assumption of responsibility for one's behavior in the community? Treatment would be more meaningful and more productive if it explored the "unexpressed emotional needs" of the inmate in the circumstances described, with the emphasis on the unique manner in which each individual experientially responds to the factors confronting him in a given situation. The question, in brief, comes down to this: Assume that an inmate experiences mounting anxiety as the time approaches for him to assume responsibility for his own behavior in the "free world." Assume, further, that his past history reflects considerable impoverishment, both physical and emotional. Increasingly disturbed by his mounting anxiety, he acts out to relieve his inner tension, let's say by verbally assaulting an officer in the prison, or by physically engaging a fellow inmate in fisticuffs. What course of action would wisdom dictate in this situation, in a correctional treatment frame of reference? What would you do if you had the authority to act? Why?

TREATMENT-ORIENTED PRISON PROGRAMMING

Institutional treatment, in the broadest context, includes educational, vocational, recreational, spiritual, social, and psychological assistance. It has practical as well as therapeutic dimensions, and it involves a lot more than merely being told that you have an Oedipus complex. One of the major demands made by the rioting prisoners during the bloody uprising at Attica was for a "realistic rehabilitation program." The broad definition of treatment involves any and all restorative efforts, with constructive reintegration of the offender in his community as the end objective. As the American Correctional Association said, in trying to avoid the pitfalls encountered in defining treatment, "it might be better to say simply that treatment is a *specific systematic effort directed toward correcting the offender.*"[64] (Italics in the original).

[64]Charles F. Campbell, "Principles and Prerequisites for Treatment of Committed Offenders," in Leonard J. Hippchen (ed.), *Correctional Classification and Treatment,* compiled by the American Correctional Association (Cincinnati: The W. H. Anderson Company, 1975), p. 117.

The essence of the broad definition is also implicit in Dr. Sturup's definition: "The term *treatment* covers the different acts and attitudes which are used in attempts to help patients—the treated—to arrive at a more realistic solution to their basic problems of accepting themselves and relating to others."[65] The essence of the definition remains when the medical model terminology is removed, and when "inmate" is substituted for "patient." This broad definition of treatment is, of course, an arbitrary one. There are those who would consider such activities as vocational and educational training as adjuncts to therapy, restricting "treatment" to "explicit procedures deliberately instituted to alter those conditions believed to be responsible for unlawful behavior."[66] One of the principal drawbacks in the corrections–medical model alliance is the failure to realize that rehabilitation is not always a clinical proposition. Providing an individual with survival skills, which is not a clinical matter, can also enhance the reintegration process and reduce unlawful behavior.

There is another key ingredient in the treatment formula: "The criminal's own attitude and active participation in the process are essential if a satisfactory maturation of his personality shall result in an experienced independence."[67] This principle is in conformity with the reintegrationist model which we examined in Chapter 5. The reintegrationist model sees the correctional or treatment effort as a joint endeavor, bringing the inmate-client and the professional practitioner together in a partnership in the common quest of human reintegration.

We will conclude this chapter with a selective review of specific examples of rehabilitation or treatment programming that may be found in correctional institutions. It is worth reiterating that treatment outcomes would be greatly improved if major changes in structure and philosophy were introduced into the correctional system. Despite the wide criticism of treatment and rehabilitation in corrections, evidence is accumulating that success is not an illusion. One study, for example, showed that inmates who have active contacts with the community are more responsive to treatment programming than are the socially isolated inmates.[68] This provides another argument for the open prison, and for programs such as those at Canningvale Prison in Western Australia, and the European programs which we have earlier examined.

Corrections will also have to take another look at the way it utilizes staff in the treatment endeavor. Those individuals who bear the formal title of "treatment professional" are in reality those who have the least

---

[65]Sturup, "Indeterminancy as Individualization," p. 1040.
[66]Sheldon Salsberg, "Treating Offenders: Some Suggestions for Improving the Efforts of Change Agents," in Edward Sagarin and Donal E. MacNamara (eds.), *Corrections: Problems of Punishment and Rehabilitation* (New York: Praeger Publishers, 1973), p. 19.
[67]Sturup, "Indeterminancy as Individualization," p. 1040.
[68]Blake McKelvey, *American Prisons* (Montclair, N.J.: Patterson Smith, 1977), p. 369.

amount of contact with the inmate population. The staff members who have the most to contribute to the reconstructive process are actually the correctional officers. Glaser's notable study[69] pointed up the importance of the correctional officer as an agent of rehabilitation. The custody staff should be integrated into the correctional thrust, instead of being insulated from it by a narrow custodial role. Indeed, it has been observed that, "The dichotomy between the treatment and custody staff produce [such] organizational chaos and splintering of efforts that the treatment staff efforts are largely negated."[70] Johnson expressed the opinion that while some custodial individuals could play combined treatment-custody roles, their contribution is limited "in part because they typically receive little support or assistance from treatment professionals."[71] The contention here is that it is time to put aside professional sniping and to holistically attack the challenge of corrections—which means tapping into the reservoir of potential in the custody staff.

One hidden advantage in mobilizing the custodial staff in the rehabilitation or treatment thrust is that it will neutralize the subversion of the treatment staff by the larger, unsympathetic bureaucratic system. Therapists, after all, are on the agency payroll. As a minority, they can be more readily manipulated at the expense of professional ideals. "Psychiatrists and psychologists who work in public or private mental institutions, those on the payrolls of public schools and private corporations, and prison psychiatrists, are all clearly agents for those who pay their wages."[72] Loyalty to the agency is an expected condition of employment, and it can seriously interfere with professional integrity. The ethics of confidentiality is a case in point. It is breached so often by prison psychiatrists and psychologists that it led Northwestern University sociologist, Arlene Kaplan Daniels, to label codes of ethics as "window-dressing."[73]

Some Examples of Prison Treatment

Despite the fact that the prison and its environment has been constantly attacked for its aridity, it is not completely a desert. Earlier we spoke of the

[69]Daniel Glaser, *The Effectiveness of a Prison and Parole System* (Indianapolis, Indiana: Bobbs-Merrill Co., Inc., 1964).

[70]Richard E. Hardy and John G. Cull, *Introduction to Correctional Rehabilitation* (Springfield, Ill.: Charles C Thomas, Publisher, 1973), pp. 16–17.

[71]Robert Johnson, "Ameliorating Prison Stress: Some Helping Roles for Custodial Personnel," *International Journal of Criminology and Penology*, 5, No. 3 (August 1977), 271.

[72]Fred Powledge, "The Therapist as Double Agent," *Psychology Today*, 2, No. 2 (July 1977), 44.

[73]*Ibid.*, p. 47. The American Psychological Association is also quite concerned about the question of loyalty (client vs. agency) in the bureaucratic setting. In 1978, as a consequence, the APA's Board of Social and Ethical Responsibility for Psychology (BSERP) commissioned a task force to explore the role of psychology in the criminal justice system. The issue of

concept of the therapeutic community, in which the total staff is considered part of the treatment milieu. The first therapeutic community in the Federal Bureau of Prisons was established at Danbury, Connecticut, for drug addicts committed under the federal Narcotic Addict Rehabilitation Act of 1966. From 1968 to 1969, a program was instituted in the federal institution at Marion, Indiana, to teach inmates transactional analysis. The inmates were then dispersed to other institutions to develop therapeutic communities. In 1978, there were ten federal correctional institutions with this type of program.

The "team treatment" concept was first introduced into the federal reformatory at El Reno, Oklahoma, in 1961. In team treatment, inmates and staff work together in decision making related to institutional classification and program development. This approach was adopted by the Missouri correctional system with the emphasis on decentralization of decision making. Inmates and staff develop a personalized plan for the inmate, covering not only work and housing assignments, but such things as furloughs, education, and work release. It has been found that an efficiently run treatment team classification process "is significantly associated with more favorable inmate attitudes towards living assignment, work assignment, staff, and a lower level of inmate alienation . . . [and] is significantly related to more favorable staff attitudes towards inmates. . . ."[74]

Transcendental Meditation has been introduced into the prison setting, as a "scientific" treatment tool at the federal correctional institution at Milan, Michigan, and at Folsom prison in California, a maximum security institution. At Folsom, 115 male inmates participated in the experimental study. After being apprised of the philosophy and method of TM, the participants were assigned to experimental and control groups. Each inmate in the experimental group was taught the TM technique and given a "mantra," a meaningless, but special sound. It was reported that the participating inmates showed "significant reductions in anxiety, neuroticism, hostility, insomnia, and behavioral infractions—to support the claim that the TM program is a scientific method of personal development applicable to rehabilitation."[75] In fact, it was asserted that "the TM program may be the most effective agent for producing a stable and integrated condition in the mind and personality."[76]

---

professional loyalty was the first concern expressed by that task force. See "Report on the Task Force on the Role of Psychology in the Criminal Justice System," *American Psychologist*, 33, No. 12, December 1978, pp. 1099–1113.

[74]John R. Hepburn and Celesta A. Albonetti, "Team Classification in State Correctional Institutions," *Criminal Justice and Behavior*, 5, No. 1 (March 1978), 71–72.

[75]Allan I. Abrams and Larry M. Siegel, "The Transcendental Meditation Program and Rehabilitation at Folsom State Prison," *Criminal Justice and Behavior*, 5, No. 1 (March 1978), p. 15.

[76]*Ibid.*, p. 17.

Employment Training

Because we live in a society that places great emphasis upon remunerative employment, both as a duty and as a status symbol, satisfying employment is a prerequisite for social adjustment. In earlier times, vocational training in prisons was largely limited to tailoring or shoe repairing. Considerable vocational diversification has subsequently been introduced into the prisons of the United States, from the computer career training program at the Massachusetts Correctional Institution, to the deep sea diver's program at the California Institute for Men. Nevertheless, a national survey conducted for the U.S. Department of Labor has concluded that "vocational preparation in correctional institutions is generally inadequate."[77] The major criticisms are that present training does not emphasize job skills, there are insufficient vocational training programs, the training is unrelated to the outside job market, and budgetary allocations are meager. In the English penal system, where "work is officially regarded as a major plank in any rehabilitation programme," similar distress has been expressed concerning the "potentially incompatible objects set for work in prison. . . ."[78]

Progress is being made. In 1976, Canada launched a new vocational program after deciding that the choice was a simple one:

> Let inmate employment continue to be a passive patchwork and inefficient arrangement or go all out to establish a realistic and viable system of penitentiary industries that would truly prepare inmates to cope with the pressures and pace of commercial industry.[79]

The result was the Joyceville pilot factory, constructed to produce metal products and to train inmates to meet completely the vocational requirements and pace of the commercial world once they are released. Joyceville is located near Kingston, Ontario, but plans are on the drawing board to construct similar factories in as many as twelve of Canada's penal institutions.

Canada's pioneering work is going to be emulated in the United States. Following a study by the National Institute of Law Enforcement and Criminal Justice, which supported the negative assessment of prison industry, the Law Enforcement Assistance Administration (LEAA) developed a new concept for prison industries which has been termed the

[77]*Criminal Justice Newsletter,* 7, No. 7 (March 29, 1976), p. 3.
[78]Karen Legge, "Work in Prison: The Process of Inversion," *British Journal of Criminology,* 18, No. 1 (January 1978), 8, 20.
[79]Public Affairs Division of the Canadian Penitentiary Service, "A New Approach to Inmate Employment," *American Journal of Corrections,* 38, No. 6 (November–December 1976), 10, 28.

"Free Venture Model." The Free Venture Model "is designed to emulate the outside world of work as closely as possible within the prison setting. . . . "[80] This will involve realistic work hours and job conditions. In 1978, LEAA awarded grants to the correctional systems of Minnesota, Colorado, Iowa, Illinois, South Carolina, Washington (state), and Connecticut to develop and implement Free Venture projects.

Educational Training

Just as we are a work-oriented society, so we are a society that largely relates achievement to education. It is significant that the average inmate's educational level approximates the ninth grade. Education in the American prison system has had a record similar to that of vocational training in the prison. It has an ancient history, but "education within prison walls has been abysmally slow in developing,"[81] particularly in view of the fact that the first prison school was opened in the Walnut Street (Philadelphia) Jail in 1784. As recently as 1972, 28 percent of 150 correctional institutions surveyed (60 percent of the total) had no complete educational programs through the elementary level.[82]

Countermeasures are also developing in the field of education. On May 11, 1978, the Federal Bureau of Prisons issued a policy statement in which uniform standards for inmate education were spelled out. All inmates during their incarceration (depending on their previous background), should complete an Adult Basic Education Program, the Adult Secondary Education Program, and one or more Postsecondary Education Activities. The policy declares that the educational program will operate twelve months of the year, and provision is made for bicultural and bilingual education.

The New York correctional system has an extensive college education program which permits inmates to attend college in the community. It also sponsors coeducational educational facilities within prisons, with academic credits that are transferable in the state university system.[83] In South Carolina, an extensive education release program is in operation, with inmates being released to community centers to pursue their higher educational objectives. The University of South Carolina is an active partner in this correctional-educational venture. There are numerous other

---

[80]*Corrections Compendium*, 3, No. 3 (October 1978), 1 (published by CONtact, Lincoln, Nebraska).

[81]Benedict S. Alper, *Prisons Inside-Out* (Cambridge, Mass.: Ballinger Publishing Company, 1974), p. 83.

[82]Frank Dell'Apa, "Educational Programs in Adult Correctional Institutions," *A Survey* (Boulder, Colorado: Western Interstate Commission for Higher Education, undated but c. 1973).

[83]Alper, *Prisons Inside-Out,* p. 85.

programs that could be cited, but space does not permit further digression. We will, instead, close this chapter with a look at a new federal prison, which is doing some exploratory work on treatment approaches in corrections.

THE FEDERAL CORRECTIONAL INSTITUTION
AT BUTNER

The Federal Correctional Institution at Butner, North Carolina, was actually first conceived in the late 1950s.[84] It was planned as an institution in which the diagnosis and treatment of emotionally disturbed offenders would take place. To facilitate this purpose, the institution site was selected in proximity to two major universities, each possessing excellent programs in psychiatry and psychology, Duke University and the University of North Carolina. The mission of the institution was conceived as twofold: "(1) to provide a facility for severely psychotic and acutely suicidal Federal offenders and (2) to develop and evaluate a variety of treatment approaches."[85]

Before the institution could be opened, public opposition began to develop because of the belief that behavior modification tactics, inclusive of experimental mind-control techniques, would be undertaken at Butner. Warden Gilbert L. Ingram contends that the "controversy arose as a result of totally unfounded comments. . . . "[86] In any event, the institution opened in the spring of 1976, and the population grew to 380 males by 1978.

Almost half of the inmates at Butner have been committed for a serious, violent offense, including murder, bank robbery, air piracy, and extortion with threats. The average age of the inmate population is 33, and the average sentence being served is just over 7 years. Almost one-third (28 percent) are serving sentences in excess of ten years, and 35 percent have had eleven or more prior arrests.

A great number of practices endorsed by progressive thinkers in the field of corrections are being implemented at Butner. Inmates wear civilian clothing if they want to, can have family visits five days per week, live in rooms without bars, and have their own keys. For the better part of the day, movement is unrestricted. The philosophy is to maintain a secure institution, but one that maximizes freedom. There are no guard towers.

[84]Gilbert L. Ingram, "Butner: A Reality," *Federal Probation,* 42, No. 1 (March 1978), p. 34. This is the definitive recent article on Butner, and the data in this section is largely taken from Ingram's account.
[85]*Ibid.*
[86]*Ibid.*

The inmate population is classified as Research Population, Mental Health Population, or General Population.

The Research Population

A little under half of the total population is in this category. These are the violent and hard-core offenders, which are the high risk group in terms of community standards. They are computer-selected for admission to Butner, and must be recidivists, with a fixed parole date, and having from 8 months to three years remaining before being eligible for release from custory. The research design is credited to the ideas of Norval Morris, Dean of the University of Chicato Law School. According to Morris, rehabilitation cannot be coercively accomplished. Inmates, instead, should be provided with the necessary resources and the opportunities to learn. They should also have a fixed parole date, that is, the indeterminate sentence is expressly repudiated.

All the inmates in this program have been given fixed dates by the U.S. Parole Commission. A control group of inmates has been spread throughout the federal prison system. Two basic elements constitute the nub of the program: (1) Any inmate can elect to drop out of the program, without retaliatory action, after ninety days. In other words, after the ninety-day cutoff period, all participants in the program are in it voluntarily. (2) Inmates participate in only those programs in which they choose to take part.

There are only three mandatory requirements for the research population: obey the rules, become involved in group discussions in the unit, and work at least one half of the day. The actual program consists of a wide spectrum of therapeutic, educational, vocational, and community-oriented programming. The team treatment concept is applied in the unit, and the team works out individualized contracts with each inmate, spelling out expectations with regard to all activities, institutional and extra-institutional. Each inmate is also subjected to a graduated release plan, being phased back into the community rather than being abruptly dumped into it. The program is being evaluated by research faculty at the University of North Carolina.

The Mental Health Population

Approximately one-fourth of the inmate population is in this group. These are the individuals with serious emotional or mental problems. They have been referred by other federal correctional institutions because they cannot be accommodated at the sending institution. A panoply of psychiatric services are provided by psychiatrists on the faculty of Duke

University, including crisis intervention and short-term therapy in addition to standard program services. In this particular program, the staff endeavors to maintain a therapeutic community, and the inmate-patients are encouraged to maintain as normal an existence as is possible. When their treatment is concluded, they are sent back to their parent institutions.

The General Population

The remainder, about 125 inmates, constitute the general population. They come to Butner by direct commitment from the courts, or are transfers from other institutions who normally live in or near North Carolina. The Federal Bureau likes to house inmates as close as possible to the states from which were committed. These inmates are involved in routine institutional programming, but can become involved in any self-help activity that is available to other inmates.

In a recently conducted "Social Climate Study" at the Butner institution, it was "found that staff favorably exceed national norms on all nine dimensions measured, and that inmates favorably exceed national norms on seven dimensions. This means that staff and inmates are probably in greater agreement as to how they perceive their social environment than is generally the case."[87] The nine dimensions measured were as follows:

1. Involvement in work
2. Support (from others)
3. Open expression of feelings
4. Autonomy
5. Practical orientation and job training
6. Personal problem orientation
7. Order and organization
8. Clarity (in re staff expectations)
9. Staff control (reliance on rules)

SYNOPSIS

In this chapter, the negatives of the prison environment are paraded for inspection. Prisons are found to represent brutal, costly, violent, old, and overcrowded penal instruments. The culture of the prison tends to be

---

[87]U.S. Department of Justice, Federal Prison System, *Monday Morning Highlights* (September 19, 1977) 3.

antithetical to treatment overtures. The concept of "prisonization," coined by Clemmer, is examined and found wanting. The functional model and the importation model represent more recent attempts to explain the prison society, the former on the basis of the inmates' collective *ex post facto* adaptation, and the latter on the basis of the influence of prior life experiences.

From Goffman's idea of the "total institution," to the modern "open prison," it becomes clear that the type of institution, and the philosophy it embodies, are crucial factors in defining its treatment potential. The Scandinavian, West Australian, and Dutch systems are reviewed, in terms of cultural dictates and the possibility of cross-cultural assimilation. Neglected aspects, such as the unique challenge of the female in the system, and the emotional repression that is overlooked in prison life, are explored.

The need to involve total staff, expecially the correctional officers, in the treatment endeavor, becomes obvious in our discussion, as well as the need to imaginatively innovate in terms of correctional treatment components. Employment and education, being cultural imperatives, are given especial comment, and we conclude with a look at a modern treatment oriented correctional facility, the Federal Correctional Institution at Butner, North Carolina.

When sufficient, definitive data have been compiled at Butner, we will either discover that breakthroughs have occurred, or that we have simply added additional millions to the funds that have already been spent to prove the correctional inefficacy of the American prison.

10 Community-Based Strategies

When they show the shiny new prisons on the news, with the spotless kitchens and the smiling staff, they should show the mangled bodies, twisted minds and perverted souls that these million dollar human zoos have created and will continue to produce.

Ex-convict Fred C.

The bitter ongoing controversy over the prison raged anew with the flaming riots of the memorable seventies. On September 9, 1971, Attica became a household word after four days of bloody uprising left 43 dead and a prison in a shambles. A month earlier, on the opposite side of the country, San Quentin's day of infamy took place, when George Jackson made his abortive attempt to escape from the Adjustment Center. Jackson, three guards, and two inmates were slain in the bloody outburst, and two other guards were wounded. Prison unrest also took place in dozens of other prisons across the land—in Idaho, Louisiana, New Jersey, Wisconsin, Georgia, Indiana, Hawaii, Illinois, Texas, Virginia, Iowa, Tennessee and Washington, D.C. Canada, England, and other foreign lands were also wracked with prison disturbances. The prison was being forced to appear in the court of public opinion, but it arrived with many friends and did not always appear as if it was the defendant.

The radical school of thought sees the prison as a correctional atavism, which should be summarily and totally abolished. At the other extreme, which has the support of a long tradition and the emerging punishment model, prison is viewed by the man in the street and some notable scholars as a necessary instrument of the criminal justice process. While it is true that some sort of secure incarceration will be indefinitely necessary for bizarre, violent, acting-out offenders such as Charles Manson, David Berkowitz, Richard Speck, and similar outrageous offenders, the evidence is overwhelming that the prison in an ineffectual, brutalizing, costly, and irrational tool for rehabilitation.

Volumes could be written and, indeed, have been written, which document the history of horror epitomized in the maximum security prison. What can be said of the appalling circumstances surrounding the elderly, black inmate, VanDyke Grigsby, who was paroled from the Indiana State Prison at Michigan City in 1974 after serving 66 consecutive years in prison? Grigsby was convicted of second degree murder in 1908, a stabbing in a bar that would not have constituted more than a manslaughter by today's standards. He was 89 years old when he was released from the longest sentence ever served by an American prisoner. Or Stephen Dennison? At the age of 16, Stephen stole a box of candy valued at five dollars. He was sent to a reformatory in New York for this offense in 1925. Because of minor disciplinary actions while institutionalized, his sentence was periodically extended. He was released from prison in 1959, after serving 34 years for the theft of a box of candy. He had committed no other crimes.

RATIONALE FOR COMMUNITY-BASED CORRECTIONS

It is unnecessary to develop an extensive indictment of the prison. It already exists, being merely amplified by data provided in this text. Reason tells us that the precipitants of criminal behavior are *in the community,* the goal is to return the offender *to the community,* and protracted absence *from the community* will only compound the problem of reintegration. It logically follows that the community is the ideal locus for the correctional treatment effort. A prisoner is a prisoner is a prisoner, as Gertrude Stein would say. That is his role. That is his status. That is his identity while he is incarcerated. But, as Goethe so wisely observed, "If you treat an individual as he is he will stay as he is, but if you treat him as if he were what he ought to be and could be, he will become as he ought to be and could be."

The rationale for community-based corrections was clearly articulated by the President's Commission on Law Enforcement and Administration of Justice:

> The general underlying premise for the new direction in corrections is that crime and delinquency are symptoms of failures and disorganization of the community as well as individual offenders.
>
> The task of corrections therefore includes building or rebuilding solid ties between offender and community, integrating or reintegrating the offender into community life—restoring family ties, obtaining employment and education, securing in the larger sense a place for the offender in the routine functioning of society . . . . [1]

In this chapter, we will examine the major correctional treatment efforts that take place in the community, the traditional as well as the innovative, within the context of the broad definition of treatment given earlier. A wide variety of activities come under the umbrella of "community-based corrections." The guiding assumption is that the bulk of the correctional effort should, and ultimately will, move to the community.

A second fundamental premise is that community-based corrections is not for every offender and, for the forseeable future, the prison will have to service the serious offender. The prison of the future, however, will be quite unlike the concrete and steel-celled edifice with which we are accustomed today. Its design will reflect not only advances in the behavior sciences, but also advances in technology and architecture. It is certain that we simply cannot continue to build prisons, which immediately become congested, *ad infinitum.*

The Dutch "subsidiary principle," of minimal use of the prison, will have to be adopted. A mass of data supporting this principle is available. From 1972 through 1977, for example, the Federal Bureau of Prisons, which spends $1.5 billion on its system annually, built or acquired nine new institutions, which provided space for an additional 3,800 prisoners in the federal system. Despite this, by the end of 1977 the federal prisons contained approximately 7,500 prisoners in excess of the rated capacity of those prisons. The director of the Federal Bureau of Prisons, Norman A. Carlson, quite succinctly declared, "The major problem facing most prison administrators today in this country is 'The Body Crunch,' the pressure of a rapidly increasing inmate population."[2] Overcrowded prisons not only compromise meaningful treatment efforts; they are powder kegs waiting to explode.

---

[1]President's Commission on Law Enforcement and Administration of Justice, *Task Force Report: Corrections* (Washington, D.C.: U.S. Government Printing Office, 1967), p. 7.

[2]Federal Prison System, *Monday Morning Highlights,* U.S. Department of Justice, Washington, D.C., October 11, 1977, p. 1.

In 1973 Minnesota enacted a Community Corrections Act. Minnesota's then Commissioner of Corrections, Kenneth F. Schoen, made some comments about that act which go to the heart of rational community corrections:

> A number of assumptions underlie the Community Corrections Act. The first of these is that, in the case of the serious offender, incarceration within the prison setting will continue to be necessary. The act is not intended to empty our institutions. Instead, it is an attempt to restrict confinement in penal institutions to those persons who have committed acts which the community regards as intolerable and who require some extended period of incarceration.
>
> A second assumption. . . is that crime and delinquency should be seen as symptoms of failure and disorganization at the community level. . . .
>
> The third major assumption. . . is that most offenders pose no threat to the community.[3]

The most obvious way to neutralize the inimical influence of the prison, and to "restrict confinement in penal institutions," is to divert individuals *from* the system.

DIVERSION FROM THE PRISON SYSTEM

There are a number of solid reasons to support some form of diversion from the system. Diversion, for one thing, aborts the stigma that results from incarceration. Furthermore, it retains the person in the nurturing environment of the community, where his major resources are located. It also puts emphasis upon the fact that the problem of criminally deviant behavior is a community problem. Additionally, it prevents the criminalization process that takes place in the prison environment. But one of the most important reasons has to be that it is a positive way of counteracting the shame of our criminal *justice* system's inequitable sentencing. As Senator Kennedy said, "Criminal sentencing today is a national scandal."[4]

Pre-Trial Diversion

While the principal reason for diversion is to preserve the present and future well-being of humans, there are also practical considerations. Diversion takes pressure off such institutions as jails and prisons. It also

[3]Kenneth F. Schoen, "The Community Corrections Act," *Crime and Delinquency*, 24, No. 4 (October 1978), 461.
[4]Quoted in *U.S. News & World Report*, September 5, 1977, p. 47.

contributes to a reduction of the courts' workload. Still, the human must be the central focus. A pertinent study contends that four basic considerations are embedded in the rationale for diversion, here paraphrased:

1. The criminal justice process, with its stigma and the consequent liabilities imposed on the defendant, acts as an inducement rather than as a deterrent to further crime.
2. The criminal justice system is a progressively expensive system. Expensive methods should be reserved for serious offenders, which will help curtail the burden on the various components of the system.
3. The criminal justice system is not always the appropriate system to deal with individuals who are so often routinely processed into it. Other social agencies, such as health, welfare, education, or civil law entities, would be more appropriate. Mentally disturbed individuals and certain drug abuse offenders are examples of individuals who should be diverted.
4. The application of the criminal law and the administration of law enforcement descend unevenly upon the community, with the least advantaged getting disproportionate attention.[5]

There are technical problems associated with pre-trial diversion. This type of program requires by-passing the system, and consequently requires broad support from various vested interests, such as the prosecutor, the courts, and the public defender. Of more concern is the legal question of due process safeguards, such as the constitutional right to a speedy trial. It can be assumed that the benefits of diversion will bring resolution of this type of problem. The American Bar Association, through its Commission on Correctional Facilities and Services, has established a National Pre-trial Intervention Service Bureau in Washington, D.C., and has pilot programs operating in a dozen cities. The Bar Association's involvement should presage resolution of some technical legal problems.

Notable programs also exist in Hawaii, Connecticut, Oregon, and Ohio. In Hawaii, the diversionary program has been made a part of the court operation. As I have commented in another source, "With the court's protective mantle, the technical, legal questions of custody, jurisdiction, preventive detention, disposition without trial, and diversion itself are in greater likelihood of being definitively clarified."[6] In Connec-

---

[5]John J. Galvin and others, *Instead of Jail: Pre- and Post-trial Alternatives to Jail Incarceration, Volume 3, Alternatives to Prosecution,* October 1977 (Washington, D.C.: U.S. Government Printing Office, 1977), pp. 1–3.

[6]Louis P. Carney, *Corrections and the Community* (Englewood Cliffs, N. J.: Prentice-Hall, Inc., 1977), p. 72.

ticut, the pre-trial intervention program has an eclectic base, drawing its membership from the Bar Association and the Yale School of Law, as well as the various components of the criminal justice system. The Connecticut program focuses on providing counseling and vocational services to the diverted. Specific, arbitrarily selected programs in Oregon, Ohio, and Florida will now be briefly reviewed.

The Oregon program, in Multnomah County, was actually created by a judge who was dissatisfied with the limited sentencing alternatives available to the court. In December 1972, the Honorable Richard L. Unis, presiding judge of the Multnomah County District Court, established what has been termed the Alternative Community Service Program. In this program, individuals are sentenced to perform certain amounts of work for non-profit agencies of the community. The defendant is permitted to accomplish this work in a manner that does not interfere with his or her regular job responsibilities. In the first eighteen months of the program, almost 35,000 hours of community service were contributed by approximately 1,200 individuals.

Although it is restricted to the resolution of minor disputes, and certain check offenses, the Night Prosecutor Program, established in Columbus, Ohio, in 1971, is of considerable significance. This is because it contributes both to the unifying of the community and to the aborting of the stigma of a penal disposition. In this program, out-of-court settlements are engineered in family disputes and neighborhood altercations. The cases are screened by the prosecutor's office, with the mediation role being performed by law students who are specifically trained for that function. Counseling services are provided by social work graduate students, and the individuals are helped to find solutions to problems without having recourse to the judicial process. From a practical viewpoint, it has been determined that the Night Prosecutor Program has reduced the cost of prosecution by 80 percent for each case handled through out-of-court mediation. During 1976, 6,429 cases were scheduled, 3,478 were actually heard, and criminal affidavits were filed in only 2 percent of the cases scheduled.[7] The Night Prosecutor Program has been designated an "Exemplary Project" by the National Institute of Law Enforcement and Criminal Justice.

In 1975, the Office of Court Alternatives was established in Florida's Orange County, and it has saved the county $2 million annually. It consists of a Pre-Trial Diversion Unit, County Probation, and a Court Alternative Center. Selected first offenders are offered alternative dispositions in the Pre-Trial Unit. They must waive a speedy trial and sign a contract agree-

---

[7]Office of Development, Testing, and Dissemination, National Institute of Law Enforcement and Criminal Justice, LEAA, *Exemplary Projects* (Washington, D.C.: U.S. Government Printing Office, 1977), p. 18.

ing to conditions of participation. When the program is completed, the original charges are dropped. County Probation, of course, provides the alternative where unsupervised release is contraindicated. Those who need a structured live-in situation are referred to the Court Alternative Center, a 45-man residential center, which has work training and release, and school release available as program components.

The Office of Court Alternatives has significantly reduced the burden of the court and the prosecutor's office, in addition to the financial savings. Reportedly, "less than five clients out of 100 are known to again become involved as offenders."[8]

Pre-trial diversion programs have begun to proliferate, and hundreds of such programs actually exist across the country today. In a nation which annually arrests approximately 10,000,000 individuals, it is self-evident that some sort of diversionary apparatus should be operating. Those that do exist, however, are not characterized by administrative uniformity, and they are usually at the mercy of erratic and unpredictable funding. Still, as one surveyor declared, "those programs which have survived seem to be proving some unwritten law of bureaucratic Darwinism."[9] Perhaps it's really the law of irrepressible wisdom.

COMMUNITY-BASED TREATMENT

When we speak of community-based correctional treatment efforts, we are literally speaking of a considerable variety of approaches. Some have endured to become traditional ways; some are transitory; the prosaic and the innovative compete; there are programs for adults, and those for juveniles; some are ambitious, and some are modest in scope; they are public and they are private. Collectively they represent the modern thrust of corrections, which is toward the community. It would be neither judicious nor possible to attempt any sort of comprehensive overview. Instead, we will focus on the major community correctional efforts represented by the residential center, work release, and probation and parole.

The Residential Center

By "residential center" we mean that facility which has been described as "standing [m]idway between the captivity of prisons and the relative freedom of probation and parole,"[10] and in which the program partici-

---

[8] American Correctional Association, *On The Line*, September 1978, p. 7.

[9] Paul F. Dunn, *Pretrial Release, Diversion Agencies, and Training: One View*, National Council of Crime and Delinquency, August 1974, p. 3.

[10] Harjit S. Sandhu, *Modern Corrections* (Springfield, Ill.: Charles C Thomas Publisher, 1974), p. 278.

pant is at least temporarily domiciled. We include the diversified community correctional center, as well as the single- or multiple-purpose halfway house. The residential correctional center provides a transitional, live-in phase in the offender's reintegration, or an alternative to imprisonment for those for whom diversion is appropriate.

The Federal Bureau of Prisons has listed five basic principles which must be put into practice if success with a residential center is to be anticipated.[11] In abbreviated form those principles are:

1. *The residents must have ready access to the community's resources,* including job opportunities, educational programs, professional services, and public acceptance.
2. *The welfare and safety of the community cannot be neglected,* which means that there must be careful selection of the residents, and of the purpose for which the center exists.
3. *Residents can be neither favored nor exploited.* They must participate with community members on an equitable basis.
4. *Residents of a center who are on a pre-release (from a prison) status are still in technical custody.* If they abscond from the program, they must be treated as escapees.
5. *The responsibility for the decisions respecting admission, and removal from the facility, should be vested in an official of the agency who is accountable for the residential center's operation.* But whether a public or a private agency is the sponsor, close collaboration with public agencies and officials is imperative.

Each residential or community correctional center provides at least one specific service, and most are diversified. Some meet a wide range of human needs, including the clinical.

The residential center is not a curative waystop. It is an instrument of reintegration. As the director of the Federal Bureau of Prisons stated, "The success of a community residential center depends upon a carefully conceived program, resolutely and skillfully administered."[12]

The Halfway House

The halfway house is the most familiar residential center. Perhaps the best known is Dismas House in St. Louis, founded by the "Hoodlum Priest," Father Charles Dismas Clark, with the backing and support of his long-time friend, the prominent Jewish businessman, Morris A. Shenker. Launched as a residential center with employment assistance as its sole

[11]United States Bureau of Prisons, *The Residential Center: Corrections in the Community,* (Washington, D.C., 1978), p. 1.
[12]*Ibid.* (Preface).

purpose, Dismas House eventually became the complete community correctional center, with a staff of professionals and the ability to meet most of the client's major needs. Both the federal Bureau of Prisons and the Missouri Department of Social Services (corrections) utilize Dismas House.

Pointing out that the halfway house, in colonial times, was a place where the weary traveler might pause to rest and refresh himself, Doleschal and Geis add that it "has been incorporated into corrections for essentially similar restorative purposes, that is, to allow an offender or potential offender some respite from pressures and strain."[13] Since the resurgence of the halfway house as a correctional device, following the establishment of Dismas House, it has grown rapidly. In 1963, an International Halfway House Association was founded, and in 1968 it became an affiliate of the American Correctional Association. There are presently over 400 correctional halfway houses listed in the IHHA directory, with approximately 10,000 individuals in residence.[14]

The correctional halfway house is not only extending the scope of its service to many different types of clients, it is becoming innovative and imaginative. The Orange County Halfway House, for example, eschewed the traditional downtown location and was established, instead, in suburban Anaheim, California, in a modern apartment complex. In addition to providing a wide range of services, including professional and recreational activities, the Orange County Halfway House caters to drop-in traffic. Employment assistance and other services are proferred to any ex-offender. Residency is not a prerequisite. For the residents, who are coeducational, the emphasis is on normalization, with all of the amenities usually associated with apartment living in the shadow of Disneyland. A private, non-profit enterprise, the facility is used by the Federal Bureau of Prisons as a pre-release center and by the local parole staff of the California Department of Corrections.

INTEGRATED COMMUNITY CORRECTIONS

As community-based corrections broadens, some interesting and significant ventures have been undertaken. We have space to mention only two in any detail, but they are selected because they epitomize the concept of the community directly participating in the treatment of the correctional

[13]Eugene Doleschal and Gilbert Geis, "Halfway House," in Burt Galaway, Joe Hudson, and C. David Hollister (eds.), *Community Corrections* (Springfield, Ill.: Charles C Thomas Publisher, 1976), p. 126.

[14]Carolyn Johnson and Marjorie Kravitz, *Halfway Houses: A Selected Bibliography* (Washington, D.C.: U.S. Government Printing Office. 1978), p. v.

client. It has been said that, "Ideally, all community-based correctional activities would be located in one center, providing the services necessary for the reintegration of the offender."[15] While the following programs do not provide all of their services from one center, they do have a cohesive program which has the same effect.

Polk County, Iowa

In 1973, the community-based corrections program in Polk County (Des Moines), Iowa was added to the list of Exemplary Projects established by the National Institute of Law Enforcement and Criminal Justice. The Des Moines program is a coordination of four services for both defendants and convicted offenders. The four services are (1) Pre-trial release on recognizance. (2) Pre-trial release with supervision. (3) Probation. (4) Residence at Fort Des Moines, a work and education release center.

The important thing about the Polk County program is that it synchronizes services, thereby substantially reducing the cost, while permitting a flexible response to a wide range of client needs. In 1973, savings accrued to the state and county correctional systems of Iowa in the amount of $454,229, with $154,000 of the total savings coming from pre-trial activities.[16] The Polk County program has been a notable success, and it is particularly interesting to discover that the high-risk clients (recidivists) did not have a higher recidivism rate than the low-risk (no prior difficulties) clients. "Because of the Des Moines Program's demonstrated success, the Iowa State Legislature voted to assume total funding of the Project and adopted 'community-based corrections' as the model for future Iowa correctional programs."[17]

PORT Program, Minnesota

Another community-based program that has drawn considerable attention is the PORT program, located in Rochester, Minnesota. Like the Alternative Community Services Program in Multnomah County, Oregon, PORT was conceived by two judges who were dissatisfied with their sentencing options. PORT is an acronym for Probational Offenders Rehabilitation and Training. It has been described as a "live-in, community-based, community directed, community-sponsored treat-

[15]Kevin N. Wright, "An Exchange Strategy for the Interface of Community-Based Corrections into the Service System," *Human Relations*, 30, No. 10 (October 1977), 881.

[16]Office of Development, Testing, and Dissemination, National Institute of Law Enforcement and Criminal Justice, LEAA, *Exemplary Projects* (Washington, D.C.: U.S. Government Printing Office, 1977), p. 13.

[17]*Ibid.*

ment program for both adults and juveniles."[18] A private, non-profit corporation, PORT has four primary objectives:[19]

1. To control criminal and delinquent behavior without resorting to institutional or probationary programs.
2. To reduce commitments to state institutions from the area served by PORT.
3. To provide a new and less expensive method of rehabilitation.
4. To test the efficacy of the PORT concept and see if it could be replicated in other areas.

Candidates for the program are referred by the local district and municipal courts. For every adult diverted from a prison commitment, the county must pay the state the equivalent of the per diem cost of institutionalization, which in 1974 was $16 per day for adults and a little over twice that for juveniles. Participants in the program must sign contracts of performance, and restitution to the victim can be made a part of that contract.

The program consists mainly of group treatment in combination with behavior modification with the extensive use of group counseling. There are five stages in the program, permitting the client to progress from minimal to maximal freedom. Before the client can advance through the various stages, however, merit points must be earned, and favorable decisions received from the group. Because it is a community-based program, heavy reliance is placed upon community resources, with various social agencies and educational institutions cooperatively involved. All types of skills and professional guidance are available to the program through its 65-member citizens advisory committee. Preliminary research data indicate that the PORT program has been more successful with adults than with juveniles. The recidivism rate for adults who have been in the program is 23 percent, while it is 45 percent for juveniles. Nevertheless, the PORT program has been sufficiently successful to have won wide recognition and to have been widely emulated.

FURLOUGH

Miller describes the furlough as "an authorized, unescorted absence from a correctional institution for a specified period of time."[20] To that bald

[18]*PORT 1971*, undated report by the Hon. O. Russell Olson, President, PORT of Olmsted County (Minnesota), p. 2.
[19]Nevin Doran Hunter, Robert M. Pockrass, and Luanne Hostermann, *Probationed Offenders and Rehabilitation Training: An Evaluation of Community Based Corrections* (Mankato, Minn.: Urban Studies Institute, Mankato State College, undated, c. 1974), p. 3.
[20]E. Eugene Miller, "Furloughs as a Technique of Reintegration," in E. Eugene Miller

definition must be added rationale, purpose, and scope. The basic rationale behind any type of furlough is that imprisonment is a temporary state of affairs; therefore some effort should be made to facilitate resumptive contact with the community on a graduated basis. The purpose is to enable the inmate to engage in those productive activities which will enhance his ultimate, post-prison adjustment, the most important of which is the restoration of family ties. The scope of the practice is basically covered by home visits, education release, and work release. The eligibility, extent, duration, and nature of the furlough are controlled by law and policy in the respective states.

The most liberal law is undoubtedly that of Alaska, which permits the Department of Corrections to grant furloughs for any period of time, for any purpose that advances the cause of rehabilitation.[21] On the other end of the spectrum, furloughs are not permitted in Hawaii, Montana, Oklahoma, West Virginia, Wyoming, and Texas. In terms of gross numbers of furloughs, the most liberal jurisdictions appear to be New Jersey, Florida, Oregon, North Carolina, Washington, D.C., and the Federal Prison System.[22] For comparative purposes, the federal Bureau of Prisons granted 26,285 furloughs in 1977, whereas the New York State Department of Correctional Services furloughed 7,500 inmates in that same year. New Jersey, incredibly, grants over 8,000 per month.[23]

The furlough concept receives its share of criticism, and it is particularly controversial when an incident occurs involving a furloughed inmate. A series of such events clouded the program in Washington, D.C. in 1974. One event was particularly explosive. Inmate Calvin F. Smith had been committed to the District of Columbia correctional facility at Lorton (which is actually located in nearby Virginia) in 1973, following convictions for first degree murder, robbery, and burglary. The victim in the murder was shot to death in his own home, which was being burglarized by Smith and his crime partner. Smith was sentenced to 20 years to life on the murder charge, and 15 years for the remaining offenses.

Only 20 months after he was convicted and committed, Smith was arrested by FBI agents at a railroad station in Washington, D.C. He had in his possession a box, which contained a sawed-off shotgun, a federal offense. Smith was on furlough at the time, and it was discovered that he had been making numerous unescorted trips to the community as the prison's "entertainment coordinator."[24] The result was an intensification of the attack that had been mounting against the poorly administered furlough

---

and M. Robert Montilla (eds.), *Corrections in the Community* (Reston, Va.: Reston Publishing Company, Inc., 1977), p. 201.

[21]*Ibid.*

[22]*Corrections Magazine,* 1, No. 6 (July/August 1975), 5.

[23]*Ibid.*

[24]*Corrections Magazine,* 1, No. 4 (March/April 1975), 53.

program at Lorton. Work furlough is an essentially sound idea, but one that can be sabotaged by incompetent selection and inept administration.[25]

WORK RELEASE AND WORK FURLOUGH

Furloughs from prison permit the reestablishment of family ties, the acquisition of advanced educational training, and the opportunity to develop release programming. Work release, however, is the most practical application of the principle of graduated re-entry. While work release and work furlough are used interchangeably, there is a technical distinction to be made. Work release indicates the practice of releasing an individual to work in the community, usually in the daytime hours and during weekdays, with return to the institution obligatory in the evenings and on the weekends. Work furlough, on the other hand, normally refers to a temporary release, the purpose of which is to develop employment prospects. Although our present discussion is limited to work release, it accepts the synonymous use of work release and work furlough.

The origin of work release is usually attributed to the so-called Huber Law, sponsored by Senator Henry Huber of Wisconsin. Enacted in 1913, the Huber Law permitted Wisconsin misdemeanants, serving sentences of up to one year in jail, to continue to work at their regular jobs in the community. While work release gradually infiltrated all the counties of Wisconsin, it did not have much of a national development until after World War II. In fact, "Prior to 1950, only four states [sic], Wisconsin, Nebraska, West Virginia, and Hawaii had provisions for work release programs."[26] On the federal level, the Prisoners Rehabilitation Act, authorizing work release for inmates of the Federal Bureau of Prisons, was signed into law by President Lyndon B. Johnson in 1965.

Zalba considers work release to be "a therapeutic contribution" to corrections, because it provides the blend of necessary institutional control and the opportunity "to perform in socially desired roles and ways in the free community."[27] Because work furlough programs have proliferated, and there is no central agency for the collection of data, it is difficult to get a definitive profile of the practice. Over 30,000 furloughs are granted each month to adult inmates of correctional facilities throughout the

---

[25]For recommended guidelines, and an expansive bibliography pertaining to work release, consult Correctional Research Associates, *Community Work—An Alternative to Imprisonment* (Washington, D.C.: U.S. Government Printing Office, 1973).

[26]Eugene Doleschal and Gilbert Geis, "Work Release," in Burt Galaway, Joe Hudson, and C. David Hollister (eds.), *Community Corrections* (Springfield, Ill.: Charles C Thomas Publisher, 1976), p. 99.

[27]Serapio R. Zalba, "Work Release—A Two-Pronged Effort," *Crime and Delinquency,* 13, No. 4 (October 1967), 508.

United States, and over 6,000 to juveniles.[28] They are not, however, all *work* furloughs. According to Zalba, who studied four work release programs (one in Wisconsin and three in California), the escape rate ranged from 12 percent in the Wisconsin program to 1 percent in one of the California programs.[29] These were work release programs operated out of *jails*, however. For comparison, the California *prison* work furlough program had only a 2 percent escape rate over a five-year period (1969–1974).[30]

When problems arise in a work release program, they can usually be traced to one or a combination of the following factors: improper selection of candidates, defects in the organizational structure of the work release program, a lack of commitment by staff, hostility from an ill-prepared community. The community should be adequately prepared in advance of such a program and brought into partnership with it. The most rational way of doing this is to involve the business sector and labor organizations in supportive roles and to establish rapport with community and social agencies, particularly including law enforcement. Presuming that the program is carefully designed and capably administered, the advantages of work release far outweigh the disadvantages.

A man on work release earns wages. He can, thereby, contribute to the maintenance of his family, and to his own upkeep while institutionalized. Most programs have that provision—that a percentage of the furloughee's wage is used to defray the expense of his own maintenance. Participants are charged $5 per day for room and board in South Carolina and in Toronto, Ontario, work release programs. In the Montgomery County, Maryland, Work Release/Pre-Release Program, 20 percent is levied on all paychecks, up to $200 per month.

The individual, by working in the community, is subjected to a normalizing influence that is absent in the prison.[31] He is able to observe and emulate the norms and roles esteemed in the community. He also pays taxes on his earned income and contributes to the lessening of the burden of welfare required for dependents of those who are incarcerated. It will help to take a closer look at a representative work release program.

Milwaukie, Oregon: An Example

The Milwaukie Work Release Center was the first of its kind established in Oregon, and it is jointly operated by the Oregon Division of

[28]*Corrections Magazine*, 1, No. 6 (July/August 1975), 3.
[29]"Work Release—A Two-Pronged Effort," p. 511.
[30]Louis P. Carney, *Corrections and the Community*, p. 126.
[31]For an interesting study of work furlough in Israel, in which the author questions the efficacy of normalization for furloughees, see Yael Hassin, "Prisoners' Furlough: A Reassessment," *International Journal of Criminology and Penology*, 5, No. 2 (May 1977) 171–78.

Corrections and the Vocational Rehabilitation Division. It has a capacity of approximately fifty residents. The residents in the program are taken from the Oregon State Penitentiary and the Oregon State Correctional Institution, each located in Salem. The facility itself has office space for staff and for counseling and is equipped with kitchen, laundry, washroom, two dormitories, and a large area that is used both for dining and as a general day room. While the residents are monitored 24 hours per day, the doors to the work release center are never locked. Like the Montgomery County, Maryland program, the Milwaukie program integrates both work and education release. Approximately one-third of the residents are in educational programs. The Vocational Rehabilitation Division pays the tuition and incidentals, such as books and fees, for those in school.

Apart from the major goals which are inherent in such a program, specific "subgoals" have been established to "facilitate the emphasis on maturation and personal development" and to provide the framework within which the resident can be progressively evaluated.[32] The subgoals are as follows:

1. *The development of a personal sense of responsibility.* This is accomplished by granting the individual increasing responsibility in functions within the center.
2. *The development of adequate inner controls* such that respect for law and regulation will result. This is achieved by giving the resident opportunities to learn from the consequences of his own irresponsible behavior as a resident.
3. *The development of a more constructive method of dealing with reality.* This is accomplished through group psychotherapy, which is provided by a psychologist on retainer to the Vocational Rehabilitation Division.
4. *The development of genuine feelings of self-worth.* To accomplish this, staff consciously endeavors to avoid negative references to past criminal behavior and to reward behavior that is positive. Verbal commendation is regularly resorted to.
5. *The development of the individual's unique potentialities.* This is largely accomplished by emphasizing community participation by the resident, since the resident is ultimately destined to participate in his own community.

Certain unique features have been integrated in the program at Milwaukie. To help the resident make more appropriate decisions, his

[32]Gordon Bird, "Community Centered Treatment of Offenders," in Edward M. Scott and Kathryn L. Scott (eds.), *Criminal Rehabilitation...Within and Without the Walls* (Springfield, Ill.: Charles C Thomas Publisher, 1973), pp. 133–35.

decision-making options are severely restricted during the initial part of his stay. His options are enlarged as time goes by, and passes to the community are more liberally granted. After one week in the program, the participant is given a four-hour pass. In time he may earn a twelve-hour weekend pass and is finally permitted overnight passes.

The unit is organized as a team, the team consisting of the residence manager, the work release representative, the rehabilitation counselors, and the counselor aide, who is a resident. Discipline is administered by the team. Serious breaches can result in a return to the institution of origin. There is also a house advisory committee, which includes five of the residents. The advisory committee makes recommendations as to how the program should be run. Approximately 10 percent of the residents are drug cases, and a drug surveillance unit is part of the overall program. As an additional control, urinalyses are randomly taken. Flexibility is emphasized in the overall program. Residents, for example, can be put in work training programs as well as in actual work programs.

From March 1970 to January 1972, a total of 211 active cases were serviced, with 84 failures. Only four of those failures, however, commited new felonies. As one of the professional staff members associated with this program said, "When one considers the failure rate for the correctional system as a whole as approximating 75 percent, it would appear that the Milwaukie program has effected a significant decrease in the recidivism rate of these offenders."[33]

Evaluating Work Release

According to Johnson and Kotch, "The expansion of work release in recent years is one of the remarkable trends in corrections in the United States," and is part of what they term "a multi-faceted movement . . . to make the walls of correctional institutions more porous to permit the two-way flow of interaction between inmates and the residents of outside communities."[34] From a pragmatic point of view, overcrowded prisons have been the inadvertent ally of community-based corrections. It has been unequivocally stated, for example, that the British Community Service Order, which was established to develop alternatives to imprisonment, "owes its origin to the overcrowding of Britain's prisons . . . . "[35] If the courts are convicting and committing more individuals than the correctional institutions can accommodate, then diversion is forced upon the

[33]*Ibid.*, p. 142.

[34]Elmer H. Johnson and Kenneth E. Kotch, "Two Factors in Development of Work Release: Size and Location of Prisons," *Journal of Criminal Justice*, 1, No. 1 (March 1973), 44.

[35]Louis Blom-Cooper, ed., *Progress in Penal Reform* (London: Clarendon Press, 1974), p. 245.

system. But community-based corrections, and work release in particular, can be defended on many grounds besides the purely practical, as our discussion should have clearly indicated.

In a November 1976 press conference, Massachusetts Correction Commissioner Frank A. Hall announced that his research department had completed a study of all prisoners released in 1973. That study revealed that the 1973 recidivism rate was 30 percent, compared to the 43 percent rate for 1966. Commissioner Hall then stated that the study "formally demonstrated that participation in the Furlough Program is the most important variable in accounting for the reduction of recidivism rates that has occurred in Massachusetts."[36]

THE FUTURE OF COMMUNITY CORRECTIONS TREATMENT

Correctional logistics are necessarily behind the thrust toward the community. But the philosophic reasons for redirecting the bulk of the correctional effort are even more compelling. The prison not only brutalizes and dehumanizes, it constitutes an unnatural and abnormal environment. The President's Task Force on Prisoner Rehabilitation said that the argument for community-based corrections was a simple one: "What is wrong with most offenders is that for any number of good or bad reasons they are unable or unwilling to respect the standards of the community, to adhere to its customs, to fulfill their obligations to it, or use to advantage the opportunities it provides. . . . The way to learn how to solve the problems of community living is to tackle them where they exist. The way to learn to understand and appreciate community life is to become immersed in it."[37]

Minnesota, which probably has the most progressive correctional system in the United States, exemplifies the commitment to community-based corrections. In 1973 it passed its Community Corrections Act, and it has subsequently endeavored to retain most of its offenders in correctional treatment programs in the community. The Community Corrections Act, in fact, was authored by Minnesota's Commissioner of Corrections, Kenneth Schoen. One of the pilot programs resulting from the act enabled Olmsted, Dodge, and Fillmore counties to develop a tri-county correctional system, with liberal subsidy from the state. "Two years after becoming community corrections counties [1974], the Dodge-Fillmore-

---

[36]Quoted in *Criminal Justice Newsletter*, 7, No. 24 (December 6, 1976), 6.
[37]The President's Task Force on Prisoner Rehabilitation, *The Criminal Offender—What Should Be Done?* (Washington, D.C.: U.S. Government Printing Office, 1970), pp. 20–21.

Olmsted Community Corrections System has treated 338 of the 347 offenders referred to it—98 percent—in community corrections programs."[38]

It has been alleged that community corrections is now in decline after a decade of enthusiastic development.[39] The negative philosophy implicit in the punishment model has, it is true, become rather infectious, but it has also been alleged that "A quiet revolution is underway in programs and services for incarcerated persons . . . . The quiet revolution of moving people out of institutions and back to the community . . . .Community-based treatment facilities are replacing prisons. . . ."[40]

Community-based treatment programs are expanding. Restitution is being looked upon with favor and increasingly integrated into sentencing practices. In 1967 the United States Bureau of Prisons established a Division of Community Services. There are innumerable local community-based projects springing up, such as Cincinnati's Comprehensive One-Stop Offender Aid Program (COSOAP), which provides a complete range of services for the ex-offender at one location. The Hennepin County (Minnesota) Department of Court Services has an extensive array of community resources for the offender, as well as a highly organized Volunteer Division.

The Offender Aid and Restoration organization (OAR) is a Virginia-based national "community-based program bringing volunteers into the lives of offenders and into the struggle for a more just corrections system."[41] In the Seattle-Tacoma area, Interaction/Transition is a new, community-based effort collaboratively developed by citizens and inmates, the latter at the federal penitentiary at McNeil Island. Group interaction and a five-phase program operates to help the offender develop self-awareness and be able to cope with the problems which will confront him upon release. A credit union and a halfway house are adjunctive features of this program.

An endless litany could be recited, but it suffices to note the transnational nature of the community correctional effort and the program proliferation. It is even more important to recognize the compelling, underlying philosophy. In the final analysis, if a program is not cost-beneficial, the bureaucrats will eventually eliminate it. Hopefully, the good will not be interred with the bones.

---

[38]John Blackmore, "Minnesota's Community Corrections Act Takes Hold," *Corrections Magazine*, 4, No. 1 (March 1978), 46.

[39]*Ibid.*, p. 47.

[40]Mercedes M. Miller, ed., *Evaluation Community Treatment Programs* (Lexington, Mass.: D. C. Heath and Company, 1975), p. xiii.

[41]*OAR NEWS*, 2, No. 1 (May 1978) (from the Masthead).

PROBATION AND PAROLE

Because so many community-based correctional treatment efforts are of recent origin, it might be assumed that the concept of correctional treatment in the community is a modern development. This is not so. Two correctional stalwarts have been community-based for well over a century, probation and parole. They continue to be the major representatives of community-based corrections. We will conclude this chapter by examining the diversionary tactic of probation and the transitional practice of parole.

The Scope

It is surprising that, despite their venerable age, the first comprehensive survey of probation and parole was not accomplished until 1976. At this time the Law Enforcement Assistance Administration (LEAA) engaged the Bureau of the Census to undertake a state by state analysis of these services. It was discovered that there were almost 1.5 million individuals under either probation or parole supervision as of September 1, 1976.[42] The breakdown was as follows:

	On Probation	On Parole	Total
Juveniles	328,854	53,347	382,201
Adults	923,064	156,194	1,079,258
Total	1,251,918	209,541	1,461,459

Males deominated the statistics, constituting 86 percent of the adult probationers and 90 percent of the adult parolees. Males also made up 77 percent of the juvenile probationers and 80 percent of the juvenile parolees. Approximately half of those on probation were felons, the remainder being misdemeanants. During the calendar year 1975, state and local probation and parole agencies had almost 2.4 million people under supervision. Those agencies had a total of 55,807 employees and were assisted by 20,263 volunteers. Sixty percent of the probation and parole staff were engaged in direct supervision and counseling, with an average caseload of 48 clients. In the United States, nationally, there are 680 individuals per 100,000 of the population on probation or parole. Four states

[42]LEAA, National Criminal Justice Information Service, *State and Local Probation and Parole System* (Washington, D.C.: U.S. Government Printing Office, 1978). For the student interested in the salaries paid to probation and parole officers in the various systems throughout the nation, the results of a recent survey are contained in the *American Journal of Corrections*, Vol. 38, No. 2, March-April, 1976.

significantly exceeded that norm: District of Columbia (1,366), Massachusetts (1,353), California (1,114), and Maryland (1,018).

Standards and Principles

In 1957 the California Special Study Commission, describing the California correctional system as "an aggregation of institutions and services," further stated that "there is extreme variation in correctional practice, indicating a strong need for the development and publication of standards and principles of corrections."[43] It took twenty years, but voluntary standards were finally propounded for probation and parole in 1977 by the Commission on Accreditation for Corrections of the National Council on Crime and Delinquency. In keeping with the ineradicable human penchant for excessive legislation, 208 standards have been incorporated in a *Manual of Standards for Adult Probation and Parole Field Services.* They will provide the basis for *voluntary* accreditation.

Some of the more important standards pertain to educational requirements, case services, and caseload size. Entry level educational requirements would necessitate a bachelor's degree in the behavioral sciences. Case services would be available 24 hours per day, and specialized caseloads would be constituted for such problems as alcoholism and drug addiction. Caseloads would be based on differential supervision needs, and not on numbers. There are also standards designed to eliminate patronage, which will undoubtedly cause the biggest obstruction to adoption.

Probation and parole have received their share of abrasive criticism in the general attack that has mounted against correctional rehabilitation. They have also been singled out as "most significant developments." Addressing the Chicago Institute for Juvenile Research, Francis A. Allen stated:

> Although one is sometimes inclined to despair of any constructive changes in the administration of criminal justice, a glance at the history of the past half-century reveals a succession of the most significant developments. Thus, the last fifty years have seen the widespread acceptance of three legal inventions of great importance: the juvenile court, systems of probation and systems of parole.[44]

While probation and parole are separate and distinct services, in terms of their place in the correctional system, the standards of the Com-

---

[43]Special Study Commission on Correctional Facilities and Services, *Second Interim Report: Probation Jails and Parole,* Sacramento, California, January 16, 1957, p. 9.
[44]Francis A. Allen, *The Borderland of Criminal Justice* (Chicago: The University of Chicago Press, 1964), p. 25.

mission on Accreditation for Corrections are generically applicable to both. The Commission's executive officer declared, "The Commission's position is that there are more similarities than differences in probation and parole field supervision and activities. Therefore, we developed one set of standards for both that allows for the discrete and necessary legal and administrative differences."[45] As further evidence of their consanguinity, probation and parole have been supported by the same three basic theories, and a fourth that is in embryo.

Theories

Both probation and parole pose dilemmas from a legal point of view. In its infancy, probation was attacked on the grounds that the power to suspend a sentence did not repose in the court. The court, it was felt, had no option but to mandatorily impose the prescribed penalty for the offense in question. As a matter of historical fact, the United States Supreme Court ruled, in a notable decision,[46] that *the federal courts* did not have the power to indefinitely suspend sentences. This decision was later invalidated, but it well reflected the controversy surrounding the legal basis of probation.

With respect to parole, the courts have struggled to reconcile the release (parole) of prospective threats into the community, when the sentencing process ostensibly aims at the effective removal of these threats from the community. The dilemma again involves the nature of the sentencing process. The following theories have aspired to resolve the dilemma, theoretically, at least.

The Theory of Grace

According to this theory, the state has the inherent right to require a convicted person to serve the full sentence prescribed by law. Where probation or parole is granted, therefore, the state is acting *ex gratia,* that is, out of its benevolence. Conviction follows due process; so it follows that probation or parole is a privilege and not a right.

The Theory of Contract–Consent

This theory is similar to the grace theory, in that both see the restoration of liberty (probation or parole) as being a result of the state yielding its power to hold the individual for the duration of the sentence. The theory

---

[45]Quoted in *Criminal Justice Newsletter,* 8, No. 19 (September 16, 1977), 3.

[46]*Ex parte United States,* 242 U.S. 27-53 (1916). In its decision, the court did, interestingly, suggest that the dilemma should be resolved by "probation legislation or such other means as the legislative mind may devise . . . ."

of contract–consent differs in that it does not see this as a matter of grace, but as a contractual matter. The state yields its power to exact the full sentence in exchange for the individual's submission to conditions imposed by the state.

The Theory of Custody

In the custody theory, there is no presumption that the probationer or parolee has been given liberty. On the contrary, through a legal fiction, the individual is considered to be in constructive custody. In parole, for example, the parolee's room in the community is considered to be an extension of his cell, and the parole officer is the agent of the warden.

The Restraint of Liberty Theory

This is not a clearly articulated theory, but one that can be considered *in embryo*. It can be inferred from the judicial disposition. In a fairly recent Supreme Court decision of pertinence, the court used the term "restraint of liberty" rather than custody, suggesting an effort to sidestep the custody-liberty controversy.[47] In view of the fact that the courts have been affirming the rights of prisoners, "it might be said that this country is moving toward a theory which could be christened 'the legal restraint theory.' Such a view would see the released prisoner as essentially free but with certain conditions restraining that freedom."[48]

Each of the three major theories can be criticized for rather obvious reasons. The *grace theory* is out-dated and of questionable constitutionality. The *contract–consent theory* is obviously vulnerable because it would permit the state to impose unlimited conditions on the individual, raising the prospect of unconstitutionality. *The custody theory*, although the one with probably the biggest following, is based on a legal fiction. It is obviously stretching credulity to consider probation or parole as the equivalent of incarceration. The *restraint of liberty theory* is an embryonic concept and is not, therefore, susceptible to critical analysis.

PROBATION

It is generally believed that probation began in the United States. The truth is that probation was first *legally* instituted in this country, but it derived from many ancestors. Among the more significant of those ancestors were benefit of clergy, suspension of judgment, recognizance, bail,

---

[47] *Jones v. Cunningham,* 83 Sup. Ct. 373 (1963).
[48] Louis P. Carney, *Probation and Parole: Legal and Social Dimensions* (New York: McGraw-Hill Book Company, 1977), p. 143.

filing of cases, and indenture. The practice of benefit of clergy developed in the thirteenth century and resulted from a conflict between the Church and the monarchy as to who would have trial jurisdiction over miscreant clergy. Under Henry II, it was agreed that clerics who were in violation of the civil law could plead benefit of clergy and be tried in the ecclesiastical courts. The benefit of being tried in the ecclesiastical courts was that the bishop's penalties were less severe than the crown's. In fact, it is this lessening of the penalty that explains why benefit of clergy is considered a predecessor of probation. Probation is a classic correctional device for mitigation of sentence.

The other forerunners of probation have an affinity with probation because they, too, reflect mitigation of sentence—or involve supervision, or suspension of sentence. In fact we can say that "The thread which linked the forerunners of probation was the persisting English common law tradition that the courts had an inherent right to *temporarily* suspend sentences."[49] (Italics in the original).

The first probation officer was an American, John Augustus. Spectating at the Boston Police Court in 1841, Augustus was moved to intercede for a derelict who was in court on a "common drunkard" charge. He importuned the judge to release the man to his custody. Augustus wrought such a remarkable change in the defendant's appearance that, upon return to court three weeks later for sentencing, the astonished judge imposed a nominal fine of one cent. For this act, and 18 successive years working with almost 2,000 individuals, John Augustus earned the title of "first probation officer." His philosophy undergirds probation and parole: "The object of the law is to reform criminals and to prevent crime and not to punish maliciously, or from a spirit of revenge."[50]

It was fitting that the first probation law was passed in Massachusetts, in 1878, although it was limited to the city of Boston. The mayor of Boston, under this statute, was empowered to appoint a paid probation officer, to be chosen either from the police force or from the citizenry. Captain E. H. Savage, a former ranking police official, is generally recognized as the first statutory probation officer in the United States. In 1880, Massachusetts passed legislation extending the power to appoint probation officers to every municipality and township in the state.

The Essence of Probation

Any definition of probation must include the four essentials that comprise this professional service: (1) The suspension of a sentence. (2)

---

[49] *Ibid.*, p. 75.
[50] Ronald L. Goldfarb and Linda R. Singer, *After Conviction* (New York: Simon & Schuster, Inc., (1973), p. 208.

The creation of a status. (3) The imposition of conditions. (4) Supervision.[51] The rationale for probation is that it retains the individual in the community, aborts the stigma and the criminalization that would ensue from imprisonment, and is more economical than institutionalization. In its Standards Relating to Probation, the American Bar Association declares that probation is the preferred form of sentencing, where the safety of the community is not jeopardized, and where the manifest need is not for incarceration of the individual.[52]

The Pre-sentence Investigation

According to Abadinsky, a probation agency provides three basic services, namely, *juvenile, pre-sentence investigation,* and *supervision.*[53] Juvenile services were instituted with the creation of the juvenile court in 1899. Supervision is administered through the professional relationship, and it combines surveillance and case services. The juvenile will be dealt with in detail in the chapter which follows, and the essence of supervision should be well understood by this time. A word or two on the pre-sentence investigation is all that remains necessary in order to round out the dynamic of probation.

The pre-sentence investigation is that exploratory action of the probation officer which results in the *pre-sentence investigation report.* This report contains an encapsulated profile of the defendant, which is designed to facilitate a just judicial disposition. The probation officers pulls together the essentials of the defendant's legal, social, familial, and criminal history for the court's edification. Most authorities speak favorably of this tool, although it is optional in most jurisdictions.

Unfortunately, probation officers, who are ordinarily overburdened with excessively large caseloads, tend to compile superfluous information. This was borne out in a very recent study of 735 state and local probation agencies, in which it was confirmed that there has been an increasing emphasis on the quantitative collection of data.[54] This is obviously self-defeating.

Innovations in Probation

In 1965, Ohio passed a statute authorizing "shock probation." This law permits a judge to send an individual to prison and then to order his

---

[51]Carney, *Probation and Parole: Legal and Social Dimensions,* p. 84.
[52]Sec. 1.3.
[53]Howard Abadinsky, *Probation and Parole Theory and Practice* (Englewood Cliffs, N. J.: Prentice-Hall, Inc., 1977), p. 27.
[54]Robert M. Carter, *Presentence Report Handbook* (Washington, D.C.: U.S. Government Printing Office, 1978), p. v.

release from 30 to 130 days after the imposition of sentence. The theory behind this practice is that the brief incarceration will have a salutary effect on young offenders and deter them from further criminality. The law precludes the "shock probationer" from serving more than 130 days in prison. The growth of this practice is evidenced in the fact that while only 85 cases were granted shock probation in 1966, the number had grown to 1,478 in 1976.[55] Violent offenders are excluded from the program. Authorities in Ohio claim that only 10.3 of shock probationed cases have recidivated, although this figure has been questioned. It costs $5,000 per year to keep a man in prison in Ohio but only $500 a year to maintain him on probation. If the recidivism figures are not convincing, the economics are.

In concert with the increasing concern for the long neglected victim, courts have been showing a predisposition to impose restitution obligations upon probationers. This is not direct restitution to the victim, but vicarious restitution to the community. Chief Justice Bailey Brown of the U.S. District Court in Memphis, Tennessee, instituted a program in 1976 in which a probationer would be required to work without pay for the equivalent of one eight-hour day each week. The theory is that "his being required to do work without pay for a good cause should have some therapeutic effect since this would make him atone for his misdeed in a concrete and constructive way."[56] This practice has been in effect since the mid-1970s in Ontario, Canada, where judges issue what are known as community service orders (CSOs). In October 1977, the Ministry of the Attorney General announced that several pilot projects had been developed to further stimulate the use of CSOs.[57] Just as in the Memphis District Court program, the Canadian probationers are required to donate work to the community, but the work is undertaken during the probationer's leisure time, and it cannot be of such a nature that it would displace a community member. Getting the community involved in the justice system is a major objective of the Canadian program.

Probation and parole officers have traditionally been buffeted between the roles of law enforcement representative and social work exponent. The profession itself has been unable to clearly establish an identity, and so the profession vacillated. As sentiment against the rehabilitation model increased, probation and parole officers found it harder and harder to develop an image. The resolution may have come with the emergence of the reintegration model, and with the concept of team

[55] Joan Potter, "Shock Probation: A Little Taste of Prison," *Corrections Magazine,* 3, No. 4 (December 1977), 48.

[56] Bailey Brown, "Community Services as a Condition of Probation, *Federal Probation,* 41, No. 4 (December 1977), 7.

[57] *Contact Newsletter,* 15, No. 10 (October 1978), 1.

supervision. In 1975, the Western Interstate Commission on Higher Education, funded by a grant from the National Institute of Corrections, developed the concept of the Community Resources Management Team (CRMT). It has been called "a coming mode of operation for probation and parole throughout the United States."[58]

Two key concepts are incorporated in this new thrust. First, the central function of the probation or parole officer is to be a broker or manager of community resources. Second, the approach of probation and parole will be on a team basis, with shared decision-making. The CRMT essence "is a synthesis of four elements: needs-assessment, resource brokerage, pooled caseloads, and team management."[59] The individual probation or parole officer will "specialize in one "needs subsystem," such as alcohol or drug abuse, mental health or job placement."[60] He or she will no longer have to be the professional alpha and omega of the client's existence. It should be noted that this concept of community resources broker had been previously suggested by the National Advisory Commission, which specifically said, with respect to the parole officer, that they "should be selected and trained to fulfill the role of community resource manager."[61]

Evaluating Probation

One of the most difficult things to do is to evaluate the results of correctional treatment. The ordinary rule of thumb is the rate of recidivism, but this is a most unsatisfactory device. An individual could have experienced considerable growth, yet constitute a failure on technical grounds. It has often been said that probation really has not been tried, because probation officers have excessive caseloads, which makes innovative and individualized treatment impossible. A General Accounting Office study of probation in four different areas of the country, involving 1,400 cases, led to the conclusion that probation is in a state of crisis.[62]

In contrast, the President's Crime Commission said, "The best data available indicate that probation offers one of the most significant prospects for effective programs in corrections."[63] On the assumption that selection and community assistance would be improved, the National Ad-

---

[58]Rob Wilson, "Probation/Parole Officers as 'Resource Brokers,' " *Corrections Magazine,* 4, No. 2 (June 1978), 48.

[59]*Ibid.,* p. 49.

[60]*Ibid.*

[61]National Advisory Commission on Criminal Justice Standards and Goals, *Task Force Report: Corrections* (Washington, D.C.: U.S. Government Printing Office, 1973), p. 430.

[62]*Criminal Justice Newsletter,* 7, No. 12 (June 7, 1976), 3.

[63]President's Commission on Law Enforcement and Administration of Justice, *Task Force Report: Corrections* (Washington, D.C.: U.S. Government Printing Office, 1967), p. 27.

visory Commission indicated that probation could reach its full potential. It predicted that probation, "which is now the largest community-based program, will become the standard sentence in criminal cases."[64] It is to be expected that some of the innovative ideas touched upon, particularly the CRMT concept and prospective variations on this theme, will bring increasing success to probation. In the interim, it is more than justified on both humanitarian and economic grounds.

PAROLE

At the opposite end of the correctional spectrum stands parole. The individual who is on parole has passed through the prison en route to that status and is permitted the privilege of serving the unexpired portion of his sentence in the community. Where probation is a diversionary tactic, aimed at keeping the individual out of the system, parole is a transitional mechanism for easing the offender back into free society.

Two men loom large in the history of parole, Captain Alexander Maconochie and Sir Walter Crofton. Maconochie is famous for putting the "marks" system and the "ticket of leave" into operation in the penal colonies of Australia in 1840. The "ticket of leave" is the direct ancestor of parole. Sir Walter Crofton, upon becoming head of the Irish prison system in 1854, introduced refinements to Maconochie's concept of graduated release. The first parole officer, in fact, was a Dubliner, James P. Organ. Crofton's refinements included job assistance for parolees, home and employment visits, and a graduated release to parole from his so-called "intermediate prison system." His system so enamored American penologists that the "Irish System" was adopted in the United States.

Parole had earlier predecessors and, in truth, a great many influences and developments led to what ultimately became parole as we know it. Indenture could be included, as well as the early practice of giving aid to discharged prisoners, which philanthropic societies began to take upon themselves, especially in the early middle of the nineteenth century. The ability to have one's sentence reduced by good time was another influence, and commutation laws, the first of which was passed by the New York Legislature in 1817, were also precursors.

The Scope of Parole

As of December 31, 1977, it was estimated that there were 181,000 conditionally released offenders under parole supervision in the United

---

[64] *Executive Summary—Reports of the National Advisory Commission on Criminal Justice Standards and Goals* (Washington, D.C.: U.S. Government Printing Office, 1974), p. 50.

States. This figure includes about 5 percent "mandatory releases," that is, individuals for whom the law mandates release after a certain portion of the sentence has been served. The majority of these were federal cases. The actual number of non-mandatory parolees under supervision on December 31, 1977 was 173,000. A total of 54 agencies, some of which were joint probation/parole agencies, were providing the parole service. During the preceding two-year period, the parole population had increased 10.1 percent, or a total of an additional 16,600 cases. The greater part of that increase, or 8.2 percent, occurred during 1977.[65] The assumption is that the increase was due to liberalized paroling practices. In the face of growing criticism of parole, it is interesting to note that the ranks of the paroled have been swelling.

The Essence of Parole

While probation is a judicial function, parole is an executive function and it is really part of that development known as "aftercare." While we normally think of aftercare with respect to hospital patients, or juveniles, the philosophic shift from punishment to rehabilitation led to concern for discharged prisoners. "The most characteristic feature of the aftercare movement was that it was local in nature. Most prisoners in earlier times served their sentences in local prisons, on the county level. It was a natural development for the philanthropic to consider it a duty to give financial assistance to released prisoners."[66]

The definition of parole given in the *Attorney General's Survey of Release Procedures* is often considered the classic definition, which is that parole is "release of an offender from a penal or correctional institution, after he has served a portion of his sentence, under the continued custody of the state and under conditions that permit his reincarceration in the event of misbehavior."[67] The basic criticism of this definition is that it is purely legal and does not take into account the aspect of social readjustment intended by the practice. If this were to be integrated with the legal aspects, an acceptable definition might be that parole "is a correctional device through which an offender, after serving less than his or her total sentence, is conditionally released from a penal facility, under active supervision, with social reintegration as the objective."[68] Conditional release implicitly indicates that revocation and return to prison would be the penalty for breach of the conditions.

[65]James L. Galvin and others, *Parole in the United States: 1976 and 1977* (San Francisco: Research Center West, National Council on Crime and Delinquency, July 1978), pp. 11–12.

[66]Louis P. Carney, *Probation and Parole: Legal and Social Dimensions* (New York: McGraw-Hill Book Company, 1977), p. 141.

[67]*Ibid.*, p. 154.

[68]*Ibid.*, p. 155.

The Indeterminate Sentence

Both parole and its handmaiden, the indeterminate sentence, were introduced in the United States at the Elmira Reformatory in New York. Until quite recently, it was considered that parole and the indeterminate sentence were inseparable, for the theory of parole partly hinged on the supposition that an indeterminate, rather than a fixed sentence, would enable a group of experts (the parole board) to definitively assess the progress of an inmate, so that he might be paroled at the optimum point.

The indeterminate sentence dominates the sentencing structure of the United States at the present time.[69] It is characterized by having a minimum and a maximum limit, rather than being precisely fixed, as is the determinate sentence. Schmidt sees the indeterminate sentence, from what is loosely called the revolutionary viewpoint, as "a further step in increasing control over prisoners," relating it to the misguuided medical model and the concept of criminals being sick, which "originated in the nineteenth century, with the ideas of determinism replacing those of free will."[70]

In the 1970s, attacks began to mount on parole as it became increasingly clear that the indeterminate sentence, instead of being a "treatment" tool, was, instead, the source of psychological anguish for the imprisoned. If parole could be indeterminately postponed by a parole board, looking for a condition of rehabilitation that really was not observable, then the only result was conflictual uncertainty for the inmates. In 1973, a popular magazine carried an article by a reputable professor urging the abolition of parole.[71] In 1975, the Citizens' Inquiry on Parole and Criminal Justice issued a stinging report, condemning not only the (New York) parole board, but the very concept of parole itself. In the 1977 American Bar Association proposed draft of *Standards Relating to the Legal Status of Prisoners,* the abolition of parole was proposed, as it was in the federal Criminal Code Reform Act, when hearings were held on that bill in 1977.

One immediate result of the onslaught of criticism in the 1970s has been a notable shift toward the determinate sentence. On July 1, 1977, California rescinded its "model" indeterminate sentence and substituted a determinate sentencing structure. In the preceding year, Maine had made a similar reversal, and Indiana followed later in 1977.[72] There has not exactly been a stampede, but about a dozen more states are in the

[69]The Twentieth Century Fund Task Force on Criminal Sentencing, *Fair and Certain Punishment* (New York: McGraw-Hill Book Company, 1976), p. 11.

[70]Janet Schmidt, *Demystifying Parole* (Lexington, Mass.: D. C. Heath and Company, 1977), p. 4.

[71]Herman Schwartz, "Let's Abolish Parole," *Reader's Digest,* August 1973, pp. 185–90.

[72]Stephen Gettinger, "Fixed Sentencing Becomes Law in Three States; Other Legislatures Wary," *Corrections Magazine,* 3, No. 3 (September 1977), 16.

planning (to change) stage. Parole, itself, though embattled is still fairly well entrenched. There is every likelihood that, in due time, parole may cease to be. But for the present, it remains a major correctional effort that is trying to become more meaningful.

Innovations in Parole

Among the major problems besetting parole is the difficulty of deciding when to parole an individual. With wide latitude under the indeterminate sentence, parole boards were more often capricious than scientific. In an effort to counteract this condition, several jurisdictions have begun to develop and apply variations of risk tables, usually based on a statistical formula. There is a twofold purpose. First, there is a need to be able to screen out the higher risks from being paroled. Second, there is a critical need to make parole board decisions equitable.

The federal system, Minnesota, Michigan, and Oregon are some of the jurisdictions engaged in this fashion. Oregon, for example, employs a "matrix system," which "assigns parole dates, not on the basis of rehabilitation, record, prediction of dangerousness or "feel," but according to two scores."[73] These scores are the Criminal History/Risk Score and the Offense Severity Rating. Numerical weights are assigned to various crimes and background factors, so that a consistent formula is applied in releasing individuals. The intent is to take the guesswork and the manipulation out of parole decision-making. The matrix system has been in operation in Oregon since 1976. Following a major reorganization in 1974, the United States Board of Parole adopted a "Salient Factor Score," which is an actuarial device, comparable to that in use in Oregon, which assesses the "risk factor" before an inmate is paroled.

In 1971 the American Correctional Association sponsored an innovative approach to parole which was based on the stated importance of shared decision-making and that the supposition that involvement of the inmate, through the decision-making process, would enhance the parole prospect.[74] Called MAP, for Mutual Agreement Program, it requires the inmate, the correctional institution, and the parole board to jointly develop a legally enforceable contract, to which all three are bound. A date is set in the contract for the completion of the inmate's obligations under the contract, which could include such activities as getting educational or vocational training. When the program completion date is reached, then

---

[73]John Darling, "Oregon's Parole Matrix," *American Journal of Corrections,* 40, No. 3 (May–June 1978), 14.

[74]Leon Lieberg and Bill Parker, Resource Document #3, *The Mutual Agreement Program* (College Park, Md.: American Correctional Association, 1973). See also, *Corrections Magazine,* 2, No. 1 (September/October, 1975), 3–8, 45–50.

that date becomes the parole date, providing that the inmate has fulfilled his contractual obligations. This is a controversial program, mainly because of the rigidity of the contract (it binds the system as well as the inmate), the fear that it will put undue pressure on the inmate, and other technical reasons. Approximately a dozen states have MAP programs currently.

Only in recent times has it been recognized that the parole system contains a unique reservoir of talent that can be applied to the correctional effort. It is the talent that resides in the offenders themselves. First of all, the experience behind jail or prison bars gives the ex-offender a rapport with those on parole, which the parole officer simply cannot possess. Second, every individual has certain skills and talents, and offenders are no exception. Theirs include insight into the mind and motive of the criminal and into the feelings of the parolee with respect to programming for reintegration. Third, a program that utilizes the ex-offender's talents makes rehabilitation meaningful and gives integrity to the system.

An outstanding example of such an endeavor is the Ohio Parole Officer Aide Program. In this program, which began in 1972, ex-offenders are screened and trained for employment with the Division of Parole and Community Services and work under the supervision of senior parole officers. The parole officer aide position is now a permanent civil service position in Ohio, and the parole aides have contributed not only to their own self-sufficiency, but have also been able to give a great deal of individualized attention to the parole aide's role as a job resource developer. The aide is also encouraged to continue his professionalization by attending appropriate courses of study at the undergraduate and graduate levels in local colleges. Up to ten hours per week is allowed for this purpose during regular work hours.

Through the first three years, 29 parole aides were hired. The unique aspect of the Ohio program is that each aide is actually given a caseload, with instructions to provide a level of supervision that would be comparable to that provided by professional parole officers. At the beginning of the program, the caseload was 30, but in 1974–1975, the caseload was increased to 50 parolees. Ohio law precludes a parole officer aide from possessing a weapon, arresting a parolee, or transporting an offender who is under arrest, nor can total supervision be assumed over the cases by the aide. It is mandatory to staff all cases regularly with the senior parole officer or the unit supervisor.

Evaluation of the program is being conducted by the Program for the Study of Crime and Delinquency at Ohio State University. At this stage, it has been said that:

> Overall, Ohio's Parole Officer Aide Program has been given positive, often superlative, ratings from almost everyone associated with it. The aides have

performed well in their two years of employment with the Ohio Adult Parole Authority. Regardless of whether parolees, supervisors, or others are evaluating their work, aides have received outstanding praise and acknowledgement for their contribution to the field of corrections.[75]

Evaluating Parole

As we have stated, parole has come under severe attack recently, and the attack has extended to include capricious, autocratic parole boards and a psychologically tormenting indeterminate sentence. It may be said that parole is fighting for survival, or at least for the opportunity to demonstrate its true worth. So a flurry of innovations may be anticipated.

In Washington and California, unemployment compensation is paid to paroled inmates. Direct financial assistance to parolees has also been experimented with in California[76] and in Connecticut. The Young Lawyers Section of the American Bar Association launched an ambitious program in which lawyers would spend at least six hours a month with selected parolees in various states, on the premise that "having a friend is helpful in coping with the problems of life . . . ." Neither this type of association[77] nor the direct financial assistance programs have shown any appreciable success.[78] On the other hand, some heartening success has been demonstrated in a project involving a residential program in the community that combines intensive parole supervision with a requirement for restitution.[79] A New York study found that consistent employment was positively correlated with parole success, and that "parole casework treatment was an essential concomitant factor which substantially assisted in the progress of the parolee's behavior."[80] A very recent Connecticut study of 173 inmates released on parole concludes that "parole was probably effective in preventing those offenders from returning to crime."[81]

There is a mixed message coming from parole. There have been grave deficiencies and promising indices. A great deal of innovative pro-

[75]Joseph E. Scott, *Ex-Offenders as Parole Officers* (Lexington, Mass.: D. C. Heath and Company, 1975), p. 98. This is a definitive study.

[76]Craig Reinarman, *Direct Financial Assistance to Parolees: A Promising Alternative in Correctional Programming,* Research Report No. 55, Research Unit, Department of Corrections, State of California, May 1975.

[77]John Berman, "The Volunteer in Parole Program," *Criminology,* 13, No. 1 (May 1975), 112.

[78]Malcolm Feeley, "Can More Gate Money Improve a Parolee's Chances?" *Beyond Time,* Spring 1974, pp. 104–14.

[79]Joe Heinz, Burt Galaway, and Joe Hudson, "Restitution or Parole: A Follow-up Study of Adult Offenders," *Social Service Review,* 50, No. 1 (March 1976), 148–56.

[80]John M. Stanton, "Parole Effectiveness," Bureau of Research and Statistics, State of New York, Division of Parole, August 15, 1969, p. 12 (mimeographed).

[81]*Connecticut Study Suggests Release of Criminals on Parole Prevents Return to Crime,* Connecticut Department of Corrections, News Release, undated (1977).

gramming must be undertaken if the real contribution of this major community correctional effort is to be vindicated. Despite the onslaught of criticism, there must be some substantial merit in parole when the arch-critics of correctional rehabilitation are constrained to say, "The evidence seems to indicate that the abolition of parole supervision would result in substantial increases in arrest, conviction, and return to prison."[82] Actively expressed concern for the reconstruction of another, expressed in this instance through parole supervision, is intrinsically meritorious. Demonstrating that empirically, or at least convincingly, is the challenge facing parole.

SYNOPSIS

Correctional treatment, to a great extent, must ultimately move to the laboratory of the community. The prison is an inimical environment, and the rehabilitation nutrients are in the community. The National Advisory Commission and numerous other reputable agencies have urged this. Community-based corrections is a correctional policy in Minnesota. It is suggested that the Dutch "subsidy principle" (minimal use of prisons) should be adopted.

Diversion from the prison aborts stigma, keeps families intact, retains the individual in the community with its nurturing resources, and emphasizes the community's stake in the correctional endeavor. A specific type of diversion, pre-trial diversion, is aimed at economic as well as altruistic objectives. Intermediate forms of diversion include work release and work furlough.

Residential treatment centers and halfway houses are prime examples of community correctional treatment efforts. Integrated community corrections are exemplified in Polk County, Iowa and the PORT Program in Minnesota.

Probation and parole, heretofore the main pillars of community-based corrections, have been found relatively wanting, parole particularly. These strategies hold great promise for corrections, but they must be professionalized and innovatively developed. Approximately 1.5 million individuals are on probation or parole. Newer developments include "shock probation" and a matrix system for determining parole eligibility (used by the Federal Bureau of Prisons and the states of Oregon, Michigan, and Minnesota).

Probation and parole are compelling tactics, but they have yet to demonstrate their full potential.

[82]Robert Martinson and Judith Wilks, "Save Parole Supervision," *Federal Probation*, 41, No. 3 (September 1977), 26–27.

11 The Juvenile Justice System

The childhood shows the man as morning shows the day.

John Milton
Paradise Regained

In the spring of 1978, Tom Beach* filed what was believed to be the first suit ever brought against a parent by a child for "psychological malparenting." The suit asked for $350,000 for medical expenses because of "intentional infliction of emotional distress." The estrangement started when young Beach was expelled from a private school in Hawaii for smoking marijuana. The expulsion, plus his use of other drugs such as LSD, brought his value system and his father's into a collision course. Even advocates of the rights of children considered the suit frivolous, and a representative of the ACLU was led to comment that this area was one that

*Not his real name.

should be left "untouched by the outside world." Letters to the editor overwhelmingly condemned the legal action, calling the plaintiff such things as a "horrible man-child," "repulsive," and similar epithets. The father was devastated, the mother heartbroken, and the plaintiff, who lived on a trust fund the parents had previously set up for him, saw psychiatrists frequently and played his guitar most of the time. The court ultimately ruled against the plaintiff.

And professionals continued to probe, unsuccessfully it seems, the labyrinthian corridors of the juvenile mind, in the attempt to understand the behavior that is increasingly shocking to a great many people.

JUVENILE DELINQUENCY: SCOPE AND NATURE

In Detroit, a 17-year-old stabbed a Wayne State University professor to death in a robbery, which netted him $2. It was the second murder he had committed in his young life. In Los Angeles, another 17-year-old was arrested after bludgeoning a mother and three of her daughters to death. He was on probation when he committed these crimes, and had been arrested eight previous times for a variety of mostly violent crimes. In Miami, a 15-year-old boy was sentenced to life in prison with no possibility of parole for 25 years, following a murder conviction. He killed an 83-year-old neighbor who caught him ransacking her home. The youth's defense was that he had become temporarily intoxicated by the violence which he had witnessed on TV. In Lanett, Alabama, a 13-year-old child shot his school principal twice, following a paddling for fighting with another student in the classroom. In 1978, an 83-year-old woman testified before a Senate subcommittee that she lived in an area terrorized by juvenile gangs and that she had been beaten, choked, and robbed of her social security money.

In Ventura, California, a judge described a 16-year-old rapist-murderer as "a savage and a sadist" and publicly regretted that he had to commit the defendant to the Youth Authority, because of his age, rather than to prison for life. And in Burlingame, California, a judge sent two teen-aged kidnappers, who had threatened to send the fingers of their 11-year-old victim to his parents if their ransom demand was not met, to county jail instead of prison. He said he was influenced by psychiatric testimony that the defendants could be rehabilitated. The victim's mother was furious. And, in 1978, the youngest person in modern American judicial history was indicted for murder, and processed as an adult, in New York. He was thirteen years old.

These few woeful cases present a fragment of the problem posed by contemporary juvenile delinquency. Sentencing inequity is as patently evident in the juvenile arena as it is in the criminal courts, and in both the challenge of reconstruction is enormous.

The prodigious research team of Sheldon and Eleanor Glueck spent a lifetime probing into the mind and the heart of the juvenile delinquent, while trying to unravel juvenile delinquency. After more than forty years of companionate research, the team was broken by the death of Eleanor, who passed away while the couple was preparing a panoramic recapitulation of their "search and research." Sheldon Glueck completed that work, and in the preface he said that "just as it is not likely that law-abidingness can be explained by any single discipline so delinquency cannot be accounted for by any single 'cause.'"[1] To understand the phenomenon of juvenile crime and delinquency, the philosophy of "reasoned eclecticism" must be adoped. But before reasoned eclecticism can be applied, some empirical dimensions of the problem must be constructed.

Statistical Dimensions

Over 2,000,000 juveniles are arrested annually in the United States. The 1975 census showed that 2,151 public and private juvenile correctional facilities and detention centers were in existence, with approximately 40 percent of those facilities being operated by state or local governments. In the twelve-month interval between the 1974 and 1975 censuses, the number of long-term correctional facilities increased by 6 percent, while detention centers grew by 4 percent. There was a dramatic growth in treatment-oriented group homes during the same period, going from 166 to 195, a 17 percent increase. While there had been a gradual decline for several years in the number of training schools (the traditional long-term institution), they experienced a 2 percent expansion from 1974 to 1975. Forty percent of all public facilities in the period surveyed were detention centers.

On June 30, 1975, a total of 46,980 juveniles were housed in public detention and correctional facilities in the United States, a figure that was 5 percent higher than that which obtained a year earlier. After a declining trend that had set in during the early seventies, which "bottomed out" in 1974, an upturn began in 1975. The June count, however, was still 14 percent below the peak of June 30, 1971. An additional 27,290 youngsters were housed in the more numerous but traditionally smaller private establishments. In 1975, the "annual expenditure by juvenile detention and

---

[1]Sheldon and Eleanor Glueck, *Of Delinquency and Crime* (Springfield, Ill.: Charles C Thomas Publisher, 1974), p. vi.

correctional facilities, both public and private, totaled $867.9 million, an amount about 8 percent higher than that revealed in the 1974 census."[2]

Defining Delinquency

A number of authorities have offered a wide range of explanations for juvenile delinquency, defining it in terms of incomplete socialization, the prevalence of illicit opportunities, and various forms of deprivation. Matza has suggested that one literally drifts into delinquency, "drift" being defined as "episodic release from moral constraint."[3] The individual begins to drift when he begins to realize that there are a number of rationalizations that can be employed to neutralize moral responsibility.

Public opinion, which varies from time to time and place to place, also controls the definition of delinquency, through its tolerance or intolerance of certain forms of behavior. Thus Cavan and Ferdinand note "that delinquent behavior is really part of a continuum ranging from extremely antisocial actions to extremely conforming behavior which elicits a variety of public responses ranging from outraged condemnation through mild disapproval to strong approval."[4]

There is also dispute over whether or not delinquency should be defined as specific behavior, detected or undetected, or as a status legally adjudicated in a court of competent jurisdiction. In a government sponsored study of quite recent vintage, in which over 600 boys were sampled, a compromise of sorts was made: "Delinquency was operationally measured as having a police and/or juvenile court record (i.e. official delinquency)."[5]

It really depends on the purpose at hand. Academicians must, perforce, travel in and out of the realm of theoretical speculation. Practitioners, and those engaged in empirical research, deal with more concrete dimensions. But in the application of the treatment art, the mind must be permitted to consider a great many more dimensions, philosophic as well as sociologic, in trying to grasp the human condition that is a "tangle of profoundly interwoven problems that are inseparable from the social system in which we live."[6]

[2]U.S. Department of Justice, LEAA, *Children in Custody, Advance Report on the Juvenile Detention and Correctional Facility Census of 1975,* October 1977 (U.S. Government Printing Office, 1977), p. 5 *et passim.*

[3]David Matza, *Delinquency and Drift* (New York: John Wiley & Sons, Inc., 1964), p. 69.

[4]Ruth Shonle Cavan and Theodore N. Ferdinand, *Juvenile Delinquency,* 3rd ed. (Philadelphia: J. B. Lippincott Company, 1975), p. 28.

[5]Leonard D. Savitz, Michael Lalli, and Lawrence Rosen, *City Life and Delinquency— Victimization, Fear of Crime and Gang Membership* (Washington, D.C.: U.S. Government Printing Office, 1977), p. 3.

[6]Gary B. Adams and others (eds.), *Juvenile Justice Management* (Springfield, Ill.: Charles C Thomas Publisher, 1973), p. 5.

A point that cannot be avoided was aptly contained in the 1970 Annual Report of the Youth Development and Delinquency Prevention Administration, an agency of the U.S. Department of Health, Education, and Welfare. It was this:

> There are different ways of looking at delinquency and its manifestations. One possible approach is to suggest that societies which place a high premium on freedom, initiative, and success should hardly expect to contain all of its members in a conventional mold. According to this approach, delinquency is one form of breaking out of the mold.[7]

A very recent survey in Illinois "demonstrated that adolescent improprieties were . . . relatively universal among adolescents,"[8] which would indicate that a great number of youths are dissatisfied with the prevailing "mold."

JUVENILE COURT

Approximately one-half of the children arrested annually in the United States, or a little over one million, appear in juvenile court. The first juvenile court was established in Cook County (Chicago), Illinois in 1899. It resulted from mounting concern in a diversity of groups about the welfare of the child, who was not at the time separated from the adult in the criminal justice process. Despite its noble birth, little of innovative significance has been produced by the juvenile court and, indeed, it perpetuates the myths and discriminatory practices that are prevalent in the criminal justice tradition in this society.

The court operates under the doctrine of *parens patriae,* that is, it acts as the parent surrogate "in the best interests of the child." But according to the Twentieth Century Fund Task Force on Sentencing Policy Toward Young Offenders, "The theory behind the juvenile court is not merely obsolete; it is a fairy tale that never came true."[9] The court, the task force asserts, instead of being indiscriminately concerned with the "best interests" of every child, should make a consistent distinction in the severity of sentencing for those under and those over the age of 18 years, waiving the seriously violent offenders into adult court.

The traditional discrimination of the court—or the juvenile justice system—was reaffirmed in a survey in New York, covering five counties and 431 children whose cases were disposed of in the Family Court of the City of New York:

[7]*Ibid.*
[8]*Target,* Vol. 6, Issue 7, July/August 1977.
[9]Quoted in *Criminal Justice Newsletter,* 9, No. 8 (April 10, 1978), 1.

It has long been established that the children brought before a juvenile court come, for the most part, from the ranks of the poor and underprivileged, from the minority groups in the geographical area concerned. This is true in New York City where the majority of court related children are Black and Puerto Rican, the City's two largest minority groups living in poverty.[10]

Growing discontent with the juvenile court and juvenile justice processes led to some recent landmark court decisions, which have radically altered these institutions. The most momentous was Gault.[11]

The Historic Gault Decision

Under the concept of chancery and the doctrine of *parens patriae,* traditional constitutional safeguards had been dispensed with in the juvenile court. The Gault decision mobilized these neglected safeguards and brought them into the juvenile court. From that memorable date when the decision was handed down (May 15, 1967), juveniles have been entitled to counsel, to cross-examine adverse witnesses, to receive appropriate notice of hearings, and to all of the protections implicit in the Fifth Amendment, which prohibits self-incrimination. The controversy over the nature of the court, however, was re-ignited. Those with a rigid social work disposition saw the specter of a juvenile criminal court, turning back the clock on progress; but the constitutionally minded saw equity introduced. One pertinent opinion sees both elements present and says that Gault views "a delinquency proceeding as the counterpart of a criminal proceeding for the purpose of mandating certain trial-centered procedural safeguards. On the other hand, preadjudication procedures and, even more plainly, postadjudication procedures and goals of juvenile justice are dominated by the pathological condition–therapeutic response view."[12]

It is of historical interest to note that, two years after the Gault decision, the United Kingdom Parliament passed the Children and Young Persons Act to govern justice in England and Wales. It is an emphatic effort to decriminalize the English juvenile courts. Among its provisions are these: No child under fourteen years of age can be prosecuted for an offense other than homicide; "civil care" cannot be enforced upon a child, unless there has been an offense and a court finding that the juvenile is in need of care that he cannot receive; children should not have to go to

---

[10]Office of Children's Services, Judicial Conference of the State of New York, *Juvenile Injustice,* October 1973, p. 2.

[11]*In re Gault,* 387, U.S. 1 (1967).

[12]J. Lawrence Schultz and Fred Cohen, "Isolationism in Juvenile Court Jurisprudence," in Margaret K. Rosenheim (ed.), *Pursuing Justice for the Child* (Chicago:: The University of Chicago Press, 1976), pp. 21–22.

court when they commit an offense, whenever possible, because treatment should be voluntary, and with the parent's agreement.[13]

Sending children home under supervision, in lieu of putting them in detention centers, is beginning to have some modest support in this country. "Home detention," as it is called, has been utilized in Louisville–Jefferson County, Kentucky and in Hennepin County, Minnesota. The intent of these programs is twofold: to reduce pressure at detention centers and to use an economical alternative. A study of these programs revealed the ironic fact that even with "home detention," the county detention centers remained crowded.[14]

THE INSTITUTIONAL SIDE OF JUVENILE JUSTICE

In the light of the appalling conditions that are rather widespread in juvenile institutions in the United States, it approaches blasphemy to suggest that treatment could take place in those facilities. It is also a matter of grave concern that children are still being incarcerated in adult jails. The Children's Defense Fund made a nine-state study and found that children were jailed in adult facilities in every state visited. Worse, the "overwhelming majority" were not violent offenders, nor could they be considered a threat to the community.[15] The report documented incidents of forcible sodomy and unimaginable brutalization. It is inconceivable that such conditions exist anywhere in the United States in the late nineteen-seventies. Unfortunately, they are widespread.

Kenneth Wooden's survey of institutionalized children, in the early nineteen-seventies, was described as "a modern horror story." It is an unbelievable account of savagery toward defenseless children, rapacity by those to whom these children are entrusted, shameless greed by members of the medical profession, and blatant political corruption.[16] It was only fitting that Wooden quoted the remark of Chief Judge David L. Bazelon of the United States Court of Appeals, who told the American Academy of Child Psychiatry, in 1973: "It's time for all of us caretakers to stop hiding the smell of society's outhouses. No matter how hidden by bushes or how deodorized, it still smells like an outhouse!"[17]

[13]For a detailed analysis of the Children and Young Persons Act see A. E. Bottoms, "On the Decriminalization of English Juvenile Courts," in Roger Hood (ed.), *Crime, Criminology and Public Policy, Essays in Honour of Sir Leon Radzinowicz* (New York: The Free Press, 1974), pp. 320–45.

[14]National Council on Crime and Delinquency, *Youth Forum*, 2, No. 3 (Fall, 1978), 1.

[15]Children's Defense Fund, *Children in Adult Jails* (Washington, D.C.: Washington Research Project, Inc., 1976), p. 3.

[16]Kenneth Wooden, *Weeping in the Playtime of Others* (New York: McGraw-Hill Book Company, 1976).

[17]*Ibid.*, p. 100.

The Massachusetts Experiment

Two years before Judge Bazelon made his blunt comment to the American Academy of Child Psychiatry, Dr. Jerome Miller, the young, idealistic commissioner of the Department of Youth Services in Massachusetts stunned the correctional world by closing the juvenile institutions in that state. Predicting a new era of humane, community-based corrections, Miller had planned for two years to bring institutionalization of juveniles to an end in Massachusetts. There was no evidence that the state's juvenile institutions had effected any measure of rehabilitation, and they were unconscionably costly to the taxpayer, so Miller reasoned that more productive community substitutes could be found.

On January 17, 1972, the Lyman School for Boys, the last of the juvenile institutions, was closed down. The Lyman School For Boys had been the first institution of its kind in the nation when it was opened in 1846. Before its closing, "reformers had repeatedly denounced Lyman as a brutal and dehumanizing institution, a school of crime whose residents were almost always worse threats to society when they left than when they went in."[18] The closing was described as "a spectacular event, in which a caravan of cars and motorcycles descended on the institution, picked up the thirty-nine remaining youngsters and sped off to the University of Massachusetts at Amherst, where the youngsters stayed until other homes were found for them."[19]

Considerable controversy has subsequently erupted over what has now become known as "deinstitutionalization." Miller has been both praised and damned. Administrators in juvenile corrections in other states "generally take a dim view of the closing of institutions. Very few believe, as do Dr. Jerome Miller and his successors, that institutions are inherently destructive and should be eliminated."[20] This is undoubtedly a political stance rather than one based on any profound knowledge of the behavioral sciences, for the destructive influence of the institution has been well documented.[21]

The Massachusetts "experiment" is under close scrutiny by many other systems, but Massachusetts does not consider deinstitutionalization an "experiment." On the contrary, it is considered "a major reform effort. It represents a pioneering approach to juvenile *corrections,* not simply an alternative form of service delivery or sentencing."[22] It is also being

---

[18]Richard Kwartler (ed.), *Behind Bars* (New York: Vintage Press, 1977), pp. 100–101.
[19]*Ibid.,* p. 100.
[20]*Corrections Magazine,* 2, No. 2 (November/December 1975), 7.
[21]Besides the material cited, two good recent references are: Clemens Bartollas, Stuart J. Miller, and Simon Dinitz, *Juvenile Victimization* (New York: Sage Publications, 1976); and Yitzhak Bakal, *Closing Correctional Institutions* (Lexington, Mass.: D. C. Heath & Co., 1973).
[22] Commonwealth of Massachusetts, Department of Youth Services, *The Issue of Security*

evaluated by research faculty at Harvard University's Center For Criminal Justice. In a preliminary report, this definitive statement is made: "To many observers, the history of the reforms in the Massachusetts Department of Youth Services appears to be a collection of bewilderingly accidental, crisis-filled events, impossible to replicate. We have found, however, that the reforms followed what seems to be a clear, replicable pattern common to many other conflict and change situations."[23]

The Massachusetts Department of Youth Services now contracts with more than 200 private agencies to provide its correctional services. Despite the skepticism that may exist in other jurisdictions, "The conviction that community correctional programs for juveniles work is nowhere stronger than in Massachusetts . . . .Everyone associated with the community system . . . is convinced that the experiment is proving successful."[24] In 1978, the federal Office of Juvenile Justice and Delinquency Prevention announced that it planned to "persuade a few other States to deinstitutionalize statewide their large juvenile correctional institutions" following the lead of Massachusetts.[25]

DIVERSION

A concomitant of the modern emphasis on community-based corrections has been the call for diversion. Several reasons are given. There are those who are beginning to adopt the Dutch philosophy, or "subsidiary principle," which we encountered in Chapter Nine. That is, the correctional system should be the last resort, for its trauma, as Menninger implied, is practically incapable of being surmounted. It is particularly important to prevent the criminalization process and social stigma from infecting the young. Economic reasons also exist, because institutionalization is a very costly business for the taxpayer.

There are practical reasons, too. The system is overcrowded and diversion can defuse the explosive potential generated by congestion. Furthermore, diversion is a method of exercising discretion, and discretion, besides being a long-time tradition in the criminal justice system, constitutes a sort of safety valve for the total system. One writer expressed the additional, broad opinion that "the argument for diversion is a negative argument against the existing system. The assumption is that the present justice system is sufficiently bad that any alternative for diverting offen-

in a Community-Based System of Juvenile Corrections, The Final Report of the Task Force on Secure Facilities, November 1977, p. 104.

[23]Lloyd E. Ohlin, Alden D. Miller, and Robert B. Coates, *Juvenile Correctional Reform in Massachusetts* (Washington, D.C.: U.S. Government Printing Office, 1977), p. 93.

[24]*Corrections Magazine,* 1, No. 5 (May/June 1975), 33.

[25]Cited in *Criminal Justice Newsletter,* 9, No. 9 (April 24, 1978), 1.

ders away from it is better than any that will move the offender further into it."[26]

It would seem that so many positive reasons can be advanced in favor of diversion that no negative criticism can be reasonably brought to bear against it. There is, however, at least one serious criticism, and that is that diversion widens the net of the juvenile justice system. As community corrections programs proliferate, the opportunity for contact with the juvenile justice system is simultaneously widened. American Justice Institute studies of California Youth Authority diversion programs, serving 3,871 "diversion clients," showed that while "51% of the clients were diverted from deeper involvement with the juvenile justice system, the other 49% apparently were given more processing than they would have received had the programs not existed."[27] In an earlier study, Gibbons and Blake had come to a similar conclusion, after reviewing ten diversion studies. They were quite blunt: "Diversion, growing out of the sociologist's recommendation of 'radical nonintervention,' 'benign neglect,' or 'judicious nonintervention,' has become perverted in practice into a strategem that swells the population of acted upon offenders!"[28] Equally blunt was the comment of some contemporaries who said that "diversionary programs currently in vogue are potentially as abusive as the programs they seek to reform."[29]

Clearly, the threat of a widening net is very real, and the criticisms have merit. The primary intent of diversion should be to prevent the individual's deeper penetration into the juvenile justice and criminal justice systems, and not merely to create new programs in an ever-widening correctional net. Those who plan community-based corrections programs should keep this in mind. A controlling principle has recently been suggested. "To prevent the possibility of an unintended expansion of the juvenile justice system's confinement capacity, it may prove necessary to close institutional facilities at the same time as opening new programs; otherwise, we will be left with both."[30]

The Sacramento Diversion Project

Before concluding our review of diversion, we will take a brief look at two projects, for which success has been claimed, to enhance our perspec-

[26]Robert L. Smith, "Diversion: New Label—Old Practice," *New Approaches to Diversion and Treatment of Juvenile Offenders* (Washington, D.C.: U.S. Government Printing Office, 1973), p. 41.
[27]Cited in *Criminal Justice Newsletter* 9, No. 12 (June 5, 1978), 6.
[28]Cited in *Criminal Justice Newsletter*, 7, No. 21 (October 25, 1976), 3.
[29]Bruce Bullington and others, "A Critique of Diversionary Juvenile Justice," *Crime and Delinquency*, 24, No. 1 (January 1978), 59–71.
[30]*Ibid.*, p. 70.

tive. The Sacramento Diversion Project was instituted in 1970 and reflects a collaborative effort by the Sacramento County Probation Department and the Center on Administration of Criminal Justice, a University
of California (at Davis) research group. The objective of the program was
to test whether certain status offenders, such as runaways and "incorrigi-
bles," could be more productively handled through short-term family
crisis therapy at the time of referral, rather than through the traditional
method of juvenile court referral. Four main goals were set for the project:

1. Reduction in the number of cases going to court,
2. Reduction in the number of repeat offenders,
3. Decrease in overnight detentions, and
4. Accomplishment of these goals at no greater cost than that which prevailed in the existing system.[31]

The family counseling approach was based on the Virginia Satir
model.[32] Two principles are crucial in this approach. One is that problems
should be dealt with as soon as they occur, and the second is that problems
are best dealt with in the family matrix.[33] Satir considered the family to be
the critical, intervening variable between society and the person. In
California, the Welfare and Institutions Code is regulatory with respect to
juveniles. Section 601 of that code covers the less serious delinquent behavior of juveniles. The subjects for the Sacramento Diversion Project
were selected from this type of case. An experimental and a control group
were established.

During the first nine months of the project which ran from 1970–71,
1,361 cases were screened in, of which 803 became project cases; the remaining 558 were designated control cases. In the first year of the project,
only 3.7 percent of the project cases were referred to court, as opposed to
19.8 percent of the control cases. At the conclusion of the first year, only
13.9 percent of the project youths had spent at least one night in juvenile
hall, as compared to 69.4 percent of the control group. The relative cost,
which includes the cost of training the diversion unit for a period of a year,
was also significant. The average cost for each project youth, which
included handling, detention, and placement, was $284, whereas the com-

---

[31]National Institute of Law Enforcement and Criminal Justice, LEAA, U.S. Department of Justice, *Juvenile Diversion Through Family Counseling,* An Exemplary Project (Washington, D.C.: U.S. Government Printing Office, 1976), unpaginated brochure.
    [32]Virginia Satir, *Conjoint Family Therapy* (Palo Alto, California: Science and Behavior
Books, Inc., 1967).
    [33]Roger Baron and Floyd Feeney, *Juvenile Diversion Through Family Counseling* (Wash-
ington, D.C.: U.S. Government Printing Office, February 1976), p. 5.

parable cost for each of the control cases was $562.[34] In 1973, the experimental phase ended, and this program became standard operating procedure for all runaway and incorrigible cases in the county.

Because of the success of the "601 Project," in April 1972, a similar program was instituted with cases falling under Section 602 of the Welfare and Institutions Code, which covers more serious behavior. Similar success was experienced. Specifically, in the first 2 years of the 602 project, only 6 cases were petitioned into juvenile court out of a total of 982 cases serviced in the project, whereas 62 petitions were filed on cases in the control group.

The Memphis Diversion Project

The Memphis Diversion Project has comparable objectives, but a somewhat different approach. It might be called constellation programming, for a wide variety of services are provided for the children selected for the diversion project. First, upon intake, the staff attempts to determine the cause of the participant's problem and then attempts to tailor a program for correction of the problem, while the child remains at home. The child can be referred to any of a number of agencies for specialized assistance, such as drug, family, or individual counseling. In addition, the project program provides "parent effectiveness training, crisis intervention, temporary shelter care, homemaker services, after school and summer care, community education, and advocacy."[35] The participants are free to drop out of the program if they wish to, but so far none has.

The target group consists of those youngsters who have committed one or two offenses of such a serious nature that they would ordinarily be processed through the juvenile justice system. Of the first 385 children seen in the project in 1977, a recidivism rate of 10 percent was recorded, compared to a rate of 35 percent for juvenile offenders who were not in the program. A most important feature of this program is the high level of cooperation that has been generated between the project and community leaders and agencies, specifically including the police and the juvenile court.

Despite legitimate criticism, the promise offered by diversion is clear. If diversion can be adopted without enlarging the system, as an authentic effort to abort penetration into the system, with human and cost benefits as exemplified in the programs discussed above, it should become a crucial plank in the juvenile corrections of the future. In 1978, the State of

---

[34]*Ibid.*, pp. 8–16.
[35]*LEAA Newsletter,* 7, No. 1 (February 1978), 7.

Washington passed the first legislation in this nation's history which set down specific guidelines for sentencing juveniles. Significantly, that legislation included provisions for *mandatory diversion* of designated juveniles into community-based programs.

THE STATUS OFFENDER

One major group for which diversion has particular applicability are those juveniles in the system known as "status offenders." Status offenders are individuals whose delinquent acts are defined as such because of the minority status of the juvenile. The behavior at issue would not be considered a crime if the individual were an adult. Running away from home, breach of curfew, drinking alcoholic beverages, "incorrigibility," and "ungovernable behavior" constitute some examples. Approximately half of all juveniles arrested are taken into custody for so-called status offenses. We say that diversion has particular applicability for status offenders, because it is all the more imperative to prevent this type of minimal offender from being stigmatized by the system. The behavior involved is more symptomatic of behavioral or inter-family difficulty, rather than delinquency. Status offenders should be *treated* by excluding them from the juvenile justice system.

In 1974, Congress enacted the Juvenile Justice and Delinquency Prevention Act, which was amended in 1977. The original bill required states to deinstitutionalize status offenders within two years, that is, by 1977, in order to be funded under the act. A major change in the amended act was the extension of the period of compliance, for an additional year, with further flexibility built in to accommodate those states which have been in substantial compliance, but which have not been able to complete the deinstitutionalization process. The first published study (1978), sponsored by LEAA's Office of Juvenile Justice and Delinquency Prevention and HEW's Office of Youth Development, revealed that considerable progress in deinstitutionalization had taken place. Data were collected from 10 states, among which California registered the most dramatic progress. This was primarily because a bill (AB 3121), which became law on January 1, 1977, mandated the deinstitutionalization of status offenders. In the first two years following the passage of this law, almost 50,000 fewer status offenders were detained.

The American Correctional Association and the Commission on Accreditation for corrections have developed, and promulgated, a set of standards for juvenile probation and aftercare services. The standards reflect the Commission's position that status offenders should be removed from the juvenile corrections system. There are some critics who challenge the removal of status offenders, feeling that the system can help them in-house. But the arguments for removal are more compelling, from human as well as from economic motives. For one thing, the removal of such a large number of minimal offenders, many of them neglected children, from the system will enhance the possibility of instituting meaningful treatment for those remaining under the professional patronage of the system.

TREATMENT THEORY IN THE
JUVENILE JUSTICE SYSTEM

In Chapter Six we reviewed the major psychotherapeutic strategies, and we have touched upon various aspects of treatment throughout the preceding chapters. All have applicability to the juvenile offender in a given context. There is no specific juvenile treatment *per se,* but there are special considerations that pertain to the juvenile offender. In this section we will narrow the focus to deal with some of the needs and problems peculiar to the youthful offender, and in the section following we will highlight some selected programs that have generated optimism.

Characteristics of Delinquent Behavior

Juvenile delinquency is, to be sure, an overt form of nonconforming behavior, but it is symptomatic of a great deal more. To understand delinquent behavior, one must have an understanding of the dynamics of growing up. There are physiological and psychological processes associated with puberty and pre-puberty that give a unique character to juvenile delinquency. En route to mature adulthood, one must learn to contain or appropriately channel aggressive strivings, impulsivity, and immediate gratification. Responsibility must be gradually assumed, guilt must be experienced in a healthy fashion, and myriad relationships must be established. Childhood must be shed and adulthood embraced. It is a rocky road in the American culture, and it makes adolescence a very painful proposition. Delinquent behavior is characterized by its sporadic, malicious, non-utilitarian, and often purposeless nature.[36]

While the adult criminal is ordinarily profit-motivated, the delinquent engages in rebellious nonconformity. Sandhu says that three themes color juvenile delinquency with "marked regularity":

[36]For an elaboration of this theme by one of its notable exponents, see Albert Cohen, *Delinquent Boys: The Culture of the Gang* (Glencoe, Ill.: The Free Press, 1955).

1. Delinquents restlessly search for thrills or "kicks."
2. The juvenile delinquent has a disdain for the work ethic.
3. Delinquency is centered on aggression.[37]

Halleck, who maintains that certain children enter adolescence with a greater predisposition to commit crime, says that it is one of the important questions of our time why so many youngsters are so willing to engage in antisocial activity. For Halleck, it is implicitly an existential problem, for "it must be admitted that our era is characterized by an increasing number of people who feel and admit to themselves that their lives are meaningless." And the adolescent is not immune. "He . . . demonstrates similar doubts in many of his behaviors and attitudes. When he searches for "kicks" and "coolness," he implies a lack of commitment to any belief or ideology."[38] This is the condition that Viktor Frankl described when he spoke of the existential vacuum.

An Analysis of Successful Treatment

Philosophically, treatment cannot be denigrated. The restoration of one to wholeness, or the remediation of deprivation, is a noble obligation. But that does not mean that the path to successful treatment is clearly mapped. In trying to ascertain what works in the treatment of juvenile offenders, one researcher made a particularly cogent comment: "Enthusiasts for one treatment modality or another have sometimes made claims of nearly universal efficacy. We found no such sufficient interventions."[39] But neither was total failure encountered. In exploring four broad modes of treating—clinical, sociological, educational, and vocational—it was found that there was "*limited success with each of the four treatment modalities.*"[40] (Italics in the original). This points up the importance of having a broad-based knowledge of treatment theory and tactic, as well as a working understanding of human development.

The research patriarchs in the field of child development, men such as Freud, Piaget, and Erikson, speak of phases or stages of development, with maturity representing the culmination of a successful journey through those stages. The importance of the parent in shaping the child has received preeminent emphasis, so much so that we must truly have a

[37]Harjit S. Sandhu, *Modern Corrections* (Springfield, Ill.: Charles C Thomas Publisher, 1974), p. 21.
[38]Seymour L. Halleck, *Psychiatry and the Dilemmas of Crime* (Berkeley: University of California Press, 1971), p. 125.
[39]Dale Mann, *Intervening with Convicted Serious Juvenile Offenders,* July 1976 (Washington, D.C.: U.S. Government Printing Office, 1977), p. viii.
[40]*Ibid.*

legion of guilt-ridden mothers and fathers in our midst. Psychologists have been retreating toward infancy in determining the boundary which marks the point at which the "crucial" influences have been imprinted on the child. It is currently the fifth year. By the fifth year, the parents have accomplished their good or their evil work, because by then the core personality has been formed, we are told.

Recent research, however, by a team at Harvard University, calls this psychological dogma into question. The Harvard group did a follow-up on a study of parenting conducted a quarter of a century earlier, also by social scientists at Harvard. The contemporary researchers interviewed 78 of the children of the parents from the first study, and a number of their children. Each individual was rated on 37 "outcome variables." They were also rated on the basis of how they ranked certain values in their lives. An important objective was to discover how the individuals surveyed rated other influences in their lives besides the influence of their parents. Specifically, they were evaluated on the basis of what importance each gave to the values in Erikson's stages of psychosocial development. Erikson's four stages are *Receptivity* (respect for tradition and appropriate behavior), *Autonomy* (self-reliance), *Assertion* (succeeding at educational and vocational skills; exerting influence on others), and *Mutuality* (understanding the viewpoints of others and serving the *summum bonum,* or common good).

The research team

> concluded that most of what people do and think and believe as adults is not determined by specific techniques of child-rearing in the first five years. ... parents should rest assured that what they *do* is not all that important in how their children turn out; many other influences in later life serve to shape what adults think and do.[41]

This does not mean that parents do not have an impact on their children. The impact, however, comes from intangibles such as love. It was determined that how the parents *felt* about their children was important, and "when parents—particularly mothers—really loved their children, the sons and daughters were likely to achieve the highest levels of social and moral maturity."[42] The poet, it seems, not only preceded the psychologist, but also succeeds him!

The lack of precise knowledge should not be misconstrued as an invitation to cease exploring avenues of hope. Even if we knew precisely

[41]David C. McClelland and others, "Making It to Maturity," *Psychology Today,* 12, No. 1 (June 1978), 45.
[42]*Ibid.*

what caused delinquent acting out, it would not mean that there would be but one specific treatment approach. There are many approaches, and this permits the professional to selectively individualize his treatment method. There are also some basics that should be in the professional's repertoire, including familiarity with the concepts of peer pressure, self-concept, and alienation.

Peer Therapy

There are only two broad treatment approaches, individual and group, whether the client is an adult or a juvenile. Of course, they can blend; one is often used as an adjunct to the other. Individual therapy takes place on a one-to-one basis. Trojanowicz said that "The individual method is generally used by psychiatrists, psychologists, and social workers, while the group method involves school teachers, recreation specialists, and social workers."[43] But this distinction is not definitive because a vast amount of group work is done by psychiatrists and psychologists.

Because of the pioneering success of the group method at Highfields, it has become a favored technique in working with youngsters. It has been considered the most promising on the basis of both cost and effectiveness.[44] The "peer-oriented treatment model," which was instituted at Highfields as "guided group interaction," was subsequently refined by one of the staff members at Highfields into a "comprehensive and specific treatment methodology, now known as Positive Peer Culture." It is not rule-oriented, but value-oriented. It is designed "to mobilize the power of the peer group in a productive manner.... In contrast to traditional treatment approaches PPC does not ask whether a person wants to receive help but whether he is willing to give help."[45] It is based on a phenomenon that is by now rather well known to students of human behavior, namely, that of all the age groups, the one most susceptible to the pressure of its peers is the adolescent group. Treatment is a combination of knowledge and techniques. It requires an awareness of human dynamics, as well as knowledge of strategies to deal with human problems. It is neither permissive nor autocratic, but with juveniles particularly, structures and limits are necessary adjuncts. It is the position of Trojanowicz that, "The setting of limits and restrictions and reprimands are a necessary element

[43]Robert C. Trojanowicz, *Juvenile Delinquency: Concepts and Control,* 2nd ed. (Englewood Cliffs, N.J.: Prentice-Hall, Inc., 1978), p. 264.

[44]Paul A. Strasburg, *Violent Delinquents,* A Report to the Ford Foundation from the Vera Institute of Justice (New York: Monarch, 1978), p. 42.

[45]Harry H. Vorrath and Larry K. Brendtro, *Positive Peer Culture* (Chicago: Aldine Publishing Company, 1974), p. 3.

in any method of treating and handling the youngster."[46] Limits should be set by the therapist or counselor in the one-to-one setting. In the group contact, the counselor subtly guides the group, but an effective peer pressure group will set the limits for the individual members.

Self-Concept and Alienation

Treatment in the criminal or juvenile justice system has one major handicap to overcome, and that is the system itself. The correctionalist has to take cognizance of the impact that the system has upon the client, particularly as it relates to self-concept. It has been shown that the deeper the juvenile is involved in the system the more likely he is to consider himself "bad." Fifty-nine percent of those incarcerated, 32 percent of those on probation, and only 14 percent of non-delinquents felt this way.[47] The impact of the system has to be evaluated in the context of the axiom that "A person's self-concept is in large part a reflection of the images others have of him."[48] It must be admitted, however, that it has not been decisively established that the individual is made vulnerable to delinquency because of a poor self-concept.[49] The point that we are making is that a poor self-image is an inhibitor of rehabilitation more than it is necessarily a cause of further delinquency. It may be more accurate to say that the difference between delinquents and nondelinquents is that the former largely feel "that they have very limited opportunity to achieve the rewards that are available to middle class children."[50] This, of course, can result from a number of developmental experiences besides a lack of self-esteem.

Another important ingredient is the degree of powerlessness felt by the individual, that is, the loss of ability to control one's destiny, which is also referred to as "alienation." It has been shown, in a reformatory study, that alienation is inversely correlated with social learning. The greater the alienation, the less the capacity for learning, irrespective of the level of intelligence.[51] It is this pervasive sentiment that causes so many young-

[46]Trojanowicz, *Juvenile Delinquency,* p. 264.

[47]Dennis C. Bliss, *The Effects of the Juvenile Justice System on Self-Concept* (San Francisco: R & E Research Associates, 1977), p. 42.

[48]Martin R. Haskell and Lewis Yablonsky, *Juvenile Delinquency,* 2nd ed. (Chicago: Rand McNally & Company, 1978), p. 12.

[49]Sandra S. Tangri and Michael Schwartz, "Delinquency Research and the Self-Concept Variable," *The Journal of Criminology and Police Science,* 58, No. 2 (June 1967), 182–90.

[50]Frank R. Scarpitti, "Delinquent and Non-Delinquent Perceptions of Self, Values and Opportunity," *Mental Hygiene,* 49, No. 3 (July 1965), 403.

[51]Melvin Seeman, "Alienation and Social Learning in a Reformatory," *The American Journal of Sociology,* 56, No. 3 (November 1963), pp. 270–84.

sters to "drop out" of society. They will not drop back in until they can feel a sense of meaningful involvement in society and personal fulfillment.

Getting Down to the Essentials

When treatment is attempted in a correctional or juvenile justice context, the least that must be done is to develop a therapeutic milieu, that is, a climate in which the individual can experience the concern of the therapist and the freedom to examine his or her own being. Follow-up is equally essential. We have spoken at length of the need to divert and deinstitutionalize as treatment tactics, but these strategies are not remedial in and of themselves. Deinstitutionalization, for example, "has often resulted in releasing persons into the community with virtually no follow-up or supportive services, little concern for their social and physical well-being, and woefully inadequate housing and economic support. Such conditions may contribute to recidivism."[52] That can hardly be stipulated as the objective of treatment.

The family is a nurturing matrix, and it should be integrated into the treatment design if at all possible. Practical treatment must be provided by the enhancement of vocational and educational skills. Where deinstitutionalization or diversion occurs, transitional facilities should be available in the community to house or service the juvenile during the process of reintegration. And the modern treatment professional in the field of corrections, the community resources broker, should consummate the process by leaving the juvenile in a state that renders him or her capable of surviving in modern society, with no impairment of dignity. Treatment is implicit in each of these activities. We can begin to remediate human misery and human inadequacy without knowing the causes.

EXEMPLARY TREATMENT PROGRAMS

Innovative corrections programs for juveniles have been proliferating in the community and, to a lesser degree, in institutions. The failure of past treatment efforts, the increasing cost of crime and delinquency, the unconscionable fiscal burden of the present institutional system, and the seemingly limitless funds being pumped into programs by the Law Enforcement Assistance Administration (LEAA), are among the more persuasive reasons. A number of primising programs have shown encouraging results. A brief, inevitably arbitrary, mosaic follows.

---

[52]Dale Mann, *Intervening with Convicted Serious Juvenile Offenders*, p. 39.

Operation Sisters United

Filling a critical need for community-based services for "delinquent girls in trouble with the law," Operation Sisters United, started in 1973, administered by the National Council of Negro Women, and funded by LEAA's Office of Juvenile Justice and Delinquency Prevention, has established alternative resource programs in Washington, D.C.; Dayton, Ohio; Greenville, Mississippi; and St. Thomas in the Virgin Islands. Operating out of restored homes, the nonresidential programs service delinquent girls aged 11 through 16. Girls stay in the program from six months to one year and are engaged in a wide range of social, recreational, and vocational activities. Heavy emphasis is placed upon service to community. Referrals come from public agencies as well as the juvenile court. The Greenville program was the first alternative care center established for female delinquents in that city. The annual cost of service to each girl has been calculated at $2,313.63, which is far less than it would cost for institutionalization.[53]

Community Arbitration Program

The emphasis on helping the community is an integral part of the Community Arbitration Program which was instituted in 1974 in Annapolis, Maryland. The Juvenile Law of Maryland, as a matter of fact, requires community arbitration as well as conventional intake. The Annapolis program was set up to deal with misdemeanant types of offenses. The juvenile is not arrested, but given a citation by the police (see Figure 11-1), which requires an appearance before the Community Arbitrator within seven working days. The youth, his parents, and the complainant, who has also received a citation to appear, attend the hearing. The usual options are open, including dismissal, informal supervision for counseling, and, in extreme cases, referral to the State's Attorney. Only 2 to 2.5 of the cited youngsters are "no-shows," and 50 percent of the complainants appear, which compares with 10 percent in the regular intake inquiry.[54]

But the emphasis is restorative. "A new aspect of the program is the volunteer work assignment, in which a youth agrees to work for a specified number of hours with an agency or group working for community improvement."[55] Over 70 community groups and agencies have participated in the program, providing the opportunity for the volunteer work. By the end of September 1975, a total of 363 youths had donated

[53]*LEAA Newsletter,* 6, No. 15 (November 1977), 12.

[54]David Larom, "The Arbitration Experience: Improving the Process of Intake Screening." Department of Juvenile Services, Annapolis, Md., undated (mimeographed), p. 4.

[55]Department of Juvenile Services, Juvenile Court Services Division, "Community Arbitration Program," Annapolis, Md. Undated Information Sheet (mimeographed).

FIGURE 11-1
Anne Arundel County Juvenile Citation

NO: 26520

ANNE ARUNDEL COUNTY JUVENILE CITATION

JUVENILE'S LAST NAME   FIRST   MIDDLE

ALIAS

ADDRESS

RACE   SEX   AGE   HGT.   WGT.   HAIR   EYES   COMP.

DATE OF BIRTH   TELEPHONE NUMBER

SCHOOL AND GRADE AND/OR PLACE OF EMPLOYMENT

PARENT/GUARDIAN

PARENT/GUARDIAN ADDRESS

OFFENSE   CASE NO.

DATE OF OFFENSE   TIME   LOCATION

COMPLAINANT.S NAME AND ADDRESS

YOU ARE HEREBY NOTIFIED TO APPEAR on the_____day of _____, 197_, at _____o'clock__M. before the JUVENILE COMMUNITY ARBITRATOR at the DEPARTMENT OF JUVENILE SERVICES, 50 Cathedral Street, Annapolis, Maryland, phone 268-4300, Ext. 291.

Your failure to appear may result in the issuance of a Juvenile Petition and/or Summons.

I HEREBY ACKNOWLEDGE RECEIPT OF THIS CITATION AND PROMISE TO APPEAR ON THE DATE AND TIME SPECIFIED. I FURTHER HAVE BEEN ADVISED OF MY RIGHT TO HAVE COUNSEL APPEAR WITH ME.

MdStP
AA Co PD   JUVENILE'S SIGNATURE
APD   PARENT/GUARDIAN SIGNATURE

OFFICER _____
     ID NO.

DISTRICT   BEAT   DIVISION

OFFICER COPY

3,323 hours of volunteer work. The goals of the Community Arbitration Program are both redemptive and practical: (1) To reduce the time required to handle a misdemeanor from 4–6 weeks to 7 days. (2) To involve youths in a positive fashion in the community. (3) To demonstrate to the victim that the offense is important and that something *is* being done about it. And (4) to make an impact on the youth through an *immediate* experience in a "quasi-courtroom setting."

Neighborhood Youth Resources Center

The Philadelphia Neighborhood Youth Services Center, begun in 1971, is located in a high-crime area of the inner-city and provides assistance and resources in crisis intervention, comprehensive personal planning, educational and vocational counseling, referrals which include monitoring and follow-up, recreational and cultural programming, and legal representation. NYRC has been designated an exemplary program by the National Institute of Law Enforcement and Criminal Justice. The Philadelphia program is an exceptionally important one because Philadelphia has one of the most severe gang and gang-violence problems in the nation. There were, for instance, more than one hundred gang-related murders in the City of Brotherly Love in the three years preceding 1975.[56]

It cannot be said that NYRC is a typical referral service, because it offers a lot more and is unique in that it concentrates on both casework services and follow-up services. More than 190 community agencies are cooperatively involved providing a wide network of resources offering "an entire range of services—college scholarships, orthopedic and medical or mental health resources, emergency housing or group home care, recreation and cultural programs, drug abuse treatment—without ever losing contact with the youth or risking the danger that the youth will "slip between the cracks" during service provision."[57]

The Philadelphia NYRC program has as its objectives:

1. The reduction of drop-out rates, by providing more meaningful opportunities and roles for the participants.
2. Through diversion, to reduce the number of referrals to the juvenile court.
3. Reduction of negative labeling, by providing alternative services in the community.
4. Reduction of youth-adult alienation by involving the youth in "total community activities," thus also reducing official delinquency rates.

One measure of its success can be inferred from data pertaining to the arrest rates of target and non-target populations (see Table 11-1). It is well stated, however, that "evaluation should be perceived and conducted as a *dynamic* activity."[58] The Philadelphia Neighborhood Youth Services Program is dynamic and merits its "exemplary program" title.

Project New Pride

Denver's Project New Pride is an attempt to reach the hard-core juvenile delinquent, the serious juvenile offenders in the 14–17 year-old

---

[56]Barry Alan Krisberg, *The Gang and the Community* (San Francisco: R & E Research Associates, 1975), p. 1.

[57]U.S. Department of Justice, LEAA, National Institute of Law Enforcement and Criminal Justice, *The Philadelphia Neighborhood Youth Resources Center* (Washington D.C.: U.S. Government Printing Office, 1975), p. 3.

[58]*Ibid.*, p. 99.

TABLE 11-1 Arrest Rates (Per Thousand) for Target and Non-Target Areas in the 9th and 23rd Police Districts (February–May 1973)

	Males			Females		
	Target (N = 492)	Non-Target (N = 224)	Significance	Target (N = 520)	Non-Target (N = 226)	Significance
9th District						
Class I	9.1	51.3	.02	2.9	6.6	n.s.
Class II	3.0	2.2	n.s.	4.8	0.0	n.s.
Class III	19.7	24.6	n.s.	4.8	0.0	n.s.
Class IV	31.5	82.5	.03	18.3	24.3	n.s.
23rd District						
Class I	4.2	17.3	.01	2.2	3.4	n.s.
Class II	1.4	1.3	n.s.	0.0	1.2	n.s.
Class III	2.3	12.0	.01	0.0	1.2	n.s.
Class IV	2.3	18.5	.001	0.0	6.6	.02

group. A local crime survey in Denver in 1971 revealed an inordinate crime rate among the city's black and Spanish-speaking groups, "who were beset by a pattern of poverty and disrupted family relations."[59] Project New Pride was Denver's response. Established in 1973 by the Denver Anti-Crime Council, and originally funded by the Law Enforcement Assistance Administration (LEAA), it is currently funded by the Colorado Division of Criminal Justice and local sources.

"New Pride operates on the premise that an individual must confront his problems in his own environment—i.e., within the community. To do this the offender must be guided in adopting and maintaining a conventional life-style as an alternative to the delinquent life-style he has known."[60] It also operates on the principle that it is necessary to restore the youth's sense of self-worth through cultural enrichment. A wide range of services is utilized in pursuit of these objectives. Criteria for inclusion in the program include having had two prior convictions, preferably for assault, burglary or robbery; having a recent arrest for one of these offenses; and being a resident of Denver. Participants are those individuals "who are perhaps one step away from incarceration."[61]

Traditional juvenile services have tended to be highly specialized, inflexible in administration, and fragmented. "New Pride's approach is to integrate all services, providing comprehensive treatment to its clients . . . . For example, a single youth may receive remedial treatment for a learning disability, take courses for high school credit, be placed in a part-time job, participate in family counseling, and experience cultural events at theaters and museums."[62] The program has four primary goals: (1) Reduction of recidivism. (2) Enhanced job placement. (3) Treatment of learning disabilities. (4) Remedial academics.

For the initial three months of the program, the client receives intensive counseling and testing and remedial training. Nine months of treatment follow, which can require daily contact between staff and the individual youngster. After initial screening, participants are placed in either the New Pride Alternative School, which is located at the project headquarters, or the Learning Disabilities Center. For those without academic incentive, other programs will be developed around a specific goal.

Flexibility characterizes the program of Project New Pride. "While each youth is expected to participate in each of the treatment components, services are not rigidly structured but are formed to accommodate individual needs and interests. This principle of flexibility and accommo-

[59]*Target,* Vol. 6, Issue 6, June 1977, not paginated.
[60]Carol Holliday Blew, Daniel McGillis, and Gerald Bryant, *Project New Pride, Denver, Colorado,* July 1977 (Washington, D.C.: U.S. Government Printing Office, 1977), p. 2.
[61]*LEAA Newsletter,* 7, No. 2 (March 1978), 4.
[62]Blew and others, *Project New Pride,* p. 6.

TABLE 11-2   New Pride Differential Police Contact Data

Number of Police Contacts
(Academic Year 1974–1975)

	One Year Prior to Project	During Project
Participants	2.21	0.46
Control Group	2.25	2.25

dation is the key to the New Pride approach."[63] Professional staff in the program are committed to intensified individual services, believing this to be a paramount need for youngsters who have chronic histories of neglect and rejection. These are the youngsters who are at a crossroads, one path leading inevitably to imprisonment. New Pride considers itself the critical other path for the street-wise, delinquency-prone youngster.

New Pride has an impressive record in terms of meeting its primary goals. During a twelve-month period, the program had a recidivism rate of 27 percent as compared to a 32 percent rate for a control group for "referral offenses." Seventy percent of all clients have been placed in full-time or in part-time jobs. With respect to school reintegration, over 40 percent of the clients returned to school.[64] The data on remediation of learning disabilities and on improving academic performance are too preliminary to report upon at this time. All in all, New Pride, quite obviously, has seeded a great deal of new pride.

TABLE 11-3   New Pride General Recidivism Data

	Project Cases (percentage)	Control Cases (percentage)
Petitions filed	3.7%	19.8%
Repeat offenses (within 1 year)	46.3	54.2
Juvenile hall detention	13.9	69.4
Average detention time (nights)	0.5	4.6
Average case handling time (hours)	14.2	23.7
Average case cost	$284	$526

[63] *Ibid.*, p. 36.
[64] *Ibid.*, p. 8.

Some Other Programs

There are a great many other programs making some headway in the relentless battle to stem juvenile delinquency and later criminal behavior. An individualized treatment approach, using reality therapy, behavior therapy, and success experiences, is being implemented at the Rockville Training Center, a juvenile institution in Indiana. The program is administered through the team treatment modality and is geared to carry over into the community after the juvenile is released. A conscious effort is made to "maximize kindness and sensitivity and to minimize mechanistic, assembly-line treatment."[65] Attention—not detention—homes have been established in Colorado and Montana, to accentuate the positive aspect of community support and interaction with the juveniles. And in Miami, the police, through the Juvenile Offender Diversionary Project, actually do social work with juveniles and their families, including referral to social agencies and follow-up.

In Boston, the Community Advancement Program is a community-centered corrections program for delinquent boys who are assigned by the state Department of Youth Services. Counselors in the program develop close, intensive relationships with the boys, an interaction that carries over into community activities of both a social and a recreational nature. But "the juveniles are placed in the program . . . not to make friends but to lower the chances they will commit future delinquent acts."[66] The program is based on constant communication and the fact that the counselor does not restrict himself to the "storefront" but also goes into the juvenile's community to assist the client and to monitor his program activities and his street life.

In Iowa, a private non-profit corporation known as Youth and Shelter Services, Inc., has four community-based programs in operation which utilize a non-coercive and youth advocacy approach. A gamut of services includes crisis intervention, family counseling, immediate counseling for youngsters referred to court, drug abuse treatment, foster home placement, and a delinquency prevention program. Opposed to the tradition of removing the child from the family when he or she gets into difficulties, Iowa's Youth and Shelter Service program, according to an administrative official, emphasizes "supporting the family structure, keeping the family unit together and enhancing the ability of the family to function more efficiently."[67]

And so on.

[65]Ken Lynch and Tom Ollendick, "Juvenile Corrections—A Model Program," *American Journal of Corrections*, 39, No. 2 (March–April 1977), 6.

[66]*Youth Forum*, 1, No. 2 (October 1977), 5.

[67]Program Director George Belitsos, quoted in *Criminal Justice Newsletter*, 8, No. 22 (November 7, 1977), 6.

There is room for consolation. But we have a long, long way to go. Unfortunately we are still reconnoitering when it comes to juvenile treatment.

SYNOPSIS

More than 2,000,000 juveniles are arrested annually, and over 2,000 juvenile correctional facilities exist to cope with the phenomenon. In the wake of landmark court decisions, which have destroyed the old chancery concept and the social work climate in the juvenile court, new methods of dealing with the juvenile have to be formulated.

Conditions in juvenile institutions have been particularly appalling and scarcely conduce to effective treatment. One widely heralded counterattack was taken in the "Massachusetts Experiment," in which Massachusetts closed down its juvenile institutions and initiated community-based corrections as a substitute. Diversion is increasingly spoken of as a mode in juvenile justice, and it has been effectively implemented in the noteworthy Sacramento Diversion Project.

The status offender is a particularly meritorious candidate for diversion from the juvenile justice system.

Treating the juvenile offender requires a knowledge of the dynamics of growing up, plus an awareness of the pangs associated with adolescence in Western civilization. Some interesting research done at Harvard University indicates that parental influence may not have been as important as previously believed.

Peer therapy seems to be a particularly effective technique with juveniles. A number of successful programs are surveyed in this chapter, but there is an insatiable need for effective therapeutics for the juvenile offender.

12 Differential Treatment

One may have a blazing hearth in one's soul, and yet no one ever comes to sit by it.

Vincent Van Gogh

If anything is obvious at this stage it is that corrections is under siege, and it has a long, long way to go before it can reasonably claim that it is significantly accomplishing its objectives. It may be that it has been given an impossible task. To employ an analogy, correctionalists have been sent out in rowboats to subdue frothy whitecaps, without being able to influence the deep swells in the very incipiency of the ocean, which are the cause of the whitecaps. The modern correctionalist, like the beleaguered Dutch boy at the dike, deals with symptomatology rather than with cause. Still, the Dutch boy had a measure of success.

But corrections, to be truly effective, will have to have a great deal more collaborative assistance from the community, and not merely in support of the correctional effort. Crime will have to be attacked at its root level. Half a century ago, the renowned penologist Sanford Bates made a definitive statement about crime that is as applicable today as it was the day he made it: "Crime will abate only as the people as a whole resolve to set up within themselves higher and more unselfish standards of conduct."[1]

Crime springs from the womb of society, and culture fashions the blueprint. Criminal behavior is that behavior which is culturally defined, and which society, officially, cannot tolerate. But the master architect of crime is social disorganization, and is a product of institutionalized greed, discrimination, inequity, and concupiscent power. Until we do something meaningful about such major issues as poverty, unjust sentencing, racism, imbalanced access to the world's resources, war, illiteracy, political corruption and similar issues, we will have no significant impact upon crime. And correctional efforts, thereby, will continue to represent largely ineffectual excursions to the land of the whitecaps.

Then why try? Why make puny scratches on the *tabula rasa* of human existence? Why try to "treat" and restore if it requires modern Bengal Lancers to ride into the jaws of hostility, insensitivity, and improbability? Perhaps Sir Walter Scott's version will still suffice: "The race of mankind would perish did they cease to aid each other. We cannot exist without mutual help. All therefore that need aid have a right to ask for it from their fellow-men; and no one who has the power of granting can refuse it without guilt." Nor fail to recognize the uniqueness and individuality of the supplicant.

THE CONCEPT OF DIFFERENTIAL TREATMENT

After a broad, but penetrating inspection of correctional treatment, it appears self-evident that treatment, to be really effective, must be differentiated or individualized. Murderers, for example, share with other murderers the fact that they have committed a homicide. But the precipitating motivation is unique to the individual offender. Would any reasonable person contend that the cold-blooded murder-for-hire killing is produced by the same motivation as that of the wife who comes upon her unfaithful husband, *in flagrante delicto,* and kills him in the heat of passion? Despite our common humanity, it is our uniqueness that must be considered in the pursuit of reformation.

There is a subtle danger lurking in the background, which the student must become aware of. It is the danger of falling into the medical model

[1]Sanford Bates, *Prisons and Beyond* (New York: Macmillan, Inc., 1936), p. 307.

approach. In the medical model, the assumption is made that all criminals are differentiated from non-criminals, and the theme of "individual pathology," as Johnson phrased it,[2] permeates the medical model. Certain specific disorders, or deficiencies, be they emotional or organic, are singled out as the precipitants of crime. Specific prepackaged treatment is then applied in terms of the isolated causal factor. This is not what we mean by differential treatment.

Defining Differential Treatment

In our specific frame of reference, differential treatment will have two separate meanings. It will refer (a) to a treatment disposition or philosophy, and (b) to a particular conceptualization that has been operationalized. In the first sense, differential treatment means treatment that takes the unique needs of the individual into consideration. As Warren said, "One of the few agreed-upon "facts" in the field of corrections is that offenders are not all alike; that is, they differ from each other, not only in the form of their offense, but also in the reasons for and the meaning of their crime."[3] There is, interestingly, an International Differential Treatment Association currently headquartered in Ontario, Canada. Intelligent treatment efforts must be geared to the differences rather than molded to fit *a priori* categories.

Acknowledging this premise does not necessarily mean that it has been accomplished. As a matter of fact, the effort to develop a functional and therapeutic correlation "between the types of treatment and types of offender is relatively new as a subject of criminological research; comparatively little research has been done on the problem, and the results to date cannot be said to be very encouraging."[4] We have, in other words, a very sound principle, but little empirical evidence of its validity. The student should keep in mind that research and experimentation, even where the results are invalid or inconclusive, contribute to the advancement of learning and to ultimate solutions. Thomas Edison was once chided for having fifty failures before he invented the electric light bulb. On the contrary, he pointed out, he had discovered and eliminated fifty filaments that did not work!

While pioneering work was done in the area of differential treatment

[2]Elmer H. Johnson, *Crime, Correction, and Society,* 4th ed. (Homewood, Ill.: The Dorsey Press, 1978), p. 13.

[3]Marguerite Q. Warren, "Differential Treatment of Delinquents," in David M. Petersen and Charles W. Thomas (eds.), *Corrections: Problems and Prospects* (Englewood Cliffs, N.J.: Prentice-Hall, Inc., 1975), pp. 215–16.

[4]Roger Hood and Richard Sparks, *Key Issues in Criminology* (London: World University Library, 1970), p. 193.

in the 1940s,[5] the names most prominently associated with this development in corrections are Marguerite Q. Warren and Herbert Quay; it is their respective work that will essentially constitute the focus and the emphasis in this chapter.

THE INTERPERSONAL MATURITY LEVEL (I-LEVEL) APPROACH

In challenging the claim of critics that correctional treatment is ineffective, or lacking in evidence, Warren countered that "treatments, to be effective for some, need not be effective for all, and that effective treatment may best be identified by asking which type of treatment method is most effective with which type of offender, and under what conditions or in what type of setting."[6] That, coupled with her earlier statement about the differences of offenders in terms of their crimes and the meanings of their crimes, forms the rationale for the development of what is popularly known as the I-Level approach to treatment.

Basic Principles and History

Two specific principles are implicit in this approach. First, treatment should be tailored to the individual's particular reason for misbehavior, and, second, the individual's behavior is based on his perception of himself and his world. The genesis of this approach can be traced to two studies undertaken in California in the 1950s.[7] One involved sailors and marines at Camp Elliott, a naval disciplinary barracks, and the other involved Youth Authority wards. At Camp Elliott, a total of 511 incarcerated individuals, most of whom were naval deserters, were rated on "interpersonal maturity," on the basis of a seven-level scale first developed by Sullivan, Grant, and Grant.[8] The participants in the study were involved in three different types of group counseling, which purportedly revealed that indiscriminate lumping of individuals in treatment had a tendency to cancel out beneficial aspects for certain individuals.

It was also determined that individuals who were ranked in the higher levels of the "interpersonal maturity" scale were those who internalized

[5]L. E. Hewitt and R. L. Jenkins, *Fundamental Patterns of Maladjustment: The Dynamics of Their Origin* (State of Illinois, 1946).

[6]Marguerite Q. Warren, "Correctional Treatment and Coercion," *Criminal Justice and Behavior,* 4, No. 4 (December 1977), 360.

[7]Warren, "Differential Treatment of Delinquents," pp. 215–16.

[8]Clyde Sullivan, Marguerite Q. Grant, and J. Douglas Grant, "The Development of Interpersonal Maturity: Applications to Delinquency," *Psychiatry,* 20, No. 4 (1957), 373–85.

standards by which they judged their own actions and the actions of others. The low level cases were impulsive, ego-centered individuals, who were incapable of perceiving the impact of their behavior on others. As might be expected, the high level individuals did signally better than did their low level comrades.

In the Youth Authority study, 200 individuals in a correctional institution, who had received intensive individual counseling, were compared with a control group of the same number in the same institution. The researcher concluded that the "amenables" showed a substantially better success rate (measured in terms of return to the institution) than did the controls, which was attributed to the intensive counseling. An any event, these two studies were the incubating forces in the development of the I-Level concept. In the original conceptualization, there were seven levels on the interpersonal maturation scale, ranging from the vegetable to the perfectly adjusted individual, neither of which, understandably, is included in the working instrument. As most juveniles appear in the 2nd, 3rd, and 4th maturity levels, these are the levels that compose the Interpersonal Maturation Level Classification: Juvenile.[9] There is a cumulative total of 9 subtypes for these major maturational levels. These levels represent a continuum, and passage to higher levels assumes the solution of a major interpersonal problem. A brief description of each, with subtypes, follows.[10]

Maturity Level 2 (I_2)

This is the individual who is primarily a taker, who sees others principally as "givers" or "withholders," and whose interpersonal understanding and behavior are based on demands that the world take care of him. He has no perception of refined interpersonal interaction beyond the behavior or reaction of others. Things outside of himself are of no interest to him, beyond being a source of supply. He is impulsive and unaware of the impact that his behavior has on others. There are two subtypes at this level.

Asocial, Aggressive (Aa). This is the demanding individual who responds with open hostility or physical or verbal aggression when frustrated. He also engages in "malicious mischief."

[9]See Marguerite Q. Grant, "Interpersonal Maturity Level Classification: Juvenile," prepared for Community Treatment Project, Department of the Youth Authority, State of California, March 1, 1961 (mineographed).

[10]Adapted from Marguerite Q. Warren, "What Is I-Level?" *California Youth Authority Quarterly,* 22, No. 3 (Fall 1969), 4–5; and Marguerite Q. Warren, "The Case for Differential Treatment of Delinquents," *The Annals of the American Academy of Political and Social Science,* 381 (January 1969), 47–59.

Asocial, Passive (Ap). This individual pouts and sulks and reacts with passivity, complaining or withdrawing when frustrated.

Maturity Level 3 (I_3)

The individual who operates at the I-3 level manipulates his environment to get what he wants. He has some awareness of the fact that his behavior is somehow an influence in whether or not he gets what he wants, in contradistinction to the I-2, but he also fails to differentiate among people except on the basis of their usefulness to him. His manipulations can take the form of conformity or highly maneuverable exploitation. He tends to deny that he has any strong feelings for others or that he has any disturbed feelings. This level has three subtypes.

Immature Conformist (Cfm). This is the compliant individual who responds out of fear and a sense that he lacks social know-how when dealing with those in a position of power. He also resorts to passive resistance on occasion and is predisposed to expect rejection.

Cultural Conformist (Cfc). This is the juvenile who identifies strongly with his delinquent peers and who considers himself "tough." He likes the idea that he is a delinquent and responds with conformity to his peer (delinquent) group.

Manipulator (Mp). The manipulator is the one who attempts to subvert or undermine the power of the authority figure or attempts to arrogate it to himself. He typically does not wish to conform, either to authority or to his peers.

Maturity Level 4 (I_4)

At this level, the individual has internalized a set of standards and norms by which he judges his actions and the actions of others. He has an awareness of the influence that others have on him, and of their expectations of him, and a lesser awareness of the impact of his behavior on others. He can sense guilt if he does not meet his own internalized standards, and he would like to be like those he admires. If he does not meet his own standards, he may feel inadequate, which may consequently result in acting out of his guilt feelings in an antisocial way. He may feel conflict over values, but is without conflict or a sense of guilt over self-worth. He may admire and identify with delinquent models. There are four subtypes in the fourth level of maturity.

Neurotic, Acting-Out (Na).   He resorts to diversionary tactics to distract himself and others from his feelings of inadequacy, rejection, or self-condemnation. He plays "games," verbally attacks, and engages in "conning" those about him.

Neurotic, Anxious (Nx).   Anxiety and psychosomatic symptomatology characterize this individual. He frequently experiences emotional disturbance in diverse forms, which result from his conscious sense of guilt or his feelings of inadequacy or failure.

Situational-Emotional Reaction (Se).   This individual appears to have had a fairly "normal" childhood and preadolescence, but he responds to family, social, or personal crises by acting out.

Cultural Identifier (Ci).   An individual who tends to see himself as rather competent or a leader of his peers, the cultural identifier nonetheless expresses his identification by opposing middle class values or by adopting ways that are commonly unacceptable.

THE COMMUNITY TREATMENT PROJECT

The I-Level diagnostic system was first operationally used with individuals who had been committed to the California Youth Authority (CYA), the state correctional agency which handles the more serious youthful offenders. It was part of an experimental program established in 1961, designated the Community Treatment Project (CTP), and operated as a special parole unit under the jurisdiction of the California Youth Authority. The program was "explicitly designed to provide individually programmed, intensive treatment services in lieu of commitments to a CYA facility."[11] The experimental CTP treatment project was divided into two phases, the first from 1961, the year of inception, to 1969. The second part of the program was from 1969 to 1974.

Phase I

The first phase of the program concentrated on assessing the effectiveness of correctional treatment in the community in lieu of commitment to a training school. The participants were recidivistic youngsters from 13 to 19 years of age, essentially property offenders (violent offenders were

[11]Paul Lerman, *Community Treatment and Social Control: A Critical Analysis of Juvenile Correctional Policy* (Chicago: The University of Chicago Press, 1975), p. 3.

excluded), and totaled 1,014 subject participants. They had "an average prior offense frequency of 5.8."[12]

The experimental group, which numbered 686, was moved directly into the community, whereas the control group, numbering 328, "were sent to a training school for several months before being returned to their home communities where they received routine parole supervision as members of a regular size caseload."[13] The experimental cases were assigned to exceedingly small caseloads, no more than 12 per parole agent. The differential treatment plan was based on the I-Level diagnostics coupled with intensive programming based on the needs, capacities, interests, and special circumstances of the case. The criterion of success or failure was recidivism, measured in terms of parole revocation or unfavorable discharge from the Youth Authority. The first phase concluded in 1969 and, in terms of outcome, was a disappointment, with at least one third of the participants reinvolved in delinquency.

Phase II

"Failure was related to residence," in the first phase, "so the Youth Authority introduced another setting that offered more controls than the CTP."[14] The youths in the second phase of the experiment were divided into "Status 1" and "Status 2" types. The former were the less promising risks and were housed in residential dormitories in minimum security institutions; the latter were treated in the style prevailing under the first phase of CTP. A great measure of the lack of success with the earlier phase of the program was attributed to the fact that many staff members were not adequately grounded in the diagnostics and mechanisms of the I-Level approach. To counter this deficiency, a Center for Training in Differential Treatment was established in 1967, at which the I-Level method of classification and ward-program compatibility decision-making became the core of training. With maturation level classification, subtype reconciliation, and program-youth compatibility development, the major problem with the I-Level approach is obviously its complexity.

According to Warren,[15] insufficient data are available to be definitive about the success of subtyping, but she asserts that the benefits deriving from the I-Level and CTP experimentation are manifold and include the following: (1) An interpersonal and maturational theory has been developed. (2) The feasibility of treating large numbers of delinquents in the

---

[12]Thomas R. Phelps, *Juvenile Delinquency: A Contemporary View* (Pacific Palisades, Cal.: Goodyear Publishing Co., Inc., 1976), p. 66.
[13]*Ibid.*
[14]*Ibid.*, p. 67.
[15]Warren, "Differential Treatment of Delinquents," pp. 224–26.

community has been demonstrated. (3) The feasibility of developing a wide range of "treatment atmospheres in group home settings" has also been demonstrated, "with some degree of success." (4) "Increasingly elaborate techniques and strategies" have evolved for the management of delinquents. (5) Institutional management problems have been diminished when the I-Level classification system is used. She adds that CTP was instrumental in the development of the probation subsidy concept. The California Youth Authority now operates 5 community programs (in lieu of institutionalization) and 4 CTP units.

SOME CRITICISMS

There are credible and articulate critics of the I-Level approach and of the claims made for differential or individualized treatment. The English scholars, Hood and Sparks, are particularly critical of the claims made by Grant. In the Camp Elliott Living Groups, for example, it had been asserted that beneficial results had been obtained by some "psychodynamic oriented" supervisory teams with the high maturity delinquents, whereas "custody-oriented" teams had an opposite effect. According to Hood and Sparks, the data provided in the Grants' study does not support the conclusion that supervisory effectiveness was responsible for the improvement noted. "What the results actually showed was that for the predicted 'best' treatment, offenders' successful restoration to duty depended on their maturity levels, whereas for that predicted 'least effective,' this was not so. But we cannot conclude from this finding that any of the three Living Groups was 'better' or 'worse' for either type of offender."[16]

Paul Lerman made a detailed, book-length critique of CTP (and probation subsidy) that should be examined by anyone having a special interest in the I-Level/CTP program or a general interest in differential treatment. Lerman alleges that the program failed to show a significant difference in favor of the experimental group on any of the five criteria of effectiveness employed: (1) Parole suspension. (2) Recidivism. (3) Favorable parole discharge. (4) Unfavorable discharge. (5) Psychological test scores. He also contends that CTP deviated from its original plan to limit intensive services to but 8 months, and instead offered these services for an average of two and one-half to three years. "This change in operational strategy cost the CTP program dearly, for it wiped out the original savings and, in fact, transformed it into a more costly program than that of the control group."[17]

---

[16]Hood and Sparks, *Key Issues in Criminology,* pp. 200–201.
[17]Lerman, *Community Treatment and Social Control,* pp. 66–67, *et passim.*

ORMSBY VILLAGE TREATMENT CENTER

Despite the obvious shortcomings in the Interpersonal Maturation Classification and treatment scheme, all research in human behavior has inevitable benefit. The negation of certain assumptions is as much an impetus to learning as is the discovery of a new fact or relationship. And much has been learned, even if through negation, in CTP to stimulate other research. Already modified programs are in operation and on the drawing boards. In Louisville, Kentucky, for example, Ormsby Village, a county facility for delinquent boys and girls was reconstituted from an old-line, authority-oriented institution to a treatment-oriented facility and renamed Ormsby Village Treatment Center.

The model was an integrated model, the components of which were the guided group interaction technique developed at Highfields, New Jersey, and the California Interpersonal Maturation Classification system. The Ormsby Village Treatment Center is considered a dramatic example of the conversion of an institution from a custodial philosophy to a treatment philosophy. "Each change at Ormsby Village Treatment Center was designed to make the treatment program more possible and more successful. Most of the changes excited a sense of renewal, of improvement, of hope and of progress among wards and staff."[18] It is clear that, with respect to the I-Level, at least one affirmative opinion exists.

Correctional treatment implies an effective and an efficient classification system, and the CTP program advanced the cause of discriminating classification. Furthermore, if correctional planning is to be truly progressive, it must be impelled by innovative thrusts, and the I-Level concept was certainly that. An indirect, but nonetheless useful benefit that derived from the CTP project was the discovery of how important trained staff are in the correctional endeavor, and that can have some practical implications.

The typologies that were developed in the application of the I-Level concept were clinically constructed, that is, they were based on compatible and consistent elements detected through clinical interviews. A different approach to typology was taken by Herbert C. Quay. Rather than clinical, it was empirical.

QUAY'S OFFENDER TYPOLOGY

The notion that criminals and delinquents have distinguishing personality characteristics that set them apart from noncriminals is not a new idea.

[18]Joseph W. Scott and Jerry B. Hissong, "An Effective Structure and Program for Institutional Change," *Federal Probation*, 37, No. 3 (September 1973), 52.

The literature is replete with studies which, though inconclusive, consistently pursue the typology theme. From Quay's point of view, the development of personality theory, with more sophisticated methods, is giving credence to the suspicion that personality traits are associated with criminal and delinquent behavior. But he emphasizes that it is not so much that a given behavioral dimension dominates a given type, but rather that multi-dimensional aspects distinguish subgroups, and he comments, "It seems likely that delinquent males can now be most meaningfully studied within a four-dimensional framework."[19]

In his early thinking, Quay conceptualized that framework as follows:

> The first dimension is comprised of a constellation of attitudes, opinions, and behavior tendencies which reflect a basic lack of socialization and emotional rapport with others. The second dimension also involves overtly hostile behavior, but here this behavior is accompanied by feelings of guilt, anxiety, unhappiness, and concern . . . . The third dimension involves the acceptance of standards, values, and ways of behaving which are at variance with the legal code and with the mores of the larger community but quite in keeping with the subculture in which many delinquents find themselves. This. . . does not represent a true lack of socialization—only a deficiency in socialization from the reference point of the middle class culture. Neither does it appear that emotional disturbance . . . is involved. Finally, there is a dimension of inadequacy, immaturity, and general inability to cope with complex situations.[20]

It is the feeling of Quay that delinquency will be much more fruitfully explored by the study of homogeneous subgroups, and not by continuing the belief that delinquents are "psychologically homogeneous."

In contrast to most typological theorists, Dr. Quay and his colleagues eschewed a clinical approach to the dimensions of deviant behavior and, instead, took an empirical and statistical tack. Through this method, rather than categorizing individuals, scores were assigned on the basis of the dimensions previously discussed. These scores were obtained by three "thoroughly researched instruments: (1) a 44-item check-list of behavior problems completed by a correctional officer who observes and rates the subject as he interacts in his present environment; (2) a 100-item true-false self-report questionnaire filled out by the subject himself; and (3) a 36-item check-list for the analysis of the subject's life history completed by the offender's caseworker based on available records of the youth's past behavior."[21] In this fashion data is secured pertaining to the past, the present, and the self-concept of the individual.

[19]"Personality and Delinquency," in Herbert C. Quay (ed.), *Juvenile Delinquency: Research and Theory* (Princeton, N.J.: D. Van Nostrand Company, 1965), p. 165. This article also provides an excellent review of the literature.

[20]*Ibid.*, pp. 165–66.

[21]U.S. Department of Justice, Federal Bureau of Prisons, *Differential Treatment. . .A Way to Begin,* Washington, D.C., September 1970, p. vi.

The Robert F. Kennedy Youth Center

The approach of Quay undergirded the program at the Kennedy Youth Center, a federal Bureau of Prisons facility in Morgantown, West Virginia, when that institution was opened in 1968. The Robert F. Kennedy Youth Center is a facility for juvenile and youthful offenders, ages 14–26 at the time of commitment, and has a capacity for 328 males. From many research studies involving the use of the three instruments mentioned above, "four factors or dimensions have consistently emerged":

1. Inadequate-immature
2. Neurotic-conflicted
3. Unsocialized aggressive or psychopathic
4. Socialized or sub-cultural delinquency[22]

It is to be noted that these dimensions are not exclusively associated with delinquents; they occur also in the normal population. The difference is one of degree. "The personality factors underlying criminal behavior appear to be quantitatively but not qualitatively different from that displayed by others."[23] Although it might be an extreme analogy, we might recall our discussion of the sociopathic personality. The sociopath is not always a criminal or a delinquent.

At the Kennedy Youth Center, the objective was to classify new admissions into "homogenous, treatment-meaningful groups." Each new admission was placed in one of four categories, based on the dimension for which he received the highest score. The four behavior categories (BC), which correspond to the four dimensions discussed earlier, are as follows:

BC-1. These youth are lazy and inattentive, showing a general lack of interest in most things around them. Their actions may be described as childish in nature, and correctional officers usually label them as blundering or helpless. They are weak and naive. Although they lose their tempers, they are not assaultive. Frequently they seem preoccupied and may give the impression of being "out of it."

BC-2. Youths in this category feel very guilty and genuinely sorry for what they have done, but they are quite likely to repeat the same thing tomorrow. Despite being very selective about their friendships, they usually are willing to talk about their problems. These individuals frequently

---

[22] *Ibid.*
[23] *Ibid.*

have nervous or anxious ways. They may impress you as feeling sad or unhappy much of the time.

BC-3.   This type of youth is very hostile and aggressive, showing little, if any, concern for the welfare of others. These people have a high need to create excitement since for them things quickly get too boring. Attempts to control them verbally are not very effective. They are frequently both verbally and physically aggressive. They will be without qualms and manipulate others to gain their own ends.

BC-4.   These individuals have usually been involved in gang activities and demonstrate a high degree of loyalty to that peer group. They are relatively unconcerned about adults because their pleasure is obtained by going along with their friends. Except for their delinquent acts, these youths appear quite normal. They are able to get along reasonably well in correctional institutions, but generally revert to their prior behavior following release.[24]

Although conceptually different, the Behavior Category (BC) approach and the I-Level approach seek to individualize treatment. Ideally, when the effort takes place in an institution, the integrated team treatment modality would be operating. But there are problems with each approach, some shared and some unique. The Behavior Classification system of Quay has not proven quite as effective as was anticipated at the Robert F. Kennedy Youth Center. The staff at that institution, for example, has questioned whether youths can actually be so differentiated, and, after the program was introduced into this experimental institution, the escape rate increased.[25]

The Endless Search

Meanwhile, further research and development of the Quay typology goes on. After 2½ years of specific research, Quay developed a comparable classifications system for adult offenders. Similar instruments were employed in developing the categories: a 204-item (true-false) personality questionnaire; a life-history analysis check-list applied to life history records, containing 50 items; and a 63-item "correctional adjustment" check-list. Five factoral dimensions have emerged and have been termed (a) Aggressive-Psychopathic, (b) Neurotic-Anxious, (c) Immature-

---

[24]*Ibid.*, pp. vi–vii.
[25]Roy Gerard, "Institutional Innovations in Juvenile Corrections," *Federal Probation,* 34, No. 4 (December 1970), 37–44.

Dependent, (d) Situational, and (e) Manipulativeness. The Quay Adult Typology has been implemented in two federal institutions—in Oxford, Wisconsin and at Seagoville, Texas.[26]

Exploratory research must go on, and the criticisms effectively dealt with if progress is to be made in understanding and dealing with delinquent and criminal behavior. The typology approach has serious flaws to overcome, some of which have already been discussed. The sophistication of the delinquent and the criminal is a variable that has not been too well considered. If we devise a classification for Manipulator, can we not also assume a capacity for manipulation of the instrument itself, the results, and the staff? Further, in "type-casting," we run into that hoary problem of labeling. When we categorize and classify, we label. And when we label we often set up a behavioral *circulus vitiosis*.

Still, the (re)search must go on. The best treatment approach for offenders continues to be sought. Imaginative, innovative, exploratory research is the only key available. While the results thus far have been dismal, the challenge is seductive. As the Director, speaking for the Federal Bureau of Prisons, said, in addressing the House Committee on the Judiciary; Subcommittee on Courts, Civil Liberties, and the Administration of Justice, in 1974:

> We candidly admit that we know relatively little about how to assist offenders in changing their lifestyle so that when released from custody, they can live a law-abiding life in society. It is our hope, however, that through innovation we can significantly improve the effectiveness of the Federal Prison System.

And that is just the minimal goal for correctional treatment.

SYNOPSIS

The concept of differential treatment is based on the recognition that as each human is an individual person, so treatment ought to be tailored to individual uniqueness.

The most notable undertaking in regards to differential treatment utilized the I-Level (Interpersonal Maturity Level) approach, developed by researchers in California. The essence of this approach is that juvenile delinquents can be categorized and then treated accordingly. The I-Level was first operationally used in an experiment with the California Youth

---

[26]For a more elaborate description of Adult Typology, see Robert B. Levinson, "Differential Treatment and Adult Typology," *Proceedings of the One Hundred and Fourth Annual Congress of Correction of the American Correctional Association,* Houston, Texas, August 18–22, 1974, pp. 373–92.

Authority, begun in 1961, designated as the Community Treatment Project (CTP).

Despite wide acclaim, the I-Level modality has been criticized for failing to prove that its success actually resulted from its approach, and because it fails its own criteria of success.

A comparable typological system was developed by Herbert C. Quay, which is experimentally in use in the Federal Bureau of Prisons. It had been previously used, with little success, at the Robert F. Kennedy Youth center in West Virginia.

There is a great need for enlightenment and a great need for additional research in the field of juvenile correctional treatment.

13 Special Treatment Problems

> *... I say that even as the holy and the righteous cannot rise beyond the highest which is in each of you, so the wicked and the weak cannot fall lower than the lowest which is in you also. And as a single leaf turns not yellow but with the silent knowledge of the whole tree, so the wrong-doer cannot do wrong without the hidden will of you all.*
>
> **Kahlil Gibran**
> *The Prophet*

Somewhere between the thinking of those who would convert our correctional system into a vast psycho-medical sybsystem and whose who would "lock 'em up and throw the key away," there must stand a middle-ground in which a rational, balanced philosophy is espoused. In this philosophy, the majority of offenders would be held accountable for their optional criminality, which would not preclude auxiliary treatment. Secure control would be ordained for those particularly dangerous or outrageous criminals. And for some, treatment would be the high priority approach. In some instances, the individual's behavior is aggravated, mitigated, or complicated by "special" behavioral problems, which compound the treatment challenge. In this chapter we will briefly examine four of the more significant of these—alcohol abuse, drug addiction, sexual pathology, and psychopathy/sociopathy—because they are profoundly represented in the world of corrections.

ALCOHOL ABUSE

If the prison world is, according to the cliché, a microcosm of the larger society, then a great many of its inmates have been scarred or criminalized through the abuse of alcohol. Estimates on the number of individuals with serious drinking problems in the United States may vary, but no one underestimates the gravity of the problem. In its third special report to the Congress (1978), the National Institute on Alcohol Abuse and Alcoholism estimated that 10 million Americans are "problem drinkers," and that they are probably responsible for 205,000 deaths each year from disease, accidents, and violent acting out. In 1975, it was further estimated, drinking problems cost the American taxpayer somewhere in the neighborhood of $43 billion in medical expenses, accidents, lost production, and related expenditures.

The problem is no longer an adult problem exclusively. Approximately 3.3 million youngsters between the ages of 14 and 17 have serious drinking problems. While alcohol abuse has always been considered primarily an urban phenomenon, a recent study revealed that alcohol and drug use among rural high-school teenagers in Vermont ranks "among the highest in the nation."[1] A survey of 413 students, ages 13 through 18, showed that 58 percent of the group were "regular drinkers." Almost a quarter of the sample "reported having drunk a six-pack or more of beer at one sitting; an additional 29 percent reported having drunk three to five bottles at one sitting; nearly 10 percent said they had consumed five to eight shots of liquor at a sitting; and another 11 percent reported having drunk a pint or more at a time."[2]

Alcohol Abuse And Criminal Behavior

The excessive addiction to alcohol in the United States, and its frequent association with criminal behavior, quite naturally brings up the question whether there is a *causal connection* between the use of alcohol and the commission of crime. It is an important question for the professionals in the criminal justice system. If there is a causal connection, then

---

[1]National Clearinghouse for Alcohol Information of the National Institute on Alcohol Abuse and Alcoholism, *NIAAA Information & Feature Service,* IFS No. 50 (August 11, 1978), p. 2.
  [2]*Ibid.*

alcohol abuse is something to be attacked in order to reduce crime, and it is also something to be treated in order to reduce recidivism. The criminal justice system has indeed been burdened with the drunk offender. In 1977, a total of 1,208,525 individuals were arrested for drunkenness.[3] Furthermore, the National Institute on Alcohol Abuse and Alcoholism estimates that alcohol is involved in as much as 50 percent of all murders and traffic deaths, and "alcohol is now suspected to be a major factor in child abuse and marital violence," as well as rape.[4]

The question of the link between alcohol and crime is related to the broader question of whether there is a link between drugs in general, which includes alcohol, and crime. In the broader context, the evidence is not generally imposing, except that we know that drug addiction precipitates a great deal of property crime in order for the addict to sustain his habit. Despite the questionable evidence pertaining to all drugs, "some evidence suggests that of all the popular drugs now taken for nonmedicinal purposes, *alcohol is most consistently and strongly linked with crime,* especially assaultive crimes such as homicide, aggravated assault, rape, and child beating."[5] (Italics in the original). Approximately 33 percent of the inmates entering Ohio prisons have admitted that drinking was related to their crimes.[6] Half of the prisoners released from the New Hampshire State Prison become affiliated with the New Hampshire Program on Alcohol and Drug Abuse,[7] which speaks of significant addiction to alcohol as well as other drugs. The intemperate use of alcohol by so many offenders amply confirms an interaction, if not a causal connection between alcohol and crime, and it is a phenomenon well known to practitioners in the field.

The Alcoholic's Right to Treatment

Interestingly, the American Medical Association did not designate alcoholism as a disease until 1956. In recent times, the courts have begun to assert the rights of alcoholics to treatment. It has been held, by a United States District Court of Appeals, that "alcoholism is a defense to a charge of public intoxication, and therefore is not a crime."[8] In a Virginia case, a chronic alcoholic who had been arrested 75 times for drunkenness appealed his incarceration on the basis that he was not getting any treatment.

---

[3]Federal Bureau of Investigation, U.S. Department of Justice, *Crime in the United States 1977: Uniform Crime Reports for the United States,* p. 173.

[4]*Los Angeles Times,* October 18, 1978.

[5]Hugh D. Barlow, *Introduction to Criminology* (Boston: Little, Brown & Company, 1978), p. 329.

[6]*NIAAA Information & Feature Service,* IFS No. 38 (July 21, 1977), p. 3.

[7]New Hampshire Program on Alcohol and Drug Abuse, *Annual Report,* September 1977, p. 58.

[8]*Easter v. District of Columbia,* 361 F. 2d 50 (1966).

The court indicated in its discussion that prisoners with special problems, such as alcoholism, might have a constitutional right to treatment for the problem.[9]

Legislative bodies are also coming around to this viewpoint, if rather slowly. Chicago has no drunkenness law. In Georgia, drunkenness is an offense only if it is accompanied by boisterous behavior. In 1973, Massachusetts removed public drunkenness from the status of a crime. Public drunkenness has also been decriminalized in Wisconsin and Minnesota. And in 1978, New York City passed a law banning discrimination against recovered alcoholics. The conviction of behavioral scientists was concisely expressed by an English authority, "that alcoholics should no longer be sent to prison for drunkenness . . . ."[10] But thousands of individuals with drinking problems remain within the correctional system and require a specialized knowledge, on the part of the correctionalist, of the resources that may be enlisted on behalf of the offender with a drinking problem.

Nature or Nurture?

Among alcohologists, the debate still rages as to whether nature or nurture is responsible for alcoholism. Up until the nineteenth century, heredity was the basis for explaining away differences. The work of the behaviorists was mainly responsible for the shift to environmentalism, in which the major impact on the human is seen as coming from the exterior environment. The enduring nature of this view has been captured in the opinion of one commentator: "Today many behaviorists tend to define man as a mindless automaton totally controlled by his environment."[11] Few fields have experienced so much written speculation and so little clearcut agreement as that of alcohology. As one writer complained, "Much has been written on the subject, with opinions varying about as widely as men differ in their reactions when intoxicated."[12]

Treatment for Alcohol Abuse

For the treatment professional in corrections, particularly the probation or parole officer, a brief acquaintance with the academic issues and controversies is advantageous. But it is more important to know what resources or techniques can be mobilized on behalf of the correctional client with a drinking problem.

---

[9]*Rakes v. Coleman,* 318 F. Supp. 181 (E.D. Va. 1970).

[10]Richard V. Phillipson, *Modern Trends in Drug Dependence and Alcoholism* (New York: Appleton-Century-Crofts, 1970), p. 189.

[11]William Madsen, *The American Alcoholic* (Springfield, Ill.: Charles C Thomas, 1974), p. 6.

[12]J. M. Thomas, quoted in Madsen, *The American Alcoholic,* p. 15.

Aversive Therapy

When prescription drugs become a part of the treatment strategy, the medical profession will have to become a partner in the endeavor. This is expressly so in those instances in which aversive therapy is employed and drugs have to be prescribed. In aversive therapy, a drug is used which induces an unpleasant reaction whenever alcohol is imbibed. Antabuse (disulfiram) is most commonly used in this regard and has its widest use in the United States.[13] Antabuse is ordinarily used in conjunction with out-patient treatment, but it must be voluntarily ingested by the patient, and therein lies its fatal flaw. "The efficacy of disulfiram treatment is obviously dependent on the patient's willingness to continue taking the medication."[14] Antabuse causes nausea, flushing, headaches, and general discomfort, so the individual has to be strongly motivated to subject himself to that experience, voluntarily, when he could, instead, enjoy the pleasure of alcohol.

This brings up an issue that has received, unfortunately, too little attention,[15] and that is the question of the client's perception-motivation. Programs and pontifications abound when it comes to alcohol abuse, but not enough attention has been paid to how the alcoholic himself perceives his problem, nor why he opts to abuse alcohol. People drink, and they drink to excess for different reasons. The correctionalist should never lose sight of the uniquely individual aspects of an alcoholic's problem, despite all the sweeping generalizations which are made.

In aversive therapy, some success has also been claimed with long-acting neuroleptics, drugs which produce symptoms which resemble those experienced in nervous disorders. Whereas antabuse is normally administered on an ambulatory basis, the neuroleptics are usually administered under supervision in a hospital.

Alcoholics Anonymous

Although most "authorities" maintain that a multidisciplinary approach must be taken to the problem of alcoholism, the best known program is not only not multidisciplinary, it is not too enamored of traditional therapy. Alcoholics Anonymous, founded by Dr. Bob and Bill W. in Akron, Ohio in 1935, is literally a household word in the United States. Its disdain for traditional therapies is matched by the hostility of a great many

[13]David J. Armor, J. Michael Polich, and Harriet B. Stambul, *Alcoholism and Treatment* (New York: John Wiley & Sons, 1978), p. 32.

[14]*Ibid.*

[15]This issue *is* definitively dealt with in Jean J. Rossi and William J. Filstead, "Treating" the Treatment Issues: Some General Observations About the Treatment of Alcoholism," in William J. Filstead, Jean J. Rossi, and Mark Keller (eds.), *Alcohol and Alcohol Problems* (Cambridge, Mass: Ballinger Publishing Company, 1976), pp. 193–227.

therapists for AA. "Professionals typically have mixed feelings about AA. On the one hand, nearly everyone acknowledges the superior effectiveness of AA in comparison with professional mental health treatment for alcoholics. On the other hand, for varying reasons, counselors tend to have negative feelings or at least serious reservations about the AA approach."[16]

AA, as it is popularly known, operates on what can be generally described as a variation of milieu therapy. The basic principles include a manifestation of genuine caring, an *esprit de corps,* which enables the individual to recognize that his problem is widely shared, and frequent "testimonies" from abstinent members. AA recognizes the group nature and needs of humanity and is a very successful form of group therapy. A great number of penal institutions in the United States now have AA chapters, or at least regular visitors from AA chapters in the community. Every sizable community has AA organizations, including Al-Anon, for family members, and Ala-teen for youngsters with drinking problems. Correctionalists, particularly probation and parole officers, should become acquainted with these facilities and organizations and maintain close rapport with their representatives. AA constitutes a very productive resource for the offender with a drinking problem.

Some Other Programs

Programs to assist the offender with a drinking problem are beginning to proliferate in corrections. The Florida correctional system has a program called Operation Reach Out, which is comparable to California's Prison Preventers, but with a different emphasis. Operation Reach Out sends inmates into the community to engage in "rap sessions" with youths who have come to the attention of the court because of alcohol or drug abuse. Inmates selected for the program must be articulate, but they must also have had prior adverse experiences with alcohol or drugs.

The STAR Unit is an alcoholic treatment project at the Federal Correctional Institution at Fort Worth, Texas. It exclusively emphasizes alcoholic treatment, and participation in the program must be voluntary. A wide variety of activities is undertaken, inclusive of group and individual counseling, in what could be called a responsibility-privilege system. The philosophy that motivates the program is that the individual must assume responsibility for his own behavior. Texas has a comparable effort in its correctional institutions known as Chemical Abusers Rehabilitation Program, and Wisconsin's Division of Corrections operates an Alcohol Education and Treatment Program, involving short-term, intensive learning

---

[16]Jon Weinberg, "Counseling Recovering Alcoholics," in Francis J. Turner (ed), *Differential Diagnosis and Treatment in Social Work* (New York: The Free Press, 1976), p. 180.

with the emphasis on the acquisition of skills needed for survival in the community. There are many others.

Counseling

It must be recognized that "alcoholism is a complex, cnronic disorder without an established etiology,"[17] but, as we have said earlier, we do not have to know an obscure cause in order to initiate remediation. The correctional counselor has an additional measure of authority over his client, because of the latter's status in the correctional system. This is not necessarily a disadvantage, as the alcoholic certainly needs structure in his existence, and structure comes through authority. Over and above this, however, some basic casework tactics are applicable.

Because alcoholism tends to be a chronic problem, it does not readily succumb to amelioration, so *patience* must be a cardinal virtue in the repertoire of the counselor. With compulsive and addictive problems, it must be recognized that it is far from a simple matter to effect resocialization. It must always be remembered that drugs are a substitution for orthodox need satisfactions and are not readily replaced. Consequently, *relapse* must be expected. It is not the end of the line, and it does not mean the failure of rehabilitation. When dealing with the alcoholic, or the drug addict, it is more important to achieve increasingly protracted periods of abstinence than to expect sudden conversion. All addicts must lie and manipulate and rationalize. They cannot be fortified in these mechanisms. The counselor must facilitate a *confrontation* between the offender and his inappropriate behavior. It is a social work cliché that the counselor must not moralize. Of course, one should not superimpose his subjective value standard on a client, but it is not moralizing to communicate to an alcoholic that his behavior is destructive.

One of the most interesting of correctional phenomena is the development of the concept of paraprofessionalism. A paraprofessional is an individual who brings certain skills and abilities to the adjunctive assistance of the professional. For example, a ghetto resident could open lines of communication and understanding to the inner city and enable the professional to reach more people and more effectively. Paraprofessionalism has also developed in the field of alcoholism, with the great majority of paraprofessionals so employed being recovered alcoholics.[18] In a very real sense, AA is a reservoir of paraprofessionals waiting to be tapped by the treatment person in corrections.

[17]*Ibid.*, p. 173.

[18]There is one good reference source extant in the area: George E. Staub, *The Paraprofessional in the Treatment of Alcoholism* (Springfield, Ill.: Charles C Thomas Publisher, 1973).

DRUG ABUSE

Alcohol abuse is such an extensive problem that it had traditionally been dealt with as if it were a separate and distinct pathology. We have followed that tradition purely for convenience and to permit a more compact discussion of the problem. But alcohol is a drug, and the student must understand that, in ordinary circumstances, it would be subsumed as such in any broad classification of drugs of abuse, including the opiates. In titling the present section "drug abuse," we are merely extending the convenience, and for the same reasons.

The common practice is to include all of the opiates, hallucinogens, barbiturates, and amphetamines in the loose confederation known as drugs. It is not our purpose to deliver an exhaustive treatise on drugs of addiction and habituation, so we will take a very generalized approach. The student should remember, however, that these different substances are more scrupulously distinguished as (1) Opium and its derivatives (such as heroin and morphine). (2) Psychotomimetics or psychoactive drugs (such as LSD, DMT, and cannabinol). (3) Sedatives, or general depressants (such as alcohol, PCP, the barbiturates, and tranquilizers). (4) Stimulants (such as cocaine, benzedrine, and methedrine). (5) Hydrocarbons (such as ether and airplane glue).

Some Dimensions of the Problem

As an ever-increasing number of Americans strive desperately to make an honored prophet out of Oswald Spengler, who foretold *The Decline of the West,* addiction to a wide variety of drugs has become widespread in the United States. Drug abuse ranks fourth among the causes of death of young men in the 18–24 year-old-group in this country, and world production of heroin and other drugs continues to increase. The main source of heroin continues to be the so-called Golden Triangle— Burma, Laos, and Thailand, with significant support from Pakistan, Afghanistan, and Mexico. It was reported in 1977 that a "Moscow Connection" had been set up to facilitate the flow of heroin from Asia to the United States, but the vigilant Russian authorities closed the route and stopped the traffic.[19]

Heroin has been the drug of preference among American addicts, and authorities variously estimate that somewhat between 500,000 and 700,000 individuals are hooked on the deadly mistress of euphoria. It is difficult to estimate how many inmates in our prisons are there because of drug-related offenses. The percentage would be higher in those states in

[19] *Los Angeles Times,* February 8, 1978.

FIGURE 13-1

which there is a high rate of addiction, such as California, New York, Michigan, and Illinois. In California, as of June 1977, the percentage of all male prisoners incarcerated for "controlled substance and marijuana" offenses was 12.5; for females it was 26.9 percent. As most drug offenders are not committed to prison for drug offenses, the true rate is concealed behind other crimes, usually property offenses.

The drug addict is becoming a very significant part of the correctional system. The heroin addict is ever compelled to find the wherewithal to satisfy his craving. An average habit can range from $75 to $100 per day, on up. No ordinary addict can afford to maintain a "mainline" habit without resorting to criminal behavior. Some authorities estimate that drug-related crime totals $6 billion a year, and that a single addict may cost the citizens $100,000 per year from his criminal activity. To support a $50 a day habit, it has been estimated, would cost a "junkie" at least $18,000 annually. And so, a vast addict-criminal army prowls this land and purloins from its citizens. When he or she is eventually caught and put into the criminal justice system, it becomes the responsibility of the correctional component to attempt to thwart recidivism. It is a very frustrating responsibility.

The Philosophic Battleground

The correctionalist who has to deal with a drug addict in a treatment context has a captive client. Before the client reaches the caseload of the probation officer, the correctional counselor, or the parole officer, a journey had to be taken through at least part of the criminal justice system. That system is not only a process, it is also part of the machinery that most articulately expresses prevailing community values. Drug abuse is negatively valued by the dominant culture, which generally views drug abusers as criminally disposed rather than as medically or psychologically disabled individuals.

But for every dominant—or dominating—value, there is a minority viewpoint. There are critics who feel that drug addiction is a personal option, or a religious prerogative, or at best a civil matter that should be decriminalized. Cocaine, which became the most popular drug of abuse in the 1970s, is widely used by the "beautiful people," music stars, and Hollywood celebrities. Actor Robert Blake is quoted as saying, "The whole town of Hollywood is coked out of its head."[20] Because cocaine abuse is clothed with the prestige of its users, it is obvious that its devotees feel that it is far from a criminal matter. At $100 per gram, it is an expensive illusion.

Many Indian tribes use various drugs in their sacred religious ceremonies. The Incas, for instance, believed that the divine child of the sun gave the coca leaf to the Incas as a gift to restore the strength of the weary and to dispel unhappiness. It is from the coca leaf that we get cocaine. And from June 1977 to July 1978, the U.S. Customs reported the confiscation of $78 million worth of cocaine at Los Angeles International Airport alone.

Many tribes of Mexican Indians have developed a "psychedelic way of life," and the Toapura Indians have a "pure peyote culture."[21] Drug use

[20]Quoted in Long Beach, California *Independent, Press-Telegram,* October 19, 1978.
[21]John C. Lilly, *Simulations of God* (New York: Bantam Books, 1975), p. xv.

FIGURE 13-2
Papaver somniferum: the opium poppy

FIGURE 13-2
Papaver somniferum: the opium poppy

and religious experience were linked in Carlos Castaneda's *The Teachings of Don Juan,* which was a much read work when published in 1968, and the quasi-religious minority of drug users became a thunderous minority when the pied piper of escapism, Timothy Leary, urged the restless and the disenchanted to "Drop out, tune in, and turn on" in the bewildered 1960s.

Regardless of one's subjective opinion about drug abuse, when criminal behavior is an accessory of this way of life, confrontation with the criminal justice system is not far off. But the options have broadened. In

1962, the United States Supreme Court ruled that drug addiction is not a crime,[22] providing the necessary impetus for civil processing of addicts, which has long been practiced in New York and California. A strong sentiment for decriminalization has also developed. Still, the vast majority of addict–correctional clients have been processed as felons, and the vast majority of these were criminals before they became addicts.

Endemic Heroin Addiction

Heroin addiction is such a serious problem that "endemic heroin use" is becoming a more commonly used phrase. "Endemic" is a term that signifies extensive occurrence, or that which is native to a particular people or region. Heroin addiction is endemic in California. In 1975, the highest level of heroin addiction occurred in San Francisco, where it peaked at 916 addicts per 100,000 of the population. Following in order were Los Angeles (864), Phoenix (796), Detroit (792), San Diego (788), and Chicago (677).[23]

An indication of how widespread the problem is can be gleaned from the fact that, throughout the world, "heroin seizures... reached an unprecedented level in 1976," as was reported to a special session of the United Nations Commission on Narcotic Drugs by the president of the International Narcotics Control Board.[24] The expense and futility of policing the drug trade is clearly revealed in the budget of one major West Coast city. The Los Angeles City budget for 1976–1977 contained *fifteen and one-half million dollars* for the Los Angeles Police Department Narcotics Division alone, including salaries, expenses, and equipment.

Heroin is the most addicting of drugs, but it is not the only drug problem. Our drug-saturated culture seems both insatiable and insensitive. A seven-year-old child came home from grade school in a Southern California city during the peak of the drug revolution, vocalizing some lyrics that obviously did not go with the tune (*Frère Jacques*). When his mother asked him to sing the lyrics for her, the modern American grade school student recited the following:

> Marijuana, marijuana,
> LSD, LSD,
> Scientists make it,
> Teachers take it,
> Why can't we, why can't we?

[22]*Robinson v. California,* 370 U.S. 660, 666–68 (1962).
[23]Milan Korcok, "Heroin Addiction Highest in West Coast Cities: NIDA," *The U.S. Journal of Drug and Alcohol Dependence,* 1, No. 7 (August 1977), 1.
[24]Quoted in *The Journal,* Vol. 7, No. 4, Toronto, Ontario, Canada, April 1, 1978.

Marijuana

While the danger posed by heroin is clearcut, controversy swirls about the presence or absence of harm from marijuana. When the Mexican government began to spray its marijuana and opium fields with paraquat in 1975 to control the flow of illegal drugs, an outcry developed because paraquat impregnated the marijuana with its toxicity, with consequent danger to the marijuana user. Where once considerable animosity existed for those who indulged in "weed," the use of paraquat brought some distinguished people to the defense of the marijuana users, men such as Senator Percy of Illinois, who was among the first to draw attention to the poisonous aspects of paraquat. The West Coast director of the National Organization for Reform of Marijuana Laws (NORML), which favors complete decriminalization, said that the use of paraquat would serve to inspire more home-growing of marijuana.[25]

There are impassioned pleas for the legalization of marijuana[26] and treatises that say that no research has substantiated "physiologic damage" from marijuana.[27] But a 13-nation conference of 41 scientists, meeting in France in 1978, disclosed research findings which repeatedly indicated that cannabinol, which is the derivative essence of marijuana, is a dangerous substance.[28] In various experiments with rodents and monkeys, notably the rhesus monkey because it has a reproductive system quite similar to the human's, it was established that cannabinol, administered orally, was an embryocidal (fetus-killing) agent. It was also revealed that the use of marijuana has harmful effects on the brain, lungs, and other body cells and will interfere with the hormones which control the function of the ovary.

It is estimated that about 12 million American adults regularly use marijuana.[29] The Institute for Social Research secured data on high-school students which revealed that 56 percent of all seniors had at least tried marijuana, and one in eleven high school students were daily users of the drug.[30] While the use of this non-addicting but habituating drug increases steadily, decriminalization has become the legislative mood, and federal marijuana penalties, approved by the senate, provide neither arrest nor jail for possession of up to one ounce of marijuana. If the amount

[25]Cited in *The Journal*, Vol. 7, No. 6, Toronto, Ontario, Canada, June 1, 1978.

[26]John Kaplan, *Marijuana—The New Prohibition* (New York: Pocket Books, 1971).

[27]Alexander B. Smith and Harriet Pollack, *Some Sins Are Not Crimes* (New York: Franklin Watts, Inc., 1975), p. 152.

[28]*Los Angeles Times*, August 6, 1978.

[29]Gary Seidler, "Legalization Would Reap $1.6 Billion," *Focus*, 1, No. 2 (March–April, 1978), 14.

[30]Institute for Social Research, The University of Michigan, *ISR Newsletter*, Summer 1978, p. 5.

FIGURE 13-3
Cannabis sativa: marijuana

is under one ounce, it is considered an "infraction," and the police record is expunged upon payment of the fine. The age level of marijuana users is constantly lowering. In 1978, six 9-year-olds were arrested in Willimantic, Canada for the possession or sale of marijuana.[31]

[31] *The Journal,* Vol. 7, No. 5, Toronto, Ontario, Canada, May 1, 1978, p. 3.

PCP

With heroin-addict concentration, per capita, the highest in California, and marijuana as plentiful as tobacco, it is not surprising to discover that another of California's cities, San Jose, has earned the title of the "PCP capital of the United States." Seizures of a chemical that has been "widely considered to be the most dangerous drug seen on the streets in a decade,"[32] phencyclidine (PCP), were 100 times greater in 1977 than they were in 1975. Also known as "angel dust," PCP ranks second only to marijuana in the extent of its use. One research physician estimated that "more than 7 million Americans had used PCP at least once."[33] PCP is particularly dangerous because its effects are unpredictable. It is used for its hallucinogenic properties, but it also causes serious disorientation, violent acting out, and psychotic episodes. When it is chronically abused, it can take the afflicted individual as long as two years to recover full cognitive functioning. The usual dose of PCP ranges from 2–10 mg, but "joints" can contain as much as 75 mg. Seven milligrams is considered an anesthetic dose.

PCP was developed during the 1950s as an anesthetic and marketed under the trade name Sernyl. Its use was discontinued by the medical profession in 1967 because of its side effects, but it began to be used by veterinarians in 1968 as a tranquilizer for animals, under the trade name Sernylan. "The first reported "street" use of phencyclidine was in San Francisco's Haight-Ashbury district in 1967 where it was illegally marketed as the *PeaCe Pill*."[34] Ordinarily sprinkled on mint leaves and smoked like marijuana, PCP also comes in crystal and in liquid form. It produces incoherence, auditory hallucinations, visual distortion, agitation, immobility, and seizures among other effects. An individual under the influence of PCP obviously needs medical treatment, possibly followed by protracted therapy.

The drugs causing the greatest concern in the United States today, in terms of illicit use, are the opiates, the amphetamines, the barbiturates, cocaine, PCP, and the hallucinogens, which include marijuana. Where bizarre behavior is associated with abuse of drugs, medical and/or psychiatric treatment is indicated. The average correctional client, who has a drug history, will ordinarily have been a poly-drug user. Marijuana use may not automatically lead to heroin abuse, but it is a rare "junkie" who has not used marijuana. Because it is literally impossible to go into

---

[32]Long Beach, California *Independent,* August 9, 1978.
[33]*Ibid.*
[34]Los Angeles County Sheriff's Department, "Phencyclidine (P.C.P)" (*sic*). Undated, mimeographed educational material, c. mid-1970s.

any detailed account of the many proposed treatment approaches for the many types of drug abuse, we will limit the remaining discussion to the treatment of heroin addiction. Inferences can be drawn in terms of the broad range of drug abuse. For a more detailed description of the methods employed in supervising drug addicts, the student can consult another source in which I have given this matter its first detailed treatment.[35]

Basic Approaches to Heroin Addiction

Anyone with an interest in the drug problem has to be immediately impressed with the wide variety of treatment approaches[36]—and the signal lack of success in all of these programs. Millions and millions of dollars are being spent on the battle against illicit drug addition, and the returns are paltry. The fact is there will not be any significant redemptive incursion into the ranks of the "boot and shoot hypes" until some substance or some belief is found which transcends the "high" of heroin. That is why religiously oriented efforts seem to have the most success and why solution of the drug addiction problem will have to come, in the main, from biochemistry and pharmaceutics, and not from psychotherapeutics. "Talk therapy" is ineffectual with heroin addicts, whether from a parole officer or a psychiatrist. At present, the critical need is for preventive education. The profound ignorance of so many youngsters about the pitfalls of illicit drug use is appalling. I once had a thirteen-year-old quite seriously ask me if smoking marijuana would result in pregnancy.

Punitive Approach

There are five basic approaches to drug addiction, if we wish to loosely include the punitive as a "treatment" approach. This is the "law and order" persuasion that sees the breach of any section of a penal code as a *de facto* crime, and which feels that while an individual may have a secondary problem, such as alcoholism or heroin addiction, the criminal justice process is just that, a *criminal* justice process—without responsibility for psychomedical concomitants.

---

[35]Louis P. Carney, *Probation and Parole: Legal and Social Dimensions* (New York: McGraw-Hill Book Company, 1977), cf. Chapter 13, "Supervising the Drug Addict."

[36]There are numerous works available on the subject of drug addiction. For an eclectic overview of a number of programs, see John G. Cull and Richard E. Hardy, *Organization and Administration of Drug Abuse Treatment Programs* (Springfield, Ill.: Charles C Thomas Publisher, 1974).

This is epitomized in New York's harsh narcotic law, which provides a life sentence as the ultimate penalty for possession of the slightest amount of a controlled substance. A related view has often been expressed, namely, that all heroin addicts ought to be quarantined on some island permanently. Ironically, quarantine would be the most effective way to deal with the spreading disease of heroin addiction, but it is far from a simple proposition. There are questions of due process and human rights, not to mention the issues of family dislocation or relocation. And permanent exile does violence to any hope of restoration. Heroin drug addiction is so patently a psychomedical problem that a purely punitive approach is an indefensible rejection of the wisdom of other disciplines.

Legalization

At the polar end of the spectrum from the punitive approach is that of legalization. The British system is rather widely known as a pioneer effort at wide-scale legalization. England's Dangerous Drugs Act was passed by Parliament in 1920. Significantly, it did not prohibit physicians from prescribing opiates in the treatment of addict patients. England's early drug problem was one of morphinism. The English drug problem was limited to somewhere in the vicinity of 600 addicts in the 1950s, which was a small problem compared with that in the United States.

Liberally disposed individuals are vocal in their support of the "British system," and it has been praised because "it is believed that not more than 3 or 4 percent of the addicts in Great Britain are unknown to the authorities."[37] But the system had to be modified because of abusive prescription of drugs by English physicians, which literally aggravated the country's drug problem. As an English authority has pointed out, "To a large extent, because of the overprescribing of heroin (and cocaine) by a small number of London GPs under this now abandoned overpermissive 'British System', a heroin–cocain epidemic arose in England in the early 1960s."[38]

In the present English system, opiates may be legally dispensed by physicians only at fifteen "Treatment Centres" in London and a few in the provinces. It is first determined if the individual addict wants to terminate use of drugs, and if so, a treatment program is developed to achieve this goal. If not, methadone will be suggested, since the au-

[37]Smith and Pollack, *Some Sins Are Not Crimes,* p. 99.
[38]M. M. Glatt, *A Guide to Addiction and Its Treatment* (St. Leonardgate, Lancaster, England: Medical and Technical Publishing Co., Ltd., 1974), p. 255.

thorities feel that methadone addiction is preferable to heroin addiction. If the addict is not interested and wants only heroin or cocaine, he is accommodated. By 1969, the addict population had grown to 1,466.[39] The British Home Office announced that at the end of 1976 there were 1,881 *known* addicts in England.

Custody, Followed by Treatment

The punitive/treatment approach is a hybrid modality, in which custody or incarceration is secured so that treatment can be administered. The so-called civil commitment of addicts exemplifies this approach, and it is featured in California's program at the California Rehabilitation Center. Inmates in this penal institution are referred to as "residents." Prosecution on their criminal offenses is held in abeyance, and they are diverted in civil proceedings for treatment. "Treatment" consists of individual and group counseling in a community therapy milieu, parole to small caseloads, and obligatory urinalysis testing. Discharge from the program can occur after two drug-free years in the community or three "drug-free" years on a methadone program.

Although reams of laudatory material fill the journals concerning this program, it has been a signal therapeutic failure. The one main advantage is that a number of addicts are *quarantined* for a brief period of time, which might suggest some fiscal savings. But the therapeutic or hospital setting is particularly vulnerable to the influx of illicit drugs. Yochelson and Samenow mentioned this problem in their celebrated research at St. Elizabeths Hospital,[40] and innumerable addicts have told me that illicit drugs were readily available at the California Rehabilitation Center. Three California researchers, who were involved in the civil addict program, said that civil commitment of addicts should only be an interim measure—between the adoption of a punitive or a nonpunitive posture toward the addict.[41]

In one list of 36 cases publicized as "discharged" from the civil addict program at the California Rehabilitation Center, leaving the implication of success, 12 had died from drug overdoses, 2 had been discharged by parole board resolution, 2 had their commitments expire, and 1 died from causes other than drugs. That scarcely constitutes success. It can be

---

[39]*Ibid.*, p. 256.

[40]Samuel Yochelson and Stanton Samenow, *The Criminal Personality, Volume II: The Change Process* (New York: Jason Aronson, Inc., 1977), p. 477.

[41]J. C. Kramer, K. A. Bass, and J. E. Berecochea, cited in Jerome J. Platt and Christina Labate, *Heroin Addiction: Theory, Research, and Treatment* (New York: John Wiley & Sons, 1976), p. 229.

predicted, as I have previously intimated,[42] that this program will come to an inglorious end. It cost a lot and achieved little, and the confidence of the judiciary is evidenced in a declining commitment rate. From July 1977 through February 1978, a monthly average of 71 male addicts and 20 female addicts were committed to CRC by the courts. This compares with 143 men and 35 women, which was the monthly average committed during 1976.[43] The civil commitment of addicts can be criticized on the grounds of economics—because it is an expensive operation without a commensurate return on the investment. But the National Council on Crime and Delinquency has also condemned the civil commitment of addicts because "it creates an illusion that treatment is being given" and has called for its repeal in a formal policy statement.[44]

Residential Treatment

The residential effort at treatment of drug addiction is probably epitomized in Synanon. Programs of this nature are often called self-help endeavors, and they rely on variations of the therapeutic community. Synanon was founded in 1958 in Ocean Park, California, by an ex-alcoholic, Chuck Dederich. A comparable program, Daytop Lodge (later Daytop Village), was founded in New York, in 1963, and was generally patterned on Synanon, but with variations. It is interesting to note that while "outsiders" consider Synanon a treatment program, its members consider it a social movement.[45] Dederich, in fact, considers the family to be in the process of reverting to the primitive clan system and he has sponsored mass mate-swapping within the "family" of Synanon.

Synanon is a closed community which "exists in order to keep addicts off drugs, not for purposes of recreation, vocational education, etc."[46] Group cohesion is emphasized, and great stress is laid on the family nature of the Synanon organization. In the heated and ruthless encounter sessions, which are a part of the program and which are known as "haircuts," attack therapy is employed. It can be said of Synanon, as of similar

[42]Louis P. Carney, *Introduction to Correctional Science* (New York: McGraw-Hill Book Company, 1974), p. 111.

[43]California Department of Corrections, *Quarterly Research Report for CAP Task Force,* March 27, 1978 (mimeographed).

[44]*Crime and Delinquency,* 20, No. 1 (January 1974), 4.

[45]James J. Murray and Ann B. Trotter, "Treatment in Drug Abuse: Counseling Approaches and Special Programs," in Richard E. Hardy and John G. Cull (eds.), *Drug Dependence and Rehabilitation Approaches* (Springfield, Ill.: Charles C Thomas Publisher, 1973), p. 147.

[46]Rita Volkman and Donald R. Cressey, "Differential Association and the Rehabilitation of Drug Addicts," in Stuart Palmer and Arnold S. Linsky (eds.), *Rebellion and Retreat* (Columbus, Ohio: Charles E. Merrill Publishing Company, 1973), p. 334.

residential treatment programs, that the success rate is notable during the in-house period but negligible once the member leaves the security of the residential program.

In the Daytop Village program, which now has six facilities in and around New York City, the candidate for admission must literally battle to get into the program. He is ridiculed, ostracized, and tested before he gains entrèe. After acceptance in the program, he is initially treated as if he were less than mature, but he is credited with increasing maturity and responsibility as he proceeds through the phases of the program. Group sessions are standard fare in the program, and marathon sessions, extending beyond 24 hours in duration, have a particular popularity. The resident is held to high standards of behavior, and "gut-level" participation in the group sessions is expected. As the resident earns his way back into the community, he is obliged to return and contribute to the program, giving testimony similar to that given in Alcoholics Anonymous.

Methadone Maintenance

The fifth and final "treatment" approach to drug addiction is a highly controversial one, methadone maintenance. It is controversial because methadone is itself a highly addicting drug, and the right of the government to maintain an individual in a condition of obligatory addiction is most certainly a critical ethical question. Methadone hydrochloride, or methadone, to use its popular name, is a water soluble opiate antagonist. It was first developed in 1945 by a German research scientist who was seeking a substitute for opium derivatives which had been in short supply because of World War II. It was first employed in a maintenance program for drug addicts by Drs. Vincent P. Dole and Marie Nyswander in a 1963 pilot project conducted in New York City. An evaluation of the project by Columbia University's School of Public Health and Administrative Medicine was favorable, and an expansion of the program was recommended. The New York State Medical Society, in February 1970, "passed a resolution recognizing the Dole-Nyswander methadone maintenance program as a valid treatment approach...."[47]

The argument offered in favor of methadone is that it blocks the euphoria produced by heroin and permits an individual to have a "normal," ambulatory existence when fortified with methadone. This philosophy necessarily implies that it is futile to try to free the addict from drugs and, instead, views the condition of addiction as a "deficiency disease"

---

[47]Jerome J. Platt and Christina Labate, *Heroin Addiction: Theory, Research and Treatment* (New York, John Wiley & Sons, 1976), p. 265.

which can be managed, as diabetes is managed with insulin.[48] Of course, this also implies "a return to the medical model of treatment . . . for drug dependence,"[49] a model that has been well discredited in contemporary corrections.

The arguments against methadone reveal, as do the criticisms of other programs, the resistance of the problem of drug addiction to any definitive solution. Methadone is a powerfully addicting drug. Withdrawal from methadone is considered more devastating than that from heroin. The ethical issue has already been mentioned. There are other cogent issues. One major concern is that addicts maintained on methadone are not really being rehabilitated, but merely "maintained." As an ex-methadone client commented to me on one occasion, "They are just creating a bunch of Zombies." Methadone is big business today, and it takes thousands of dollars to maintain *each* addict annually. Methadone programs have grown prodigiously and, "as a result of the proliferation of methadone programs, problems related to competition for funding are being experienced."[50] And once again the venal discredit the Hippocratic.

The challenge is almost insurmountable. With the obvious implications of financial windfalls being made at the expense of human misery, a good argument could be made for decriminalizing drug addiction (not the criminality that accompanies it) and placing the therapeutic emphasis on the education of the young, so that the problem can be aborted if it cannot be *ex post facto* extirpated. The iconoclastic psychiatrist, Thomas Szasz, vehemently condemns what he terms the "ritual persecution" of drug addicts[51] and caps his indictment by saying that "we cannot choose to prohibit drugs or force people to undergo therapy to 'cure' them of their desires without abandoning the ethic of autonomy the Founding Fathers intended to be the backbone of our society."[52] To be or not to be—or how to be—that is, indeed, the question.

SEXUAL PATHOLOGY

History has well recorded the fact that it is the human's gift to soar above the eagle and to enchant the universe with incomparable acts of creativ-

[48]Wolfram Keup, *Drug Abuse* (Springfield, Ill.: Charles C Thomas Publisher, 1972), p. 175.

[49]Carl N. Edwards, *Drug Dependence* (New York: Jason Aronson, Inc., 1974), p. 10.

[50]Jerome J. Platt and Christina Labate, *Heroin Addiction,* p. 273.

[51]Thomas Szasz, *Ceremonial Chemistry* (Garden City, New York: Anchor Press/ Doubleday, 1975).

[52]Thomas Szasz, "Our Despotic Laws Control the Right to Self-Control," *Psychology Today,* 8, No. 7 (December 1974), 21.

ity. But it has also recorded the fact that it is within the power of this self-same human to reduce itself to an unutterable level of degradation and to plummet into the Stygian bowels of unimaginable pathology. As I write, Norman Rockwell perishes and leaves a heritage of treasured imprints upon the sands of time; and Charles Manson, who precipitated a human slaughter, makes his first appearance before the parole board.

And in Colton, California, a man who was on probation following a sex perversion conviction was arrested for the mutilation deaths of two young women; and a 23-year-old sex offender, one week out of a Colorado jail on a work release program, murdered all five members of a family that had befriended him. The mother and the two daughters had also been raped. Tragically, this recital of criminal sexual perversion and brutalization could go on endlessly. How do we penetrate the brooding recesses in the twisted minds of the perpetrators of these misdeeds? How do we contain those evil impulses?

The Professional's Role

Because of the tremendous power of the sex drive, it is obviously doubly difficult for the disturbed individual to contain his pathological impulses, and the behavioral sciences have contributed little toward the resolution of serious sexual pathology. Notwithstanding, probation and parole officers are constantly called upon to supervise individuals with deviant sexual histories, and they are ordinarily infinitely less qualified to do so than their colleagues in the psychiatric profession. In some correctional jurisdictions, psychiatric therapy is prerequisite for release, or at least mandatory upon release. In any event, wisdom dictates that the probation or parole officer enlist the professional assistance and counsel of a psychiatrist or a clinical psychologist when supervising offenders with a history of psychosexual pathology.

But the corrections professional should also be conversant with the fundaments pertaining to sexual pathology, particularly of the types of cases that would most likely be represented in his or her caseload. Serious pathology can easily escape detection by the clinical staff in a prison. Sometimes there has been no *overt* prior history of sexual pathology. Sometimes the institutional staff is less than competent or is overburdened. I recall one case in which an individual had been released on parole from a midwestern prison, where he had been incarcerated for a property offense. The "jacket" gave no indication of any pathology, nor was there any psychiatric or psychologic intimation of clinical concern. But a perceptive parole officer, pursuing intuitive feelings, and with skillful interviewing techniques, induced the parolee to reveal his inner feelings. Those feelings included the ambition to "cut open a woman to see what she looked like inside, because I have already done it to rabbits and cats." Steps were immediately taken to have that very sick individual committed to a state hospital for appropriate treatment.

It is an extremely difficult thing for the average individual to feel sympathetically disposed toward a person who has sexually abused a child, committed a rape-murder, or performed some other sexual offense. But that is why a professional is called a professional. He or she is obliged to control subjective feelings and to provide objective supervision and treatment where possible. The sexual offender who is on probation or parole has been through the adjudication process, and the corrections professional is not a surrogate judge or jury.

Treatment for the sex offender must include surveillance, for the professional responsibility is twofold: It is to afford maximum protection to the public and supportive therapy for the client. In concert, surveillance and therapeutic supervision will, hopefully, reduce the acting out potential. There is a wide array of sexual offenses, but it would serve no purpose to dwell on the rarer pathologies such as necrophilia. Instead, we will take an all too brief look at the two major types of sexual offender most likely to be represented in the correctional caseload, the rapist and the child molester, and examine some of the treatment dispositions in vogue.

Rape

Rape is defined as the forcible carnal knowledge of a female against her will. During 1977, the FBI reported, "there was an estimated total of 63,020 forcible rapes" committed in the United States. That represented an 11.1 percent increase over the preceding year.[53] This total does not include "statutory" rapes, nor can it be considered in any way a precise estimate. It is a common belief among professionals that rape is underreported significantly, perhaps as much as ten times, because of the embarrassment and shame associated with the offense and the public trial that must ensue. One fact is certain, there has been a steady increase in the number of rapes. In 1964, for example, there were 11.1 rapes per 100,000 of the population. In 1977 there were 57.0, which constituted a 10 percent increase over 1976.[54]

The common view is that rape is an offense of sexual gratification. Nothing is further from the truth. While sexual gratification is accom-

---

[53]FBI Uniform Crime Reports, *Crime in the United States 1977* (Washington, D.C.: U.S. Government Printing Office, 1978), p. 14.
[54]*Ibid.*

plished, rape is essentially an act of physical degradation, or, as one writer expressed it, "a ritual of power."[55] It is an act of violence expressed sexually. In a survey of 73 "excessively violent" rapists at the Atascadero State Hospital in California, the Queen's Bench Foundation (a non-profit organization of female judges and lawyers in San Francisco) revealed that not one of the rapists gave sex as his motivation. Instead, they said that "power, dominance or revenge" were the motivating factors.[56] Although Eldridge Cleaver claimed that rape was "an "insurrectionary act," degradation and domination clearly characterized his activity, as inferred from his statement, "It delighted me that I was defying and trampling upon the white man's law . . . and that I was defiling his women. . . . I felt I was getting revenge."[57] The motive for rape should be fairly clear by now, but what types of individuals are disposed to commit rape?

Characteristics of a Rapist

Occasionally the rapist is produced by peculiar and unusual pathology. Most readers will have some familiarity with the phenomenon of multiple personality, because of the best-selling works *The Three Faces of Eve* and *Sybil*. An equally remarkable case was that of William M. who, in 1978, was revealed to have ten different personalities constantly at war within him. Psychiatric testimony confirmed that these were actual and not spurious personalities. One was that of an 18-year-old lesbian, another was a screaming 9-year-old boy, still another was a British poet—and one was a rapist who attacked four university coeds. But rapists ordinarily are not of such esoteric textbook caliber.

One useful classification categorizes rapists according to the following types:[58] (1) The rapist who assaults his victim because he is impotent. (2) The inadequate individual who tries to induce his victim to "love" him so that he can act out his fantasies. (3) The predatory, criminalized, streetwise prowler who calculatingly stalks his prey and is given to other criminality as well. (4) The sadistic, often psychotic rapist who becomes sexually aroused by the victim's resistance and is the one most disposed to torture or kill. These are *general* categories, not precise clinical typologies, so the usefulness of this classification, for probation and parole officers, is basically for anticipatory case planning.

---

[55]Deena Metzger, "It Is Always the Woman Who Is Raped," in Deeana R. Nass, *The Rape Victim* (Dubuque, Iowa: Kendall/Hunt Publishing Company, 1977), p. 4.
[56]Carol R. Benfell, "Power, Dominance, Revenge, Not Sex—Motive for Rapist," *Prosecutor's Brief*, 3, No. 3 (Sept.–Nov. 1977), 28.
[57]Eldridge Cleaver, *Soul on Ice* (New York: McGraw-Hill Book Company, 1968), p. 14.
[58]Adapted from J. L. Barkas, *Victims* (New York: Charles Scribner's Sons, 1978), p. 107.

Recidivism

We will review treatment efforts with the sex offender shortly, but before doing so it would not be inappropriate to consider the issue of recidivism. The development of meaningful recidivism data on sex offenders is complicated by a number of factors, including contradictory research findings. Further, the nature and precipitants of rape, and the etiological factors associated with it, are still not clearly understood.

In a study of Denver rapists, it was asserted that recidivism was as high as 85 percent,[59] whereas a study conducted by the Institute for Law and Social Research (INSLAW) drew the conclusion that "Defendants arrested for sexual assault appeared to have arrest records no more frequently than other defendants. In addition, as a group, they were not found to be highly recidivistic in terms of subsequent rearrests . . . or reconvictions for serious crimes. . . ."[60] Denver, it should be noted, and for reasons not clearly understood, has one of the highest per capita rape rates in the United States. One serious flaw in the recidivism index is that it does not provide for the variable of opportunity. In other words, how many rapists are constrained from recidivating because the opportunity to offend does not present itself? The recidivism rate measures only what has happened *and come to the attention of the authorities.* As treatment in the narrower sense implies a change in the individual, a true reduction in recidivism would signal a transformation of the person.

Pedophilia

The individual who uses a child for sexual gratification, that is, the pedophile, is an object of particular revulsion in our society. The common image is of a skulking stranger lurking around movie houses and playgrounds. While it is true that a great number of child molesters do prowl in those locations where children tend to congregate for recreation, the belief that strangers are predominantly the culprits is wrong. Research in this particular field of deviance has determined that, in the majority of cases, the offender and the victim are acquainted.[61]

Increasing evidence points up the fact that sexual abuse of children within the family is "prevalent in every segment of society." From 65 to 85

[59]John D. MacDonald, *Rape Offenders and Their Victims* (Springfield, Ill.: Charles C Thomas Publisher, 1971), p. 56.

[60]*LEAA Newsletter,* 7, No. 7 (September 1978), 8.

[61]In the Sexual Assault Center in Seattle, Washington, only 15 percent of the youthful victims had been assaulted by a stranger: *Target,* Vol. 7, Issue 8, September/October 1978, p. 5.

percent of the offenders are known to the victim, and 55 to 58 percent are either family members or close friends of the family.[62] This was only too poignantly borne out in a "Child-Porn" trial that took place in Los Angeles in 1978. An 11-year-old girl testified that her father sold her for illicit sexual purposes in an international child prostitution and pornography ring. It is a sign of the insensitivity of our times that the newspapers can depict the horror to which a child has been subjected with such quaint terms as "Child-Porn."[63]

Child abuse covers the gamut and is not limited to passive, manual sexual molestation. The "lewd and lascivious" adult so frequently encountered in the correctional world is prototypically passive and inadequate. According to most standard psychiatric interpretations, he is operating in an arrested state of development in the psychosexual sphere. But passivity is not the exclusive hallmark of the child abuser, and serious violence, including fatal violence, is frequently visited upon the child victim. Thus, it can be dangerously disarming to consider the molester as purely a passive and inadequate being. Sagarin says that, in addition to the dirty old man stereotype, "two other types are recognized: the over-sexed individual and the extraordinarily timid."[64] The former is the compulsively aggressive, and the latter is the one who is diverted to the helpless child because of his inability to relate to adult females. Passive or aggressive, however, where passion is involved, the threat of identification haunts the offender and too frequently precipitates the killing of the victim to preserve immunity from apprehension.

Recidivism

The same general comments which have been applied to the rapist apply equally to the child molester with respect to recidivism, with some qualifications. It must be remembered that the child is particularly vulnerable to the manipulations of an adult. First of all, the adult stands in the position of authority over the child. Secondly, perverse sexual behavior is covered by a blanket of secrecy and fear, and the child is often intimidated into silence by threats not only of physical abuse, but of the withdrawal of love. There is unquestionably a horrifying amount of sexual abuse of children that never comes to light because of these factors. Barlow feels that "most incidents of child molestation will remain hidden from re-

[62]Marianne E. Cahill, "Sexually Abused Children," *Youth Forum,* 2, No. 1 (January 1978), 4.

[63]See, for example, the *Los Angeles Times,* November 22, 1978.

[64]Edward Sagarin, "Sexual Criminality," in Abraham S. Blumberg (ed.), *Current Perspectives on Criminal Behavior* (New York: Alfred A. Knopf, Inc., 1974), p. 148.

search scrutiny, particularly those offenses in which physical force and abuse are not employed and which involve offenders and victims who are familiar with one another and are associated in continuing relationships of a nonsexual kind."[65] This iceberg syndrome will necessarily affect the validity of the data available as well as the conclusions drawn therefrom.

Much research has focused on the sexual offender in general, and recidivism data is usually provided for the sex offender as a class, without a breakdown in typology. In one significant six-year follow-up study of sex offenders, conducted by the California Department of Mental Hygiene (now the Department of Mental Health), 1,921 subjects, released from the Atascadero State Hospital, were assessed for recidivism. A most important statement was made in that study which had practical implications for the correctional practitioner: ". . . it is particularly important to know *when* re-offending is most likely to occur in the different categories of the deviant behavior."[66] This indicates that the recidivism rate it related to the particular type of offending behavior. Other findings in the study showed that for the male pedophile, the highest recidivism rate occurred during the second year in the community; for the "sexual aggressors," most recidivism occurred within the first two years; and, overall, the recidivism rate was a low 20 percent for the six years under study (1955–1961). One particularly interesting finding was that pedophiles who were married and whose victims were females had a higher recidivism rate than unmarried pedophiles whose victims were males.

Treatment for the Sex Offender

It has been said that attempts "to develop a meaningful evaluation and treatment program for convicted rapists long have frustrated those engaged in the rehabilitation of offenders."[67] That statement does not have to be restricted to rapists. It can be applied to the wide range of sex offenders. A particularly difficult problem in dealing with the institutionalized sex offender is the universal contempt felt for this individual, not only in the "free world," but specifically in the world of the prison inmate. As one Canadian convict persuasively expressed it, "If you live long enough in one of these institutions, you come to the realization that what really makes things tick here is hate. The inmates hate the

---

[65]Hugh D. Barlow, *Introduction to Criminology* (Boston: Little, Brown & Company, 1978), pp. 354–55.

[66]Louise V. Frisbie and Ernest H. Dondis, *Recidivism Among Treated Sex Offenders*, Research Monograph No. 5, California Department of Mental Hygiene, 1965, p. 81

[67]National League of Cities, United States Conference of Mayors, *Rape*, Washington, D.C., April 1974, p. 23.

guards, the guards hate the inmates, and together they hate the sex offenders. The sex offender is considered to be the lowest form of life and is treated as such almost universally."[68]

Once in a while a bizarre practice in treatment will make the newspapers. It was reported, for instance, that transsexual inmates at the California Medical Facility (a state prison) were being given hormones and brassieres, although the quoted spokesman was quick to point out that they are not allowed to wear skirts![69] But the vast majority of sex offenders in the nation's prison systems are mixed indiscriminately with the regular prison population and not singled out for any special treatment. Nevertheless, some dramatic developments are taking place in this area. One researcher, who surveyed sex offender treatment programs, was compelled to say that "The rich array of innovative approaches unearthed in the course of this survey came as a surprise to its author, and to authorities on sex offenses whom he consulted."[70] For some obvious and some not so obvious reasons, treatment programs for the sex offender tend to be unpublicized.

The most impelling reason for treatment of the sex offender is to reduce recidivism. But Brecher adds that research is also served, and he offers another, rarely thought of reason: service to the sexual offender. Society has a number of functions, a primary one being the provision of various services to its constituent members. The sex offender is in need of the service of treatment, and society should provide it.

ROARE Program

In 1969, a program for the treatment of sex offenders known as ROARE (Reeducation of Attitudes and Repressed Emotions) was instituted in the Rahway State Prison in New Jersey. A controversial program, it was developed by psychologist William Prendergast and concentrates on having the participating patients relive their past sexual experiences. It is the conviction of its founder that these past traumata are the precipitants of later sexual offenses. ROARE is a voluntary program, "because the inmates must cooperate fully for it to be effective."[72] Certain assumptions undergird the ROARE program. Compulsion is a prominent concern, for most of the offenders are unable to explain the precipitation of their

[68]Anthony M. Marcus, *Nothing Is My Number* (Toronto, Canada: Genral Publishing Co., Ltd., 1971), p. 1.
[69]*Los Angeles Times,* April 15, 1978.
[70]Edward M. Brecher, *Treatment Programs for Sex Offenders* (Washington, D.C.: U.S. Government Printing Office, 1978), p. 1.
[71]*Ibid.,* p. 10.
[72]Michael S. Serrill, "Treating Sex Offenders in New Jersey," *Corrections Magazine,* 1, No. 2 (November/December 1974), 14.

crimes, and thus it is accepted that deep, unconscious compulsive urges drive them to the acts. "The purpose of therapy is to force the inmate to dredge up the "repressed" hatred, fear, and insecurity that led to his crimes."[73] The basic technique employed is that of regressing the patient into a forced and painful reliving of past negative experiences. This is not a new technique, but the interesting thing about the ROARE program is that it is done without the assistance of adjunctive drugs or hypnotism. Further, the therapy sessions take place without therapists being in the room, because of the belief that the presence of a therapist would be an inhibitory influence on the process. Sufficient data is not available to make a definitive assessment of the ROARE program. The preliminary findings were allegedly highly successful, but considerable skepticism has also been expressed. Abstinence from overt forms of negative behavior, for example, does not necessarily mean that the undesirable behavior has been excised from the repertoire of the offender.

Group Therapy in Washington State

Self-treatment is also the significant characteristic of the program at the Treatment Center for Sexual Offenders which is located in the Western State Hospital at Fort Steilacoom in the State of Washington. When a new member enters this program he is assigned to a small group of sex offenders, and he remains with that group as long as he is in the program.[74] In his initial contact with his group, his efforts at rationalizing his deviant behavior are rejected, and he is advised that he will not be permitted to "justify." He then observes "merciless" group confrontations. He is also advised precisely what is expected of him, verbally and in writing. The emphasis is on understanding the self and gaining a recognition that there are many behavioral factors behind sexual aberration, not all of which are purely sexual. Considerable pride in the group is nurtured, and group therapy is literally operative. Privileges are controlled by the group, and where there is a breach, the group descends *en masse* upon the recalcitrant. It is hammered at the individual that he must assume responsibility for his own behavior, and he will not be permitted to engage in deceptive practices and games. Sexual deviation is considered to be a way of escaping emotional stress, a way that is consciously and habitually resorted to by the members in the group. Therapy must break this pattern, but it must also deal with the feelings of inferiority possessed by the individual which have prevented the development of healthier modes of reaction to stress.

[73] *Ibid.*, p. 16.

[74] For further elaboration of this program, see Brecher, *Treatment Programs for Sex Offenders;* and *Corrections Magazine*, 1, No. 2, November/December 1974. Brecher is especially useful for its discussion of a wide range of programs.

Since 1966, the Western State Hospital treatment program has been designated as the sole program in Washington for the treatment of sex psychopaths. The same evaluative qualifications are applicable as were applicable to ROARE, but the program directors claim a high success rate. From 1958 through 1968, for instance, only 8.9 percent of the releasees were rearrested, but not one for a crime similar to their original offense. This compares with a 25 percent recidivism rate for sex offenders released from correctional institutions in Washington over a one-year period.[75]

Behavior Modification in Connecticut

Space limitations have permitted only a brief look at treatment programs for sex offenders. There are many others, some traditional, some innovative, and some highly controversial. A behavior modification program, featuring aversive conditioning, is in operation at the Connecticut state prison at Somers. Hypnotism, electro-shock, and visual material of adults and children in provocative poses are employed. The sex offender lies on a couch with his pants down, and a device which permits the transmission of electrical shocks is strapped to his thigh, in close proximity to his genitals. Aversive conditioning is introduced by showing the provocative pictures and simultaneously shocking the offender. Hypnosis is then employed to take the patient through a sexual fantasy involving a child. Unpleasant consequences are implanted through hypnotic suggestion as the patient becomes engrossed in his sexual fantasy. Considerable controversy, as might be expected, surrounds this program, and the ACLU instituted legal action to block the use of behavior modification on prisoners on the general premise that it constitutes an unwarranted control of the human mind.[76]

The treatment component in corrections, and especially the probation and parole officer, should maintain an ongoing interest in these developing programs. They represent sources for the enhancement of knowledge, as well as prospective resources in the continuing effort to contain and neutralize the sex offender.

PSYCHOPATHY/SOCIOPATHY

The terms "psychopath" and "sociopath" have been used with representative frequency and will confuse the student without an introductory word of clarification. They are to all intents and purposes interchangeable.

[75] *Corrections Magazine, supra,* p. 56.
[76] For a more elaborate discussion of this program, see *Corrections Magazine* 1, No. 3, January/February 1975.

Some Preliminary Distinctions

The only difference is an implicit one, although some writers, such as Greenwald, make distinctions. Psychopathy indicates the influence of psychology and sociopathy reveals the sociological influence. Godwin said that "sociopath" is the present psychiatric term of preference only because it is "less blunt" than "psychopath." "It delineates exactly the same personality disorder, which they can identify and render harmless through sedation but cannot cure. It is not a mental illness but rather a character defect so severe that it amounts to a lobotomy of the moral sense or conscience or whatever it is that gives us empathy with our fellow creatures."[77] As far as the present work is concerned, it accepts the interchangeability of these terms and considers both as descriptive of the same pathological phenomenon. The use of one term will subsume the other and vice versa in the following discussion.

The significance that the psychopath/sociopath has for corrections is profound and multi-faceted. In the present context, our concern is with the sociopath who is criminally oriented and who becomes a part of the practitioner's caseload. The probation officer and the parole officer, in particular, need some specific guidelines for handling this type of individual. More important, correctional systems will have to recognize that supervising a highly manipulative, ego-centered, unregenerative individual can have an emotionally devastating effect on a professional case carrier who is ill-trained to recognize and deal with this pathology. No system that I am aware of makes any provision for the separation, or selective supervision, of the probationed or paroled sociopath. The prognosis is bleak, where the criminal sociopath is concerned, and the probation and/or parole officer should not have to fruitlessly expend effort in attempting to "treat" this type of offender. The clinical sociopath should not be included in traditional correctional treatment endeavors. For this type of individual, a strictly structured program with collateral surveillance should be the "treatment" option, with psychiatric expertise mobilized as needed.

Defining the Psychopath/Sociopath

Psychopathy was early described by the English psychiatrist, J. C. Prichard, as "moral insanity," but the term itself was first used in the latter part of the nineteenth century by J. L. A. Koch who described severe behavior disorders as "psychopathic inferiority."[78] It is generally conceded that the classic work in the field is Hervey Cleckley's *The Mask of*

[77]John Godwin, *Murder U.S.A.* (New York: Ballantine Books, 1978), p. 300.
[78]Samuel Yochelson and Stanton E. Samenow, *The Criminal Personality Volume I: A Profile for Change* (New York: Jason Aronson, Inc., 1976), p. 89.

Sanity, which contains an unsurpassed definitive discussion of the psychopath. While considerable controversy continues over the etiology of psychopathy/sociopathy, the descriptive features of this behavioral phenomenon are generally agreed upon. The diagnosis of psychopathy will reveal the following features:

1. A failure to profit from experience
2. The absence of a sense of responsibility
3. An inability to form meaningful relationships
4. A lack of control over inner impulses
5. A defective moral sense
6. A history of chronic or recurrent antisocial behavior
7. Not responsive to punishment in terms of alteration of behavior
8. Emotional immaturity
9. Inability to experience guilt
10. Self-centeredness[79]

These can be said to be the features which are common to psychopathy (sociopathy) and commonly accepted as such. Beyond that, there is little diagnostic agreement among behavior scientists. For a long time, psychopathy was called the "psychiatric wastepaper basket." In other words, if you had some inexplicable behavioral disorder which did not fit neatly into pre-ordained categories, then you threw it into the wastepaper basket of psychopathy.

It should be clearly understood that all psychopaths are not necessarily criminals. They can be charming, articulate, intelligent, non-criminal, and devouring. Many an unsuspecting female has had a psychopathic boyfriend who exploits, uses, and manipulates her wholly within the parameters of the law, but he is psychopathic nonetheless. Sometimes the psychopath acts out his perversity through sexual misbehavior; he is then termed a "sexual psychopath." Sex psychopathy laws are sometimes all-encompassing, and offenders processed under these laws may be labeled psychopaths when they are, in fact, disturbed but not psychopathic individuals.[80]

The Etiology of Psychopathy/Sociopathy

While the etiology of psychopathy or sociopathy is not precisely known, Lemert pointed out that "The deviant person is a product of differentiating and isolating processes. Some persons are individually dif-

[79]Adapted from Yochelson and Samenow, *The Criminal Personality,* p. 90.
[80]For a good discussion of sex psychopathy laws, see Linda Sleffel, *The Law and the Dangerous Criminal* (Lexington, Mass.: D. C. Heath & Co., 1977).

ferentiated from others from the time of birth onward . . . ."[81] Lemert, a symbolic interactionist, reveals the influence of this viewpoint in his statement: "The importance of the person's conscious symbolic reactions to his or her own behavior cannot be overstressed in explaining the shift from normal to abnormal behavior or from one type of pathological behavior to another, particularly where behavior variations become systematized or structured into pathological roles."[82]

Hartman says that three basic explanations prevail in the attempt to explain the asocial person.

1. The individual has had "insufficient mothering during the first years of life."
2. The asocial person has had a completely rejecting mother who overcompensated because of her guilt, and consequently overindulged and overprotected the child. This in turn absolved the youngster from assuming responsibility, and he grew to consider the world a mechanism solely for his gratification. He takes but never gives.
3. The asocial personality structure develops when attempts *are* made to inculcate a sense of discipline in the child, but fail because the discipline is inconsistently imparted, or there is such a delay between misbehavior and consequent punishment that the child cannot make the proper connection between the two.[83]

Treating the Psychopath/Sociopath

Harold Greenwald once said that we do not hear much discussion about the *successful* psychopath because if we did, "we would then have to discuss many of the rulers of our world."[84] In keeping with his character, Dr. Greenwald expresses more hope and optimism for therapeutic success with psychopaths than possibly any other authority, and certainly more than the overwhelming majority. Instead of accenting differences, Greenwald stresses human similarities in his treatment approach to the psychopath. This means convincing the patient that the therapist has similar problems as well as similar attributes. But the problem of control is the central problem in the therapy, that is, the necessity of teaching the psychopath to control his impulses. The acquisition of control means the

[81]Edwin M. Lemert, *Social Pathology* (New York: McGraw-Hill Book Company, 1951), p. 73.

[82]*Ibid.*, p. 74.

[83]Henry L. Hartman, *Basic Psychiatry for Corrections Workers* (Springfield, Ill.: Charles C Thomas Publisher, 1978), pp. 153–54.

[84]"Treatment of the Psychopath," in Harold Greenwald (ed.), *Active Psychotherapy* (New York: Jason Aronson, Inc., 1974), p. 364.

acquisition of freedom and, according to Greenwald, this "becomes one of the most ego-building experiences they have ever known."[85] The therapist who would work with the psychopath, says Greenwald, must be non-moralizing, secure in himself, certain of his own controls "and free to be in contact with his own antisocial, manipulative, and psychopathic trends."[86]

There is no question but that correctional systems have a number of individuals possessed of the quoted attributes. The problem is that they are in scarce supply at the case-carrying level, where the treatment effort is such a critical challenge. Probation and parole officers should assiduously pursue an understanding of psychopathy. By learning how to constructively and therapeutically cope with the psychopath/sociopath, they will, indubitably, lighten the burden of the compassionate few who presently try. More important, they will have demonstrated that

> The ability to deal with psychopathy is an example of the ability really to deal with the dark destructive forces that stand ever ready to destroy the individual and society.[87]

SYNOPSIS

A substantial number of correctional clients are afflicted with compounded behavioral problems, such as drug abuse, sexual deviance, and psychopathy/sociopathy. It behooves the correctionalist to become conversant with the dynamics of each disability, as well as the resources for coping with these afflictions. On the periphery of treatment, the researcher ponders the causal connection between such elements as alcohol and crime. The nature-nurture controversy continues to rage.

The primary approaches to alcoholism are aversive therapy and Alcoholics Anonymous.

Drug abuse is widespread in the U.S., with about 700,000 heroin addicts alone in the country. The drug abuser is becoming a very significant segment in the correctional system. The philosophic approach to drug addiction ranges from a commitment to complete legalization to an equation of drug abuse with crime. In either event, drug abuse is practically endemic in the U.S. The treatment of drug abuse necessarily involves medical personnel and often adjunctive psychiatry.

Diverse treatment approaches have been attempted with the heroin addict, from civil commitment (residential treatment) to methadone

---

[85] *Ibid.*, p. 373.
[86] *Ibid.*, pp. 376–77.
[87] *Ibid.*, p. 377.

maintenance. Self-help groups like Synanon, a closed community, profess a high degree of success, but the success of such programs is mainly in-house success.

Sexual pathology, particularly that of a violent nature, is a singularly perplexing phenomenon. Child molestation and forcible rape are reprehensible acts to the average citizen, but the professional is obliged to deal with these individuals in an objective, detached manner. Accumulating evidence confirms that rape is a crime of violence and degradation more than a sex offense. A useful classification of rapists is offered.

Newer thrusts in treatment of the sex offender are reviewed, with the focus on the ROARE program in New Jersey, the group therapy program in Washington State, and Connecticut's effort with behavior modification. This chapter closes with a look at the psychopath/sociopath and sees these terms as essentially interchangeable and the individual as highly resistant to treatment.

14 The Past Is Prologue

> *The case of the People vs. Delinquency and Crime in the Court of Public Opinion is continued from year to year without final judgment. At times fresh arguments are advanced. Gradually new viewpoints are accepted and new procedures tried, but the challenge of an unsolved case remains.*
>
> **Charles L. Chute**

During the critical, trilateral negotiations on the Middle East, when President Carter was acting as mediator between Egypt's President Anwar Sadat and Israel's Prime Minister Menachem Begin, President Carter went on television to announce the results of the negotiations. His subject was peace, the peace that had been promised. As a result of his television appearance, the ABC station received 800 complaints in its New York and Washington Offices alone. The complainants protested the President's pre-empting the Battlestar Gallactica program to make his Mideast peace announcement! If the promise of peace is afforded such a reception, what kind of reception should be expected for the restless plea for correctional reform?

THE MOOD AND TEMPER OF THE PUBLIC

In a democracy, it is the "will of the people" that constitutes the authority for institutional change. Consensus must be obtained. Unfortunately, it is also a fact that ignorance multiplied by 200,000,000 does not necessarily result in good government. The theoretical beauty of democracy is often less than convincing to scholars who consider themselves, rightly in most cases, to be much better informed than the public. But there is no place in a democratic society for an elitist viewpoint, so even the insights of the scholars must be subjected to the grand test—public acceptance. When it comes to the necessity of good education, efficient public transporation, or full employment, the public speaks with one voice, and it is an affirmative voice, But when the issue is "socialized medicine," treatment for the psychotic, or rehabilitation of the criminal, the public speaks ambiguously, changing its mood on such controversial matters rather frequently, and not always on the basis of sound scientific evidence. The mood of an uninformed public can be the biggest barrier to progress in criminal justice reform.

On the other hand, the public can be excused for much of its cynicism and hostility, in the face of the failures of the criminal justice system, and in the face of the frightening amount and violence of American criminality. A few trenchant examples will more than make the point. In Chicago, while her thirty students looked on in horror, a teacher was attacked by a man who attempted to rape her in front of her young students, and that was but an infinitesimal speck in the symphony of violence being played across this land. Approximately 5,000 teachers are attacked *each month* in the nation's schools, 1,000 of whom consequently require medical attention. Violence in the Los Angeles city schools is so great that the security force for the school system is the third largest security force in the county, exceeded only by the sheriff's office and the Los Angeles City Police Department.

In New York, two teenaged "hit men" shotgunned a stranger to death on contract. The killers were 13 and 14 years of age. The fee for the killing was $500, and the terms were $50 down for each of the young killers, and the balance when the job was done. Wanton, violent, murderous crime is not designed to enlist the community's sympathy, despite whatever merit there might be in correctional therapeutics. And there seems to be more and more crime. Not just acquisitive or situational offenses against the person, which we will never completely eradicate, but the crime that displays a sociopathic insensitivity to the sacredness of life. This morning's paper added to the list. Two garbage men were wantonly shot and critically wounded by a robber who wanted their garbage truck as a getaway vehicle. He had just held up a fast food restaurant, fleeing with $400, and shot his victims without warning. Another robber, whose loot was just half of the amount taken at the restaurant, cold-bloodedly executed two gas station attendants, one of whom was only 16 years old. It is obvious that the relationship between punishment and treatment can no longer be explained in terms of a divorce. The relationship is clearly a connubial one.

PUNISHMENT, TREATMENT, AND FREE WILL

There is a natural tendency to polarize or dichotomize our thinking, so that black becomes the separable opposite of white. We fail to remember that black and white are the parents of grey. In a similar manner, punishment becomes the endogamous opposite of treatment, and the marriage of the two becomes inconceivable. But wisdom, history, and tradition show, to the contrary, that they are irretrievably wedded. Punishment for the sake of punishment is, of course, to be condemned. But punishment which rebukes the culpable transgressor and holds him responsible for adopting acceptable behavioral patterns is not punishment for the sake of punishment. It is, rather, as the psychiatrist, Halleck, termed it, "that punishment which must coexist with any effort at social control."[1]

Determinism and Positivism

This brings us back to the issue of personal responsibility and free will. The social sciences have long been under the dominance of the determinists and the positivists, for whom free will is a fiction. The revolution in sociological thinking,[2] which coincided with all of the other "revolutions" in the sixties and seventies, and the revolution within correctional theory, has led many thinkers to what we have earlier described as "soft determinism." The term should really be "soft *indeterminism,*" because it would put the emphasis where it belongs—on freedom of the will. As we slip from the grasp of the hard determinists, we necessarily move toward an acceptance of the doctrine of personal responsibility. As Halleck concisely states,

> it is difficult to imagine the existence of a society which did not hold its citizens responsible for their actions. By simply creating a legal code, society implies that a man must be held accountable for his actions. All theology teaches us

[1] Seymour L. Halleck, *Psychiatry and the Dilemmas of Crime* (Berkeley: University of California Press, 1971), p. 206.

[2] For a scholarly discussion of some of the major trends, see David C. Thorns, *New Directions in Sociology* (Totowa, New Jersey: Rowan and Littlefield, 1976).

that man has choice. Indeed, it seems impossible for man to survive without some belief in his capacity to exercise free will.[3]

Teleology and Volition

There is increasing evidence of a trend toward a teleological and volitional point of view in the social sciences, and specifically in the criminal justice area. The venerable Karl Menninger, patriarch of a psychiatric dynasty, unashamedly titled one of his most recent books, *Whatever Became of Sin?*[4] Sin, as everybody knows, is a culpable (volitional) breach of a divinely instituted code of behavior. The staid *American Journal of Corrections* also deferred to the trend by giving prominence to an article by a prison chaplain which deplored the fact that God (viz., moral responsibility) has been "left out of the prison system."[5]

There are, of course, many individuals in conflict with the criminal justice system who are incapable of free choice, either by virtue of intellectual or organic impairment, and reason dictates that responsibility be mitigated in their cases. But those who are not exempted by competent medical or psychiatric diagnostics must assume responsibility for their actions and be prepared for the consequences of their irresponsible behavior. This is a bedrock proposition of Dr. Glasser's reality therapy, but it is also a fact which is beginning to be empirically validated.

In their epochal study, Yochelson and Samenow pointed out that they had begun their intensive, in-depth research, with over 200 long-term criminals, along traditional lines. That is, they searched for "root" causes of the individual's behavioral problems basically through a psychoanalytic bias. In time they came to the conclusion that the *criminals* were "very much in control of their actions."[6] As a consequence, the researchers abjured permissiveness in favor of firmness, unhesitatingly employed the term "criminal," and discarded "mental illness," replacing it with "personal responsibility."[7]

Corrections must recognize that it has a prime responsibility to inculcate its clientele with a sense of personal responsibility. Rational treatment efforts cannot exempt the rational person from responsibility for his or her actions. If unacceptable behavior is condoned rather than condemned, rewarded rather than punished, explored rather than deplored, it merely provides excuses for criminal behavior and will not alter criminal

---

[3]Halleck, *Psychiatry and the Dilemmas of Crime,* p. 208.

[4]Karl Menninger, *Whatever Became of Sin?* (New York: Hawthorn Books, Inc., 1973).

[5]Charles Repole, O.F.M., C.A.P., "God Left Out of Prison System," *American Journal of Corrections,* 39, No. 4 (July-August 1977), 10.

[6]Samuel Yochelson and Stanton E. Samenow, *The Criminal Personality, Volume I: A Profile for Change* (New York: Jason Aronson, Inc., 1976), p. 19.

[7]*Ibid.,* p. 28.

patterns. It must be stressed that a realistic assessment of criminal behavior does not preclude a compassionate commitment to human reconstruction, nor is a firm approach in dealing with the offender incompatible with a reformative philosophy. The system also needs reforming.

THE CRIMINAL JUSTICE SYSTEM

A veritable torrent of books, articles, and journal treatises has appeared in
recent times depicting the moribund state of the criminal justice system
and enumerating all its imperfections. It has many. We have no intention
of adding to the many detailed indictments, but cannot refrain from some
comment on aspects that are relevant to the correctional endeavor. A lot
can be inferred from the raw data that is available. Where is the equity, for
example, in a system which has imprisoned about 300,000 individual felons to expiate for the tens of millions of *de facto* felons who have not been
processed into the institutional system?

As a functional entity, the criminal justice system can only stem the
tide. It can never approach efficiency when it is beset by political manipulation, goals that are not precisely articulated, contrapuntal philosophies,
and fiscal impoverishment. The Law Enforcement Assistance Administration was established to improve the criminal justice system and,
thereby, to reduce crime. Its budget in fiscal 1978 was in the vicinity of
$646 million, which its Acting Director, Henry S. Dogin, said would be
enough to run the New York City Police Department "for a couple of
days."[8] This fact not only supports our premise, but suggests the incredible amount of money needed for the mission of the criminal justice system. Expenditures in the public sector for criminal justice increased 9.3
percent during 1977, reaching a record $21.5 billion, up from $19.7 billion in 1976.[9] Justice in the justice system is compromised in many ways,
beyond the lack of money to see it realized (or the excess of misspent
monies). Its compromise is particularly poignant in the judicial phase.

The Courts and Sentencing

In a major address on criminal justice, as the Democratic presidential
nominee, Jimmy Carter chastised LEAA for not allocating sufficient
funds to the state and local courts (only 6 percent of the total disbursed
from 1968 to 1976), and accused that agency of "a grossly misdirected set
of priorities."[10] The courts are the fulcrum in the justice system. If justice

[8]Quoted in the Long Beach, California *Independent,* November 23, 1978.
[9]*LEAA Newsletter,* 7, No. 8–9 (October/November 1978), 5.
[10]Quoted in *Criminal Justice Newsletter,* 7, No. 17 (August 30, 1976), 3.

is not administered here, where will it be dispensed? Unfortunately the same crisis faces the courts as faces every other component of the system. On April 7, 1976, Chief Justice Warren E. Burger, addressing the National Conference on the Causes of Popular Dissatisfaction with the Administration of Justice, in St. Paul, Minnesota, quoted a statement uttered by the distinguished American jurist, Roscoe Pound, seventy years earlier. We have been "tinkering where comprehensive reform is needed."[11] The broad references are to inequitable sentencing and protracted processing of justice in the context of diminishing public esteem for the court system.

An English jurist once made the statement that trying a man was as easy as falling off a log compared with deciding what to do with him once he has been found guilty. The insoluble dilemma of appropriate punishment in corrections is matched by the insoluble dilemma of an appropriate sentence in the court system, and that dilemma pertains only to that discriminated minority that finally arrives before "the bar of justice." In the United States that is approximately 20 percent of offenders. The English have just announced that the British system is similarly afflicted. In 1977, only 21 percent of the "serious crimes" were cleared by arrest in England.[12] The percentage of offenders who have their day in court becomes microscopic after plea bargaining and other devices take place. Yet, "[a] trial is the most visible and dramatic event in the criminal process, the most formal and sustained display of the majesty and authority of the law."[13] Farther down the line, when corrections enters the process, the offender must wonder at his good fortune at being plucked from the vast army of criminal Americans to be afforded specialized reformative attention.

Indeterminate v. Determinate Sentencing

Narrowing the focus, the indeterminate sentence has been the vogue in America for the better part of a century. In the seventies, again, dissatisfaction with the indeterminate sentence grew markedly. It is another one of those practically insoluble, highly controversial issues. The renowned superintendent of the equally renowned Danish Detention Center at Herstedvester, Dr. Georg K. Sturup, speaks for indeterminancy when he comments, "Although the indeterminate sentence seems at first glance to be inhumane, it may be more valuable for the most recalcitrant

[11]Quoted in Howard James, *Crisis in the Courts* (New York: David McKay Co., Inc., 1971), p. iii.

[12]See the comments of the head of New Scotland Yard, Sir David McNee, in *LEAA Newsletter*, 7, No. 8-9 (October/November 1978), 2.

[13]Lloyd L. Weinreb, *Denial of Justice* (New York: The Free Press, 1977), p. 87.

group of offenders than is presently believed by some reformers."[14] Indeterminacy, according to Dr. Sturup, equates with individualization.

The opposition is substantive and vociferous. The Coordinating Council of Prisoner Organizations set up a committee in 1973 to study the matter, coming out in favor of determinancy.[15] Fogel's "justice model" is based on determinancy in sentencing.[16] Harvard's James Q. Wilson maintains that disparities in sentencing will be eliminated by limiting judicial discretion.[17] The judiciary, of course, has a contrary view, expressed by one United States District Court judge when he said, "The shortcoming of mandatory sentences is that they do not limit discretion; they simply move it around."[18] The Model Sentencing Act of the Council of Judges of the National Council on Crime and Delinquency is built on individualized (ergo, indeterminate) sentencing.

The Victim

The plight and position of the victim is one of the most neglected areas in the criminal justice system. If the victim cannot be convinced that there is justice in the system, then the system is imperiled, and additional barriers will understandably be erected against the thrust of correctional treatment. The California Probation, Parole and Correctional Association has formally taken the position "that the serious plight of victims in crimes must be drastically changed and that the agencies of the criminal justice system must assume leadership in bringing about the change."[19] Fortunately, victim compensation, restitution, and community service are infiltrating the sentencing process[20] and the relationship of the criminal to his victim (or the victim "and his criminal," as Schafer phrased it) is receiving increased study.[21] There is another forgotten victim, for whom little understanding or assistance has been available, and that is the innocent survivor of the incarcerated offender, the family member who faces

[14]Georg K. Sturup, "Indeterminacy as Individualization," *San Diego Law Review*, 14, No. 5 (July 1977), 1039.

[15]Coordinating Council of Prisoner Organizations, "Determined Sentencing Proposal" (Pasadena: American Friends Service Committee, January 1975).

[16]David Fogel, "The Case for Determinancy in Sentencing and the Justice Model in Corrections," *American Journal of Corrections*, 38, No. 4 (July-August 1976), 25, 28.

[17]James Q. Wilson, "Changing Criminal Sentences," *Harper's*, November 1977, pp. 16–21.

[18]Jon O. Newman, "A Better Way to Sentence Criminals," *American Bar Association Journal*, 63 (November 1977), 1563–66.

[19]*Crime Prevention Review*, 5, No. 2 (January 1978), 3.

[20]An excellent resource work is Joe Hudson and Burt Galaway (eds.), *Considering the Victim: Readings in Restitution and Victim Compensation* (Springfield, Ill.: Charles C Thomas Publisher, 1975).

[21]Stephen Schafer, *Victimology: The Victim and His Criminal* (Reston, Va.: Reston Publishing Company, Inc., 1977).

added deprivations as well as the hostility of a world that likes to attribute guilt by association.[22] Restoration and reconstruction cannot be terms reserved exclusively for the offender. The victims also need to be restored.

The Police

Considerable reformation is also needed in the police role and function. A tremendous amount of time and money is wasted fighting so-called "victimless crime." A recent study in Washington, D.C. revealed that 21 percent of all persons appearing in superior court in the first half of 1976 were charged with this type of offense. Approximately half were acquitted and 83.8 percent of those convicted never went to jail. The enormous and pointless expense attendant on such criminal justice activity is self-evident. The study itself was one of a number of projects funded at $1.5 million![23]

As serious and violent crime proliferates, the specialized police function must be devoted to that type of human behavior which most seriously threatens to undermine social stability and tranquility. Picking up a pathetic streetwalker *as a criminal* or raiding neighborhood bingo games does not do much for either crime control or public morale. When police raided a neighborhood trailer park bingo game in San Mateo, California in 1978, one of the disgruntled, elderly participants bitterly complained that eight murders could go unsolved but the police had time to raid "a bunch of little old ladies trying to have some fun."

THE OFFENDER

On a purely mathematical basis, we simply cannot continue to offer incarceration as the paramount instrument for the resolution of the crime problem. We will run out of room, building materials, and people. What is needed, instead, is a more discriminatory knowledge of the criminal offender and his motivation, a constant consciousness of the cultural determinants of crime, and programs that are tailored to take cognizance of both. Karl Menninger, in a lecture at the University of Southern California in the late fall of 1978, commented: "We can almost define sin, crime and disease as being adverse and unsatisfactory ways of expending energy, of dealing with stress."[24] This suggests that correctional treatment should be an educative process more than a therapeutic process. In fact,

---

[22]A sensitive article in this regard is: Laura J. Bakker, Barbara A. Morris, and Laura M. Janus, "Hidden Victims of Crime," *Social Work*, 23, No. 2 (March 1978), 143–48.

[23]*LEAA Newsletter*, 7, No. 8–9 (October/November 1978), 20.

[24]Quoted in Long Beach, California *Independent, Press-Telegram*, November 26, 1978.

Yochelson and Samenow said that they considered themselves educators rather than therapists. It is not that we are witnessing a great schism between therapy and education, but rather that we are coming to recognize the therapeutic nature of education.

The Dangerous Offender

Rational corrections does not preclude the use of incarceration for dangerous or otherwise serious offenders. But it has to recognize the cumulative wisdom of many thoughtful sources with respect to the non-dangerous offenders. The President's Task Force on Prisoner Rehabilitation recommended "conducting as much of the correctional process as possible in the community rather than in custodial institutions. . . ."[25] The National Council on Crime and Delinquency, in a policy statement, declared: *"Confinement is necessary only for offenders who, if not confined, would be a serious danger to the public."*[26] (Italics in the original). And, as we learned earlier, the American Bar Association has declared probation (diversion) to be the preferred form of sentencing.

The dangerous offender is a separate proposition. He causes inordinate stress on the community because the result of his criminality is physical harm or injury. Human aggression is far from clearly understood. But one thing is clear, cultural imperatives have a great deal to do with crime, both violent and non-violent. Silberman, for example, leaves little doubt but that he considers urban crime in the United States to be largely a race problem.[27] The American culture is a violent culture. So is that of New Guinea, whose natives engage in bloody wars. But the Warao tribe in Venezuela has a ritual arena in which contestants merely shove one another until one falls down. No blood is shed. This practice indicates that violence can be culturally controlled. People are programmed into violence. It is interesting to recall that Freud said that there is little likelihood that we will be able to suppress the aggressive tendency in humanity.

Correctional treatment must address itself to defusing the rage that results in violent acting out. Violent people are almost always the products of violent backgrounds and are not strangers to brutal treatment. Unfortunately, some of these offenders have been so damaged in their childhoods that they are, to all intents and purposes, beyond recovery. But those who are responsive to intelligent treatment must be the subject of

[25]"The Criminal Offender—What Should Be Done?", *The Report of the President's Task Force on Prisoner Rehabilitation,* April 1970.

[26]National Council on Crime and Delinquency, "The Nondangerous Offender Should Not be Imprisoned: A Policy Statement," *Crime and Delinquency,* 21, No. 4 (October 1975), 315.

[27]Charles E. Silberman, *Criminal Violence, Criminal Justice* (New York: Random House, 1978).

continual study—both to help them to contain their aggressive impulses, and also to enable the releasing authorities to more perceptively determine when parole is warranted.

Relevant research in Michigan, involving a little over 2,000 offenders, has uncovered some surprising data. It has been found, for example, that neither the number of prior commitments nor the number of crimes committed by an individual is an accurate predictor of post-prison violence. Offenders in the most dangerous group, however, did share the following characteristics: Their commitment offense was an assaultive offense, they had never been married prior to their commitment offense, and they had served "at least half their prison sentences in involuntary segregation."[28]

There were additional variables that were present significantly more often in the dangerous offender than in the nondangerous offender. The dangerous offenders were raised almost exclusively by their mothers prior to the age of twenty, had a juvenile commitment (not a status offense), and were first arrested prior to their fifteenth birthday. This type of research is useful. It will eventually give us deeper insights into the dynamics of violence and permit intelligent correctional treatment for the assaultive offender.

The Career Criminal

Loosely speaking, criminals can be divided into situational criminals and career criminals. The former could also be loosely termed amateur criminals. In recent times more attention and recognition have been given to the individual who makes a full-time occupation out of crime. While a comprehensive treatment approach would also aspire to recover the career criminal, realism dictates that the emphasis must be on neutralizing the predatory threat posed by the career criminal. On September 15, 1977, California passed pioneering legislation setting up the California Career Criminal Prosecution Program, which became law five days later. The law appropriates $3 million annually to fund career criminal units in the district attorney's offices in the state. Comparable, locally funded programs are now in operation in Ohio, Illinois, Texas, Colorado, Florida, and Washington, and LEAA has funded additional programs in 23 states.

The Juvenile Offender

One of the most distressing characteristics of modern delinquent behavior is the frequency of extreme and often senseless violence. In New

[28]*Criminal Justice Newsletter*, 7, No. 14 (July 5, 1976), 5–6.

York, for instance, three youths manipulated their way into a church by pretending that they wanted to be baptized and then shot a 76-year-old priest to death in a robbery that netted only $50. Countless other incidents could be related. The end result is that the public and many professionals are calling for adult treatment for seriously criminal juveniles. In an address to the International Association of Chiefs of Police in New York on October 8, 1978, Senator Edward Kennedy said that "unrealistic" humaneness with violent youths had backfired, and he recommended "some significant punishment" for violent youthful lawbreakers.

Juvenile gangs are becoming a growing phenomenon and an increasing threat because of their violent behavior. They differ from gangs in the early 1900s in that they are exceedingly violent and amoral. It has been estimated that there are 10,000 gang members in the city of Los Angeles, and about 25 percent of those gang members are under twelve years of age. From 1972 through 1974, juvenile gangs in Philadelphia, Los Angeles, Chicago, New York, and San Francisco committed a collective 525 murders.[29] It is evident that decisive action is called for and that amoral insensitivity to life and indiscriminate violence toward others cannot be permissively tolerated. One writer, indicating that his research failed to confirm that violent behavior in juvenile offenders can be predicted, rhetorically asked: "If we cannot reliably predict violent behavior, how can we justify our continued detention of juveniles evaluated as violent?"[30] Assuming the validity of his premise, the only reasonable answer is for either the protection of society and/or punishment, deterrence, *and* treatment thereby.

In Chapter Twelve we examined the Community Treatment Program in California, which employs the I-Level classification scheme. We also took some note of Lerman's critical view of the CTP program. One rather interesting fact uncovered by Lerman was that the experimental (treatment) cases were actually subject to longer periods of detention than were the control group subjects, leaving the unavoidable impression that punishment (detention) was an inescapable part of treatment.[31] It is, of course, hazardous to generalize without developing empirical data to support our generalizations.

In a report to the Ford Foundation by the Vera Institute of Justice, several basic propositions about the violent delinquent and his prospective treatment were made:

[29]Reported in the *Los Angeles Times*, May 1, 1976.
[30]Stephen E. Schlesinger, "The Prediction of Dangerousness in Juveniles: A Replication," *Crime and Delinquency*, 24, No. 1 (January 1978), 48.
[31]Paul Lerman, *Community Treatment and Social Control* (Chicago: The University of Chicago Press, 1975).

1. There has not yet been developed a specific treatment approach to violence, but tentative evidence indicates that some forms of treatment are more effective than others with certain types of offenders.
2. It is a very rare occasion when one specific form of treatment is effective; effective treatment will ordinarily be multimodal treatment.
3. Group techniques appear to be the most promising approaches to the juvenile offender.
4. It is a fallacy to expect rapid "cure" within a short period of time.

"Incremental progress toward constructive reintegration into society is a more reasonable goal, and one that may require social and therapeutic supports long after the delinquent's legal debt to society has been repaid."[32] One promising development, in terms of the reduction of violence, was not mentioned in this report. Between 1970 and 1977, the under-age-17 population decreased by 5.5 million children!

Deinstitutionalization

Meanwhile, with respect to the non-violent juvenile offender, the controversy over deinstitutionalization and status offenders continues, but with some promise. John Rector, head of LEAA's Office of Juvenile Justice and Delinquency Prevention, said that 85 percent of all juveniles now incarcerated should be deinstitutionalized.[33] The effort to remove juveniles, particularly status offenders, from institutional constraint is reflected in New Mexico's Children's Shelter Care Act, which mandates the removal of non-delinquent juveniles from secure detention. There are allied forces at work. Basically as a result of the adoption of the diversionary philosophy, the number of juveniles in secure and semi-secure detention in the United States dropped from 34,242 on January 1, 1965 to 26,000 on January 1, 1978, or more than 25 percent.[34]

Under Roman law, a father had absolute power over his children, literally the power of life and death. As the concept of chancery evolved, the seed of concern for the rights of children was planted, although it took many years to bear fruit. In contemporary times, the cause of children's rights is gaining advocacy. One advocate asserts that "children have a special right to the protection of the state by reason of their dependency."[35]

---

[32]Paul A. Strasburg, *Violent Delinquents,* A Report to the Ford Foundation from the Vera Institute of Justice (New York: Monarch, 1978), pp. 162–63.

[33]Cited in *Criminal Justice Newsletter,* 9, No. 23 (November 20, 1978), 5.

[34]*Corrections Magazine,* 4, No. 3 (September 1978), 4.

[35]Bernard J. Coughlin, S. J., "The Rights of Children," in Albert E. Wilkerson (ed.), *The Rights of Children: Emergent Concepts in Law and Society* (Philadelphia: Temple University Press, 1973), p. 7.

As emancipation displaces dependency, and as serious violence supplants "delinquency," a criterion becomes available for the differential approach to the youthful offender.

THE ATAVISTIC PRISON

The contemporary attitude toward the prison is clearly schizophrenic. Reputable individuals and organizations call for the abolition of the prison, on the one hand, and correctional agencies pour millions into new construction, on the other. On April 25, 1972, the National Council on Crime and Delinquency adopted three policies designed to stimulate reform in the nation's corrections systems. The first of those policies declared: "No new detention or penal institution should be built before alternatives to incarceration are fully provided for. Specifically, the National Council on Crime and Delinquency calls for a halt on the construction of all prisons, jails, juvenile training schools, and detention homes until the maximum funding, staffing, and utilization of noninstitutional correction have been attained."[36]

In 1973, the National Advisory Commission called for a ten-year moratorium on prison construction, and in 1977 the Director of the American Foundation's Institute of Corrections made a similar plea.[37]

Meanwhile, the Federal Bureau of Prisons plans to add 62,000 beds to its prison system by 1982, at a cost of $1.4 billion.[38] In mid-1977, the House Appropriations Committee estimated the cost of *one* cell in a new prison to be $42,100.[39] The economics of maintaining the prison system, apart from any other consideration, is staggering.

The Character of the Prison

A perceptive reporter once termed the female prison "the concrete womb."[40] The prison is more than that. It is a facility that breeds the seeds of its own iniquity, despite well-meaning efforts to abort that possibility. The CIA, for example, conducted secret medical experiments on prisoners at the California Medical Facility (a state prison). The superintendent of that facility, without denying the tests, said that "neither the prison nor the inmates knew that the experiments were financed by the spy

[36]National Council on Crime and Delinquency, *Policies and Background Information,* September 1972, p. 5.

[37]William G. Nagel, "On Behalf of a Moratorium on Prison Construction," *Crime and Delinquency,* 23, No. 2 (April 1977), 154–72.

[38]*Criminal Justice Newsletter,* 21, No. 8 (October 24, 1978), 1.

[39]*Criminal Justice Newsletter,* 8, No. 12 (June 6, 1977), 4.

[40]Kathryn Watterson Burkhart, *Women in Prison* (New York: Popular Library, 1976).

agency."[41] In 1976, the board of directors of the American Correctional Association called for the end of medical experimentation on prisoners.

The European Court of Human Rights condemned Britain, in 1978, for "inhuman and degrading treatment" of Irish prisoners in the North of Ireland. Twenty years earlier, the United Nations had promulgated its Standard Minimum Rules for Treatment of Prisoners, which proscribed the dehumanization wilfully practiced by the British *in a prison*. In 1977, the president of the American Bar Association called conditions in state prisons "sickening."[42] In addition to the disabilities imposed from without, the prison atmosphere and experience impose their own disabilities. Studies have shown, for example, that there are negative psychological correlates associated with long-term imprisonment, which, in effect, cause human deterioration, and it has been suggested that this deterioration may be irreversible.[43] The prison, in other words, works at cross-purposes with the correctional intent. The capper is provided by an ex-inmate:

> Fighting crime and rehabilitating prisoners is a very complex business with no easy solutions. One thing is clear: we can't build prisons that keep inmates in and society out. If a man has to return to society he has to feel part of it even when locked up. We have to stop looking for panaceas and start making changes. Almost anything would be more than has been accomplished in the last hundred years.[44]

DIVERSIONARY ALTERNATIVES

To offset the thoroughly documented, inimical nature of the prison as a correctional device, diversionary alternatives have begun to mushroom. Diversion from jail is as much desired as diversion from the prison. In 1976 there were 7,098 inmates in the Monroe County Jail in upstate New York. Of this total, only 1,087, or 15 percent, were actually sentenced prisoners. The balance, almost 6,000 individuals, were awaiting disposition of their cases. An astonishing 60 percent of the total, or 4,261, were released within 5 days. It was appropriately reasoned, "If they could be released in so short a time, need they have been locked up at all?"[45] It cost

[41] *Los Angeles Times,* October 13, 1978.

[42] *Criminal Justice Newsletter,* 8, No. 14 (July 4, 1977), 6.

[43] See, for example, K. J. Heskin and others, "Psychological Correlates of Long-Term Imprisonment," *British Journal of Criminology,* 14, No. 2 (April 1974) pp. 150–6; and R. J. Sapsford, "Life-Sentence Prisoners: Psychological Changes During Sentence," *British Journal of Criminology,* 18, No. 2 (April 1978) pp. 128–45.

[44] Ken Jackson, "Story of an Ex-Con," in David Malikin (ed.), *Social Disability* (New York: New York University Press, 1973), p. 166.

[45] Judicial Process Commission, Genesee Ecumenical Ministries (New York) *Monroe Alternatives Project,* undated descriptive booklet, c. 1978.

$12,929 to maintain one person per year in the Monroe County Jail. Because some concerned citizens became aware of these facts, the Monroe Alternatives Project was developed, a community action plan to save human and community resources. A broad spectrum of diversionary programs are now developing in Monroe County.

There are numerous alternative programs operating in the United States, and substantial resource material is available. Some of that material has been cited throughout this text. California's probation subsidy program, instituted in 1966, is fundamentally a diversionary program. Michigan has a successful Community Treatment Project for Repeat Offenders in Oakland County. Not only is it unusual in that it is for recidivists exclusively, but it is also unusual in that preliminary data reveals a recidivism rate of only 2.5 percent.[46] Halfway houses, community service in lieu of incarceration, and pre-trial diversion all fall within the broad intent of diversion. This thrust, indeed, has been termed "the New Justice."[47]

THE MISSION OF CORRECTIONS

The mission of corrections is not obscure. It is to recover fallen humanity; to diminish recidivism; to render the public more secure; to constantly probe the dynamics of crime and delinquency; to be part of the machinery that constantly battles crime to prevent it from homesteading further territory. All noble sentiments. Many more can be added. The problem is that these are, for the most part, sweeping generalizations whose credibility can be seriously questioned. If the correctional system itself weren't a vested, quasi-political enterprise, the American Correctional Association would not have to call for an end to patronage in corrections, which it did at the plenary session of its annual convention in Denver, Colorado, in 1976. The kind of political abuse and misuse that is such a distinguishing characteristic of institutional American life has not exempted corrections. The clarion call goes out, the legion of committed respond, and the hopelessness of the task soon seduces multitudes. Nothing will more effectively throttle enterprise than cynicism. The real mission of corrections is to conquer erosive cynicism by mobilizing sufficient energy, idealism, and verifiable evidence that corrections can do better and that rational correctional treatment is a vital element in the achievement of its mission.

[46]National Council on Crime and Delinquency, *Instead of Prison,* undated descriptive booklet, c. 1974.
[47]David E. Aaronson and others, *The New Justice: Alternatives to Conventional Criminal Adjudication* (Washington, D.C.: U.S. Government Printing Office, 1977).

FIGURE 14-1

Vox Populi

Americans are deeply and understandably concerned about crime. The interesting thing is that while Americans are deeply concerned, they tend to have a much greater anxiety about the national crime trend than they do about crime in the local neighborhood. In a major survey conducted by the Law Enforcement Assistance Administration and the Bureau of the Census, approximately 22,000 individuals (in 10,000 households) were interviewed in each of the following cities: Atlanta, Baltimore, Cleveland, Dallas, Denver, Newark, Portland (Oregon), and St. Louis. A substantial 82 percent of the respondents felt that crime had increased nationally,[48] whereas only 40 percent felt that crime had gone up in the local neighborhood.[49] This has several implications. Corrections must be supported by the local community if it is to be effective. If there is less anxiety on the part of the residents of the community, there is a greater likelihood that their positive, reconstructive support can be enlisted in the corrections mission. It is imperative that the correctional effort be a unified effort, a community effort. "When people begin to pro-

[48]James Garofalo, *Public Opinion About Crime* (Washington, D.C.: U.S. Government Printing Office, 1977), p. 34.
[49]*Ibid.*, p. 36.

tect themselves as individuals and not as a community, the battle against crime is effectively lost."[50]

Treatment, Rehabilitation, and Reason

The attacks on treatment and rehabilitation in corrections, which became vociferous in the 1970s, were largely the result of rising crime rates, disenchantment with the medical model, the paucity of empirical verification of the claims of corrections, and a shift in public philosophy toward the punishment model. But any practical, realistic evaluation of correctional endeavors must lead to the conclusion that a great army of concerned professionals and a multiplicity of restorative programs cannot be wholly ineffectual. There is no ironclad restorative formula, or it would have long since been patented. But each individual engaged in correctional treatment has the potential to be a catalytic agent, and, by definition, a catalyst is something that makes something transform into another substance. Transformation has the greatest promise of happening during a professional encounter. While an agency must satisfy cost effectiveness, the magic that enables one individual to inspire and redeem another is beyond the pale of cost effectiveness.

We cannot abide ruthless punishment either on economic or on philosophic grounds. Because we simply cannot institutionalize all of our offenders, we are impelled to seek alternative methods, both of treatment and dissuasion. We also find excessive punishment philosophically and legally untenable. The United States Supreme Court emphatically demonstrated this at the beginning of the significant seventies, when it declared the entire Arkansas penal system to be unconstitutional and violative of the Eighth Amendment, which bars crual and unusual punishment.[51] Economics and philosophics notwithstanding, the correctional profession must zealously endeavor to become more effective. It must discard the ineffective. It must not fear critical scrutiny of its activities. Above all, it must become innovative, imaginative, and creative. It must pursue wise legislative action in the halls of government, and humanitarian sensitivity in its actual operation.

A Balanced Mission

Corrections must, in the final analysis, define its mission in terms of balanced and achievable goals. It must respond to its attackers with reason

---

[50]O. Newman, *Defensible Space: Crime Prevention Through Urban Design* (New York: The Macmillan Company, 1972), p. 3.

[51]*Holt v. Sarver*, 309 F. Supp. 362, (E.D. Ark. 1970).

and with results. During the height of the furious attack on correctional treatment, in the mid-seventies, "it appeared that programmed rehabilitation of criminal offenders was about to become an extinct process—a type of social action without a future."[52] But the hard opposition has melted, and corrections has a new opportunity to prove itself.

Realism and balance must be the foundation of corrections. Rehabilitation cannot be the sole reason for the existence of the correctional agency. As Adams has said, "Correctional managers are...being reminded that there are now other goals for their agencies other than rehabilitation."[53] Some offenders do have to be incapacitated. Rational punishment is not a dirty word. Prisoners are not "sick." Functional reintegration of offenders back into the community is the comprehensive goal. Treatment, in its broadest sense, encompasses every activity that aims at this objective. Treatment must also be widened in its definition. In corrections it is more than esoteric therapeutics; it is an educational process. It is a pedagogic act in the ultimate.

Corrections is only a segment of the criminal justice system, a system that has to deal with a malady whose roots are buried deep in society's wellsprings. But that does not excuse it from assiduous efforts to counteract the malady of crime and criminality. Offenders must be provided with a real stake in society if they are to be diverted from continuing criminality. Society contains the means to maximize its own protection, and corrections is one of its handmaidens. Whatever qualitative meaning we give to "rehabilitation," it is an inescapable truism that "A system that fails genuinely to rehabilitate the criminal also fails to provide protection to society. Justice and social order are intertwined."[54] But justice and social order, without catalytic altruism, are merely intellectual abstractions. Corrections, in the final analysis, must make some small but significant response to Alfred Lord Tennyson's plaintive inquiry:

> When shall all men's good
> Be each man's rule
> And universal peace
> Be like a shaft of light
> Across the land?

[52]Stuart Adams, "Evaluating Correctional Treatments: Towards A New Perspective," *Criminal Justice and Behavior*, 4, No. 4 (December 1977), 323.

[53]*Ibid.*, p. 326.

[54]Khoren Arisian, "Social Order Requires Social Justice," *The Urban Review*, 6, No. 3 (1973), 19.

Index

A